New Directions in the Study of African American Recolonization

Southern Dissent

UNIVERSITY PRESS OF FLORIDA

Florida A&M University, Tallahassee
Florida Atlantic University, Boca Raton
Florida Gulf Coast University, Ft. Myers
Florida International University, Miami
Florida State University, Tallahassee
New College of Florida, Sarasota
University of Central Florida, Orlando
University of Florida, Gainesville
University of North Florida, Jacksonville
University of South Florida, Tampa
University of West Florida, Pensacola

NEW DIRECTIONS IN THE STUDY OF AFRICAN AMERICAN RECOLONIZATION

EDITED BY BEVERLY C. TOMEK
AND MATTHEW J. HETRICK

Foreword by Stanley Harrold and Randall M. Miller

University Press of Florida
Gainesville · Tallahassee · Tampa · Boca Raton
Pensacola · Orlando · Miami · Jacksonville · Ft. Myers · Sarasota

Publication of this paperback edition made possible by a Sustaining the Humanities through the American Rescue Plan grant from the National Endowment for the Humanities.

Copyright 2017 by Beverly C. Tomek and Matthew J. Hetrick
All rights reserved
Published in the United States of America

First cloth printing, 2017
First paperback printing, 2022

27 26 25 24 23 22   6 5 4 3 2 1

Library of Congress Cataloging-in-Publication Data
Names: Tomek, Beverly C., editor of compilation. | Hetrick, Matthew J., editor of compilation. | Harrold, Stanley, author of foreword. | Miller, Randall M., author of foreword.
Title: New directions in the study of African American recolonization / edited by Beverly C. Tomek and Matthew J. Hetrick ; foreword by Stanley Harrold and Randall M. Miller.
Other titles: Southern dissent.
Description: Gainesville : University Press of Florida, 2017. | Series: Southern dissent | Includes bibliographical references and index.
Identifiers: LCCN 2017005517 | | ISBN 9780813054247 (cloth) | ISBN 9780813080109 (pbk.)
Subjects: LCSH: African Americans—Colonization—Liberia. | American Colonization Society. | Liberia—History. | United States—History.
Classification: LCC DT633 .N49 2017 | DDC 325/.666208996073—dc23
LC record available at https://lccn.loc.gov/2017005517

The University Press of Florida is the scholarly publishing agency for the State University System of Florida, comprising Florida A&M University, Florida Atlantic University, Florida Gulf Coast University, Florida International University, Florida State University, New College of Florida, University of Central Florida, University of Florida, University of North Florida, University of South

University Press of Florida
2046 NE Waldo Road
Suite 2100
Gainesville, FL 326099
http://upress.ufl.edu

Contents

Foreword vii
   Stanley Harrold and Randall M. Miller

Introduction: The Past, Present, and Future of Colonization Studies 1
   Beverly C. Tomek

Part I. Reconsidering the Missionary Dimensions of Colonization

1. Race, Sympathy, and Missionary Sensibility in the New England Colonization Movement 33
   Gale L. Kenny

2. "The Heathen Are Demanding the Gospel": Conversion, Redemption, and African Colonization 50
   Ben Wright

3. "He Be God Who Made Dis Man": Christianity and Conversion in Nineteenth-Century Liberia 70
   Andrew N. Wegmann

4. "Teaching Them to Observe All Things": African American Women, the Great Commission, and Liberia in the Nineteenth Century 90
   Debra Newman Ham

Part II. Reconsidering the Political and Diplomatic Dimensions of Colonization

5. The American Colonization Society's Not-So-Private Colonization Project 111
   David F. Ericson

6. James Monroe and the Practicalities of Emancipation and Colonization   129
   Daniel Preston

7. The Missouri Crisis and the "*Changed* Object" of the American Colonization Society   146
   Nicholas P. Wood

8. Situating African Colonization within the History of U.S. Expansion   166
   Brandon Mills

9. Experiments in Colonial Citizenship in Sierra Leone and Liberia   184
   Bronwen Everill

10. The American Colonization Society and the Civil War   206
    Sebastian N. Page

Part III. Redirecting the Field and Offering New Answers to Old Questions

11. The Cape Mesurado Contract: A Reconsideration   229
    Eric Burin

12. "A Desire to Better Their Condition": European Immigration, African Colonization, and the Lure of Consensual Emancipation   249
    Andrew Diemer

13. The End of Emancipation Street: "Civilization," Race, and Cartography in Colonial Liberia   267
    Robert Murray

14. Rewriting Their Own History; or, The Many Paul Cuffes   288
    Matthew J. Hetrick

15. The Changing Legacy of Civil War Colonization   303
    Phillip W. Magness

16. Rethinking Colonization in the Early United States   329
    Nicholas Guyatt

List of Contributors   351
Index   353

Foreword

From the nation's birth in 1776 to its supposed redemption with the ratification of the Thirteenth Amendment in 1865, nothing threatened the promise and prospects of the United States more than black slavery in the South. But convincing white Americans that slavery constituted a moral, economic, and political problem was not an easy task. The South's dependence on slave labor, the Northeast's economic dependence on cotton slaves, and slaveholders' political power presented great obstacles. Just as significantly, the great majority of white Americans, northern as well as southern, feared ending slavery would create an uncontrollable free black class. Therefore, as an antislavery movement developed during the late eighteenth and early nineteenth centuries, many who supported it advocated removing free African Americans from the country. They supported the American Colonization Society (ACS), which organized in 1816 and claimed that its plan for sending African Americans to Africa would relieve white fear and prepare the way to ending slavery.

The ACS's quasi-antislavery effort drew on the British Empire's settlement of former slaves in its West African colony of Sierra Leone. It had similarities to the American government's forceful removal during the 1830s and 1840s of southeastern American Indian nations to Indian Territory west of the Mississippi River. And it reflected a belief among some black as well as white Americans that migration to areas beyond U.S. borders provided potential migrants with a path to liberty and self-improvement impossible within the racist United States. Those who hoped to send African Americans to Africa also envisioned the migrants bringing Christianity, civilization, and commerce to what they regarded as a benighted, heathen, and backward continent.

The ACS, although politically influential, never overcame resistance among southern slaveholders, nor free black opposition and practical obstacles. By the 1830s most slaveholders objected to any suggestion that slavery should be even gradually abolished. The great majority of free African Americans opposed removal from the land of their birth. Also, transporting large numbers of people beyond the country's borders would be extremely expensive. Therefore, although the ACS received U.S. government support for its Liberia colony, located in West Africa to the south of Sierra Leone, it failed to achieve its stated goals. Liberia remained a small, impoverished American colony (and by 1847 an independent country); few slaveholders freed their slaves in response to the ACS's urgings; and few free African Americans left the United States.

By the late 1820s, the small minority of white northerners who advocated immediate emancipation of the enslaved and equal rights in the United States for African Americans had joined the ACS's black opponents in rejecting colonization. In the resulting argument that persisted through the Civil War and beyond, colonizationists asserted that they aimed to end slavery by encouraging masters to free slaves. Immediatists, black and white, portrayed this claim as a ruse designed to perpetuate slavery by removing its most determined opponents—free African Americans.

Historians of American slavery, the antislavery movement, and the Civil War era have for many years investigated this debate. By the 1960s, most of the scholars agreed that, regardless of its supporters' claims, the African colonization movement appealed to racism and hampered progress toward black freedom. Yet not all who studied the movement shared this view, and a new generation of scholars has revisited questions of the ACS's purpose, politics, and possible outcomes. They have placed colonizationists within a transatlantic context, investigated African responses, and reevaluated the movement's long-term consequences. They have reexamined free African Americans' opposition to, support for, and (in some cases) hopes that colonization in Africa would produce an independent black nation beyond the United States.

All of this is finely demonstrated in Beverly Tomek and Matthew Hetrick's collection of essays on the dimensions and directions of the African colonization movement. The essays, written by a mixture of beginning and established historians, provide new insights into the movement's role in the history of race, slavery, antislavery, and black nationalism in the United States. They offer multiple perspectives and employ various methodologies.

Altogether they suggest that understanding the African colonization movement is central to understanding the role of race, not only in southern history, but in American history. This collection is a welcome addition to the Southern Dissent series.

Stanley Harrold and Randall M. Miller
Series Editors

Introduction

The Past, Present, and Future of Colonization Studies

BEVERLY C. TOMEK

William Lloyd Garrison once described African colonization as "inadequate in its design, injurious in its operation, and contrary to sound principle." He accused the "master spirits in the crusade," the slaveholders who helped found and continued to support the American Colonization Society (ACS), of tricking otherwise good people throughout the nation into joining a formidable coalition united by the desire to send black Americans to Africa. If opponents of slavery only had to fight against "men-stealers and slaveholders," he contended, "victory would be easy." Unfortunately, he concluded, they had to fight a "whole nation," including its churches, its most respected leaders, even its well-meaning reformers, some of whom actually agreed that slavery must end.[1]

When Garrison declared war on the ACS, he focused on a national organization whose appeal cannot be measured simply by examining its membership rolls and lists of donors, as some scholars have done. Although few Americans joined the ACS or donated funds to it, many did support the notion of separating the races by removing blacks to Africa.[2] Neither can the appeal be understood simply by reading the society's reports or the speeches of its most famous members.

The movement appealed to different people for different reasons. Proslavery politicians and some, but not all, slaveholders supported it from hope that removing free blacks would strengthen the bonds of slavery. Some politicians regretted the effects slavery had on the nation's development, contending that continued reliance upon bound labor encouraged the South to remain an agrarian society dependent upon a single cash crop. Other supporters saw it as a way of removing people whose presence they deemed a destabilizing social force that left white Americans (especially those in the South) in constant fear of retribution and revolt. Some gradual abolitionists supported colonization as the best means to peacefully convince slaveholders to give up their human property and the best way to avoid civil war. Finally, some social reformers supported colonization as the only means for black Americans to break free of the racism that held them down in the United States, and some black Americans agreed.

Garrison did not agree with colonization on any level. He decided to battle this hydra in 1832 because he wanted to convince Americans that slavery was a sin, that it must end immediately, and that "men-stealers" deserved no compensation for doing the right thing and freeing their captives. He wanted to re-chart the nation's moral course in a way that would transform society by forcing white Americans to admit and atone for their sins and then offer black Americans equal citizenship and opportunity. His dream has yet to be fulfilled.

Garrison dedicated himself to opposing the African colonization movement, but his real enemy was more fundamental—a cultural current of racism that permeated every aspect of society in the United States from before the ACS emerged in 1816 to well beyond the death of Reconstruction in 1877. The ACS clung to life until the 1960s, and the legacies of suspicion, division, and separation it fostered still haunt the United States today. What were the true intentions of those who supported this movement? How did African colonization come to dominate the discourse of antislavery and race relations in the United States? How was the idea able to last so long? Why have racial separation and various forms of de facto and de jure segregation been so difficult to move beyond? The essays in this collection address these and other key questions.

Historical Background

The story of African colonization begins with the enslavement and forced migration of Africans to the New World. As European leaders began to exploit the Americas for wealth—whether precious metals or cash crops—they encountered unprecedented labor needs. The easiest solution was to enslave indigenous peoples, but Native Americans knew the land and could escape fairly easily. More importantly, they lacked immunity to European diseases and died in great numbers, so European colonizers in British North America turned to the poorer people in their own nations, enticing them with passage to the colonies in exchange for a set labor contract that generally included four to seven years of indentured servitude, after which time the servants would receive "freedom" dues of some sort. This labor source also had its problems, primarily because landowners could only exploit these workers for a limited time, and servants resisted and ran away from the abuses.

At the same time that some explorers headed to the New World, others sailed down the African coast seeking trade opportunities. They began to buy human beings to use as forced laborers in the American colonies, creating the Atlantic slave trade. Landowners in the New World colonies learned the value of African strength and knowledge in their quest for labor, and as the African population grew and its labor value increased, white colonial leaders began to construct the social and legal framework of race-based chattel slavery. Of course, as Frank Tannenbaum has shown, this framework differed according to the social and political customs and ideologies of the home countries, with perhaps the strictest racial divisions being drawn in the English colonies. Unlike Spanish and Portuguese colonists, who were strongly influenced by Iberian customs and the Catholic Church, the English colonists developed a strong racial caste system that forbade "interracial" marriage and discouraged the type of personal interaction that would favor cooperation and ease white attitudes toward manumission.[3]

Opposition to slavery arose immediately. Africans resisted capture and rose up in slave factories and on ships. Slaves rebelled and ran away and otherwise disrupted masters' efforts to control them completely. During the eighteenth century, especially during the Revolutionary Era, free blacks argued passionately and articulately for freedom. They pointed out that slavery violated human rights and God's law.[4] Some Europeans and European colonists also argued against slavery early on, maintaining that a system based on human bondage carried grave danger, defied scripture, and bode ill for progress. In the English North American colonies, most opponents of slavery belonged to the Society of Friends, called Quakers.

Quakers and others who opposed slavery for a variety of reasons created the first abolitionist groups in the New World. Some of these early abolitionists considered the immorality of capturing human beings and selling them as objects, but others worried more about the notion that such behavior would eventually earn slaveholders as well as their non-slaveholding neighbors retribution from an angry God. Others who opposed slavery maintained that, no matter how hard slaveholders tried to keep control over their human property, the enslaved would eventually break free and wreak vengeance, not only on those who had oppressed them, but also on those who had stood by and allowed it to happen. Finally, other opponents of slavery insisted that members of a biracial society would inevitably mix, leading to what they called "amalgamation." The focus on white safety in these arguments illustrates the self-interested side of some early antislavery efforts.[5]

From Pennsylvania northward, slavery existed in varying degrees of importance to local economies through most of the colonial era, but it was not integral to the economic and social structure as it was in the southern colonies. During and because of the American Revolution, northern states adapted various programs of emancipation, most of which were gradual. These plans provided for freedom of enslaved people, but only after they had worked long enough to compensate the financial losses their freedom would bring their masters. Many who supported this type of abolition argued that, during the period before their release, slaves could be prepared for productive citizenship.

Northern states took different paths toward gradual abolition. Vermont eliminated human bondage through its state constitution, which freed men at the age of twenty-one and women at eighteen. Pennsylvania passed a state law in 1780 that provided for the eventual end of slavery in the state. It allowed owners to keep their current slaves and free their offspring only after periods of indenture, and lawmakers required owners to post bonds of thirty pounds each on all manumitted slaves to provide for their care in the case of indigence. They also passed laws prohibiting vagrancy, interaction with slaves, and racial mixing. In 1783, Massachusetts took a third path to abolition when the state supreme court ruled against slavery—ending it immediately.[6]

Historians have generally agreed that most Americans, even those in the southern states, claimed to oppose slavery on some level or another during the early years of the Republic. In the South, however, slavery had become an integral part of the economic and social fabric. Thus, although tobacco cultivation had sapped the land of key nutrients, leaving it exhausted and slavery less profitable in the tidewater Chesapeake region by the late 1700s, slaveholders remained reluctant to release their laborers.[7] They switched to wheat and other crops and hired out or sold their "excess" slaves, thereby maintaining slavery.

Thomas Jefferson's often-quoted complaint of holding a "wolf by the ear" has reached the status of cliché, but it remains the best way to illustrate the position of slaveholders. His wealth and status depended upon forced labor, yet he realized that slaves could revolt. He also knew well the temptation to "amalgamate," as historians have shown that he very likely had multiple children with one of the women he owned. Jefferson and others of his generation realized that slavery was as much a social as an economic system. Black bondage was what enabled them to keep the races separate on a psychological level, if not physically, and it provided them the means of controlling black behavior as much as possible. They looked to the northern states to illustrate the problem with general emancipation, arguing that freed blacks relied on the public dole and committed a variety of crimes.[8]

These claims forced abolitionists to grapple with the racial implications of freedom. During the years of the Early Republic, gradualist organizations such as the Pennsylvania Abolition Society (PAS) took censuses of blacks and worked to prove wrong assertions of black misbehavior. Initially these efforts appeared to succeed in defending free blacks from racist arguments, but as the free black population grew, so too did white resistance to black freedom. By the early 1800s black and white abolitionists found themselves under increasing attack from resentful whites. At that time the PAS began to consider what should be done with freedpersons. The group considered colonization in the western territories of North America but rejected it, choosing instead to continue fighting for abolition in the District of Columbia and other federal jurisdictions and to fight in court against those who kidnapped free blacks to enslave them. They also worked to educate free blacks and help them find jobs that offered independence and success.[9]

As they began to seriously consider African colonization, white and black Americans took their cue from English reformers. British humanitarians and abolitionists founded the African colony of Sierra Leone in the 1790s with poor blacks from London and black loyalist refugees from the American Revolution. The effort gained official sanction when the British government assumed control of the colony in 1808 and began to send "recaptives," or people who had been rescued from the illegal slave trade, to the colony. Sierra Leone provided an example for American reformers who founded the American Colonization Society (ACS) in 1816 and the colony of Liberia in 1822. In both cases colonization provided an outlet for an unwanted population while also promising a means to end slavery and "redeem" Africa through the spread of Christianity, commerce, and Western civilization.[10]

Reformers in Great Britain and the United States worked in part out of self-interest, but the selfishness was more acute in the United States, where abolition without colonization would have more direct effects. For example, someone in London could support colonization for the selfish reason of wanting to keep poor relief to a minimum, but the black population there was never large enough to change the social order. For white Americans, especially southerners, that prospect was real.[11] Thus, men like Jefferson, who feared both the prospect of trying to maintain control over the wolf *and* that of freeing it, colonization offered the only viable solution. As a result, many slaveholders helped create, joined, and supported the ACS.

Like their British counterparts, American colonizationists argued that their goals involved stopping the slave trade at its source while also "civilizing" Africa, and some blacks in both nations initially supported the colonization endeavor. Believing the humanitarian rhetoric, they saw the movement as an antislavery effort to send a select number of the most educated and skilled blacks to Africa to serve as colonial leaders of a society that would influence the indigenous population to put an end to the slave trade. They drew hope from the efforts of British philanthropist Granville Sharp, who saw the project as nothing less than "the chance to construct the perfect society on Earth." He donated 1,735 pounds and wrote a plan for the settlement that would have provided self-government by the settlers, had it been adopted.[12]

The idea may have sounded good in theory, but Ottobah Cugoano, a former slave then living in England, realized that the British government had provided funding and would eventually govern the colony. Unlike the humanitarians such as Sharp, the government was concerned only with alleviating the problem of a growing population of poor blacks in London. Cugoano argued that many black people in Britain would have "embraced the opportunity . . . to reach their native land." He pointed out, however, that sufficient preparations for the success of the colony had not been made, that no legitimate treaty had been reached with Africans as to the terms and location of the settlement, and that the settlers had not been provided for and "were to be hurried away at all events, come of them after what would." He saw maltreatment of the proposed colonists as evidence of sinister motivation behind the settlement plans and argued that potential settlers would not participate in such a government-supported, white-initiated scheme because they had learned from centuries of forced captivity and exploitation not to trust Europeans.[13] For Cuguano, colonization was not permanently out of the question, but a settlement initiated by whites and funded and promoted by the British government could not be trusted.

Former slave Olaudah Equiano's experiences gave credence to Cuguano's arguments. When asked by the government to serve as commissary of stores for the expedition, he expressed reservations but accepted. He soon learned his initial thoughts were right after uncovering evidence of agents pocketing money and provisions allotted for the settlers. He also witnessed the "most wretched" conditions of the prospective settlers as they waited on board for the ships to set sail for the colony. He reported the abuses to the Navy, and the government dismissed him from his post. Equiano concluded that the government was using free blacks as pawns. He also began to realize that "even the supporters of abolition could be unfeelingly paternalistic, and insulting," as whites remained unwilling to allow blacks true leadership roles.

By the time the British government cleared Equiano of any wrongdoing and paid his lost wages, he had learned that white abolitionists were willing to fight on behalf of the slaves but, whether they knew it or not, their faith in blacks' ability to help themselves was insincere.[14] Realizing their marginal status within the white abolitionist movement, Equiano, Cugoano, and other blacks living in England came to reject colonization.

African Americans of this generation also felt initial hope for Sierra Leone. Paul Cuffe of Massachusetts and James Forten of Pennsylvania tried to recruit qualified representatives of the American free black community to emigrate to Sierra Leone to open businesses and help ensure the colony's self-sufficiency. Cuffe, a leading merchant sailor, took one group of settlers but died before he could contribute more to the colony. Forten worked as a recruiter until Cuffe's death left the movement void of black leadership and revealed the extent to which it was a white initiative. This, plus the development of a similar colonization scheme by American whites, caused Forten to question both schemes.

When the ACS was formed in 1816, it overshadowed Cuffe's efforts and turned most black Americans against African colonization. The last thing they wanted was to be taken back across the Atlantic by whites who had exploited black labor for centuries but now deemed those laborers and their descendants unfit for citizenship in the nation they had helped forge. When blacks supported emigration, they focused on select and temporary migration to create model societies under black leadership, not full-scale exodus. Successful black republics with black leaders could showcase black capability, but large-scale removal to a distant land where they would remain under white leadership did nothing for their cause.

Just as Equiano and Cugoano had realized that the Sierra Leone project was partly fueled by a government desire to rid England of blacks, most black American leaders saw a similar motivation behind colonization and argued strongly against the ACS's plans. By the late 1820s, increasingly vocal opposition emerged from the black community in the United States. Although the ACS founded Liberia as a private colony and never enjoyed support from the government comparable to that the British government extended to Sierra Leone, black Americans lived in fear that the government would adopt the colony and initiate forced removal to it. The ACS's repeated attempts to gain official sanction and support did little to assuage such concerns. Slaveholder involvement with the ACS, and the organization's constant striving for government support, led many black Americans to question the ACS's true intentions.

This concern was justified given government treatment of Native Americans. Soon after the American Revolution, debate ensued as white Americans tried to decide if Indians should be assimilated or removed. George Washington was the first president to consider a removal policy, seeing Native Americans as savages in the way of white settlement. Thomas Jefferson also considered removal, but he did so partially out of anthropological concern for preserving indigenous culture. Beginning soon after the War of 1812, the government began forcing Native Americans westward, but full-scale removal did not begin until Andrew Jackson's 1830 Indian Removal Act. The government cloaked removal in humanitarian terms by insisting that it would save Native groups from extinction and preserve their culture. In theory this migration was to be voluntary, but in policy it was forced.[15]

There were obvious parallels between Indian Removal and colonization, and some black Americans opposed any notion of forced removal to Africa. David Walker, a black abolitionist in Boston, publicly articulated serious concerns over colonization in his 1829 *Appeal to the Colored Citizens of the World*. In this pamphlet he argued that colonization was a scheme whereby slaveholders hoped to send free blacks away, thus removing the most vocal abolitionists and securing slavery.

Many white abolitionists began their antislavery careers by supporting colonization, but black resistance such as Walker's led them to reconsider. The most studied example is Garrison and his 1832 pamphlet, *Thoughts on African Colonization*. Through this work he influenced contemporary debate as well as a generation of historians who relied heavily upon it in assessing colonization in the aftermath of the twentieth-century civil rights movement. Garrison, the most vocal white anticolonizationist, is often cited as the father of immediate abolition, but he took cues from black leaders who resisted colonization after determining its potential to become a government-sponsored, forced migration similar to Indian Removal.[16]

Though most black Americans rejected colonization, some held on to the idea of emigration. Enforcement of the Fugitive Slave Act of 1793 and then the more aggressive Fugitive Slave Act of 1850, combined with continued racial discrimination in the free states, led some blacks to reassess their prospects in America. They thought that only by leaving the United States could they be sure of their freedom and secure their rights. Settlements in Canada suggested a route to freedom and security for some black Americans. Others placed their hope in Africa.

A new generation of black leaders emerged in the 1850s to carry forth Cuffe's plans to build an independent African nation with the goal of proving black equality. Some, like Alexander Crummell, focused on carrying forward the civilizing and Christianizing agenda earlier colonizationists had advocated, but others, like Martin Delany and Henry Highland Garnet, wanted to use emigration to create economically successful colonies that would replace the U.S. South as the top producer of cotton. Determined to avoid the ACS in many cases and unaware of—or at least willing to forget—Equiano's mistreatment, some of these emigrationists turned to Great Britain for funding.[17]

Emigrationists like Delany developed a coherent set of goals that focused mainly on the idea of "free produce." British abolitionists had argued that purchasing goods produced by slave labor encouraged the slave trade, and they called upon people to boycott the rice, sugar, and cotton grown by slaves in order to make slavery unprofitable. When black American emigrationists heard manufacturers voicing concerns about the cotton supply, they refined the free-produce argument by concentrating on that crop. Even as emigrationists sought British support, they continued to insist that the colonies being settled were first and foremost ventures in black independence and would remain free from white rule.[18]

The appeal for assistance seemed to work at first, with British textile manufacturers showing interest, but they eventually abandoned support of black-led emigration and pressured the British government to simply extend its sphere of influence in West Africa with direct and swift imperialistic intervention in the autonomous governments in the area. Choosing exploitation over paternalism, the textile interests abandoned black emigrationist leaders in favor of adopting goals that were strictly commercial. Just as white abolitionist motives were co-opted by the British government in the 1790s, so were black abolitionists overcome by commercial interests in the 1850s. Both groups learned how easy it was for former allies in their colonization schemes to transform the proposed colonies into self-serving entities with little or no regard for black interests. Black Americans saw the results as a warning against what could be if the ACS and the U.S. government were to join forces.[19]

Black Americans' interest in colonization waned during the Civil War and the early years of Reconstruction. As biographers of Martin Delany have shown, this was a period of hope that the situation in the United States would improve and that blacks might eventually be able to achieve equality in the nation they had helped to build. Only after the Compromise of 1877 and the failure of Reconstruction would black Americans again look toward Africa, but even then not in large numbers. Delany devoted the last years of his life to reconsidering colonization. By that point Liberia had gained diplomatic recognition from the United States and was seen by many as a legitimate free black republic, but the violent resistance to Reconstruction and meaningful black freedom in the United States left him and other leaders disheartened. At that point he even embraced the ACS and Liberia, but he died before he could return to Africa.[20]

Historiography of African Colonization

In both cases—British colonization in Sierra Leone and American colonization in Liberia—historians have offered mixed assessments of the movements' motives and results. Some have heeded Garrison and black abolitionists' warnings against the ACS, dismissing it as a proslavery organization, while others have argued for its role in the antislavery movement. Some historians have shown that these two arguments are not mutually exclusive, seeking to understand the movement's complexities and its various stages of development.

Some historians of British abolition question government motives for involvement in Sierra Leone. They argue that the effort stemmed from a desire to limit the relief rolls by removing poor blacks. Other historians highlight the humanitarian efforts of men like Granville Sharp. One of the first historians of the colony, J. J. Crooks, served as governor of Sierra Leone from 1891 to 1894. He emphasized that British interest there was to introduce "civilisation into the African continent" and to stop the slave trade. Crooks credited philanthropists such as Sharp, a founder of the Sierra Leone Company, with the purest of motives.

Crooks's close involvement in the colony may leave his scholarship suspect, but other historians concur with his assessment. In 1991 Howard Temperley examined the papers of abolitionist Thomas Fowell Buxton and concluded that evangelical conscience played a large role in Buxton's support for colonization. He argued that Buxton and his fellow abolitionists believed that Britain had a duty to create a new Africa based on a trinity of Christianity, civilization, and commerce. Even scholars who are critical of government efforts to remove blacks for selfish reasons agree that humanitarians labored under the best intentions, at least in Great Britain.[21]

Matters were more complicated in the United States, and the historiography of the ACS is more divided. Historians who agree with abolitionist accusations that the ACS was proslavery usually stress the southern origins of the society. Writing soon after the Civil War, Herman von Holst contends that the organization originated in Virginia and that southern slaveholders tricked northern philanthropists into supporting a proslavery movement. Many abolitionist specialists agree. Vincent Harding, a historian and an active participant in the civil rights struggle during the 1960s, stresses the domination of southern leaders and claims that the ACS sought to encourage voluntary emigration of free blacks because they were "thorns in the side of slavery." Paul Goodman concurs. His 1998 study, *Of One Blood: Abolitionism and the Origins of Racial Equality*, relies heavily upon abolitionist writings and concludes that colonization was a ploy by southerners to "forestall and repress latent agitation against slavery in the free states." While he accuses the ACS of providing "political and ideological cover for an expansionist slave South," Goodman gives the colonization movement credit for motivating black abolitionists to speak up and convert important white leaders like Garrison.[22]

Not all black Americans immediately opposed African resettlement, and some historians have pointed to the complex relationship between blacks and colonization. A number of authors connect American efforts in Africa to the legacy of Paul Cuffe's interest in Sierra Leone. Henry N. Sherwood argues that Cuffe's efforts served as a useful example to the ACS. More recently, James Wesley Smith expanded upon Sherwood's work by emphasizing black agency in the settlement of Liberia and crediting Cuffe with providing the impetus for the formation of the ACS.[23] Historiographically, what is most important about Cuffe's participation is that it complicates many criticisms of colonization by showing that the movement held appeal not just for whites but also for some black Americans. A vibrant debate existed within the black community from Cuffe's time through the Civil

War and beyond about whether to embrace or reject the ACS, or to attempt parallel black-led emigration movements.

Few scholars continue to believe that black resistance to white-led colonization was immediate and unified. Julie Winch argues that both Cuffe and his associate James Forten supported the British movement and showed initial enthusiasm for Sierra Leone, but that after Cuffe's death, Forten realized the limited role of black leaders in the colony and came to question the American scheme. At that point he joined the grassroots resistance to resettlement. Historians generally support the argument Richard Blackett first made in the early 1970s that this resistance turned British philanthropists against the ACS's efforts. According to this view, the society cited the humanitarian motive of removing free blacks from a debilitating racism in the United States that made equality impossible, but black abolitionists realized that the ACS was a proslavery organization seeking to remove free blacks from the country in order to strengthen the bonds of slavery.[24]

Of central importance to this debate is the difference between "colonization" as a white-led movement and "emigration" as a black-led movement. One of the first to make this distinction, in his book *The Search for a Black Nationality: Black Colonization and Emigration, 1787–1863,* Floyd J. Miller explores the origins of black nationalism to find that many African Americans embraced the chance to emigrate during the 1820s. He argues that, even though they applied to the ACS for passage to Africa, most emigrants "assumed they would be sovereign in all territorial and political matters" once in Liberia. Dickson D. Bruce Jr. agrees and adds that ideas for black-initiated colonization predated the ACS and even Cuffe's work with Sierra Leone. Finding a great deal of black agency in African colonization, he insists that, once the ACS began to take over, blacks lost interest since "a 'national identity' was not something to be imposed by others, and . . . the Colonization Society sought to do just that."[25]

Marie Tyler-McGraw makes a similar claim about black support for the ACS in Richmond. She argues that during the 1820s many free blacks sought passage to Liberia but that, once negative reports began to indicate miserable conditions in the colony and a lack of leadership opportunity for black settlers, free black immigration dwindled.[26] Clearly, in the United States as in Great Britain, some blacks were interested in African colonization when they saw potential for self-determination, but they changed their minds when they realized what awaited them in the ACS colony.

Even considering its failure to provide real opportunities for black leadership, some historians portray the Colonization Society as a moderate antislavery organization. These historians emphasize the role of northern founders such as Robert Finley, a Presbyterian minister from New Jersey; Leonard Bacon, a Connecticut minister and social activist; and Samuel J. Mills, the founder of the American Bible Society and the American Board of Commissioners for Foreign Missions. They argue that these northern philanthropists and other evangelicals who supported colonization did so for humanitarian reasons. Like gradual abolitionists, they wanted to do away with human bondage in a way that would not disrupt the peace of the nation. They walked a tightrope between their desire to free the enslaved and their hopes of maintaining sectional unity.[27]

Explaining this situation, Early Lee Fox and Frederic Bancroft, historians writing during the Progressive Era—a time when the nation sought to heal the wounds of the Civil War—argue that the ACS offered a peaceful solution that might have prevented the war by ending slavery before the matter led to armed conflict. Fox pays particular attention to the society's efforts to reach out to both sections of the nation and, in his view, work to maintain peace. He blames immediate abolitionists like Garrison not only for destroying colonization efforts but also for causing disunion. Bancroft furthers this point. Focusing on the southern reaction to colonization, he agrees that the main opposition in the North came from immediatists, but he added that southerners, particularly from South Carolina, attacked the society because they saw it as a radical plot to destroy slavery. By these accounts the ACS mirrored the Union itself, torn apart by extremists from both sides. Fox insists that the ACS became "almost aggressively anti-slavery" after 1839, but he maintains that the colonizationists, unlike the abolitionists, respected states' rights and remained unwilling to stir trouble with the South.[28]

Important works produced during the civil rights era also portray the ACS as moderate yet antislavery. P. J. Staudenraus links colonization to the larger moral reform movement and credits Finley as its chief founder. In his book *The African Colonization Movement*, the most cited and thorough study on the Colonization Society, he characterizes early ACS leaders as "sedate, honorable, judicious gentlemen" and Garrison as fanatical. His account shows that colonizationists, though antislavery, harbored a number of negative racial biases and left a legacy that combined "racism and African nationalism," but he insists that "the American Colonization Society was not a conspiracy to strengthen the chains of slavery."[29]

A preeminent scholar in the study of race and racism, George Fredrickson offers an ideological examination of the relationship between racism and colonization in his 1971 book *The Black Image in the White Mind*. He devotes a full chapter to the goals and prejudices of colonizationists in the United States, concluding that colonizationists believed that racial bias was so tightly woven into American society that the white masses would never allow the black masses to achieve equality. Distrust of the white masses is mostly what set colonizationists and emigrationists apart from abolitionists, who decided that they could use moral arguments to persuade fellow Americans of the evils of racism. Abolitionists at the time and historians since asked how former slaves, unworthy of American citizenship, would suddenly be qualified to "civilize" Africa. Fredrickson's assessment solves this puzzle. He argues that colonizationists did not claim to see inherent inferiority in blacks. Rather, they claimed to see a society that deliberately held people of color down. Once in Africa, they believed, constraints of racial prejudice would be removed and the freedpersons could prove their equality.[30]

Douglas R. Egerton moves the issue from the ideological to the political arena by further explaining how colonizationists could be antislavery yet less than altruistic. He begins by setting out to prove that Charles Fenton Mercer, a border southerner, led in the ACS's founding. Egerton argues that Mercer, like many colonizationists of the border South, wanted to remove free blacks as a first step to ridding the entire country of African Americans. According to Egerton, "it was not that the free black was a danger to slavery; it was that his skin made him a part of the permanent lower class, and thus a danger to an industrializing society."

In a follow-up article Egerton expands his argument by placing colonization into the overall framework of Henry Clay's "American System." He concludes that colonization was popular in the North and border South, regions that were more likely to foster industrialization and national development. Disagreeing with Winthrop Jordan's claim that Virginians realized "that colonization was utterly impractical," he argued that southern opponents of the scheme realized that the ACS's plans could have worked economically and genuinely feared that possibility.[31] In other words, the strongest defenders of slavery resisted colonization most vehemently, not only because it challenged slavery but because it portended a new national, industrial economy.

The works of Fredrickson and Egerton, when combined, reveal that in the United States, as in England, some humanitarians wanted to give the bondspeople, once freed, a fair chance. Others wanted to preserve their white country by keeping blacks from challenging racial and national purity. Even Americans who truly detested human exploitation feared the racial mixing, job competition, growing relief doles, and violence they assumed would accompany emancipation.

Regional and biographical studies allow historians to further test the extent to which colonization supported or challenged slavery. Eric Burin focuses on manumission rates of colonizationist slaveholders to argue that they were well-intentioned individuals who freed their slaves even when they had to overcome financial and logistical obstacles. He cites six thousand manumissions as evidence of southern philanthropy. Shifting to the North, I use Pennsylvania colonizationists and emigrationists as case studies to explore the mix of humanitarian and political reasons for supporting resettlement, and my evidence in *Colonization and Its Discontents* reveals that most Pennsylvanians who supported the movement did so out of antislavery motives, even if many of them remained concerned with limiting the state's black population for reasons of self-interest. I explain how colonization can be both antislavery and antiblack for some supporters but an extension of gradual abolition for others. I also trace, through James Forten and Martin Delany, the changes in black sentiment toward colonization and emigration over the span of two generations.[32]

Specialists in black history have long used biography to explain race and racism in the United States, and some of those studies have also dealt with colonization and emigration. Victor Ullman and Cyril Griffith wrote biographies of Delany in the 1970s, and Wilson J. Moses and J. R. Oldfield offered biographical works of Alexander Crummell in 1989 and 1990. More recently, Winston James wrote a biography of John Brown Russwurm that dealt with him as a "pan-Africanist pioneer." These are just a few of many biographies that consider emigrationists.[33]

Colonizationists, however, are not as well represented in the biographical literature. Egerton's pioneering article on Charles Fenton Mercer remains important in this field, and Hugh Davis's biography of Leonard Bacon remains unsurpassed. *Colonization and Its Discontents* contains biographical sketches of Mathew Cary, Elliott Cresson, and Benjamin Coates. The works of Lydia Sigourney, the most famous of women colonizationists, have been published in many forms, but she has yet to receive significant biographical treatment. Finally, among the many biographical works on Abraham Lincoln are some that examine his relationship with the colonization movement.[34]

When assessing the colonization movement, one issue that cannot be overlooked is its effect upon Africa. The most obvious question is why African Americans would encourage a movement that could ultimately lead to outside intervention in Africa. As historians from throughout the Atlantic world have shown in various ways, the answer is that they were Americans first and foremost. Floyd Miller, Wilson Moses, Claude Clegg, and James Campbell each focus on the role of black Americans in colonization and emigration movements. Though sympathetic to African American leaders who participated in the movement, Miller and Moses admit that a Western bias shared by black and white Americans fed into the cultural imperialism of the day in regard to African colonization. This applies to Sierra Leone as well, as John Peterson shows in *Province of Freedom: A History of Sierra Leone, 1787–1870.* He maintains that settlers shared the humanitarians' imperialist assumptions about "the heathen," but he credits them with managing to create a "province of freedom."[35]

African historians' assessments of colonization complicate the picture considerably. Monday Abasaittai explains that black settlers in Sierra Leone and Liberia emigrated in hope of achieving freedom, and he concludes that the Liberians were ultimately successful in this endeavor because the American government did not interfere with the colony. He argues that the ACS was "a philanthropic organization" and that the United States "had disavowed colonialism." Feeling less generous toward Britain, he ignores the role of philanthropists there and calls the government "an outright imperial power" that "had no scruples whatever in colonizing Sierra Leone."[36]

Lamin Sanneh shifts the focus to the role African American settlers played once they arrived. He evaluates their efforts favorably, explaining that they brought a legacy of resistance dating back to the American Revolution and maintaining that this attitude, which he calls "antistructure," led Africans to challenge their kings, do away with the slave trade, and modernize Africa. Unlike Abasaittai, he prefers the more active leadership that Britain took in Sierra Leone and argues that the British colony was more successful because it enjoyed direct support from the home government.[37]

Basil Davidson offers a more critical assessment. He examines the role of the recaptives rescued from the slave trade by the British and sent to Sierra Leone, and argues that they adopted an idea of British superiority that caused them, and the nations they created in Africa, to suffer long-term problems. Tunde Adeleke offers even stronger criticism of "un-African American" leaders who supported African settlement, arguing that "black nationalists" worked for the good of elite black Americans and Europeans and ignored the consequences for Africans.[38]

Historians of the Atlantic world also argue that colonization harmed Africa, and African Americans, in a number of ways. Svend Holsoe, an anthropologist, supports Davidson's work by highlighting the cultural imperialism that fueled African colonization and left lasting legacies in and beyond the former colonies. Similarly, a number of historians trace the role of African colonization in British and American empire building. Tom Shick switches focus to emphasize the high mortality rate suffered by black Americans who became African colonists. Most agree that the bad outweighs the good when assessing the legacies of African colonization.[39]

Reconsiderations and Redirections

The essays in this collection address many of these same questions and debates surrounding African colonization from new angles and offer new questions for scholars of colonization to ponder. First and foremost they seek to move beyond the black-and-white argument of whether colonization was proslavery or antislavery and reveal the movement's complexity. David Brion Davis recently contended that the "simple dichotomy between the ACS antichrist and the abolitionist Redeemers . . . can only obscure our understanding," and he called upon historians to place the movements within their own time when seeking to understand them. By reconsidering the missionary, political, social, and diplomatic dimensions of African colonization, the authors in this volume hope to answer his call by redirecting the field and encouraging deeper analysis not only of actions but also of implications and results.[40]

The first part of the book examines the movement's missionary elements. Whether ACS founders set out to create an antislavery organization or not, as Gale Kenny shows, they created a movement that attracted a cohort of reformers that was concerned primarily with using missionary work in Africa to foster evangelical goals. The New England reformers Kenny writes about shared a missionary zeal and, despite their physical distance from most black Americans, they embraced an interracial sympathy born of Christian feelings. Such sympathy, however, existed only in an abstract realm and did not lead to the kind of interracial friendship attributed to immediate abolitionists. Kenny also reveals how these well-intentioned reformers, despite their best intentions, inadvertently contributed to racist notions of blacks as inferior.

Ben Wright also spotlights religious motivation and missionary work, but he shifts focus to black missionaries and the importance of conversionist ideology in explaining support for the cause. He maintains that nonspecific Protestant ideology, fueled by millenialist optimism, served as the linchpin of the movement. He adds that emphasis on conversion rather than on whether the organization was pro- or antislavery allowed colonizationists to hold together an unsteady coalition of supporters in both the North and the South. His work supports those who emphasize Robert Finley's importance in founding the ACS. Though he admits that African colonization may have contributed to imperialist ambitions, in contrast to some of the chapters in part II, he warns that it would be a mistake to overemphasize this aspect of the movement.

While Kenny and Wright are concerned primarily with the religious and intellectual underpinnings of the colonization movement in the United States, Andrew Wegman and Debra Newman Ham focus on Liberia to show how the missionary zeal played out in the colony. Using Lott Cary as a case study, Wegman describes a situation reminiscent of Equiano's by explaining how Cary's missionary aims and racial identity put him at odds with the ACS as he sought to protect the settlers and his religious mission against a movement that did not necessarily share his lofty goals. Whereas Wright maintains that it is ultimately irrelevant whether the conversionist emphasis was a genuine or a pragmatic attempt to hold the coalition together, Wegman's work argues that for black men like Cary it was relevant. He illustrates important efforts by black leaders to make the movement and the colony conform to their agenda. Cary and black leaders who followed in his wake remained mindful of indigenous involvement, even when white leaders failed to do so.

Ham goes deeper into the grassroots level of the movement by examining the lives of Americo-Liberian women to tell how they fostered the on-the-ground missionary work initiated by Cary and other leaders through schools and other outreach efforts. The women she writes about built on the missionaries' efforts and worked to create an educated and benevolent society in Liberia. Collectively, part I offers an in-depth multidimensional look at the missionary aspect of the movement, revealing that, for many in the United States as well as in the colony, missionary work was central to colonization efforts.

Part II considers the political and diplomatic dimensions of the African colonization movement. David Ericson argues that, like Sierra Leone, Liberia was from the beginning intended by many to become a government-supported, if not a government-sponsored, project. He shows that the ACS gained support by emphasizing the colony's role in combatting the slave trade and that this emphasis on the trade dovetailed nicely with federal officials' desires to compete in a propaganda war with Great Britain. He also shows that it ensured federal funding for the program. Daniel Preston deepens the discussion of this theme by offering a case study of James Monroe and his relationship to the society. Of all presidents, Monroe did the most to help the ACS and the colony, and Preston explores the reasons for this support.

Nicholas Wood agrees with Ericson's assessment, going even further and claiming that ACS leaders had the ultimate goal of making colonization a government-sponsored national program that would eventually fund the voluntary removal of free blacks. Ericson and Wood remind readers why contemporary black Americans feared the society and why so many immediate abolitionists felt compelled to speak out against it. At the same time, Wood demonstrates that the debates over the Missouri Compromise led southerners to see colonization as an antislavery plot even as they led northerners to see it as a scheme to strengthen slavery. While the missionary rhetoric may have held public opinion together to some extent, Wood shows that cross-sectional support for colonization in Congress collapsed after the Missouri debates, changing the function of the ACS from the federally backed program envisioned by the founders to a decentralized network of local societies.

Brandon Mills and Bronwen Everill move the political assessment beyond the domestic realm to consider the role of Liberia in U.S. imperialism. Mills calls upon historians to reconsider the movement's impact on politics by looking at how it connected domestic racial policies with overseas expansion. He points out that early colonization proposals focused on the western territories and on the idea of creating domestic dependent nations like those created for Native Americans. He contends that it was the persistent threat of black revolt that led colonizationists to turn to Africa.

Moving overseas, however, led to the possibility of the United States turning into an imperial power like Great Britain, and Mills argues that it was concern for avoiding this situation that prevented the U.S. government from adopting Liberia the way Great Britain adopted Sierra Leone.

Americans were thus able to argue that Liberia was different because it was an independent colony—a reproduction of the United States abroad rather than a colony of it. Whereas Ericson and Wood detail government support, Mills illustrates why that support remained tenuous. His assessment supports the work of African historians and Everill, who have compared the two colonies.

Everill acknowledges that the United States did not consider itself an empire, but she places Liberia within the context of empire building to illustrate commonalities between it and Sierra Leone. In both cases, she maintains, founders experimented with new constitutional forms for ruling territories and subjects while granting some elements of self-representation. Historians before focused on emancipation, but Everill is more concerned with empowerment after freedom. Thus she explores the extent to which freedom in the colonies was genuine. She leads readers to question the notion that Liberia was somehow less of a colony than was Sierra Leone.

Sebastian Page rounds out the section by tracing the relationship between the U.S. government and the colonization movement into the Civil War years. He argues that the war provided the opportune time for the government to become strongly involved in colonization and explores why that did not happen. Overall this section offers the deepest understanding of the political aspects of colonization available and introduces a number of ideas historians should explore even further in future studies.

The final part seeks to redirect the field by offering new answers to old questions about colonization and encouraging new questions that will take colonization studies to greater depths in the future. Eric Burin begins by reassessing the notion that colonization was a pipe dream that did nothing more than allow its supporters to avoid the social and political dilemmas posed by slavery and racism. He contends that colonization was more than just a form of escapism and that proponents acted to shape society in significant ways. He adds that the movement created a new country that (whether in the ways black leaders hoped it would or not) influenced debates over slavery, race, and freedom. He looks more deeply into Americans' efforts to acquire land for the colony, and the story he shares highlights in new ways the complexity of colonization.

Andrew Diemer carries forth a point of Burin's that, no matter what black Americans feared, the colonization movement remained one based on consent. But he also challenges the idea that it was ultimately an emancipatory movement. Conceding that six thousand people gained freedom through ACS efforts, he contends that the negative effects outweighed the gains by hampering the development of a robust antislavery movement early on. Colonizationists made migration for better opportunities seem plausible by placing it in the context of European immigration into the United States. This weakened the antislavery potential of the movement by allowing proponents to imagine an emancipation that did not depend on using the coercive power of the state, as had been done in the North, and did not violate slaveholders' property rights. In essence, colonization put the brakes on the gradual abolition movement.

Combining Everill's emphasis on empowerment, Ham's focus on Americo-Liberian life, and Burin's focus on the new nation colonization created, Robert Murray looks at the geography of emancipation and whiteness. He puts colonization studies into the context of whiteness studies—a subfield that has sought to understand the development of American racism—to explore the ways movement to Africa affected racial perceptions in that continent. He finds that indigenous Africans made few distinctions between black and white Americans, classifying them all as white. His work draws on cultural analysis in new and exciting ways.

Similarly, Matthew Hetrick links colonization studies to another dynamic subfield by examining the historical memory of Paul Cuffe's role in colonization. He offers a close look at abolitionist literature and compares it to events not only to correct the record regarding black support for colonization but also to analyze the historical manipulation. Similarly, Phillip Magness revisits the historiography on Abraham Lincoln and colonization. Activists and historians have altered both Cuffe's and Lincoln's stories to distance these historical figures from a movement that is often (correctly) seen as racist. Hetrick and Magness take closer looks at sometimes forgotten, sometimes overlooked, and sometimes newly discovered primary sources to offer multidimensional assessments of these men. Magness answers the old question, "When did Lincoln abandon colonization?" with a solid "Never."[41]

Nicholas Guyatt rounds out the collection by arguing that historians must restore colonization to its historical context if they are ever to appreciate its legacy. He begins by examining the abolitionist assessment of the movement and then considers the importance of consent. He poses the question of why colonization survived as long as it did, and he concludes by assessing the long-term effects of the movement in hampering peaceful integration in the United States. Like Diemer, he considers the unfortunate consequences of colonization upon blacks in the United States.

The varying interpretations in *New Directions in the Study of African*

American Recolonization reflect continuing debates on African colonization. Some contributors argue the centrality of missionary work in colonization, while others question that notion. Some privilege the political side of colonization rhetoric, while others emphasize the cultural. Interwoven through the chapters are disagreements, though often subtle, about the legacy of colonization in Africa and the United States.

There is much to take away from this volume. It shows that colonization was often perceived as an antislavery movement, even if it tragically reinforced American racism both at home and abroad. It supports the argument that some black Americans backed the idea of spreading Christianity and civilization to Africa even if mistrust of the ACS was widespread. It also demonstrates that the ACS coalition of support was always unstable with colonizationists fighting hard to please all constituents, even at the expense of their general goals. Finally, it shows that combating the slave trade was crucial to the success of the movement.

This collection also shows that there is much for future studies to bring to the field. Mills and Everill's work encourages more exploration of the role of these colonies in fostering imperialism. This connection needs further consideration, especially in light of the ties Delany tried to form with white industrialists. Guyatt offers a number of questions for scholars to consider, and he calls upon historians to discard the notion that the ACS was divided between proslavery and antislavery interests. He suggests moving the discussion forward by looking more closely at colonization after the Emancipation Proclamation. Here and elsewhere Magness and Page have done much to tell the story of colonization during the U.S. Civil War, and there is plenty of room for scholars to join their efforts and to take the story beyond the 1870s.

Many black Americans changed their mind about Africa upon the end of Reconstruction in 1877, and there is a large and significant story to be told about that. As Magness, Page, and Michael J. Douma have also revealed in their archival work throughout the Caribbean, Central and South America, and Europe, there are plenty of sources yet to be discovered on this topic all over the world. Just as importantly, however, Hetrick and Magness show that historians need to reexamine sources that are already known and reconsider assumptions about those who supported and those who resisted the movement.

Future historians must explore even further the African perspective. Much has been written about the life of Americo-Liberians, but what of the lives of Africans inside and bordering the colonies? Some of the chapters in this collection mention various African groups and nations, and much remains to be done to tell the stories of those groups. Of course, this effort could easily lead to a volume of equal size to the current work. Such a volume would make a nice companion to this book, and we encourage scholars to pursue such a project.

Scholars should also pay more attention to other regions that supporters of racial colonization focused on—from the American West to Canada to Central and South America to the Caribbean. A fair body of work has been produced on Haitian colonization, but Haiti was not the only Caribbean destination considered. For example, historian Michael J. Douma recently discovered cases of European governments offering asylum for former slaves in hopes of convincing the U.S. government to send able-bodied workers to their colonies. He, Bo Anders Rasmussen, and others are busy uncovering documents throughout Europe and the Americas that will shed light on this subject.[42]

Colonization studies are a major branch of American foreign-policy history, as some of the essays show, and this avenue of study remains ripe for even more analysis. Colonization is heavily intertwined with parallel historical questions about imperialism, westward and southern expansion, commerce, and even the political stability of nations in the southern hemisphere, and these connections need to be explored.

Scholars will continue to ponder racial colonization for years to come, and those who do so will face many challenges. Among historians, colonization continues to be a contested topic. Those who try to understand the mindset of colonization proponents risk being labeled defenders of a racist movement. Similarly, the implications of a historical figure supporting colonization are complicated. Scholars must move beyond the notion that all who doubted whether the races could live together in peace were racists. To do this, historians have to put the movement squarely within the context of its time and work to understand it as people of that time saw it. Certainly many regarded the movement as racist at the time, and their argument has merit, but after the New York draft riots, massacres such as Fort Pillow, and the racially motivated hate crimes that followed immediately in the wake of emancipation, should readers be surprised that Abraham Lincoln considered the possibility of separating the races? Is asking this question a racist act?[43]

Finally, more biographies are needed to help understand the motives of those who supported and those who contested the movement. Biographies of supporters like Ralph Gurley, Mathew Cary, and Lydia Sigourney would add much to the discussion. Jehudi Ashmun and other colonial leaders who spent time in Liberia and worked to build up the colony should also receive biographical treatment, as should Thaddeus Stephens and other politicians who at least considered the idea at one point or another. Key white and black opposition figures in both the North and the South should also be studied in depth.

Collectively, these essays offer a sampling of the major issues historians of colonization confront while seeking new answers to questions historians have addressed for decades. They demonstrate that African colonization was intimately tied to every important issue in American history: slavery, politics, religion, economics, culture, race, national identity. All were involved in colonization, and colonization was entangled with each of them. At the same time, the essays encourage new questions about the motivations and actions of a range of supporters and opponents of colonization and emigration. They encourage comparisons of different and sometimes competing schemes. They also suggest that historians look more analytically at key figures in the movement, and they nudge the field toward a broader look at colonization in parts of the world that have not yet been considered in depth. We hope that this volume will encourage further contemplation and discussion of the colonization movement for years to come.

Notes

1. William Lloyd Garrison, *Thoughts on African Colonization: or an Impartial Exhibition of the Doctrines, Principles and Purpose of the American Colonization Society, together with the Resolutions, Addresses and Remonstrances of the Free People of Color* (Boston: Garrison and Knapp, 1832), 2, 7.

2. The essays in this collection collectively testify to the ubiquitous nature of colonization sentiment in the United States. See also Matthew Mason, *Slavery and Politics in the Early American Republic* (Chapel Hill: University of North Carolina Press, 2008), and Beverly Tomek, *Colonization and Its Discontents: Emancipation, Emigration, and Antislavery in Antebellum Pennsylvania* (New York: New York University Press, 2011).

3. Frank Tannenbaum, *Slave & Citizen: The Negro in the Americas* (New York: Vintage Books, 1946); Oscar and Mary F. Handlin, "Origins of the Southern Labor System," *William & Mary Quarterly*, 3rd ser., vol. 7 (1950): 199–222; Carl Degler, "Slavery and the Genesis of American Race Prejudice," *Comparative Studies in Society and History* 2 (1959): 49–66; David Brion Davis, *The Problem of Slavery in Western Culture* (Ithaca, N.Y.: Cornell University Press, 1966); Winthrop Jordan, *White Over Black: American Attitudes Toward the Negro, 1550–1812* (Chapel Hill: University of North Carolina Press, 1968); Edmund S. Morgan, *American Slavery, American Freedom* (rpt., New York: W. W. Norton & Co., 2003);

Kathleen Brown, *Good Wives, Nasty Wenches, and Anxious Patriarchs: Gender, Race, and Power in Colonial Virginia* (Chapel Hill: University of North Carolina Press, 1996).

4. Marcus Rediker, *The Amistad Rebellion: An Atlantic Odyssey of Slavery and Freedom* (New York: Viking Press, 2012); Graham Russell Gao Hodges, *Root and Branch: African Americans in New York and East Jersey, 1613–1863* (Chapel Hill: University of North Carolina Press, 1999).

5. See Tomek, *Colonization and Its Discontents*.

6. Gary Nash and Jean Soderlund, *Freedom by Degrees: Emancipation in Pennsylvania and Its Aftermath* (New York: Oxford University Press, 1991), 153, xiv, 156, 12, 43, 54, 13; Edward R. Turner, "The Abolition of Slavery in Pennsylvania," *Pennsylvania Magazine of History and Biography* 36 (1912), 129–42; Pennsylvania Archives, 8th ser., vol. 6: 5191, 5196, 5197, 5204, 5205–6, 521–14, 5215, 5217. For the economic side of gradual abolition, see Robert William Fogel and Stanley L. Engerman, "Philanthropy at Bargain Prices: Notes on the Economics of Gradual Emancipation," *Journal of Legal Studies* 3 (1974), 377–401. Fogel and Engerman argue that the greatest fear expressed during debates over emancipation in the Northeast centered on the concern that non-slaveholders would be hurt financially by emancipation.

7. Edward Baptist, *The Half Has Never Been Told: Slavery and the Making of American Capitalism* (New York: Basic Books, 2014).

8. For more on Jefferson and slavery, see the seminal studies—Robert McColley, *Slavery and Jeffersonian Virginia* (Urbana: University of Illinois Press, 1964), and John Chester Miller, *The Wolf by the Ears: Thomas Jefferson and Slavery* (New York: Free Press, 1977). For Jefferson's own words on the subject, see, among other printed collections, Julian Boyd, ed., *The Papers of Thomas Jefferson* (Princeton, N.J.: Princeton University Press, 1950–90). For the Jefferson quote, see Thomas Jefferson to John Holmes, April 22, 1820. This letter can be found in all major collections of Jefferson's writings. For Jefferson and Sally Hemings, see Annette Gordon-Reed, *Thomas Jefferson and Sally Hemings: An American Controversy* (Charlottesville: University of Virginia Press, 1997). See also Nash and Soderlund, *Freedom by Degrees*, and Tomek, *Colonization and Its Discontents*.

9. Tomek, *Colonization and Its Discontents*, chapter 1.

10. James Walvin, *The Black Presence: A Documentary History of the Negro in England 1555–1860* (New York: Schocken Books, 1972) 12; Peter Wilson Coldham, *Emigrants in Chains: A Social History of Forced Emigration to the Americas, 1607–1776* (Bath, Avon, U.K.: Bath Press, Ltd., 1992).

11. Seymour Drescher, *Capitalism and Antislavery: British Mobilization in Comparative Perspective* (New York: Oxford University Press, 1987), 12–13. Drescher used this proximity thesis to explain why British abolition developed, but it also works well to explain why abolition seemed a much simpler matter to the British than to most Americans.

12. Edward Scobie, *Black Britannia: A History of Blacks in Britain* (Chicago: Johnson Publishing Co., 1972), 67.

13. Ottobah Cugoano, *Thoughts and Sentiments* (London, 1787), in Walvin, *Black Presence*, 85–86.

14. Mavis Campbell, *Back to Africa: George Ross and the Maroons: From Nova Scotia to Sierra Leone* (Trenton, N.J.: Africa World Press, 1993), viii; Olaudah Equiano, *The Life*

of *Olaudah Equiano,* ed. Paul Edwards (Essex, U.K.: Longman Group UK Limited, 1988), xv; Olaudah Equiano, *The Interesting Narrative of the Life of Olaudah Equiano, Written by Himself,* ed. Robert J. Allison (New York: St. Martin's Press, 1995), 187; Scobie, *Black Britannia,* 67; Equiano, *Life of Olaudah Equiano,* xiv; Allison, in Equiano, *Interesting Narrative of the Life of Olaudah Equiano,* 14.

15. Mary Stockwell, *The Other Trail of Tears: The Removal of the Ohio Indians* (Yardley, Pa.: Westholme Publishing, 2015); Anthony F. C. Wallace, *The Long, Bitter Trail: Andrew Jackson and the Indians* (New York: Hill & Wang, 1993); Theda Perdue and Michael D. Green, *The Cherokee Nation and the Trail of Tears* (New York: Viking, 2007); Anders Stephanson, *Manifest Destiny: American Expansion and the Empire of Right* (New York: Hill & Wang, 1995).

16. James Walvin, *England, Slaves, and Freedom, 1776-1838* (Jackson: University Press of Mississippi, 1986), 178; David Walker, *Walker's Appeal, in Four Articles, Together with a Preamble to the Colored Citizens of the World* (Boston: Printed for the Author, 1829), 55; Garrison, *Thoughts on African Colonization.*

17. Martin R. Delany, *Official Report of the Niger Valley Exploring Party,* in *Search for a Place: Black Separatism and Africa, 1860,* ed. Howard Bell (Ann Arbor: University of Michigan Press, 1969), 23-148, especially 123-25.

18. R. J. M. Blackett, *Building an Antislavery Wall: Black Americans in the Atlantic Abolitionist Movement, 1830-1860* (Baton Rouge: Louisiana State University Press, 1983), 69; "The First Annual Report of the Cotton Supply Association" (Manchester, 1860), qtd. in Blackett, *Building an Antislavery Wall,* 182.

19. Blackett, *Building An Antislavery Wall,* 69.

20. See Victor Ullman, *Martin R. Delany: The Beginnings of Black Nationalism* (New York: Beacon Press, 1971), and Tunde Adeleke, *Without Regard to Race: The Other Martin Robison Delany* (Jackson: University Press of Mississippi, 2003).

21. Walvin, *Black Presence,* 9-12; Scobie, *Black Britannia*; Campbell, *Back to Africa*; James Walker, *The Black Loyalists: The Search for a Promised Land in Nova Scotia and Sierra Leone, 1783-1870* (Halifax, Nova Scotia, Canada: Dalhousie University Press, 1976); J. J. Crooks, *A History of the Colony of Sierra Leone West Africa, With Maps and Appendices* (1903; rpt., Northbrook, Ill.: Metro Books, Inc., 1972), 66-67, 27, 20; Howard Temperley, *White Dreams, Black Africa: The Antislavery Expedition to the River Niger, 1841-1842* (New Haven, Conn.: Yale University Press, 1991).

22. Herman von Holst, *The Constitutional and Political History of the United States* (Chicago: Callaghan & Co., 1889), vol. 1: 331; Vincent Harding, *There Is a River: The Black Struggle for Freedom in America* (Orlando: Harcourt, Brace & Company, 1981), 66; Paul Goodman, *Of One Blood: Abolitionism and the Origins of Racial Equality* (Los Angeles: University of California Press, 1998), 18, 16; Stanley Harrold, *American Abolitionists* (New York: Longman, Pearson Education Ltd., 2001), 26.

23. Marie Tyler-McGraw, "Richmond Free Blacks and African Colonization, 1816-1832," *Journal of American Studies* 21, no. 2 (August 1987): 209-22; Marie Tyler-McGraw, *An African Republic: Black and White Virginians in the Making of Liberia* (Chapel Hill: University of North Carolina Press, 2014); Henry N. Sherwood, "Paul Cuffe and His Contribution to the American Colonization Society," *Proceedings of the Mississippi Valley Historical Society for 1912-1913,* ed. Benjamin F. Shambaugh (Cedar Rapids, Iowa: Torch Press,

1913), vol. 6: 370–402; James Wesley Smith, *Sojourners in Search of Freedom: The Settlement of Liberia by Black Americans* (New York: University Press of America, 1987).

24. Julie Winch, *A Gentleman of Color: The Life of James Forten* (New York: Oxford University Press, 2002); Blackett, *Building an Antislavery Wall*; Richard S. Newman, *Freedom's Prophet: Bishop Richard Allen, the AME Church, and the Black Founding Fathers* (New York: New York University Press, 2009).

25. Floyd J. Miller, *The Search for a Black Nationality: Black Colonization and Emigration, 1787–1863* (Urbana: University of Illinois Press, 1975), 60; Dickson D. Bruce Jr., "National Identity and African-American Colonization, 1773–1817," *Historian* 58, no. 1 (Autumn 1995): 15–28, quote from 28.

26. Tyler-McGraw, "Richmond Free Blacks and African Colonization," 216–18.

27. Hugh Davis, *Leonard Bacon: New England Reformer and Antislavery Moderate* (Baton Rouge: Louisiana State University Press, 1998); Hugh Davis, "Northern Colonizationists and Free Blacks, 1823–1837: A Case Study of Leonard Bacon," *Journal of the Early Republic* 17, no. 4: (Winter 1997): 651–75.

28. Early Lee Fox, *American Colonization Society, 1817–1840* (Baltimore: Johns Hopkins University Press, 1919); Frederic Bancroft, *The Colonization of American Negroes, 1801–1865*, in Jacob Ernest Cooke, ed., *Frederic Bancroft, Historian* (Norman: University of Oklahoma Press, 1957). Bancroft's work on colonization was written in 1917 and published posthumously in this collection.

29. P. J. Staudenraus, *The African Colonization Movement, 1816–1865* (New York: Columbia University Press, 1961), vii, 28.

30. George Fredrickson, *The Black Image in the White Mind: The Debate on Afro-American Character and Destiny, 1817–1914* (Middletown, Conn.: Wesleyan University Press, 1971); Henry Noble Sherwood, "Early Negro Deportation Projects," *Mississippi Valley Historical Review* 2, no. 4 (March 1916): 484–508.

31. Douglas Egerton, "'Its Origin Is Not a Little Curious': A New Look at the American Colonization Society," *Journal of the Early Republic* 5, no. 4 (Winter 1985): 463–80; Douglas Egerton, "Averting a Crisis: The Proslavery Critique of the American Colonization Society," *Civil War History* 43, no. 2 (June 1997): 142–57; Jordan, *White Over Black*, 569; Tomek, *Colonization and Its Discontents*.

32. Eric Burin, *Slavery and the Peculiar Solution: A History of the American Colonization Society* (Gainesville: University Press of Florida, 2005); Tomek, *Colonization and Its Discontents*. The state auxiliaries gained a great deal of power in the 1830s, and there is more work to be done in telling their stories, but these works give us a solid start in that direction: Kenneth C. Barnes, *Journey of Hope: The Back-to-Africa Movement in Arkansas in the Late 1800s* (Chapel Hill: University of North Carolina Press, 2004); Alan Huffman, *Mississippi in Africa: The Saga of the Slaves of Prospect Hill Plantation and Their Legacy in Liberia* (New York: Gotham Books 2004); Penelope Campbell, *Maryland in Africa* (Urbana: University of Illinois Press, 1971); Richard L. Hall, *On Afric's Shore: A History of Maryland in Liberia, 1834–1857* (Baltimore: Maryland Historical Society, 2003); Randall Miller, "Georgia on Their Minds: Free Blacks and the African Colonization Movement," *Southern Studies* 17 (Winter 1978), 349–62; James Gifford, "Emily Tubman and the African Colonization Movement in Georgia," *Georgia Historical Quarterly* 59 (Spring 1975): 10–24; James Gifford, "The Cuthbert Conspiracy: An Episode in African Colonization," *South*

Atlantic Quarterly 79 (Summer 1980): 312–20; James M. Gifford, "The African Colonization Movement in Georgia, 1817–1860," PhD diss., University of Georgia, 1977.

33. Ullman, *Martin R. Delany*; Cyril Griffith, *The African Dream: Martin R. Delany and the Emergence of Pan-African Thought* (State College: Pennsylvania State University Press, 1975); Wilson J. Moses, *Alexander Crummell: A Study of Civilization and Discontent* (New York: Oxford University Press, 1989); J. R. Oldfield, *Alexander Crummell, 1819–1898 and the Creation of an African American Church in Liberia* (London: Edwin Mellen Press, 1990); Winston James, *The Struggles of John Brown Russwurm: The Life and Writings of a Pan-Africanist Pioneer, 1799–1851* (New York: New York University Press, 2010). See also Adeleke, *Without Regard to Race,* and Tunde Adeleke, *UnAfrican Americans: Nineteenth-Century Black Nationalists and the Civilizing Mission* (Lexington: University Press of Kentucky, 1998).

34. Davis, *Leonard Bacon*; Phillip W. Magness and Sebastian N. Page, *Colonization after Emancipation: Lincoln and the Movement for Black Resettlement* (Columbia: University of Missouri Press, 2011); Paul Escott, *"What Shall We Do with the Negro?": Lincoln, White Racism, and Civil War America* (Charlottesville: University of Virginia Press, 2009); Paul Escott, *Lincoln's Dilemma: Blair, Sumner, and the Republican Struggle over Racism and Equality in the Civil War Era* (Charlottesville: University of Virginia Press, 2014). See also James Oakes, *The Radical and the Republican: Frederick Douglass, Abraham Lincoln, and the Triumph of Antislavery Politics* (New York: W. W. Norton, 2008) and Lawanda Cox, *Lincoln and Black Freedom: A Study in Presidential Leadership* (Columbia: University of South Carolina Press, 1994). For a biographical sketch of a female colonizationist, see Gifford, "Emily Tubman and the African Colonization Movement in Georgia."

35. Campbell, *Back to Africa*, vi; Walvin, *England, Slaves, and Freedom*; John Peterson, *Province of Freedom: A History of Sierra Leone, 1787–1870* (Evanston, Ill.: Northwestern University Press, 1969), 18–19, 61, 46–47, 13, 229–30; Ellen Gibson Wilson, *The Loyal Blacks: The Definitive Account of the First American Blacks Emancipated in the Revolution, Their Return to Africa, and their Creation of a New Society There* (New York: G. P. Putnam's Sons, 1976); Claude Clegg III, *The Price of Liberty: African Americans and the Making of Liberia* (Chapel Hill: University of North Carolina Press, 2003); James T. Campbell, *Middle Passages: African American Journeys to Africa, 1787–2005* (New York: Penguin Press, 2006).

36. Monday Abasaittai, "The Search for Independence: New World Blacks in Sierra Leone and Liberia, 1787–1847," *Journal of Black Studies* 23, no. 1 (1992): 107–16.

37. Lamin Sanneh, *Abolitionists Abroad: American Blacks and the Making of Modern West Africa* (Cambridge, Mass.: Harvard University Press, 1999).

38. Basil Davidson, *The Black Man's Burden: Africa and the Curse of the Nation-State* (New York: Random House, 1992), 25; Adeleke, *UnAfrican Americans*, 144.

39. Tom W. Shick, *Behold the Promised Land: A History of Afro-American Settler Society in Nineteenth-Century Liberia* (Baltimore: Johns Hopkins University Press, 1980). The founding editor of the *Liberian Studies Journal,* Svend Holsoe, has produced a number of works on Liberia (www.onliberia.org/holsoe.htm). See also major works on race, nationalism, and manifest destiny, including Reginald Horsman, *Race and Manifest Destiny: The Origins of American Racial Anglo-Saxonism* (Cambridge, Mass.: Harvard University Press,

1981), and James T. Campbell, Matthew Pratt Guterl, and Robert G. Lee, eds., *Race, Nation, and Empire in American History* (Chapel Hill: University of North Carolina Press, 2007).

40. David Brion Davis, *The Problem of Slavery in the Age of Emancipation* (New York: Alfred A. Knopf, 2014), 84.

41. While George Frederickson came to this same conclusion long ago, much historical scholarship on Lincoln in the last few decades has ignored his connection to the movement or argued that he abandoned colonization during the Civil War years. See Magness's essay for the historiography of this debate.

42. Michael J. Douma, "Danish St. Croix as a Precedent for Colonization," paper delivered at Society of Civil War Historians Biennial Meeting, Baltimore, June 12–14, 2014.

43. For more on Lincoln's relationship to colonization, see Magness and Page, *Colonization after Emancipation,* and Eric Foner, *The Fiery Trial: Abraham Lincoln and American Slavery* (New York: W. W. Norton & Co., 2010).

I

RECONSIDERING THE MISSIONARY DIMENSIONS OF COLONIZATION

1

Race, Sympathy, and Missionary Sensibility in the New England Colonization Movement

GALE L. KENNY

When New England Protestants sent out their first foreign missionaries in the 1810s, distance appeared to be a challenge. Why should a Hartford mother or a Boston merchant contribute money to send a minister and his wife to the Sandwich Islands or India? The New England supporters of the American Colonization Society (ACS) met with a similar dilemma when they encouraged benevolent-minded Protestants to embrace their cause. Did white New Englanders have an obligation to an African village decimated by the slave trade? Did residents of a free state bear responsibility for the persistence of slavery in the South? As they answered all of these questions affirmatively in their appeals to their fellow New Englanders throughout the 1820s and 1830s, Protestant humanitarians redefined race and sympathy, as well as religion, and they gave African colonization a central role in their antislavery agenda.[1]

In her 1836 poem "Difference of Color," colonizationist Lydia Huntley Sigourney wrote that God judged the "complexion of the heart," not the "color of the skin." Racial prejudice had no place in Sigourney's religion because God looked within, to the heart, where feelings, including passions and moral affections like love and hate, humility and pride, and, most importantly, sympathy, resided. Nineteenth-century moral philosophers argued that feelings, not reason, motivated people to take moral action, and Sigourney knew that she had to win hearts, not just minds, to the colonization cause. The prominent Connecticut clergyman Leonard Bacon also appealed to his audiences' emotions when he urged them in 1825 to support the ACS. God called white Christians to be the "almoners of his love," and Christians needed to expand their "circle of sympathies, to include the whole family of man." In the past, an ordinary Christian could only "relieve the beggar at his door, but he could do nothing for a dying continent," but by pooling their money in a benevolent society and arranging for the transport of millions of black Americans to Africa, they could "assuage the miseries of another hemisphere."[2]

Sigourney's and Bacon's words illustrate how New England colonizationists used the missionary sensibility to define themselves as Christian humanitarians operating on a global field.[3] Like the Protestants who supported the American Board of Commissioners for Foreign Missions, New England colonizationists also believed that faithful Christians had a responsibility to civilize and evangelize the world and to cultivate sympathy for suffering others. Sigourney and Bacon represented the views of many antislavery New Englanders when they applied this missionary sensibility to the problem of slavery in the United States. As missionary conversions abroad expanded the Christian family to include people of color, ministers like Bacon and evangelical women like Sigourney urged their fellow white Protestants to reconsider their moral obligation to blacks in the United States. They presented colonization as the best course of action, and they presented the ACS as a part of the broader missionary movement. As one article in the evangelical *Boston Recorder* surmised, the ACS "in reality, though not in name, has a Missionary character, and is undertaken in the name of the Lord."[4]

Building on these connections, colonizationists borrowed missionary ideas as tested and religiously sanctioned ways to argue against slavery and racial prejudice while also perpetuating racial distinctions. These colonizationists condemned slavery and railed against "prejudice," while their plan for black Americans to leave the United States for Liberia also maintained racial boundaries. Not only did the colonization scheme put an ocean between white Americans and black people, but the missionary sensibility of white colonizationists also imposed metaphorical distance between white "helpers" and the people they saw in need of aid. As white Protestants self-consciously constructed an image of themselves as benevolent "friends" of people of color, they paid very little attention to the actual demands of black Americans. Their maintenance of color lines and the distance they placed between themselves and the objects of their benevolence contrasted markedly with another major reform group of the 1830s—immediate abolitionists.[5]

While some abolitionists shared the missionary sensibility, they offered a different application of it that challenged the necessity of distance and instead called for interracial cooperation and collaboration across color lines. The tensions concerning sympathy and interracial community became evident in the debates over black education in Connecticut in the early 1830s. The proposed Negro college in New Haven and Prudence Crandall's school for black girls in Canterbury served as the backdrop for a schism between Protestant humanitarians.[6] Beginning in the early 1830s, abolitionists redeployed the missionary sensibility to serve their own agenda, and they wondered at the "unholy prejudice" and "barbarity" of those white colonizationists who opposed the two schools. As the decade wore on, the colonization cause lost much of its support in the region, but the missionary sensibility lived on in a domesticated form as white and black abolitionist men and women embraced the sentimental aesthetics and heart appeals of their colonizationist predecessors to battle against slavery and racial prejudice for the next several decades.

Institutional Roots

In the first decades of the 1800s, Andover Theological Seminary served as the training ground for the missionary-minded men who would establish the American Board and who would serve as agents and officers of the Colonization Society. In 1811 a cohort of evangelical students at Andover organized the Society for Inquiry on the Study of Missions to investigate how American Protestants might evangelize and enlighten the world. Foreign missions affirmed white Protestants' perceptions of themselves as benevolent men and women. As a part of this tradition, the American Colonization Society, founded in late 1816, offered white New Englanders the opportunity to move from being guilty benefactors of slavery to participants in the conversion of Africa. Rather than dwelling on the fact that slaveholders had been responsible for founding the Colonization Society and served as its most active members, New England's Protestant humanitarians instead emphasized the nascent ACS's missionary objectives.[7]

Facing the daunting challenge of evangelizing the world, the American Board got off to a relatively slow start and the organization would not send a missionary to West Africa until the early 1830s. This had much to do with logistics and widespread assumptions about West Africa's insalubrious climate, but it did not mean that the missionary public was uninterested as the American Board frequently published reports from the British Church Missionary Society in Sierra Leone.[8] Indeed, in the 1820s, evangelical New Englanders welcomed the ACS as an organization with missionary potential for West Africa although it was not always clear if African American emigrants or white Americans would be responsible for evangelism to Africans. The Boston-based Baptist Board of Foreign Missions' monthly newspaper praised the "National Colonization Society" for reaching out to "a part of the world that has for ages been sunk in ignorance, bondage, and affliction." Missionary leaders and ministers also made the case for the shared goals of colonization and evangelical missions and saw the parallels between the two as a boon to both movements. The American Board's Jeremiah Evarts suggested that the ACS would "draw in the affections of people" if it presented Liberia as a missionary opening to Africa. Further, when the Andover-educated Samuel J. Mills died while working as an agent for the ACS in 1817, his friends memorialized him as a missionary martyr. Gardiner Spring, an antislavery Presbyterian clergyman in New York, published a hagiographic biography of Mills, announcing that the proceeds of the volume's sales would be donated to "missionary purposes." Like the missionary martyrs remembered by the American Board, Mills and later white agents of the ACS who died in Africa became symbols of white Christians' willingness to sacrifice themselves in the name of sympathy for distant others; they were "martyrs" who had "sacrifice[d] their lives to extend the triumphs of American philanthropy."[9]

While northern evangelicals praised the Colonization Society as a potential missionary agency, the ACS still struggled to gain a foothold in New England. The regional conflict following the Missouri Crisis of 1820 led many New Englanders to question the motives of the southerner-dominated institution. Further, many pointed to the ACS's ongoing financial problems and reports of the instability of the African colony to explain their hesitancy to donate to the cause. Unlike the flourishing culture of voluntary societies emerging during the Second Great Awakening, the ACS Board of Managers still relied on governmental aid and had done little to market the colonization cause to a wide audience. This changed, at least in part, in 1823 when two New Englanders put forward a plan to restructure the ACS to more closely resemble New England benevolence societies. Ralph Gurley and Leonard Bacon, both Andover graduates, laid out a plan for the ACS to decentralize into a large number of local auxiliaries and to rely more on private donations instead of grants from the federal government. The board of managers favored the plan and asked Bacon to work for the ACS. He declined, choosing instead to become the minister at New Haven's Center Church. Gurley accepted in his stead, and during his first few months as the assistant to the infirm Elias Caldwell, he publicized the ACS to a wider audience, including skeptical New Englanders. He expanded the organization's annual report, launched the *African Repository and Colonial Journal*, and encouraged clergymen to preach and take up a collection for the ACS on the Fourth of July. Gurley and his fellow New England colonizationists also recognized that the missionary angle was their best hope to win more supporters: "We know, indeed, that among our friends, in many parts of the country, the introduction of Christianity into Africa is the principal motive for exertion in our cause. This single motive is sufficient; though we consider it but one of many, of perhaps equal, or nearly equal strength."[10]

Christian Sympathy and the Problem of Prejudice

New England colonizationists presented missionary work and colonization as two sides of the same coin. Adhering to a Protestant humanitarian reading of the Bible, they believed all human beings to be descended from Adam and Eve and were capable of becoming "civilized" Christians. For example, in a critical review of a book by the racial scientist Charles Caldwell, Leonard Bacon argued, "if the Africans are not men in the same sense that we are," then "we have a right to hold them in bondage; we have a right to make them objects of traffic," and to enslave them as well. He made a similar defense of Native Americans and "savages," arguing that, if they were not human beings, then "our endeavours to civilize them are founded in misconception and error." Understanding humans as part of the same family was not only biblically accurate, but it justified white New Englanders' missionary work to evangelize people of color. The future abolitionist and wealthy reformer Gerrit Smith believed that those who supported foreign missions already had developed the "sympathies which we can hope to reach." Smith censured those who looked "with contempt upon all efforts to enlighten and civilize heathen nations" because "their charity begins and ends at home." Bacon would have agreed with Smith's proclamation that "all Christians" needed "a sympathy as wide as the world."[11]

Colonizationists with a missionary sensibility embraced this ideal of an interracial sympathy that bridged distances as a tenet of Christianity. One article in the *African Repository* pronounced that "the Christian looks through the shadowy and evanescent disguises of fashion, rank, manners, complexion and education" to focus on the "universal characteristics" that "prove the close relationship of all men to each other." Yet sympathy and colorblindness tended to exist in an abstract realm rather than in an actual interracial community. White Christians who had Smith's "sympathy as wide as the world" could renounce prejudice precisely because the racial others with whom they sympathized remained distant ideas rather than nearby bodies. A sermon published in the *Christian Spectator* exemplified this imagined community when it declared that Christ served as "the common bond of union" for all Christians regardless of "habits and complexions," including "every desolate but pious islander of the ocean; with every devout tenant of the wilderness, and with the millions that worship God in the four quarters of the globe."[12] Colonizationists could easily envision an interracial and transnational Christian community in which all of the world's people could be spiritually connected while the Atlantic Ocean would keep them physically separate.

Antislavery colonizationism required more than theological pronouncements against racial prejudice to recruit more members. They also needed to stir churchgoers' hearts and ignite their affections. Like other nineteenth-century writers and orators, antislavery colonizationists used sentimental aesthetics to mold their audiences' perceptions of race and to inspire them to feel sympathy for black Americans and Africans. Sentimental literature has been seen as a feminine enterprise, and colonizationists agreed with the widely held gender ideology that women were more sympathetic and selfless than men.[13] Yet in the 1820s and early 1830s, both men and women colonizationists used the sentimental tactics of the missionary sensibility to shape the emotional perceptions of both sexes.

In Fourth of July sermons, colonizationist ministers detailed the cruelty of the slave trade, the physical suffering of slaves, as well as the "degraded" state of free blacks in the North. Descriptions of pain and references to sexual violence would have affected all audience members, but ministers more specifically targeted men's patriotic feelings and emotional investment in manly independence. These sermons conflated American Christians' salvation in Christ and political freedom as they appealed for Africa. "Christians! You whom Christ has made free, what will you do for Africa?" asked one preacher. Could they not "soften some bed of sorrow, mitigate some pain, or put a Bible into the hands of some miserable African who is now a heathen!"[14]

Leonard Bacon connected to men particularly in one of his published sermons, *A Plea for Africa*. He declared that "there is nothing more oppressive to our best feelings, than the thought, that so many millions of our fellow men are the subjects of a thraldom which despoils them of the attributes of intellectual and moral, and even of social existence, and makes them the mere machines of avarice."[15] This evocative statement spoke to American men's feelings of spiritual and political independence as well as their concerns about preserving their humanity in the face of a growing market economy. Calling them "subjects of a thraldom" and "machines," Bacon showed slaves to be spiritually bound and emotionally dead. He then turned the very act of feeling sympathy for slaves into a way for white men to affirm their Christian identity and to prove that, because they could feel, they were men and not machines.

In contrast to the appeals directed at men's patriotism and independence, the sentimental texts written for a female audience reached out to readers as mothers. One of Sigourney's poems, "The African Heathen Mother at her Daughter's Grave" (1833), both emphasized the similarity between a white American mother and an African mother and reinforced difference by comparing the emptiness of "pagan" practices compared to the solace of Christianity. The first five stanzas were in the first person, putting white readers in the place of the African woman as she explained to her deceased daughter the years of suffering, including her terror as her husband and sons were "from our cabin torn, while in my blood I lay." She now felt entirely alone because the spirits of her ancestors and her lost children were mute: "When, pierced with agony, I weep," the "wildest cry" received "no reply." The final stanzas, however, switched perspectives as Sigourney called on white Americans to deliver Christianity to Africa to "soothe her bursting sighs" and "plant the hope that never dies / Deep in her tear-wet soul."

While reading these final lines, white readers moved from the tangled imaginative space in which they saw themselves as an African woman onto the clear-cut ground that distinguished white benevolent Christian helpers from distant suffering heathen. They did not have to look far to find out how they should respond. An 1831 appeal for women to donate to the ACS asked, "Mothers! Are your children spared from the grave, to blossom in beauty and cheer your hearts with the promise of intellect and of wisdom?" Then donate to the ACS on each child's birthday, as a "thank offering, a gift for Africa."[16]

The fact that Bacon and William Lloyd Garrison both printed Sigourney's "African Mother" poem in their respective newspapers points to their overlapping interest in the missionary sensibility, and Garrison would probably have agreed with Bacon's statement that slavery made men into "machines of avarice." But, unlike radical abolitionists, antislavery colonizationists did not see interracial sympathy as a pathway toward a racially integrated society. To black abolitionist David Walker, this made the colonizationists' supposed Protestant humanitarianism hardly better than slaveholders' Christianity. By working for the removal of blacks to Liberia, the ACS would spread the religion "as they have among the Americans—distinction, whip, blood and oppression." In a stark challenge to the colonizationists' claims of having sympathetic hearts, Walker urged them to repent, to "throw away your fears and prejudices" and "treat us like men." Blacks would forgive them because "we are not like you, hard hearted, unmerciful, and unforgiving."[17]

Antislavery colonizationists came prepared with a ready response to critics like Walker and Garrison. Like the foreign missionaries who used ethnographic analyses to explain why "barbarous" people had not flocked to their mission churches, colonizationists created an ethnography of black Americans and attributed their resistance to colonization on poverty, ignorance, and idleness, all of which had been exacerbated by whites' racism. Speaking to the Vermont Colonization Society in 1826, Silas McKeen worried that "in this land of gospel light" so promising for whites, blacks were "groping in darkness as thick as rests on the remotest regions of Africa." Only by leaving the stultifying climate of prejudice would they be able to advance and become a "civilized" people.[18] Colonizationists also described black Americans as emotionally damaged and incapable of developing the sympathetic hearts that were essential to civilized Christianity. Writing to a black newspaper, one white colonizationist asked why "intelligent individuals of your colour" rejected colonization and "sadden[ed] the hearts of their most ardent friends?"[19]

As colonizationists questioned free blacks' capacity to feel the right emotions, they twisted the same humanitarian sentiments used to condemn racism into the evidence of black difference. Colonizationists developed an emotional history of "Africans" that could be used to dismiss their protests against the ACS. As Leonard Bacon explained in *A Plea for Africa*, this history began in Africa, where "the basest superstition has conspired with the darkest ignorance to stupify the intellect, as well as to brutalize the affections." The slave trade worsened this dreadful situation as it destroyed towns and families and removed any sense of security that Africans had felt. The trauma was impossible to imagine, one New Englander admitted: "I cannot tell what it is to be torn away from country and home—to be carried in chains to a strange land, and doomed to a slavery worse than death." If he managed to survive the physical trauma of the middle passage and the seasoning period, enslavement only further damaged the slave's affections and feelings. Not even emancipation could transform the slave's soul. In Sarah Tuttle's children's book, *Claims of the Africans,* her character Aunt Caroline proposes that the reason why so few free blacks wanted to go to Liberia stemmed from the fact that "they have lost all self-respect and confidence in themselves."[20]

In language anticipating post–Civil War respectability politics among African Americans as well as the missionary ideology of the "civilizing mission," white colonizationists focused on education as a pathway to reform blacks' behavior and feelings, especially when it came to blacks' negative attitudes toward colonization. When colonizationists created the African Education Society in 1829, they saw schools as a chance to reconstruct black children's sensibilities so that they would lose their "prejudices" against Liberia. At the organization's first meeting, the participants decided that the proposed schools needed to isolate children from their "idle and vicious companions," and "make constant and untiring inroads on their wrong habits and propensities," as well as "inspire them with virtuous, generous and honorable sentiments." By "enlightening and enlarging their minds, and correcting and quickening their moral faculties," the proposed schools would lead them to become benevolent men and women who recognized that their "own best interests" lay in Africa.[21]

Indeed, colonizationists lavished praise on those black Americans who had elected to go to Liberia. They stood as beacons of intelligence, entrepreneurial prowess, Christian faith, and sympathetic concern for their African brethren. In Tuttle's Sabbath school book, black colonizationists Paul Cuffe, Lott Cary, and John Russwurm were praised as "sensible" by one of the children characters. His aunt responded, "If all our colored population were to obtain learning, they would never remain in the United States in such a debased condition, but would line our shores, til they were taken, and conveyed to the natural home of the African."[22]

Throughout the 1820s, antislavery colonizationists built up the idea that civilized people rejected racial prejudice and favored Christian sympathy. They valued interracial sympathy as paramount to Christian piety, and they made religious work of the practices of imaginative sympathy that asked them to put themselves in the place of a suffering slave. Consequently, as they looked at slavery and racism through a missionary sensibility, antislavery colonizationists wrote off any criticisms of the ACS—from whites and blacks—as the irrational ravings of an insensible people. Their claim to be sympathetic humanitarians, however, was arguably the point that most irritated colonizationists' black and white abolitionist critics. One repudiated colonizationists in exactly these terms when he wrote in a black newspaper, *Rights of All*, that colonizationists were nothing but "miserable comforters, cold hearted and cruel christians."[23]

"Heathenism Outdone!"

Before turning to the controversies over black education in Connecticut in the early 1830s, it is instructive to compare the ACS's pairing of interracial sympathy with distance to the American Board's failed attempt to create an interracial Christian community.[24] Beginning in the early 1820s, the American Board invited promising "natives" from its mission fields to attend their Foreign Mission School in Cornwall, Connecticut.[25] In this small New England town, the "natives"—the students in the first years included Native Americans, as well as pupils from Hawaii and India—would be trained as ministers for their people while also experiencing Christian civilization firsthand. Because the emphasis was on returning these students to the mission field, Ralph Gurley and others commended the school to the ACS as a model for how they might train black ministers for Liberia.[26]

By 1826, however, the Foreign Mission School had been closed, in large part because it had become the site of two marriages between white women and Cherokee men. Proximity had enabled the two women to exchange interracial sympathy for interracial marriage, and the couples ignited the anger of many whites who wondered at this "new missionary machinery" that seemed to sanction such unions. "How much wickedness has been committed under the cloak of religion and of a missionary spirit?" asked one writer. Another complained that the second engagement, between Harriett Gold and Elias Boudinot, stood as the "very unpleasant consequence of the excessive zeal for propagating the gospel among the heathen."[27]

When couples like those in Cornwall breached the cordon separating white helpers from the objects of their benevolence, racist white mobs reacted violently, and the missionary community faced an existential challenge to explain why exactly the marriages were wrong when they argued that all humans belonged to the "family of man." Herman Vaill, the brother-in-law of Harriett Gold, could only explain that "a thing which may be right in itself" could, "in given circumstances, be very wrong."[28] The "circumstances" that worried Vaill had to do with the ways that the interracial marriages turned public opinion against missionary work. A similar fear lay just under the surface of antislavery colonization. Just as the Gold family fractured when the question of interracial marriage arose in 1825, New England's Protestant humanitarians would divide over the question of integration in the early 1830s, and the issue of the relationship between the missionary sensibility's interracial sympathy and "amalgamation" proved to be the breaking point.

In 1831 white and black abolitionists together proposed that a black college be established in New Haven to serve both American and potentially even West Indian students. On the surface, the school appeared quite similar to the seminary that the African Education Society had proposed two years earlier, except for the fact that this school had the backing of the Convention of Free People of Color, an organization that stood against the ACS. One of the school's promoters, New Haven clergyman Simeon Jocelyn, presented the school as an example of Christian benevolence, and he even endorsed the idea of some of the school's graduates going to Liberia as missionaries. But as the proposal circulated, Nat Turner's slave rebellion in Virginia occurred, making New Haven's elite whites even more concerned about increasing the free black population of their town. The town's white leaders, many of whom supported colonization, voted down the proposed school as other whites rioted in the streets in mob violence in opposition to any interracial endeavor. The school's failure served as a turning point for race and reform in New England. It also was the first time antislavery colonizationists faced accusations from more radical whites that their self-proclaimed interracial sympathy was a sham.[29]

By the time of the annual meeting of the ACS in early 1832, colonizationists knew of the new radical abolitionist movement and the threat it posed to their moderate antislavery stance. Leonard Bacon's address to the meeting shifted his hostility away from "prejudiced" blacks and toward "fanatical" whites like Garrison. Bacon revised his earlier assessments of blacks' emotional depravity, telling the audience that "the people of color are not ignorant" of the ACS's plan: "they read—they hear—and when they are spoken of as a nuisance to be got rid of, they prove themselves men, men of like passions with us, by resenting it." Here, finally, buried within Bacon's attack on white abolitionist "demagogues" who stirred up black people's feelings, he admitted that the black opponents of colonization had a valid point.

Instead of fixating only on black men's failures, Bacon chastised white abolitionists as false friends. Men like Garrison were merely "wearing the aspect of friendship" in order to "confirm them in their prejudices, and to acquire an influence over them which may be directed to disastrous issues." In response to the radical threat, Bacon urged the ACS to adopt new practices of interracial sympathy and to befriend black people: "Let us go, then, and show these fellow-men that we are individually their friends." Through real-life interactions, colonizationists would help blacks "become better acquainted with their real interests," which was, of course, settling in Liberia.[30]

While white New Haveners feared an influx of young black men, the "amalgamation" issue fully flared up in 1833 when the recently converted abolitionist Prudence Crandall opened a school in Canterbury, Connecticut, to serve "young ladies of color." Crandall's opponents protested against the introduction of "foreigners" into their community, and some of the town's selectmen worried that Crandall's ads in the *Liberator* would overwhelm the town with free blacks: "Once open this door, and New England will become the Liberia of America!!" They also felt certain that Crandall planned "to force the two races to amalgamate." Unlike later anti-miscegenation rhetoric that focused on the threat of black male sexuality, the colonizationists who opposed Crandall's school made a different point. Black education created "a new species of gentility in the shape of sable belles," wrote one self-identified "friend of the colonization cause," and Crandall's goal was to "cook up a palatable morsel for our white bachelors." Sure to be rejected by white men, the educated black woman would "return disappointed and angry to her primitive station" and "sink into degradation and infamy." In contrast to the righteous Christianity that would educate black women in Liberia, a similar program for racial uplift in Canterbury would produce amalgamation, described as "revolting to every moral and religious feeling within us."[31]

When whites painted Crandall as a woman who had "stepped out of the hallowed precincts of female propriety," her abolitionist defenders responded with a reformulated version of the missionary sensibility. Abolitionists deftly turned Crandall's femininity and Christian sympathy to their advantage. Crandall was a "truly benevolent young lady, who has so nobly espoused the cause of suffering humanity," in contrast to the "unholy prejudices" of those who opposed her. A *Liberator* article bore the headline: "Heathenism Outdone!" and others repeated the theme: "More Barbarism!" and "Savage Barbarity!" Another put the debate over black schools in Connecticut in the context of the American Board's mission to the Cherokee, asking: "More Barbarism! Who are now the Savages? The Indians, the Georgians, or the Persecutors of the noble minded Miss

Prudence Crandall of Canterbury, and her excellent pupil Miss Eliza Ann Hammond, of Providence?" How could those who opposed her consider themselves Christians "who profess to love their neighbors as themselves, and to believe that God has made of one blood all the nations of the earth!" And all of this "barbarism" existed in the hallowed heart of New England.[32]

The debate over colonization continued to ripple through the ranks of Protestant humanitarians throughout the 1830s as more white northerners rejected the ACS. By the mid-1830s, even Leonard Bacon had begun to turn against colonization. While he remained an antislavery moderate, he focused his energies on supporting schools for the colonists already settled in Liberia rather than trying to convince black Americans of their need to leave the United States. Many white abolitionists continued to see interracial sympathy, with all of its paternalistic implications, as a vital part of their religious lives.

The missionary sensibility did not disappear from the antislavery movement. An example can be found in a letter from abolitionist Amos Phelps to his wife on the subject of colonization. An Andover graduate who had once supported colonization, the Congregationalist minister endorsed immediate emancipation in the early 1830s. Ten years after Bacon had urged his congregation to do for Africa what they once could only do for "the beggar at their door," Phelps wrote: "that man who opens his charities and sends up his prayers to send the gospel to Africa and yet spurns the negro, Africa's representatives from his door, his table, his friendships, his society, does but play the hypocrite. He is bound to feel toward that despised negro at his door, just as he would if he saw him on the coast of Africa and was going as the missionary to bear the tidings of salvation to him, and if he does not, he does but play the hypocrite in all his pretended sympathies and charities for the negro at a distance."

While Phelps supported immediate emancipation, he did not propose immediate racial equality; instead he told white abolitionists to be missionaries to black people in the United States, to domesticate the missionary sensibility. The humanitarian crisis at home must be managed before Americans could evangelize Africa. "First be reconciled to your brother," he wrote, "then—away with slavery and your prejudice, then come and offer thy gifts—send thy missions to Africa." When Phelps cofounded the American Missionary Association in the 1840s, he helped to lay the foundations for the institutionalization of the missionary sensibility in home missions during and after the Civil War and for a new era of Protestant humanitarianism abroad. Long after the ACS faded away, missionaries and humanitarians would continue to draw on colonizationists' ideas of sympathy, race, distance, and religion as they appealed to Americans to feel and act on behalf of suffering others.[33]

Notes

1. P. J. Staudenraus, *The African Colonization Movement, 1816–1865* (New York: Columbia University Press, 1961), 117–35; Hugh Davis, *Leonard Bacon: New England Reformer and Antislavery Moderate* (Baton Rouge: Louisiana State University Press, 1998).

2. Mrs. L. H. Sigourney, "Difference in Color," in *Poems for Children* (Hartford, Conn.: Canfield and Robins, 1836), 57–58, emphasis in original; "Review of Lectures on the Philosophy of the Human Mind by Thomas Brown," *North American Review* 21 (July 1825): 19–51, 21; John Corrigan, "'Habits from the Heart': The American Enlightenment and Religious Ideas about Emotion and Habit," *Journal of Religion* 73, no. 2 (April 1993): 183–99, 193; Leonard Bacon, *A Plea for Africa* (New Haven, Conn.: T. G. Woodward and Co., 1825), 21–22.

3. For theoretical work on "sensibility," see Thomas L. Haskell, "Capitalism and Humanitarian Sensibility, Parts 1 and 2," in Thomas Bender, ed., *The Antislavery Debate: Capitalism and Abolitionism as a Problem in Historical Interpretation* (Berkeley: University of California Press, 1992): 107–60. See also Elizabeth B. Clark, "'The Sacred Rights of the Weak': Pain, Sympathy, and the Culture of Individual Rights in Antebellum America," *Journal of American History* 82, no. 2 (March 1995): 463–93; Karen Halttunen, "Humanitarianism and the Pornography of Pain in Anglo-American Culture," *American Historical Review* 100, no. 2 (April 1995): 303–34; Margaret Abruzzo, *Polemical Pain: Slavery, Cruelty, and the Rise of Humanitarianism* (Baltimore: Johns Hopkins University Press, 2011), 17–18, 63–70; Daniel Wickberg, "What Is the History of Sensibilities? On Cultural Histories, Old and New," *American Historical Review* 112, no. 3 (June 2007): 661–84, 662. On Protestant missionaries' definitions of race, religion, and nation, see Derek Chang, "'Marked in Body, Mind, and Spirit': Home Missionaries and the Remaking of Race and Nation," in Henry Goldschmidt and Elizabeth McAlister, eds., *Race, Nation, and Religion in the Americas* (New York: Oxford University Press, 2004), 139–41.

4. "Colonization Society," *Boston Recorder*, August 19, 1820.

5. Susan Ryan, *The Grammar of Good Intentions: Race and the Antebellum Culture of Benevolence* (Ithaca, N.Y.: Cornell University Press, 2003), 19.

6. Hilary J. Moss, *Schooling Citizens: The Struggle for African American Education in Antebellum America* (Chicago: University of Chicago Press, 2009); James Brewer Stewart, "The New Haven Negro College and the Meanings of Race in New England, 1776–1870," *New England Quarterly* 76, no. 3 (2003): 323–55.

7. *First Ten Annual Reports for the American Board of Commissioners for Foreign Missions* (Boston: Crocker and Brewster, 1834), 9–12; William M. Blackford, "Address," *African Repository*, May 1828, 76; Douglas Egerton, "'Its Origin Is Not a Little Curious': A New Look at the American Colonization Society," *Journal of the Early Republic* 5, no. 4 (Winter 1985): 463–80.

8. On the American Board's decisions about its first missions and its history in Liberia, see Emily Conroy-Krutz, *Christian Imperialism: Converting the World in the Early American Republic* (Cornell, N.Y.: Cornell University Press, 2015), 30–47, 157–78.

9. "American Mission to Africa," *Boston Recorder,* July 17, 1819; "Colonization Society," *African Repository,* January 1826, 323; "American Colonization Society," *Boston Recorder,* May 19, 1818; "Colonization of Free Blacks: Address to the American Society for Colonizing the Free People of Color of the United States," *Boston Recorder,* February 27, 1819; "The Missionary Cause," *Boston Commercial Advertiser,* February 11, 1820; Bacon, "The Reports of the American Society for Colonizing the Free People of Colour," *Christian Spectator,* September 1823, 492. See Mary Kupiec Cayton, "Canonizing Harriet Newell: Women, the Evangelical Press, and the Foreign Mission Movement in New England, 1800–1840," in Barbara Reeves-Ellington et al., eds., *Competing Kingdoms: Women, Mission, Nation, and the American Protestant Empire, 1812–1960* (Durham, N.C.: Duke University Press, 2010), 69–93.

10. Staudenraus, *African Colonization Movement,* 76–81, 94–135; "Colonization Society," *African Repository,* August 1825, 160; "Colonization," *Boston Daily Advertiser,* September 7, 1822; "Considerations in Reference to a Mission to Africa," *African Repository,* June 1825, 119.

11. George M. Frederickson, *Racism: A Short History* (Princeton, N.J.: Princeton University Press, 2002), 56–63; Winthrop Jordan, *White Over Black: American Attitudes Toward the Negro, 1550–1812* (Chapel Hill: University of North Carolina Press, 1968), 243–52; Hugh Davis, *Leonard Bacon,* 72; James Brewer Stewart, "Modernizing Difference: The Political Meanings of Color in the Free States, 1776–1840," *Journal of the Early Republic* 19 (Winter 1999): 691–712; Bruce Dain, *A Hideous Monster of the Mind: American Race Theory in the Early Republic* (Cambridge, Mass.: Harvard University Press, 2003), 65–72, 115–23; Leonard Bacon, "Review of Thoughts on the Original Unity of the Human Race," *Christian Spectator,* March 1831, 74–75; Gerrit Smith, "Address to the Annual Meeting of the American Colonization Society," *Fourteenth Annual Report of the American Colonization Society* (Washington, D.C., 1831), viii.

12. "Colonization Society," *African Repository,* April 1825, 36; "A Sermon," *Christian Spectator,* July 1821, 343.

13. Shirley Samuels, ed., *The Culture of Sentiment: Race, Gender, and Sentimentality in Nineteenth-Century America* (New York: Oxford University Press, 1992); Glenn Hendler, *Public Sentiments: Structures of Feeling in Nineteenth-Century American Literature* (Chapel Hill: University of North Carolina Press, 2001); Christine Levecq, *Slavery and Sentiment: The Politics of Feeling in Black Atlantic Antislavery Writing, 1770–1850* (Durham: University of New Hampshire Press, 2008); Bruce Dorsey, "A Gendered History of African Colonization in the Antebellum United States," *Journal of Social History* 34, no. 1 (October 2000): 77–103. On female colonizationists, see "Mementos," *African Repository,* March 1826, 26; L. H. Sigourney, "Letter 1," *African Repository,* August 1827, 189; L. H. Sigourney, "Appeal to New England for Missions to Africa," *African Repository,* March 1829, 31.

14. "From the Boston Recorder and Telegraph," *African Repository,* May 1825, 93.

15. Bacon, *Plea for Africa,* 16.

16. "The Heathen African Mother at her Daughter's Grave," *Liberator,* February 2, 1833,

and *Journal of Freedom*, May 1833; "Address: To the Females of the United States for the Schools of Liberia," *African Repository*, March 1831, 13.

17. David Walker, *Walker's Appeal: With a Brief Sketch of his Life* (New York, 1848), 57, 80.

18. John Hough, *A Sermon, Delivered before the Vermont Colonization Society* (Montpelier, Vt., 1826), 9–10; Davis, *Leonard Bacon*, 60–61; Bacon, *Plea for Africa*, 12; Silas McKeen, *A Sermon, Delivered at Montpelier, October 15, 1828, before the Vermont Colonization Society* (Montpelier, Vt., 1828), 15.

19. A Subscriber, "Original Communication," *Freedom's Journal*, August 24, 1827.

20. Nathaniel Bouton, *Christian Patriotism: An Address Delivered at Concord, July the Fourth, 1825* (Concord, N.H, 1825), 21–22; Bacon, *Plea for Africa*, 10–14; Sarah Tuttle, *Claims of the Africans* (Boston, 1832), 175.

21. "Address," *Report of the Proceedings at the Formation of the African Education Society* (Washington, D.C., 1830), 8–9. This rhetoric of "racial uplift" correlates with the rhetoric of the civilizing mission, but it is also an iteration of what historians have called respectability politics. Both free blacks and some antislavery whites promoted racial uplift in the post-emancipation North, although historians have focused far more on the dynamics of respectability and racial uplift rhetoric among African Americans in the post–Civil War era. See, for example, Evelyn Brooks Higginbotham, *Righteous Discontent: The Women's Movement in the Black Baptist Church, 1880–1920* (Cambridge, Mass.: Harvard University Press, 1994); Kevin Gaines, *Uplifting the Race: Black Leadership, Politics, and Culture in the Twentieth Century* (Chapel Hill: University of North Carolina Press, 1996).

22. Tuttle, *Claims of the Africans*, 165.

23. "The Old Hobby, Colonization," *Rights of All*, September 18, 1829.

24. John A. Andrew III, *From Revivals to Removal: Jeremiah Evarts, the Cherokee Nation, and the Search for the Soul of America* (Athens: University of Georgia Press, 1992), 100–104; Molly Oshatz, *Slavery and Sin: The Fight Against Slavery and the Rise of Liberal Protestantism* (New York: Oxford University Press, 2012), 83–88; Charles K. Whipple, *Slavery and the American Board of Commissioners for Foreign Missions* (Boston: American Anti-Slavery Society, 1859).

25. John Demos, *The Heathen School: A Story of Hope and Betrayal in the Age of the Early Republic* (New York: Knopf, 2014).

26. Alisse Portnoy, *Their Right to Speak: Women's Activism in the Indian and Slave Debates* (Cambridge, Mass.: Harvard University Press, 2005), 1–4; Report, *Eighth Annual Meeting of the American Colonization Society* (Washington, D.C., 1825), 18.

27. Quote from *American Eagle*, Litchfield, Conn., cited in Theresa Strouth Gaul, ed., *To Marry an Indian: The Marriage of Harriett Gold and Elias Boudinot in Letters, 1823–1839* (Chapel Hill: University of North Carolina Press, 2005), 9; "Marriage of an Indian with a White Girl," *Gazette of Maine*, Portland, July 5, 1825; *Daily National Intelligencer*, August 2, 1825, 3.

28. Herman Vaill to Harriett Gold, July 29, 1825, in Gaul, *To Marry an Indian*, 93.

29. Moss, *Schooling Citizens*; Simon S. Jocelyn, "College for Colored Youth," *Liberator*, November 12, 1831; Stewart, "New Haven Negro College," 332.

30. Davis, *Leonard Bacon*, 83–85; Leonard Bacon's Address, *Fifteenth Annual Report of the ACS* (Washington, D.C., 1832), ix–x, 17.

31. Garrison, *Thoughts on African Colonization*, 1; "To the American Colonization Society," *Liberator*, April 6, 1833; "Negro School in Canterbury," *Norwich Republican*, March 27, 1833, rpt. as "Comment Is Needless!!" *Liberator*, April 6, 1833; "Look Here!" *Liberator*, July 20, 1833.

32. "Look Here!" *Liberator*, July 20, 1833; "Infamous Behavior," *Liberator*, March 9, 1833; "Heathenism Outdone," *Liberator*, March 16, 1833; "More Barbarism, *Liberator*, May 18, 1833; "Savage Barbarity," *Liberator*, July 6, 1833; *Fruits of Colonizationism* (Boston, 1833), 6; "Appeal to the Females of the United States in Behalf of Prudence Crandall," *Liberator*, August 17, 1833.

33. Amos A. Phelps to Charlotte Phelps, November 30, 1834, Amos A. Phelps Papers, Boston Public Library; Davis, *Leonard Bacon*, 90; Gale L. Kenny, "Reconstructing a Different South: The American Missionary Association and Jamaica, 1834–65," *Slavery and Abolition* 30, no. 3 (September 2003): 445–66.

2

"The Heathen Are Demanding the Gospel"

Conversion, Redemption, and African Colonization

BEN WRIGHT

On February 13, 1820, several dozen white and black bodies huddled around a flickering flame. Samuel Bacon's voice filled the crowded cabin of the *Elizabeth* with tales of Christian missionaries, past and present. Eighty-six American emigrants rocked with the swells of the Atlantic as they drifted farther from their families in America and closer to their new home in Africa. Daniel Coker, born a slave, now a free man of color, a husband, a father, and a missionary, reflected on the evening devotional. Bacon's words left him "refreshed much," and Coker reported that all on board "felt encouraged in our work, in the conversion of the heathen." Coker and eighty-five other emigrants risked everything they had in traveling to Africa, and they did so for many reasons, but it was this goal, "the conversion of the heathen," that excited him more than anything.[1]

Colonization promised salvation for Africa and moral redemption for the United States. Colonizationists—white and black—drew strength from a millennial faith in the promise of the sixty-eighth Psalm, that "Ethiopia shall soon stretch forth her hands to God." The impending conversion of Africa would redeem the sins of the slave trade by repaying the wounded continent with the gift of Christianity. In the minds of early nineteenth-century white Christians, colonization would do more than abolition, as the salvation of an entire continent weighed heavier than the emancipation of several million. Tracing the conversionist ideologies of early colonizationists reveals the goals and expectations of the men and women who invested so much capital, human and otherwise, in this ambitious venture.[2]

This study does not chronicle the establishment or struggle of these African colonies but rather restricts itself to questions of motivation. The on-the-ground reality involved tremendous suffering and all the violence of conquest and colonialism, but the motivations for these actions repeatedly circled back to religious conversion. Colonization held together men and women, North and South, black and white, in a remarkably widespread effort. Cutting across the major political and geographic divisions of white society in the early republic, the ACS coalition was wide and unwieldy but tremendously influential. The ability to transcend these divisions resulted from the ACS's use of the great unifying force of the era: conversionist Christianity. Free blacks in the North remained skeptical of colonization but largely shared the conversionist worldview of their white coreligionists.

Conversion, of course, meant different things to different people, but white colonizationists mostly avoided theological squabbles and instead offered a generic millennial promise of international religious revival. Tracy Fessenden has described the development of the "nonspecific Protestantism" that enabled reform movements like the ACS to exert so much pressure in the early republic. John Lardas Modern describes how, "Transcending both doctrinal and denominational differences, a somewhat hazy metaphysics assumed hegemonic status both within Protestant practice and across a number of other sites." These "nonspecific," "hazy metaphysics" exerted tremendous influence on early American culture, enabling the disparate colonizationist movement to hold together its unlikely coalition.[3]

Popular religious discourse during the era was ubiquitous but often theologically ambiguous. This ambiguity did not signal a lack of conviction, however. The capacious theology of popular Christianity in the early republic enabled colonizationists to espouse a simple and attractive religious message of African conversion and American redemption. Neither Fessenden nor Modern acknowledges the important role of millennial optimism in forming the hegemonic nonspecific Protestantism of the early republic. Christians have expected the return of Christ since the earliest days of the faith, but Anglo-Atlantic Christians in the late eighteenth and early nineteenth centuries looked to the millennium with an unusual intensity.[4]

Black American theologies of the era prove more elusive. While consistently employing a prophetic, liberationist critique against slavery, black Christians nonetheless shared theological similarities with whites. Both shared an evangelical soteriology, the theology of salvation, and believed that, without a transformative Christian conversion, sinful souls were bound for eternal damnation. Both also shared a millennial imagination. The millennium envisioned by African Americans often proved more capacious than that by whites, including racial equality and powerful black nationalism, but both whites and blacks privileged Africa in their providential expectations. Evangelical Christianity provided a powerful biracial discourse that colonizationists wielded to surprising success.

Colonizationist pamphlets extolled the many expected blessings of the movement, including: the removal of free black communities, the development of an American empire, the enervation of American slavery, the destruction of the Atlantic slave trade, and limitless economic growth resulting from new markets and trading networks, but another motivation was mentioned more often and with greater rhetorical intensity. Throughout the antebellum era, colonizationists almost constantly reprinted Robert Finley's 1816 tract, *Thoughts on the Colonization of Free Blacks*. The brief eight-page essay laid out a rhetorical pattern shared by nearly all colonizationists' tracts. After promising a host of benefits to spring from colonization, the most intense emotional rhetoric comes in the final paragraphs with the promise of African conversion and American moral redemption. In the final paragraph, Finley proclaims, "Nor shall Africa be forgotten. Her bosom begins to warm with hope and her heart to beat with expectation and desire." He later continues by rejoicing that through colonization the United States will surpass other nations, "in the great cause of humanity which has begun its never-ending course."[5] This "great cause of humanity" was the advance of religious conversion that would hasten the millennium. Generations of ACS propagandists copied Finley's style, overwhelming readers with a lengthy catalogue of the seemingly innumerable benefits of colonization before concluding with an emotionally heightened plea to save African souls and absolve American sins.

Africa was not the only site considered for colonization. Finley contemplated a colony west of the Mississippi and even concluded that "Africa would be a much more arduous undertaking," but he was not looking for expediency. He was after souls. Other possible locations were similarly vetoed for their lack of missionary potential. Prince Saunders, a New England black educator, pressed the case for Haiti, claiming that Christians had a duty to help the infant republic. Saunders himself arrived in Haiti in 1815 and worked as an agent for the administration of Henri Christophe.[6] Eventually over two hundred black Americans relocated to Haiti, though many returned after finding their Protestantism an awkward fit with the Haitian variant of Catholicism. Haitian plans never generated nearly as much enthusiasm or economic activity among whites as African colonization. As an embodiment of black militancy to white Americans ever fearful of slave rebellion, nearby Haiti proved a problematic site for white-sponsored colonization efforts. Often these fears remained unnamed, however, as white colonizationists framed their opposition by employing the discourse of conversion.

Boosters billed the two migrations differently. Haiti was sold as a refuge, Africa as a mission field. President Jean Pierre Boyer wrote of Haiti as "a sure asylum to unfortunate men."[7] Boyer believed that African Americans, "debased by ignorance and exasperated by misfortune, have become turbulent and dangerous." While white colonizationists often held the same opinion of American blacks, ACS materials rarely invoked this discourse, opting instead to focus on the positive potential of colonization for both Africa and the United States.

Both before and after the founding of the ACS, Americans looked to migration as a means of liberation, but white colonizationists could not divorce African American migration from the mission of Christianization. James S. Green weighed the possibility of facilitating Haitian migration in his address at the 1824 inaugural meeting of the New Jersey State Colonization Society. According to the rules established by President Boyer, immigrants to Haiti enjoyed religious liberty but were restricted from proselytizing. Green wondered how any true Christian could hold his tongue and allow his neighbors to drift through life on their way to an eternity of torment. As far as he was concerned, by prohibiting conversionist activity, Haiti nullified its candidacy as a major site for colonization. Theodore Frelinghuysen, speaking before the same society six months later, similarly appreciated the offer from Haiti but told his fellow colonizationists that "the trespass was committed against the continent—and to the continent, let retribution be made." Speaking for the United States, he claimed that "we have injured, and we must make reparation." Frelinghuysen framed the need for redemption as a millennial imperative, for what would happen "when America beholds, flaming from the eternal throne, 'The blood of injured Africa calls for judgment.' What must be our plea?" He concluded that the United States would be found "guilty before God."[8] The injury of the slave trade required reparation, and colonization promised not only eternal life for Africans but also absolution for America's sinful slave trading. Africa needed conversion; America needed redemption.

American and British Christians shared a religious imagination of Africa as blessed with a rich and often mythic Christian past. This imagination captivated white Christians in the eighteenth and nineteenth centuries on both sides of the Atlantic. Benjamin Rush took for granted that his readers would be well aware of African Christianity, asking "Who has not heard of the Christian Church in Africa?" Ezra Stiles pored over the travel accounts of James Bruce looking for remnants of ancient Christianity. Stiles even wrote Bruce, correcting the Scottish explorer's claims regarding the travels of the early apostles and asking if Ethiopia contained relics of St. Matthew. Granville Sharp's antislavery pamphlet *The Just Limitation of Slavery in the Laws of God* included an extensive history of Christianity in Africa, drawn mostly from William Cave's *Scriptorum Ecclesiasticorum Historia Literaria*, a widely reprinted literary history of early church writers. Sharp followed the interests of his grandfather in studying the major African church councils in Carthage and even provided a numerical count of 310 bishops in the West African City of Baga by 394 CE. Since the glory of the early African church, the continent had "lamentably, fallen back into gross ignorance," yet Sharp and so many others determined "to restore the heathens to their lost privileges."[9] Restoring the heathen would return Africa to her glorious past, a challenge that required immediate action.

Africa was both the location of a proud Christian past and an anticipated glorious future, but in the minds of American and British Christians, it was also an unrivaled challenge for missionaries eager to win the world for Christ. Colonizationists drew on deeply racist understandings of Africa held by Anglo-Christians for centuries. In an 1820 funeral sermon honoring two fallen ACS agents, William Augustus Muhlenberg called Africa "the strong hold of Satan," a land "enveloped in a moral night of tenfold darkness." This imagery originated in the earnest missionary pleas of conversionist Christians fretting over the souls of unreached Africans, but took on new life as justifications for imperialism. It would be a mistake to overemphasize the imperial ambitions of early American colonizationists, but the seeds of what would bear troubling fruit sprouted in even the earliest colonizationist rhetoric.[10]

Conversionist discourse enabled colonizationists to subsume early antislavery writers under their banner, including the writings of many of the most committed antislavery agitators. When Anthony Benezet reflected on the evangelical opportunities of the continent, he could not help but mourn a missed opportunity. Europeans long had favorable chances for bringing the gospel to Africa, and Benezet lamented how Christendom failed to deploy her maritime prowess in the cause of Christ and instead enriched herself through war and plunder. Benezet and others feared how "the slave trade must necessarily raise in the minds of the thoughtful and well-disposed negroes the utmost scorn and detestation of the Christian name." Benezet cited Peter Kolb, who wrote that "numbers of these people have given it as reason for their not harkening to Christianity."[11]

The greatly influential early eighteenth-century Anglican divine William Law shared Benezet's concern for the salvation of Africans, warning that the slave trade nullified the Christian witness.[12] Kolb, Benezet, Law, and numerous others feared that the slave trade had damaged the cause of conversion by linking Christ with slavery in the minds of Africans. For many reformers, slavery was seen as a tremendous obstacle to missionary activity, and the colonization movement managed to harness antislavery sentiments to a project ultimately ambivalent about abolition. By emphasizing religious conversion over either antislavery or proslavery motivations, colonizationists held together a fractious coalition. For even many of the most zealous antislavery activists, the only sounds more sorrowful than the moans of a shackled slave were the wails of a damned soul.

Conversionists had to present Africans as desperately needing the light of the gospel yet not so horribly depraved as to be unreachable. A gathering of abolitionists in 1818 opposed colonization partially because the "bold and martial race, entirely addicted to war, many of them a large size, strong and well proportioned," that occupied the African coastline was ill suited for religious conversion. In combating these claims, colonizationists relied on environmental racism, condemning the licentiousness of Africans while also offering a promise of improvement, an improvement best achieved through religious conversion. Colonization advanced the belief that African Americans could elevate themselves to at least near equality with whites if they were removed from the exploitative relationships of American society. This logic undercut the arguments of inherent African inferiority but also reinforced the widespread belief that a stable, biracial America could never exist.[13]

After researching African colonial history and observing African culture firsthand, Carl Bernard Wadström, a Swedish geographer in the service of the Sierra Leone Company, declared Africans to be "already predisposed by their natural dispositions and principles to receive Christianity." Catholic missionary success in Congo, Angola, and several other Portuguese African possessions illustrated just how fertile the African prospects could be if the Gospel was sown with care. The African American poet Phillis Wheatley likewise understood Africa as ready for harvest and praised the early colonizationist scheme of Samuel Hopkins and Ezra Stiles. In a 1774 letter to Hopkins, Wheatley assured him that Africans would zealously turn to Christianity, and she rejoiced that she could see "the thick cloud of ignorance dispersing from the face of my benighted country." Wheatley declared that African "minds are unprejudiced against the truth," and accordingly believed Hopkins's missionaries would enjoy great success.[14] Minds unprejudiced against truth and naturally predisposed to receive Christianity portended a thorough triumph for suitable missionaries willing to voyage across the Atlantic.

A half-century after Wheatley reflected on Africa's missionary potential, racist understandings of the continent as a religious blank slate flourished among British and American Christians. Ralph Randolph Gurley, addressing a Fourth of July crowd in 1825, described Africa as a land without any "formidable systems of superstition consecrated by age and authority." He dismissed indigenous beliefs as "shadowy conceptions [that] cannot fortify their minds against the arguments and appeals of the word of God." Nowhere in the world was a missionary field "more easy for cultivation, or rich in promise." He claimed that African chiefs had found Christians morally and intellectually superior and accordingly would aggressively work to help missionaries convert their people.[15] The vapidity of Africans and their alleged eagerness for Christian instruction promised great success for a concerted conversionist enterprise. Evangelical Christianity and racist assurances of Anglo-American supremacy combined to create expectations of a smooth and speedy African conversion.

Reports of conversionist advances in Africa and elsewhere assured colonizationists of missionary success. In 1774 Phillis Wheatley rejoiced, "that which the divine royal Psalmist says by inspiration is now on the point of being accomplished, namely, Ethiopia shall soon stretch forth her hands unto God." This last clause, drawn from Psalm 68:31, became a rallying cry, and nearly every colonizationist tract repeated the verse. Robert Finley looked to the missionaries in New Holland, the contemporary name for Australia, and others in Africa who had "already been so successful in teaching the Cassre, the Hottentot, the Boshemen, the means of present happiness and the way of eternal life." Christians anticipated the advance of the gospel with eager zeal and sought to join the glorious cause as it swept the globe. William Augustus Muhlenberg in 1820 was no exception but grew even more strident, thundering, "The heathen are demanding the gospel. On us hang the fulfillment of the promises. The time is come. The church is on her march to victory." The international march of conversions foretold a transformative, historic advance in the history of the church. The millennium loomed.[16]

The conversion of Africa had become an essential requirement for the fulfillment of millennial prophecy. For most Americans, and nearly all colonizationists, millennialism had little to do with precise understandings of eschatological theology but rather manifested itself as a component of the versatile, nonspecific Protestantism that dominated the early republic. Millennialism became a venue for imperial ambitions, fantasies of racial homogeneity, and the enduring optimism of messianic American nationalism. While a few painstakingly searched the scriptures for a prophetic checklist, the vast majority of Americans drifted along with hearts and eyes directed heavenward in assurance of impending radical improvement. Colonizationists harnessed millennial faith as a unifying force and read current events as signs of the times portending African conversion.

Early reports of British activity in Sierra Leone offered encouragement and illustrated the potential power of nonwhite missionaries. The story of one African prince circulated on both sides of the Atlantic as evidence of African religious potential. King Naimbanna, an African chief who ceded land for the Sierra Leone settlement in 1787, sent his son John to England where he experienced a dramatic religious conversion. John became a celebrity among evangelicals opposed to the slave trade, evincing all the characteristics of pious Christianity. After his conversion, he stopped dressing in the manner of African royalty and refused to drink more than one glass of wine per day. After several years in England, Naimbanna returned to Africa. Through the work of the Sierra Leone Company and the influence of the Christian prince's return, Britons expected to convert the continent. The vessel that carried the Christian African prince back to his homeland took the name of *Naimbanna* in honor of its prized passenger. Tragically, John Naimbanna grew ill as he drew nearer to Africa and died almost immediately after reaching shore, unable to fulfill the missionary dreams of British Christians. Information on John Naimbanna reached Americans in 1799 when Thomas Dobson of Philadelphia printed a summary of several reports from the Sierra Leone Company and then again in 1800 with British playwright, philanthropist, and moral reformer Hannah More's *The Black Prince*.[17] These sources almost assuredly distort the beliefs of Naimbanna but offer valuable insight into the preoccupations of the English and American men and women who used his tale as evidence of conversionist potential.

White missionaries signed up for the cause, but many Christians came to believe that only African Americans could truly bring the gospel to Africa. Fears of tropical climates and racist anxieties of supposed African barbarism joined with a practical awareness that many Africans understandably equated white skin with fears of slave trading, fears that would certainly impinge on missionary activities. As Anthony Benezet mourned in his antislavery tract, white slavers spoiled European opportunities to evangelize the continent. Henry Clay feared the same but believed that Americans could yet still make a difference in claiming that "the African Colonists, whom we send to convert the heathen . . . will be received as long lost brethren."[18] Imagining the encounter between an African and an African American missionary left white American colonizationists swelling with paternalist pride.

Colonization promised to transform black Americans as well as Africans. Robert Finley wanted only well-prepared migrants, those who upon arrival would "be the great instruments of spreading peace and happiness." He dreamed of assembling an army of "thousands and tens of thousands" to make the voyage. Training black American missionaries would turn a class of loathed, feared, or pitied Americans into pious servants of Christ. In the minds of white colonizationists, degenerate slaves and dangerous free blacks would become disciplined missionaries. In 1817 Edward Griffin, preaching on behalf of the African School, a Presbyterian training ground for African American missionaries, proclaimed that "it can no longer be made a question whether the elevation of the African race is a part of the new order of things. The providence of God has declared it."[19] Through the benevolence of American colonizationists, black Americans would take their place as trusted servants of God, and Africans would be brought into the kingdom of Christ.

American Christians paid close attention to British colonization, but an American colony, Finley assured, would enjoy far greater success. British action proved the viability of colonization, but according to the spiritual father of American colonization, "toward this land of liberty [Africa] turns her eyes." The settlers at Sierra Leone were refugees battered about the Atlantic World. American colonists, according to Finley, "could carry with them property, the useful arts of life, and above all, the knowledge of the benign religion of Christ." The British proved it could be done, but Americans would do it better. Christian nationalism convinced white Americans that their nation was the most holy nation on Earth, particularly anointed to bring about the Kingdom of God. Millennial energies blended easily with American nationalism. Edward Dorr Griffin implored Americans to "no longer look to Europe for the redemption of Africans: the work is laid on ourselves by the plain direction of heaven."

Elias B. Caldwell, Finley's brother-in-law and clerk of the U.S. Supreme Court, understood the millennial promise of colonization as a unifying program for an increasingly fractured American Christianity. While Caldwell acknowledged a growing difference of opinion among American believers, he rejoiced that Americans increasingly believed the "glorious and happy day is near at hand." By emphasizing this shared belief, Americans could overcome increasingly contentious economic, social, and theological divisions. Caldwell pointed to "great movements and mighty efforts in the moral and religious world" as evidence of an approaching international wave of conversions that would transcend geographic and denominational lines.[20] Colonization offered a message of unity that not only cut across political and sectional divides but also transcended denominational and theological barriers. The promise of global conversion appealed to a wide array of Americans, and through the promise of the sixty-eighth Psalm, Africa took center stage in the great millennial drama about to unfold.

By the second decade of the nineteenth century a clear majority of Americans believed the Atlantic slave trade was evil, and although it had been abolished, a moral scar endured. Finley believed that the United States had committed a grave sin, but colonization offered "the atoning sacrifice." The slave trade robbed Africa of millions of children, encouraged violence between African nations, and hindered the progress of missionaries by linking Christianity to slavery. Finley wrote, "if wrong has been done to Africa in forcing away her weeping children, the wrong can be best redressed by that power which did the injury." William Augustus Muhlenberg praised American attempts to weaken the Atlantic slave trade but regretted that the nation still owed a debt to the sons and daughters of those taken into captivity. In an 1820 sermon he proclaimed that if, by the labors of the American Colonizationist Society, "we can transmit to Africa the blessings of our arts, our civilization and our religion, perhaps we may extinguish a part of the great moral debt." Colonizationists repeated the theme of debt. Edward Dorr Griffin claimed that Americans "owe a greater atonement than any other nation to bleeding Africa."[21] This debt mocked American claims to greatness. For Americans to regain their moral capital, they must repay Africa.

The impending wave of conversions had begun. God was calling the United States to lead the charge. By doing so, Americans would erase the sins of their slave-trading past and establish themselves as the preeminent moral authority among the nations of the world. James Patterson, in a July 4, 1825, sermon, told his ecumenical audience, "we cannot conceive how this country would make a reparation to Africa for the wrongs done her." But Patterson and others wanted to do more than make reparation. They would assert American righteousness. Patterson asked, "Would this government give a Christian education to her slaves, which she is bound to do, and then return them to their native country, what greater favor under heaven could they possibly confer on Africa?" What greater favor could there be than providing "60,000,000 of souls, sunk in the most cruel heathenism, with the most efficient missionaries."[22]

The successful conversion of Africa would recast the tragedy of the slave trade as a divine step in the workings of Providence. In a curious late eighteenth-century tract, James Beattie lampooned the work of proslavery writer Richard Nisbet, mocking the claim that the slave trade "has been the principal means of heaping wealth and honors on Europeans and Americans and rescuing many millions of wretched Africans as *brands from the fire*."[23] By the early nineteenth century, however, proslavery Americans made these same points without a tinge of irony. As the nineteenth century progressed, the conflict between proslavery and antislavery thought accelerated, but both sides drew arguments from an earlier conversionist consensus. The proslavery assurance that the slave trade bore a positive good in saving African heathens from a life of barbarism and an eternity of torment received a major boost from colonizationists, some carrying antislavery convictions. By tracing the anticipated millennial revival back to the slave trade, antislavery colonizationists loaded one of the most potent weapons in the proslavery arsenal, a weapon that would be wielded repeatedly in the pamphlet wars of the mid-nineteenth century.

Absalom Jones, the first African American Episcopal bishop, made this very point. In an 1808 sermon he asked why "the impartial Father of the human race should have permitted the transportation of so many millions of our fellow creatures to this country, to endure all the miseries of slavery." His answer was that God allowed this great evil to happen in order to raise up a generation of African American missionaries. He mused, "Perhaps his design was, that a knowledge of the gospel might be acquired by some of their descendants, in order that they might become qualified to be the messengers of it, to the land of their fathers." James Green wrote in 1824 that even the horrors of the slave trade "shall eventually be made productive of the richest blessings, which the inhabitants of that quarter of the globe have ever received from the Father of Mercies." Green searched the scriptures and human history to find "the usual order of the divine dispensations" and determined that God always worked in ways contrary to the nefarious intentions of mankind. Since "from the sure word of prophecy, we know that 'Ethiopia shall stretch forth her hands unto God,'" it was clear that "Africa shall yet be Christianized."[24]

The rhetoric of national redemption emerged in surprising places. The United States was still struggling to establish an identity distinct from Great Britain. In its immediate attempt to secure funding from Congress, the ACS proclaimed "it may be reserved for our government . . . to become the honorable instrument, under Divine Providence, of conferring, a still higher blessing upon the large and interesting portion of mankind." The House of Representatives agreed, responding with a report read before the whole body on February 11, 1817. The national legislature recognized the continent as "a wide field for the improvements in civilization, morals, and religion" and expected Christianity "in process of time, to spread over that great continent." Southerners contributed to the national conversionist conversation. The ACS chapter in Loudoun, Virginia, exhibited a great interest in both the conversion of Africa and the resulting redemption of America. These northern Virginians rejoiced in 1819 that, through African conversion, "our national character will cease to wear its most marring blemish."[25] But, this mission would ultimately depend on the willingness of the black Americans expected to inaugurate the continental revival.

African Americans largely shared the conversionist mission, but an overwhelming majority had no desire to emigrate. Free black Americans found themselves in a difficult situation. Many yearned for the conversion of Africa but, like white Christians, most believed it a task best suited for someone else. The widespread African American opposition to colonization did not equate to a lack of support for the missionary cause. Free blacks understandably mistrusted the curious coalition of abolitionists and slaveholders and feared the ways in which the ACS might be used to further erode their already tenuous freedoms.

In response to the panic in Philadelphia, over three thousand African Americans gathered at Mother Bethel African Methodist Episcopal Church to draft a response. Ministers Richard Allen, Absalom Jones, James Forten, and Russell Parrott took the lead. All had made previous public statements supporting the cause of African conversion. Parrott concluded an 1812 address celebrating the abolition of the slave trade with a millennial cry for Africa, rejoicing that "Religion has unfolded [Africa's] sacred page; and while she holds the heavenly volume to the eye, by her enlivening presence she dispels the clouds of paganism and error, which had so long overshadowed her."[26] Absalom Jones, the abolitionist minister of the African Episcopal Church of St. Thomas, frequently shared his commitment to African conversion, including in an 1808 sermon where he proclaimed, "May *Ethiopia soon stretch out her hands unto thee,* and lay hold of the gracious promise of thy everlasting covenant." He then beseeched God to destroy "all the false religions which now prevail among them; and grant, that they may soon *cast* their *idols, to the moles and the bats* of the wilderness." The case with Richard Allen is more complicated. The founder of African American Methodism became a supporter of Haitian emigration and even advocated for a Canadian colony, but, in the early years, Allen was a major booster for African colonization, holding meetings in his home and laboring to support Paul Cuffe's early attempts to settle African Americans in Sierra Leone.[27]

Despite the feelings of these influential leaders, the three thousand black Philadelphians responded to colonization with overwhelming opposition. White ACS leaders clearly had a difficult task in earning the trust of potential emigrants. The language of conversionism proved to be the most effective means of forging and maintaining biracial relationships, but many African Americans who shared conversionist goals nonetheless opposed colonization. James Forten and Russell Parrott issued a statement on behalf of the three thousand African Americans who met at Mother Bethel. In evaluating this statement, historians emphasize their African American sense of ownership of the nation where they lived. Forten biographer Julie Winch provides the following quote from the document: "whereas our ancestors (not of choice) were the first successful cultivators of America, we . . . feel ourselves entitled to participate in the blessings of her luxuriant soil, which their blood and sweat manured."

Another portion of the same message reveals a reason for opposition that has not received scholarly attention. The authors asserted their support for the conversionist mission and shared the ACS's optimism regarding the religious fate of Africa but feared that an insufficient number of well-educated free black Americans would voluntarily emigrate. The intense resistance of the Mother Bethel crowd illustrated the hesitance of settled free blacks to make the journey. They remarked that, if the new colony was populated solely by uneducated former slaves, "the light of Christianity, which now dawns among that section of our species, [would] be shut out by the clouds of ignorance, and their day of life be closed without the illuminations of the gospel."[28] Philadelphia's free black community distrusted the ACS to provide the training necessary to fulfill the glorious mission. Black Philadelphians either shared the conversionist, millennial convictions of the ACS or at least recognized the potency of the discourse, and articulated their opposition accordingly.

Phillis Wheatley similarly worried about the prospect of sending unqualified missionaries. Writing to John Thornton fifty years earlier, she weighed the possibility of traveling to Africa as a missionary. Wheatley yearned for the conversion of Africa and enthusiastically supported missionary efforts to the continent, but she declined an invitation to participate. Writing that she would impair the mission, as she did not speak the language, she nonetheless gave her support and prayed for its success.[29]

Baptists provided the strongest base of African American support for colonization, as Lott Cary and Collin Teague of Richmond dreamed of "spreading through the land of Ham, the knowledge of the Redeemer." These two African American ministers successfully transmitted their dream to the First African Baptist Church in Philadelphia, and ultimately persuaded the white leaders of the Baptist General Convention to support the movement. The two sailed for Africa in 1821, and the following year Cary established Providence Baptist Church in Monrovia. Men and women like Daniel Coker, Lott Cary, and Collin Teague, who shared the conversionist mission and were willing to risk their lives in its pursuit, represented a very small minority. Colonization always held greater currency in white populations who could piously praise the conversionist mission without having to offer more than a monthly contribution to the cause. The ACS fretted over the lack of African American support but ultimately ignored the overwhelming opposition of the free black community. In fact, the ACS claimed the mantle of Paul Cuffe, the famous African American colonizationist, and used his image in their advertising campaign.[30]

Early reports from Africa encouraged Americans that the continental conversion was already underway. Ephraim Bacon sailed from Norfolk on the brig *Nautilus* in January 1821. On their very first evening in Sierra Leone, the ACS agents attended a worship service, followed by another service less than twelve hours later. The colonists stared intently at their Bibles, closely following the sermon. "Such cheering fruits" told Bacon that "surely Christians ought to feel themselves encouraged in the support of missions." He emphasized the order and cleanliness, a striking instance of "a Christian congregation in a heathen land." On a single Sunday, he recorded services at six and ten in the morning and two more at three and six in the evening. At the primary service in the morning, he recorded four hundred Christians receiving communion.[31]

Encouragement came from black colonists as well. Samuel Wilson wrote from Sierra Leone in 1818 to free blacks in America, "your fathers were carried into that land to increase strangers' treasures, but God has turned it all to good, that you may bring the gospel into your country." A joint letter crafted three days later by eleven residents of Sierra Leone echoed this idea, claiming that "all that has befallen us is of God for our good, that we may bring the gospel into our country."[32]

By 1825 a few things had changed. Optimism for a world breaking free from generations of tyranny slowed, and white confidence in the missionary abilities of black Americans waned. Later reports from Africa explained the challenges that lay ahead. The faith in imminent global transformation that rang throughout the early nineteenth century gave way to a more somber interpretation of world events. Similarly, earlier encomiums to black American piety disappeared, as many Americans grew increasingly intolerant of the expanding population of free black Americans. Ralph Randolph Gurley, the two-time chaplain for the House of Representatives, editor for the *African Repository and Colonial Journal*, and an active officer for the ACS, criticized the Christianity of northern blacks by writing that "even religion their sole benefactress seldom rouses them for their insensibility to her motives and rescues them from their captivity to the lowest indulgencies of sense. Her light shines around, but penetrates not the darkness of their minds." Despite the negative portrait of black spirituality, on the very same page Gurley asserted that the ACS would send free blacks "to the soil of their ancestors and assist them there in founding the institutions of freedom, civilization, and Christianity."[33] Gurley believed that the free black population had tremendous potential, but for now he saw them as only a degraded, licentious nuisance.

The dream of African conversion endured, and Gurley's rhetoric matched the soaring heights of earlier colonizationists. In his 1824 Fourth of July oration, Gurley told the audience "Africa appeals to us this day!" Still deploying the language of national guilt, he claimed that Africa "stretches out her hands, and implores us in the name of justice as well as of mercy and religion to remember the unparalleled wrongs which, for centuries, she has endured from Christian nations." Burned villages, stolen children, and lost property "bear testimony to the validity of her claims," and America stood in need of redemption. By bringing the gospel to Africa, the current generation would surpass even the honored revolutionaries who earned national independence. Through their mission to Africa, Americans would "erect to our national honor a monument more durable than granite, inscribed to charity, the queen of the virtues."[34]

It was one thing to harbor these dreams in 1819, before the American settlements had struggled to gain traction, but by 1825 it was quite another to pursue the conversion of Africans with the same enthusiasm. In that year, the Petersburg auxiliary society in Virginia composed a circular letter to local ministers with some of the most elevated conversionist rhetoric in all of colonizationist literature. In telling their own history, the society claims they were "instituted, principally through the instrumentality of a devoted soldier of the cross," and that the prayers of pious Christians "have never yet ceased to ascend on its behalf." It had been nearly a decade since the movement began, but now the prayers of faithful Americans were joined with "the humble but ardent *Amen*" of the infant churches in Liberia, churches that were already saving souls in Africa and honoring the United States for her benevolence. To these local ministers to whom the circular was addressed, the authors asked, "will you not be on the Lord's side?"[35] Virginians had a choice. They could either join the patriotic Christian mission of saving Africa and redeeming their nation or they could stand with Satan, allow Africans to perish for eternity, leave America sullied by the sins of the slave trade, and expose their white neighbors to the potential of a slave revolt.

In 1833 Ezra Stiles Gannett wrote to his mentor William Ellery Channing to explain his support for the ACS, an increasingly unpopular position in Boston as Garrisonian abolitionists picked up the mantel of David Walker in opposing the movement. Gannett wrote, "The effect of the Colonization Society in diminishing or alleviating slavery in this country, I have not believed would be great. I have advocated it solely on the ground of its effects in Africa, where if the colony be properly increased, it will be the instrument of extinction to the slave trade and of regeneration to the continent." Eight years later in 1841, William Hemphill, a Presbyterian minister in Abbeville District, South Carolina, extolled African colonization as "the greatest means of extending the church of Christ over the benighted regions of enslaved and enslaving Africa."[36]

As Daniel Coker sailed across the Atlantic in 1820, he called to the heavens, "Oh! my soul, what is God about to do for Africa? Surely something great." Only a few days before arriving, he rejoiced, "has not the day of Africa's salvation already began to dawn? I imagine I behold the uplifted hands of thousands, in prayer, that it may shine more and more to the perfect day."[37]

Historians have understandably assessed colonizationist movements in relation to slavery, but colonization was more than just a proxy debate about slavery. Daniel Coker, Samuel Bacon, and hundreds of others dreamed of restoring Africa to the church and expunging the national sins of the slave trade. Ethiopia would stretch forth her hands to God and, as she did, millions of saved Africans would look with gratitude on the United States for transforming the horrors of the slave trade into a blessed agent of evangelism. Africa would be saved. America would be redeemed. Religious conviction cannot be understood solely as a ruse for political ambitions, and it is ultimately irrelevant whether the conversionist emphasis flowed from genuine sentiments or pragmatic attempts to hold together a fractious coalition. Either way, conversionism united colonizationists in a way nothing else could. That their millennial vision proved a mirage does not mean we can dismiss it. If we are to understand why so many Americans and Britons gave their money, their time, and their lives to this incomparably bold venture, we must listen to their words and take seriously their religious ambitions.

Notes

1. Daniel Coker, *Journal of Daniel Coker* (Baltimore, Edward J. Coale, 1820), 12.

2. I refer to my actors as *conversionists* and their ideology as *conversionism* because other terms are too narrow. Dreams of a converted Africa transcended the theological boundaries implied by labels like evangelicalism or missionary Christianity.

3. See Tracy Fessenden, *Culture and Redemption: Religion, the Secular, and American Literature* (Princeton, N.J.: Princeton University Press, 2007), 61, and John Lardas Modern, *Secularism in America* (Chicago: University of Chicago Press, 2011), 21.

4. Nathan O. Hatch, "The Origins of Civil Millennialism in America: New England Clergymen, War with France, and the Revolution," *William and Mary Quarterly*, 3rd ser., vol. 31, no. 3 (July 1974): 407–30; Robert H. Abzug, *Cosmos Crumbling: American Reform and the Religious Imagination* (New York: Oxford University Press, 1994); Nicholas Guyatt, *Providence and the Invention of the United States, 1607–1876* (New York: Cambridge University Press, 2007).

5. Robert Finley, *Thoughts on the Colonization of Free Blacks* (Washington, D.C., 1816), 8.

6. Ibid., 2; Prince Saunders, *A Memoir Presented to the American Convention for Promoting the Abolition of Slavery, and Improving the Condition of the African Race* (Philadelphia, 1818).

7. Jean Pierre Boyer to Loring Daniel Dewey, April 30, 1824, in Loring Daniel Dewey, *Correspondence Relative to the Emigration to Haiti, of the Free People of Color, in the United States* (New York, 1824), 11.

8. James S. Green, *Proceedings of a Meeting Held at Princeton, New Jersey, July 14, 1824 to form a Society in the State of New Jersey, to cooperate with the American Colonization Society* (Princeton, N.J., 1823), 31; Theodore Frelinghuysen, *An Oration: Delivered at Princeton,*

New Jersey, November 16, 1824 before the New Jersey Colonization Society (Princeton, N.J., 1824), 12–13.

9. Benjamin Rush, *An Address to the Inhabitants of the British Settlements on the Slavery of the Negros in America, Second ed. By A Pennsylvanian* (Philadelphia, 1773), 27; Abiel Holmes, *The Life of Ezra Stiles* (Boston: Thomas and Andrews, 1798); Granville Sharp, *The Just Limitations of Slavery in the Laws of God* (London, 1776), 26, 29–31. Sharp included a passage of a sermon his grandfather delivered before the House of Commons in 1679.

10. William Augustus Muhlenberg, *A sermon in memory of the Rev. Samuel Bacon, and John P. Bankson, May, 1820* (Philadelphia, 1820), 23. For more on the relationship between missionary rhetoric and imperialism, see Emily Conroy-Krutz, *Christian Imperialism: Converting the World in the Early Republic* (Ithaca, N.Y.: Cornell University Press, 2015); Derek Peterson, ed., *Abolitionism in Britain, Africa, and the Atlantic* (Athens: Ohio University Press, 2010); and Gale Kenny, *Contentious Liberties: American Abolitionists in Post-Emancipation Jamaica, 1834–1866* (Athens: University of Georgia Press, 2010).

11. Anthony Benezet, *A Short Account of That Part of Africa, Inhabited by the Negroes* (Philadelphia, 1762), 22–23; Peter Kolb, *The Present State of the Cape of Good Hope* (London, 1731), vol. 3: 359. See also Maurice Jackson, *Let This Voice Be Heard: Anthony Benezet, Father of Atlantic Abolitionism* (Philadelphia: University of Pennsylvania Press, 2009).

12. William Law, *An extract from a treatise on the spirit of prayer, or The soul rising out of the vanity of time into the riches of eternity. With some thoughts on war: Remarks on the nature and bad effects of the use of spirituous liquors. And considerations on slavery* (Philadelphia, 1780).

13. American Convention for Promoting the Abolition of Slavery and Improving the Condition of the African Race, *Minutes of the proceedings of a special meeting of the Fifteenth American Convention for Promoting the Abolition of Slavery, and Improving the Condition of the African Race* (Philadelphia, 1818), 52; Nicholas Guyatt, "'The Outskirts of Our Happiness': Race and the Lure of Colonization in the Early Republic," *Journal of American History* 95, no. 4 (March 2009): 986–1011.

14. Carl Bernhard Wadström, *An Essay on Colonization* (London, 1794–95), 95; Phillis Wheatley, *The Collected Works of Phillis Wheatley*, ed. John Shields (New York: Oxford, 1988), 175–76.

15. Ralph Randolph Gurley, *A Discourse, Delivered on the Fourth of July, 1825* (Washington, D.C., 1825), 18.

16. Wheatley, *Collected Works*, 178; Finley, *Thoughts*, 3–4; Muhlenberg, *A sermon in memory of the Rev. Samuel Bacon, and John P. Bankson*, 25.

17. Naimbana also sent another son to North Africa to study under Islamic tutors and another to France to learn under Catholics. See *Substance of the report of the court of directors of the Sierra Leone Company to the general court* (London, 1791), 15–21; Zachary Macaulay, *The African Prince* (London, 1796). See also William Gilpin, *Moral Contrasts: or, the power of religion exemplified under different characters* (London, 1798), and Hannah More, *The Black Prince* (Philadelphia, 1800).

18. Henry Clay, *Speech of the Hon. Henry Clay before the American Colonization Society in the Hall of the House of Representatives, January 20, 1827* (Washington, D.C.: Columbian Office, 1827), 12.

19. Finley, *Thoughts*, 8; Edward Griffin, *A Plea for Africa* (New York, 1817), 30.

20. Finley, *Thoughts*, 8, 3–4; Griffin, *Plea for Africa*, 31; Elias B. Caldwell, *A View of the Exertions Lately Made for the Purpose of Colonizing the Free People of Color in the United States, In Africa, or elsewhere* (Washington D.C., 1817), 8.

21. Finley, *Thoughts*, 6–8; Muhlenberg, *A sermon in memory of the Rev. Samuel Bacon, and John P. Bankson*, 12; Griffin, *Plea for Africa*, 31.

22. James Patterson, *A Sermon on the Effects of the Hebrew Slavery as Connected with the Slavery in this Country* (Philadelphia: S. Probasco, 1825), 20–21.

23. James Beattie, *Personal Slavery Established by the Suffrages of Custom and Right Reason* (Philadelphia, 1773), 3. For a longer discussion of the irony involved in the tract, see Lester B. Scherer, "A New Look at Personal Slavery Established," *William and Mary Quarterly*, 3rd ser., vol. 30, no. 4 (October 1973): 646.

24. Absalom Jones, *A Thanksgiving Sermon, preached January 1, 1808, in St. Thomas's, or the African Episcopal, Church, Philadelphia: on account of the abolition of the African slave trade, on that day, by the Congress of the United States* (Philadelphia, 1808), 18; Green, *Proceedings of a Meeting Held at Princeton, New Jersey, July 14, 1824*, 32–33.

25. Thomas Hart Benton, *Abridgment of the Debates of Congress from 1789 to 1856* (New York, 1857), vol. 5: 712; *Address of the Colonization Society of Loudoun, Virginia* (Annapolis, Md., 1819), 4–5.

26. Russell Parrott, *An Oration on the Abolition of the Slave Trade* (Philadelphia, 1812), 10.

27. Jones, *Thanksgiving Sermon*, 20–21. For a full treatment of Richard Allen's complex views on colonization, see Richard Newman, *Freedom's Prophet: Bishop Richard Allen, the AME Church, and the Black Founding Fathers* (New York: New York University Press, 2008).

28. Julie Winch, *A Gentleman of Color: The Life of James Forten* (New York: Oxford University Press, 2003), 191; James Forten and Russel Perrott, "An Address To The Humane And Benevolent Inhabitants Of The City And County Of Philadelphia," published in *Minutes of the Proceedings of a Special Meeting of the Fifteenth American Convention* (Philadelphia: 1817), 69–72.

29. Phillis Wheatley to John Thornton, October 20, 1774, in Wheatley, *Collected Works*, 184.

30. *Proceedings of the General Convention of the Baptist Denomination in the United States, 1817* (Philadelphia: Printed by order of the Convention, 1817), 180. See for example the imaginary dialog Robert Finley wrote between Cuffe, Abaslom Jones, and William Penn in Finley, "Dialogues on the African Colony," in Isaac Van Arsdale Brown, ed., *Memoirs of the Rev. Robert Finley* (New Brunswick, N.J.: 1819), 274–75.

31. Ephraim Bacon, *Abstract of a Journal of Ephraim Bacon* (Philadelphia, 1821), 5, 10–11.

32. Letter from Samuel Wilson, May 18, 1818, in *The Second Annual Report of the American Society for the Colonization of Free People of Color* (Washington D.C., 1819), 150. This letter was signed by John Kizzell, William Martin, George Davis, George Lewis, R. Robertson, Samuel Wilson, Peter Mitchell, Perry Locke, Thomas Williams, John Kizell Jr., and Pompey Rutledge and dated May 19, 1819. Bacon, *Abstract of a Journal of Ephraim Bacon*, 152.

33. Gurley, *A Discourse, Delivered on the Fourth of July 9, 1824*, 14–15.

34. Ibid., 17–18.

35. Broadside, June 17, 1825, Brand Papers, Virginia Historical Society.

36. Ezra Stiles Gannett to William Ellery Channing, August 21, 1833, reel 2, William Ellery Channing Papers, Massachusetts Historical Society; William Hemphill, "Address on Colonization," July 1, 1840, Hemphill Family Papers, David M. Rubenstein Rare Book and Manuscript Library, Duke University, Durham, N.C.

37. Coker, *Journal*, 14, 21.

3

"He Be God Who Made Dis Man"

Christianity and Conversion in Nineteenth-Century Liberia

ANDREW N. WEGMANN

One of the first buildings ever constructed in Liberia was a church. In January 1821, while the survivors of the American Colonization Society's first voyage to West Africa sought refuge in Freetown, Sierra Leone, a group of black Virginia Baptists, led by Lott Cary, decided to unite as a church before embarking on their own voyage to Africa onboard the *Nautilus* a few weeks later. The church the group formed in the United States eventually became the first church ever built in Liberia. They called it Providence Baptist and completed construction in early 1822 at the center of Cape Mesurado, the fledgling settlement that would become Liberia's capital.[1] All of the seven founding members of Providence Baptist were free people of color—four men and three women—from Richmond, Virginia. Working-class and literate, the cohort represented the standard among the *Nautilus* group, which ranged from future Americo-Liberian elites, such as Hilary Teage and John J. Barbour, to an elderly former slave named Roderick Simpson, who had purchased his own freedom in 1820.[2] The seven Baptists led the emigrants in prayer, and held church services on Sundays in the stowage quarters of the brig. Lott Cary soon became a leader of the *Nautilus* party as his energetic sermons concerning "the search for freedom" and the hope that lay in Africa captured the attention and trust of nearly everyone on board. One of the emigrants wrote of Cary's zeal a few years later. "A sermon which I heard from Mr. Cary," he wrote in 1828, "was the best extemporaneous discourse I have ever heard; it contained more original and impressive thoughts, some of which are distinct in my memory and can never be forgotten."[3]

Cary was a good example of an early emigrationist. Born a slave in Virginia in 1780, and freed in 1813 after converting to Christianity and paying his master $850, he looked to Africa as the natural home of American blacks. He saw the Liberian experiment as a worthy cause for racial uplift and African enlightenment but did not intend to let the Liberian government remain in the hands of white American Colonization Society (ACS) and U.S. government agents forever. Like most American blacks who supported the movement, he believed that the American settlers were to establish a black settlement in their shared ancestral home and aid their "benighted brethren" with the virtues and practices of Western Christianity. "I am an African," he wrote before leaving for Liberia. "I wish to go to a country where I shall be estimated by my merits, not by my complexion." He felt "bound to labor for [his] suffering race," both in America and Africa. But, he affirmed, nothing would come of the Liberian experiment if the United States did not grow to respect the "conduct and character" of the African race.[4]

Because Providence Baptist was the only permanent settler church in Liberia until 1828, and because, as Ben Wright argued in the previous chapter, the missionary zeal transcended denominational boundaries among evangelical Protestants, Cary preached to a large portion of the settler community, regardless of denomination. The church, which doubled as a meetinghouse in the early years of the settlement, was Cary's political and religious pulpit. From it each Sunday he preached, infusing calls for settler authority and missionary ventures into scripture. In a sermon from early 1822, Cary attacked the ACS for promoting government-led colonization over missionary-minded emigration. Like the other missionaries in Wright's chapter, he labored for the higher goal of African redemption. "If you intend to do anything for Africa," he told his new congregation, "you must not wait for the Colonization Society, nor for the government, for neither of these are in search of missionary grounds, but [only] of colonizing grounds."[5] Missionary work, and the establishment of a Western Christian society in Africa, Cary believed, required racial unity and an escape from the central American notion of Negro inferiority. A white-led system, he felt, would do little toward this end.

But Cary also saw little sense in shunning all foreign support from the budding American settlement in Africa. Although he clearly supported emigration over colonization, he gained influence in the colony as an outspoken proponent of cooperation—the idea that Liberia could not grow or prosper without communal sacrifice and compromise. "All of us who are connected with the [ACS] agents, who are under public instructions," he proclaimed, "must be conformed to their laws, whether they militate against missionary operations or not."[6] The colony, he believed, was not strong enough, or organized enough for self-rule in the 1820s. Independence required social structure, a Christian foundation, and a strong sense of purpose. To Cary, the settlement, though capable, lacked both the structure and the unified purpose to exist on its own. "I am greatly afraid [that foreign oversight] will not end soon," he wrote to the United States in 1822. "Until there can be a more permanent settlement obtained, . . . we are bound to the government's agents."[7]

Cary filled a unique role in the history of both Liberia and American missionary work in Africa. As an unmixed "pure Negro," a former slave, and an emigrationist, Cary did not meet the standard descriptions of early Liberian leaders, most of whom were freeborn, mixed-race, and strongly supportive of ACS authority. As a Baptist, he represented a church that in the following decades failed to establish a meaningful presence in Liberia. And as a self-proclaimed missionary, he placed the virtues and standards of Christian thought ahead of the cultural imitation and social expansion advanced by the Americo-Liberians of later years. But Cary was also a pastor, a man of God, and a brilliant speaker. He was passionate about his people, his race, and his religion. He was opinionated and outspoken, but willing to compromise for the betterment of the community. According to a memorial printed after his death, Cary "exhibited a boldness of thought" and a sense of leadership "which no acquirement could ever have given him."[8]

The extent of Cary's influence in Liberian settler society as a whole is unclear. Though many scholars see him as a leader of early Liberian society, his death in 1828 stopped him from having any serious influence on the colony's long-term development.[9] In the early years of the settlement, Cary stood as a talismanic figure for many of the hungry, struggling settlers at Cape Mesurado. Almost larger-than-life in his civic and religious energies, he was a thorn in the side of ACS leadership while also providing for the maintenance of peace in the young colony. On at least two occasions, Cary dissuaded a large group of settlers from withdrawing to Freetown, Sierra Leone, following food shortages and complaints of abuses from ACS authorities.[10] As health officer of the colony, a position given him by the ACS, he accused agents of "hoarding" provisions and led a "riot" against the Society Storehouse to provide clean water for those dying of cholera, malaria, and the ever-present "diarhatic fever."[11] He clearly appreciated the existence of the ACS, though, and the hand it had in the creation and maintenance of Liberia; but he also recognized the evil it could do to a weak and wandering people. Between 1823 and 1828, he led the colony's defense against numerous native attacks, a point often cited to suggest his dedication to ACS leadership. Outside of wartime, however, he remained wary of ACS authority and ever committed to the emigrationist and black-led missionary cause.

If anything, Cary's influence was latent and indirect in the legacy of the young colony. The Americo-Liberian settler minority stepped into the leadership void left by Cary's tragic death in 1828, forming a meritocratic racial oligarchy that dominated colonial society unopposed for nearly thirty years. As a result, the emigrationist concepts of pan-Negroism and clerical autonomy became tools of the ruling elite, and lost nearly all meaning until the creation of the Liberian republic in 1847. Western churches also did not arrive in Liberia in any meaningful numbers until 1833, when the Methodists established a church and missionary post outside of Monrovia. Cary's memory, then, held more meaning than his lived actions. In later decades, a number of settlers looked back at his work with reverence, proclaiming him the person to whom the colony was "indebted, more than any other man."[12] But it was not until the emergence of black-run churches in Liberia years later that Cary's legacy had any real impact.

In a sense, Cary was the first settler-missionary, the first public figure who in action and thought saw Liberia as a black Christian nation, who supported black-led missionary work and civilization through Christian ideas rather than Western images. In that way, he was the ideological frontrunner for what men like Edward Blyden and Alexander Crummell proposed in the 1860s and 1870s, and what came to define the social and cultural divide between Monrovia and the interior for more than a century thereafter. The evolution of American churches in Liberia is the key to understanding how this social and religious conflict came about, and how Cary's ideas remained dormant and misrepresented for so long.

After Cary's death, religion in Liberia became part of the Americo-Liberian social structure. Although Providence Baptist remained active, and Christianity, in general, remained a major fixture in the lives of most settlers, elites stopped using the church as a political forum and social center. Under the settler elite and ACS agents, the cooperative effort that Cary promoted came to focus more on society building and organization than on racial unification and expansion through Christianity.

Some leaders, such as Jehudi Ashmun, who served as ACS agent from 1824 to 1828, emphasized Christianity as the latent foundation of colonial society, not the driving force. "My confidence in the great Christian foundation is steadfast and unshaken," Ashmun wrote to the United States in

August 1828. "[We are] building on this foundation," recognizing the "love of Christian brotherhood, unfeigned." To Ashmun, the Liberian experiment gave Americans of color the chance to grow both as individuals and as a racial unit. But this growth was not self-imposed. The settlers needed oversight in addition to education in the fundamentals of white Christian morality before they could expand into the African continent to spread the word of God, or even exemplify the very standards with which they sought to indoctrinate the natives.[13]

Ashmun's "great Christian foundation," as he termed it, replaced active church membership in the settler community.[14] Although American church leaders and white visitors to the colony continuously wrote of Africa's potential for missionary work, the rhetoric and writing did not crystallize into action until much later, in the late 1830s and early 1840s. As a result, Liberian society during the late 1820s and early 1830s relied on emotional religion and outward expressions of piety, often directly connected to material evidence of financial well-being and emerging standards of Western middle-class lifestyles. Temperance organizations, for example, flourished in the early settlement as a reaction to the natives' "love of rum," and some colonists' "clandestine" consumption of the "ardent spirits."[15]

Nearly every report and letter from Liberia spoke of the providential "journey of the Negro back to Africa" and the settlers' divine assurance that their experiment would succeed.[16] In a letter to his former master in North Carolina, Richard McMorine expressed his trust in Liberia's providential success. "It is a new Country," he wrote, "[and] it is hard to live in all new Countrys at first, . . . [but] God did not make a country for the man of collor [sic] where he could not live."[17] In similar fashion, Robert Mechlin wrote to the ACS board that he was "taken by the Great work in which [the settlers] are engaged."[18]

In spite of the "Christian foundation" and professed morality at work in the settlement, Christianity did not expand in Liberia as planned. In fact, during the five years between the death of Lott Cary and the arrival of the first official Western missionary in Liberia, the settlers founded just one quasi-permanent church in the colony: the First United Methodist Church of Liberia (1828), which lacked a permanent home and organized congregation until 1832.[19]

During that same period, the expansion of Christianity into the hinterland took the form of hapless agrarian settlements on the outskirts of Monrovia inhabited by newly arrived freedmen and returned slaves. Unlike the earliest settlers, these freedmen were, in many cases, literally forced by their masters to emigrate, or drawn to the ACS by oppressive legislation across the United States.[20] As a result, the expansion out of Monrovia lacked an active sense of community. The Americo-Liberian and ACS leadership, through new legislation, forced the new arrivals to dedicate their labor to building homesteads and food supplies before any real communal unity could occur.[21] So, while a number of new, semiorganized settlements sprouted up around Monrovia in the late 1820s and early 1830s, very few new churches formed.

In response to the "remarkable embrace" of the Second Great Awakening, though, American churches soon looked to Liberia for a permanent missionary field.[22] The Methodist Episcopal Church led the way in 1833, with the short-lived white missionary Rev. Melville B. Cox. In 1834 the Presbyterian Church completed its first permanent structure in the Monrovia area.[23] Almost immediately, small bands of white missionaries founded religious schools and built permanent churches in and around the capital. Much like American-based Methodist groups at the time, the first Methodists in Liberia focused almost entirely upon educating the settlers in Christian morality and skilled labor.[24]

Caught up in the missionary spirit and humanitarian fervor of the era, Melville Cox started planning his work for Liberia nearly two years before his departure. He planned to found a "properly *academical* primary school" for both "the Africans and the Americans." The purpose of this school, which he planned to build in Monrovia, was to aid the settlers in the work of creating a "Christianized and civilized" society while implanting the "*habits*" of Christianity into the "pagan" minds of "the Africans."[25]

Christian education was by no means restricted to Cox's plan. Throughout much of West Africa, missionary schools served as the conduit through which natives could "shed the cloth of ignorance" and become integrated members of colonial society.[26] As far north as Senegal, French Catholic missionaries founded schools devoted to the "assimilation" of native youth into the "internal and external features" of French culture.

From these schools, as well as other avenues of conversion, came a small group of native elites called the *assimilé*, or *métis*. These groups stood between the settler and native communities as "proof" of the benefits of Christian education and cultural training in Senegal and French West Africa.[27] In Sierra Leone, just north of Liberia, the Church Missionary Society of England, as well as a number of Wesleyans, Methodists, and even some Catholics, established schools as early as 1806. Promoting the so-called "Three C's"—Christianity, commerce, and civilization—the schools sought to "develop" local youth into "subjects of the Crown" through the embrace of European cultural norms—Western names, dress, language, and religion.[28]

The European-based mission schools stretching from Senegal to the Niger River Delta met reasonable success in the first half of the nineteenth century. Like any colonial venture, these schools were not necessarily voluntary institutions, as Edward Blyden later complained while in residence at Freetown.[29] In many cases, white missionaries forced children from their homes, justifying their actions by claiming the "noble sacrifice" of a single child for the enlightenment of an entire village. The schools did not simply intend to convert native children into colored colonists. They meant to create a new class of assimilated evangelicals capable of returning to their villages and recruiting their families and friends to the schools.[30] Conversion, then, was only introduced in the field. The schools were the main site of assimilation, education, and conversion to the "Three C's."

Cox's plans for Liberia, however, were nothing short of quixotic. Cox tried to transplant the revival-style mass conversions of the Great Awakening to the small settler enclave on the coast of Africa without considering the disparity between the settler and native cultures. He, like many others of his ilk, expected the indigenes to seek out Western education and Christianity. The church, and Christianity in general, would then expand from the outside inward, creating a single educated, skilled Christian society. But like most early white missionaries, Cox failed to recognize the history of Liberia's ethnic groups, or the power of the "settler standard." Few of Liberia's local ethnic groups had any meaningful interaction with Christians before the settlers arrived.[31] The Mandingo and the Vai, for example, had been devoted Muslims since the mid-sixteenth century. The Gola did not operate a coastal trade, and thus had very little exposure to foreign religions or cultures in general.[32]

As a result of this misperception, the first missionary schools in Liberia seemed to reverse the notions of self-worth and unified Christian individualism promoted through the Great Awakening and the Jacksonian Era in the United States. The schools, in essence, served as mass apprenticeships. Methodist teachers feared the "problem of 'pagan' influences on students" and required native children to don Western clothing and speak the American English of the settlers. Native students lived at the school, unlike their settler classmates. After morning classes, the settler children returned home while the native children spent the afternoon learning a skill, such as carpentry or weaving.[33]

The length of education was generally four years for both settlers and natives. However, in 1838 Methodist and Presbyterian schools started requiring nonsettler parents to "indenture," or legally apprentice, their children to the school in exchange for education.[34] In many instances, the white missionary teachers would then accept native children into their homes to immerse the students "immediately and entirely to the habits and customs of civilized society, in dress and everything, as are the children of the colonists."[35] Under this system, following the four-year educational term, the schools offered settler families the healthiest and most intelligent native children for four more years of skill training and immersion into Liberian culture. Beginning at age fourteen, most native children either returned home or became part of settler society following their twenty-second birthday.[36]

The ideas of the Great Awakening in the United States simply did not translate to the white-led Liberian missionary field of the 1830s and 1840s. Although inspired by the same rhetoric of revival, education, and uplift, the first wave of Methodist and Presbyterian missionaries engaged in practices strikingly similar to those of the Americo-Liberian elite. Missionary teachers did not simply implant the "habits" of American Christianity into the minds of "benighted" natives, as Melville Cox had planned in 1831. They forced total indoctrination through legal indenture and immersion. There was no cultural "fusion" atop a "Christian foundation." The dominant Americo-Liberian system of cultural imitation and Christian rhetoric simply absorbed the few native children who successfully completed the term of study, positioning them as third-class "pure Negroes" and "Congo children."[37]

To the natives who left their villages to join the settler schools, the Americo-Liberians and white missionaries occupied the same dominant social strata. Both were light-skinned, well-spoken, well-dressed, and in charge. As pupils and apprentices, the natives stood as listeners, not speakers, followers, not leaders. They were told how to speak, how to dress, and what to believe. In the eyes of Americo-Liberian leaders, the average native's lack of an American experience hindered his or her ability to fully accept and understand the standards of Liberia's American social order. Their dark skin and "savage" origins made it difficult for them to learn the syntax of American English, the virtues of Christian morality, and the Western model of Americo-Liberian politics.[38]

Americo-Liberian, ACS, and missionary leadership in the 1830s and 1840s often overlapped. Of the eight official colonial agents and governors of Liberia, all but two were openly pious and/or members of the clergy.[39] Men like John B. Pinney and Ezekiel Skinner, two white Methodist reverends, oversaw the colonial government while actively participating in the church's missionary organization.[40] Public schooling, which the ACS board established as early as 1827, quickly shifted to church-run religious schooling as white missionaries started to build more and more schools throughout the settlements.[41] Seeing the increasing number of white missionary schools and teachers around Monrovia, the ACS board, in 1833, decided to cut all funding to the public school system and dedicate the funds to improving the infrastructure of the colony.[42]

In the early 1840s, however, portions of the Liberian missionary establishment began to notice, and organize against, the social and political disparity at work in the Monrovia area. John Seys, the white superintendent of the Methodist mission in Liberia at the time, started looking to the black populations of both the United States and Liberia to fill empty missionary positions in the field.[43] Like Lott Cary, Seys believed that blacks should convert blacks, and that the white system of superintendency and leadership should serve the sole purpose of establishing an organized structure for a future black-run system.

To Seys, the inclusion of white missionaries in black Africa both threatened the autonomy of the settlers and erased any separation from slavery and white authority that existed in Liberian society. He recognized the problems with the status quo of the missionary enterprise, and complained of the lack of "local workers." Although black missionaries existed in Liberia before his arrival, the American churches did not recognize them as official representatives of the church and did not pay them a salary or give them any benefits. Yet these missionaries, Seys pointed out, ventured into the interior, spoke at native villages, and traveled "up rivers and creeks at their own expense to teach their brethren and neighbors the way to heaven."[44]

This same logic was used outside of Liberia, but with less success. As early as 1814, the Baptist Missionary Society in Jamaica had plans to expand their "light" into West Africa without using white missionary education. By 1838, it had received enough funding from private interests to organize the trip it had planned more than two decades earlier.

Looking briefly to the African continent, under the leadership of William Knibb, a white Briton, and Rev. John Clarke, a white Baptist priest, the group decided that an "administrative order" could only descend upon the African interior through the guise of "Africans themselves."[45] Knibb,

Clarke, and a man named John Keats, a free man of color from Jamaica, then, agreed that the "conduits of conversion" in Jamaica should likewise be "civilized and free" Jamaicans, many of whom had grown up hearing stories of the "dark continent" and had once lived lives of "abject debasment."[46] In 1843, Rev. Clarke gathered twenty-one colored Jamaicans and set sail for the Niger Delta, eventually seeking to merge his company with that of the famous Samuel Crowther.[47] After nearly three months of searching for a foothold along the Niger River, the expedition retreated to Fernando Pó, a Spanish island dominated by unfriendly Spanish agents and white Catholic missionaries.[48] Unwelcomed and hungry, Clarke and his contingent of black New World missionaries returned home in 1847, just four years after arriving, and just months before the declaration of an independent Liberian republic.

Beyond the small Baptist Missionary Society in Jamaica, very few groups along and across the Atlantic took note of this cause. In the United States, black evangelicals and missionaries, with some exceptions, served as unofficial representatives of the main church. In the tradition of the Second Great Awakening, these black men, and some women, preached to their own communities, rarely expanding into white society or the Atlantic world. Although often seen as tools of conversion by white bishops and leaders, they developed their own "Christian lineage," a sense of duty and devotion to the uplift of their own people in their own country. This devotion, however, did not stretch to Africa until much later in the century.[49] In the 1840s, John Seys stood alone with the idea of leading American blacks into the African interior.

The missionaries that Seys recruited were mainly second-class, dark-skinned, semi-literate former slaves who, after failing to properly maintain their crops, took to missionary work to fulfill their perceived Christian "destiny."[50] Recognizing the inequality at work, Seys wrote a pamphlet that challenged the authority of the white-run colonial system and its refusal to involve dark-skinned blacks in both the government and the various missionary enterprises.[51] He attacked what he called the "oppressive regulations" of the white government and Americo-Liberian council, made up largely of light-skinned settlers with free American roots. He challenged the honesty of the settler elite and the validity of their alleged Christian foundations. Most importantly, he questioned the meaning of missionary work if a section of the host population was debarred from active, recognized participation.[52]

Such rhetoric "astounded" men like Joseph Roberts who, as a member of the highest Americo-Liberian circles, viewed the "false and malicious" accusations as insults to the "chaste, sober, and honest" people of Liberia. It incited riot and social unrest, he claimed. And if such "dangerous insinuations . . . [are] the facts," he concluded, "I bid adue [sic] to Liberian Liberty."[53]

In essence, Seys was the first to promote clerical voluntarism in the Liberian colony. But far from Roberts's fears, Seys did not seek to abolish all connections with the ACS and United States. He sought clerical autonomy—freedom to enter the interior and spread the "word of God." To him, the system of stationary mission schools and cultural assimilation was not working. It converted too few souls in too long a time. Itinerancy was the key. Christianity, according to Seys and his black missionaries, could not function beneath the regulations and norms of Monrovia and a distant white leadership.[54] A successful missionary enterprise *required* black authority over black missionaries with a focus on mass conversion to Christian thought, rather than Western cultural immersion in the guise of Christian education.[55]

Seys did not have to wait long. In late 1841, white political leadership in Liberia ended. Following the death of Gov. Thomas Buchanan in September, the ACS board appointed Joseph Jenkins Roberts the first colored governor of the colony.[56] Some six years later, on July 26, 1847, the Liberian people announced their independence from the ACS and elected Roberts the first president of the new Republic of Liberia. The colonial era was over; white authority had collapsed; and in the wake of rhetorical promises of republicanism, civic equality, and racial unity out of Monrovia, John Seys left Liberia, convinced his work was done.[57]

But the ideas first posited by Lott Cary, and revived by Seys, remained in the minds of Liberia's black missionaries and second-class thinkers even as Liberia became a "Black Republic." By the time the Methodist Board of Foreign Missions granted the Liberian Missionary Convention full autonomy in July 1849, a number of disgruntled underclass Liberians had fled the Monrovia area and joined missionary groups on the frontier.[58] Almost immediately, men like Alexander Crummell emerged as leaders, promoting mass conversion, racial unity, and the importance of itinerancy in the field. No longer did missionary leaders adhere to total indoctrination or immersion into an American-style social order. Recognition of the fundamentals of Christianity was the key to civilization and moral uplift.

This new group saw mass conversion as a way to "enlighten" many natives with a simple understanding of Christian thought, allowing the natives to teach themselves the values of Christianity without apprenticeships and schooling.⁵⁹ They built churches and stations at the furthest reaches of settler territory, in Clay-Ashland, Edina, Greenville, and Cuttington.⁶⁰ They traveled distances of forty miles or more, over a number of days, to hold palavers with native chiefs and to preach to entire villages. They simplified their language, either translating scripture directly to native tongues (Kpelle and Vai), or speaking in a heavily accented pidgin English. "[The missionary] may not penetrate the mines of [the natives'] mountains and bring up from their buried deeps the gold and gems of commerce and civilization," Cyrus Hamlin wrote as early as spring 1837. "But he may penetrate the mines of [their] moral darkness, and bring from thence the gem of an immortal spirit."⁶¹

With this came more accessible lessons. Rather than focusing on the dense theology taught in settler schools and the United States, the new black missionaries spoke of a simple creation; a single, omnipotent, benevolent God; angels, rather than the native "devils," or *gree-grees*; and the unity of man through Christian faith. "He be God who make all dis man, dem bush, dem tree, dem riber," they told one village. "First time, no one man lib to dis world. Den God, he make one man and one woman. Dat man and dat woman go hab pickenniny, and dem pickenniny go hab more gen; bomby de world cum up full people."⁶² They had entirely abandoned the Americo-Liberian notion of complete cultural conversion.

Many field missionaries and leaders wrote of this move. In 1857, David Wilson, a Presbyterian missionary from St. Clair, Pennsylvania, wrote a colleague: "You are not unaware that a strong jealousy of the white man . . . [prevails] in this country."⁶³ That same year, Edward Williams, a Monrovian transplant, argued that the interior held more "hope and progress" than the urban Americo-Liberian capital. He advocated native conversion to "Gospel principles," claiming that the intense Bible studies, and "deliberate cultural distractions" of indentures and missionary schools, denied native conversion on "God's own time."⁶⁴

Alexander Crummell agreed. "I cannot write the glowing reports of the nation and of the people and condition and prospects of the Republic which many people do," wrote Crummell, a dark-skinned, New York–born Protestant minister, in 1853. "Political partisanship," along with inequality, "is unseemly, distracting and despiritualizing" in a nation founded on liberty and freedom.⁶⁵ Crummell believed that the Americo-Liberians had lost Christianity as a guide for civilization. Like the leaders of the Roman Empire, Babylon, and Egypt, they had fallen to "decadence" and "idolatry," spoiled by the "luxury [that] cloys and enervates," destroys and corrupts. They worshiped fine clothes, and drink, and food, and speech, all while preaching of temperance, virtue, and acceptance. They were, in Crummell's eyes, "as low and rude" as the natives themselves. The difference, however, was that the natives could be fixed; the Americo-Liberians were too far gone.[66]

Modesty in dress, correctly accented English, and even correct religious terminology thus gave way to a basic understanding of Christian fundamentals. The missionaries came to see their work as a constructive process, adding to what the natives already knew and believed. In 1860, Edward Blyden, perhaps the best-known and most respected early pan-Negro thinker, wrote of the Liberian mission field as "constructive rather than destructive." The missionary, he asserted, "has nothing to demolish; he only has to arrange his materials and proceed to build." Through the seeds of Christianity planted by the itinerant missionaries, the natives, Blyden believed, would learn to integrate Christian ethics and symbols into their normal lives, eventually growing into an enlightened, proud people.[67]

To thinkers like Blyden and Crummell, the Americo-Liberians, as well as white missionaries and leaders, acted on an inherently racist foundation, as if lightness of skin defined one's intellectual ability and gave him or her the right to claim Christianity as a form of racial property. To Americans, Europeans, and Americo-Liberians, "the African mind is regarded as a great blank, or worse than a blank, filled with everything dark and horrible and repulsive," Blyden wrote. "Everything is to be destroyed, and replaced by something new and foreign." But that "new and foreign" idea (Christianity), Blyden claimed, "has seemed to be the property exclusively of the European branch of the human family."[68] To break the Indo-European monopoly over Christian ideals, Liberian and African missionaries had to adopt a heuristic approach to conversion and free Christianity from the constraints of Western social and cultural standards. "Let the boys and girls in the schools eat the simple, wholesome food of their country," Blyden wrote. "Let them wear the clothing of their country made in the best style, clean and neat, that in the process of their training they may not receive the impression that the external accidents of European civilisation are the essentials of Christianity."[69]

Missionaries, according to Blyden, should likewise avoid secular jobs and politics altogether.[70] Both Blyden and Crummell believed that racial hegemony and Christian thought should define Liberia as a nation, rather than a partial imitation of Western culture and an enormous native population oppressed and degraded by those Western imitators. To Blyden, Africans and people of African descent who focused on the internalization of Christian faith and morality embodied "the ardent and enlightened love of liberty" that the Americo-Liberians wrote into their declaration of independence, but subsequently forgot.

This "love of liberty," and the right to self-definition and self-help, were the core tenets of the Liberian idyll for Edward Blyden, Alexander Crummell, and their second-class followers of the 1850s, 1860s, and 1870s.[71] Of course, the Americo-Liberians remained in Monrovia, Buchanan, and other settler enclaves, imitating the United States in speech, dress, custom, and memory. They claimed to be a nation of civilized Christians born in the image of America's "brave pilgrims." But their sensibilities stretched no further than the coast. They ventured into the interior only later, in the 1880s, to establish political control over the hinterland and its people, satisfying the demands of their colonial European neighbors.[72]

But somehow Christianity continued to grow in Liberia over the next century and a half, reaching 31 percent of the population by 1982.[73] Thus, a failure of purpose, at least on a structural level, never occurred in the Liberia mission field. Following independence, and the end of white authority, it took on a new form, a new constitution, and a new set of values opposite those at work in Monrovia and other urban centers. It took the Jacksonian notion of self-definition out of its "civilized" American context and placed it in the African interior, something the Americo-Liberians never did.[74] Founded on the basics of Christian morality and faith, the Liberian missionary enterprise under men like Blyden, Crummell, and Seys brought forth a populist Christian nationalism, rather than a political and cultural colonialism, in the interior. Civilization and belonging amounted to a basic understanding of Christian faith and ethics, not the donning of silken top hats and membership in the Liberian Masonic Order. In this way, Lott Cary and emigrationism never really died. They just went to sleep, awakened by the likes of John Seys, Alexander Crummell, and Edward Blyden and their shared dedication to making Liberia a Christian, African nation of its own.

Notes

1. Marie Tyler-McGraw, *An African Republic: Black and White Virginians in the Making of Liberia* (Chapel Hill: University of North Carolina Press, 2014), 63; J. Gus Liebenow, *Liberia: Evolution of Privilege* (Ithaca, N.Y.: Cornell University Press, 1969), 9; and *African Repository* 44, no. 3 (July 1877): 81.

2. "Information relative to the Operations of the United States Squadron on the West Coast of Africa . . . ," 28th Congress, 2nd Session, S. Doc. 150.

3. Anonymous, qtd. in George Winfred Harvey, *The Story of Baptist Missions in Foreign Lands: From the time of Cary to the present day* (St. Louis, Mo.: Chancy R. Barns, 1884), 202.

4. Lott Cary, qtd. in Liebenow, *Liberia: Evolution of Privilege*, 9; P. J. Staudenraus, *The African Colonization Movement, 1816–1865* (New York: Columbia University Press, 1961), 109; and Andrew Billingsley, *Mighty Like a River: The Black Church and Social Reform* (New York: Oxford University Press, 2003), 69. Also see Lamin Sanneh, *West African Christianity: The Religious Impact* (Maryknoll, N.Y.: Orbis Books, 1983), 93.

5. Cary, qtd. in Miles Mark Fisher, "Lott Cary, the Colonizing Missionary," *Journal of Negro History* 7, no. 4 (October 1922): 390; also, *Seventh Annual Report of the Baptist Board of Foreign Missions* (Philadelphia: Anderson & Meehan, 1822), no pagination, microform, Pullen Library, Georgia State University.

6. Cary, qtd. in Fisher, "Lott Cary," 390.

7. Cary, qtd. in J. B. Taylor, *Biography of Elder Lott Cary, Late Missionary to Africa* (Baltimore: Armstrong & Berry, 1837), 29.

8. "Brief Memoir of Rev. Lott Cary," *Missionary Register* 17 (November 1829): 481.

9. Nearly every work on Liberian and African missionary history mentions Cary as an early Liberian leader. On his leadership, see Sanneh, *West African Christianity*, 93–94; Staudenraus, *African Colonization Movement*, 96–97; Lamin Sanneh, *Abolitionists Abroad: American Blacks and the Making of Modern West Africa* (Cambridge, Mass.: Harvard University Press, 1999), 210–12; James Sidbury, *Becoming African in America: Race and Nation in the Early Black Atlantic* (New York: Oxford University Press, 2007), 182–83, 188–89; and, among others, Leroy Fitts, *Lott Cary: First Black Missionary to Africa* (Valley Forge, Pa.: Judson Press, 1978), 40–44.

10. Eli Ayres to E. B. Caldwell, August 23, 1822, in Charles Henry Huberich, *The Political and Legislative History of Liberia*, 2 vols. (New York: Central Publishing Company, 1947), 210–12. Also see Sidbury, *Becoming African in America*, 185–86.

11. His time as "health inspector" of the colony is little discussed in the existing scholarship. The ACS referred to his movement for provisions as a "riot" in its official report to Washington. See Lucius Edwin Smith, *Heroes and Martyrs of the Modern Missionary Enterprise: A Record of their Lives and Labors* (Providence, R.I.: O. W. Potter, 1856), 357–59; Fisher, "Lott Cary," 412–13; and Sanneh, *Abolitionists Abroad*, 211.

12. Samuel Wilkeson, *A Concise History of the Commencement, Progress and Present Condition of the American Colonies in Liberia* (Washington, D.C.: Madisonian Office, 1839), 38.

13. Ralph Randolph Gurley, *Life of Jehudi Ashmun, late Colonial Agent in Liberia* (Washington: James G. Dunn, 1835), 60, 91, 388–90.

14. While rhetoric of providential destiny and divine action became commonplace in speeches, letters, and reports, discussion of church-related matters or active church organizations in Liberia drastically decreased after 1828. See *African Repository* 4–10, with emphasis on the "Latest from Liberia" section; and Records of the American Colonization Society, Library of Congress (hereafter RACS), Incoming Letters, boxes 6 and 7, 1821–33.

15. *African Repository* 6, no. 4 (June 1830): 101 and no. 11 (January 1831): 333.

16. See Kenneth C. Barnes, *Journey of Hope: The Back-to-Africa Movement in Arkansas in the Late 1800s* (Chapel Hill: University of North Carolina Press, 2004), 123–25; Wilson Jeremiah Moses, ed., *Liberian Dreams: Back-to-Africa Narratives from the 1850s* (University Park: Pennsylvania State University Press, 1998), xiv–xvi; and Andrew N. Wegmann, "To Fashion Ourselves Citizens: Colonization, Belonging, and the Problem of Nationhood in the Atlantic South, 1829–1859," John Garrison Marks and Whitney Stewart, eds., *Race and Nation in the Age of Emancipations: An Atlantic World Anthology* (Athens: University of Georgia Press, 2017).

17. Richard McMorine, qtd. in Claude Clegg III, *The Price of Liberty: African Americans and the Making of Liberia* (Chapel Hill: University of North Carolina Press, 2003), 185.

18. Robert Mechlin to R. R. Gurley, May 15, 18[33], RACS.

19. The history of the First United Methodist Church of Liberia is largely a mystery. The only two scholarly works that specifically mention the church are D. Elwood Dunn, Amos J. Beyan, and Carl Patrick Burrowes, eds., *Historical Dictionary of Liberia* (Lanham, Md.: Scarecrow Press, 2001), 229, which refers to the church as "Union Church of Liberia," and Sanneh, *West African Christianity,* 102, which provides 1832 as the year the "First Methodist Church" was completed.

20. Eric Burin, *Slavery and the Peculiar Solution: A History of the American Colonization Society* (Gainesville: University Press of Florida, 2005), 17; Tyler-McGraw, *An African Republic,* 72.

21. The 1824 Constitution required settlers who accepted ACS land to build a wood-framed house and plant sufficient crops within six months of their arrival in Liberia. Failure to do so most often resulted in confiscation of land, fines, or even apprenticeship. See Amy DeRogitas, *Moral Geography: Maps, Missionaries, and the American Frontier* (New York: Columbia University Press, 2003), 2–4, 155; Huberich, *Political and Legislative History,* 319–20; and James Thomas Sabin, "The Making of the Americo-Liberian Community: A Study of Politics and Society in Nineteenth-Century Liberia," Ph.D. diss., Columbia University, 1974, 33–34.

22. Daniel Walker Howe, *What Hath God Wrought: The Transformation of America, 1815–1848* (New York: Oxford University Press, 2007), 179–88; and Nathan O. Hatch, *The Democratization of American Christianity* (New Haven, Conn.: Yale University Press, 1989), 197–200.

23. Sanneh, *West African Christianity,* 102–3; J. R. Oldfield, "The Protestant Episcopal Church, Black Nationalists, and Expansion of the West African Missionary Field, 1851–1871," *Church History* 57, no. 1 (March 1988): 31; Eunjin Park, *"White" Americans in "Black" Africa: Black and White American Methodist Missionaries in Liberia, 1820–1875* (New York: Routledge, 2001), 19–20; and Amos J. Beyan, "The American Colonization Society and the Socio-Religious Characterization of Liberia: A Historical Survey, 1822–1900," *Liberian Studies Journal* 10.2, no. 1 (1985): 2. Beyan provides dates that are different from all other works. The Roman Catholics, who had little influence throughout West Africa, and especially Liberia, arrived in Cape Mount, north of Monrovia, in 1841. The Protestants first arrived in Cape Palmas, an independent settlement far south of Monrovia, founded by the Maryland Colonization Society in 1834.

24. Park, *"White" Americans,* 21–22.

25. Melville B. Cox, *The Remains of Melville B. Cox, late Missionary to Liberia,* ed.

Gershom F. Cox (New York: T. Mason and G. Lane, 1839), 232; also see Henry John Drewal, "Methodist Education in Liberia, 1833–1856," in Vincent M. Battle and Charles H. Lyons, eds., *Essays in the History of African Education* (New York: Teachers College Press, 1970), 36.

26. Quote from George Thompson, *Palm Land; or, West Africa Illustrated* (Cincinnati, Ohio: Moore, Wilstach, & Co., 1859), 35.

27. On the *métis* specifically, see Hilary Jones, *The Métis of Senegal: Urban Life and Politics in French West Africa* (Bloomington: Indiana University Press, 2013), chap. 2; and, among others, Saliha Belmessous, *Assimilation & Empire: Uniformity in French and British Colonies, 1541–1954* (Oxford, U.K.: Oxford University Press, 2013), 47–56.

28. See Gibril R. Cole, *The Krio of West Africa: Islam, Culture, Creolization, and Colonialism in the Nineteenth Century* (Athens: Ohio University Press, 2013), 180–87; and, among others, Bronwen Everill, *Abolition and Empire in Sierra Leone and Liberia* (New York: Palgrave Macmillan, 2013), 49–53.

29. Edward Wilmot Blyden, "Study and Race," in Hollis Lynch, ed., *Black Spokesman: Selected Published Writings of Edward Wilmot Blyden* (London: Frank Cass, 1971), 200–204; also cited, in slightly different form, in Cole, *Krio of West Africa*, 182.

30. Cole, *Krio of West Africa*, 181–82; Sanneh, *West African Christianity*, 106–7, 111–13; and Sanneh, *Abolitionists Abroad*, 101–3.

31. Very few of these groups have a history on the Grain Coast before the sixteenth century. See Yekutiel Gershoni, *Black Colonialism: The Americo-Liberian Struggle for the Hinterland* (Boulder, Colo.: Westview Press, 1985), 1–6; Jo M. Sullivan, *Settlers in Sinoe County, Liberia, and their Relations with the Kru, 1835–1920* (Boston: Boston University Press, 1978), 69–71.

32. Gershoni, *Black Colonialism*, 82–90; Teah Wulah, *The Forgotten Liberia: History of Indigenous Tribes* (Bloomington, Ind.: AuthorHouse, Inc., 2005), 33–34, 52–53.

33. Gurley, *Life of Jehudi Ashmun*, 356–57; *Sixteenth Annual Report of the American Society for Colonizing the Free People of Color of the United States* (Washington, D.C.: James G. Dunn, 1833), 6–8; *Christian Advocate and Journal* 12 (1838): 34–35; and Drewal, "Methodist Education," 40–43.

34. "Missionary Department," *Christian Advocate and Journal* 24, no. 32 (1850): 126; and "Protest," *Christian Reflector*, August 3, 1838, 2–3. This "Protest," signed by such names as William Wilberforce and John Clapham, asserts that the ACS's plan for the "abolition of slavery [is] altogether delusive" because of apprenticeships, and "colored people" practicing the same "persecution" that made them emigrate in the first place.

35. *African Repository* 29, no. 7 (July 1853): 202; Drewal, "Methodist Education," 42; and *African Repository* 13, no. 7 (July 1837): 246.

36. George R. Stetson, *The Liberian Republic as it is* (Boston: A. Williams & Co., 1881), 18; Park, *"White" Americans*, 106. Also United States Bureau of Manufactures, "Liberian Law of Apprenticeship," *Monthly Consular and Trade Reports*, 1904, 127–29, Library of Congress; and "Missionary Department," *Christian Advocate and Journal* 24, no. 32 (1850): 126.

37. Americo-Liberians often referred to recaptured slaves and "converted" natives as "Congoes" because they assumed the slaves originally inhabited the Congo River area. See Tom W. Shick, *Behold the Promised Land: A History of Afro-American Settler Society in*

Nineteenth-Century Liberia (Baltimore: Johns Hopkins University Press, 1980), 72; and J. Gus Liebenow, *Liberia: The Quest for Democracy* (Bloomington: Indiana University Press, 1987), 84.

38. *African Repository* 13, no. 7 (July 1837): 246–47; Charles S. Johnson, *Bitter Canaan: The Story of the Negro Republic* (New Brunswick, N.J.: Transaction Press, 1987), 86, 94, 131–33; Joseph Mechlin to R. R. Gurley, May 15, 1833, RACS; and Joseph Jenkins Roberts, "First Inaugural Address," in Guannu, *The Inaugural Addresses of the Presidents of Liberia: From Joseph Jenkins Roberts to William Richard Tolbert, Jr., 1848–1976* (Hicksville, N.Y.: Exposition Press, 1980), 2–7.

39. Christian Abayomi Cassell, *Liberia: History of the First African Republic* (New York: Fountainhead Publishers, 1970), 411.

40. Teah Wulah, *Back to Africa: A Liberian Tragedy* (New York: AuthorHouse, Inc., 2009), 227; also see James Fairhead, Tim Geysbeek, Svend E. Holsoe, and Melissa Leach, eds., *African-American Exploration in West Africa: Four Nineteenth-Century Diaries* (Bloomington: Indiana University Press, 2003), 41–43.

41. "Foreign Intelligence," *Christian Advocate and Journal* 2, no. 10 (November 1827): 39; Drewal, "Methodist Education," 34–35.

42. Board of Managers, "Business Papers," Proceedings and Minutes, 1816–33, Book 10, RACS, 35. ACS public schools, based on the business records of the ACS, existed for no more than five years, and all but ceased to exist after the establishment of a stable missionary school system both in Monrovia and its surrounding areas. ACS public schools do not show up in any record after December 1834. See Drewal, "Methodist Education," 36–40; Board of Managers, "Business Papers," Minutes, 1834–47, Books 11 and 12, RACS; and Gershoni, *Black Colonialism*, 23.

43. There was an extremely high death rate among white missionaries in Liberia. See Park, *"White" Americans*, 198–99, for statistics on this. Also see Clegg, *Price of Liberty*, chap. 4.

44. Quote from *African Repository* 11, no. 5 (May 1835): 155; also see Park, *"White" Americans*, 127–30.

45. Sanneh, *West African Christianity*, 107–8; and William Knibb, *Memoir of William Knibb, Missionary in Jamaica*, ed. John Howard Hinton (London: Houlston and Stoneman, 1849), 364–65.

46. Knibb, *Memoir*, 156–57, 336–38; and Catherine Hall, *Civilising Subjects: Metropole and Colony in the English Imagination, 1830–1867* (Chicago: University of Chicago Press, 2002), 160–61.

47. On Samuel Crowther sources vary drastically from nineteenth-century hagiographies to more modern contextual treatments. See, among others, Jesse Page, *Samuel Crowther: The Slave Boy who Became Bishop of the Niger* (New York: Fleming H. Revell Co., 1892); Rev. Samuel Crowther, *Journal of an Expedition Up the Niger and Tshadda Rivers* (London: Church Missionary House, 1855); Myles Osborne and Susan Kingsley Kent, *Africans and Britons in the Age of Empires, 1660–1980* (London: Routledge, 2015), chap. 2; and Ibrahim K. Sundiata, *From Slavery to Neoslavery: The Bight of Biafra and Fernando Po in the Era of Abolition, 1827–1930* (Madison: University of Wisconsin Press, 1996), 67–69.

48. On Fernando Pó, see, among many others, Sundiata, *From Slavery to Neoslavery*, 27–54.

49. Jay Riley Case, *An Unpredictable Gospel: American Evangelicals and World Christianity, 1812–1920* (New York: Oxford University Press, 2012), 159–64, 188–95. Also see Andrew N. Wegmann, "Skin Color and Social Practice: The Problem of Race and Class Among New Orleans Creoles and Across the South, 1718–1862," Ph.D. diss., Louisiana State University, 2015, chaps. 4 and 5.

50. Fairhead et al., eds., *African-American Exploration*, 18–20; D. Elwood Dunn, *A History of the Episcopal Church in Liberia, 1821–1980* (Metuchen, N.J.: Scarecrow Press, 1992), 47–48; and see *African Repository* 13, no. 7 (July 1837): passim. There are many references to dark-skinned missionaries both embarking for, and already existing in, Liberia as early as 1837. On semiliteracy, see the lack of extent letters from this group, and statistics in Shick, *Behold the Promised Land*, 32–33.

51. J. J. Roberts to Samuel Wilkeson, April 6, 1841, RACS; John N. Lewis to Samuel Wilkeson, April 10, 1841, RACS; Wesley Johnson to Samuel Wilkeson, December 2, 1841, RACS; and unknown to unknown, unknown date, #15, box 154, RACS.

52. No copies of the original pamphlet remain in American archives or publications. Portions of the pamphlet were printed in *Africa's Luminary*, September 4, 1840, 47. It is mentioned specifically in a number of settler letters to the ACS. Francis Burns, the first official black missionary to Liberia, wrote of Seys's angry, impassioned sermons in a letter to the ACS from 1841. See Francis Burns to Samuel Wilkinson, April 2, 1841, RACS. Also see George S. Brown, *Brown's Abridged Journal* (Troy, N.Y.: Prescott & Wilson, 1849), 148–49.

53. J. J. Roberts to Samuel Wilkeson, April 6, 1841, RACS.

54. "Need of an Itinerant Missionary," *African Repository* 13, no. 7 (July 1837): 247.

55. Park, *"White" Americans*, 136–41; Liebenow, *Liberia: The Quest for Democracy*, 89; Liebenow, *Liberia: Evolution of Privilege*, 10–11, for background on the "Missionary Party's" stance.

56. Louis Sheridan to ACS Board, September 10, 1841, RACS.

57. Seys served as superintendent from October 18, 1834, to January 16, 1845. After 1845, he became "special agent of the ACS" until independence in 1847. He left Liberia thereafter. See Park, *"White" Americans*, 160–62, 198.

58. J. J. Roberts to William McLain, January 7, 1848, RACS. Roberts mentions an "unusual" number of settlers leaving "a tract of territory on the Sinoe River, opposite the Mississippi settlement." He feared that they had left to live with the "colored people of the free state," that is, the Protestant Maryland colony. Also see J. W. Lugenbeel to William McLain, October 9, 1847, and July 15, 1848, RACS.

59. Mass conversion worked in much the same way as high student-teacher ratios work today. For a short discussion of this, see Shick, *Behold the Promised Land*, 55.

60. Dunn, *History of Episcopal Church in Liberia*, 12. All of these towns contained churches built during the late 1830s and early 1840s, when the second-class settlers started to mimic the first-class Americo-Liberians.

61. *African Repository* 13, no. 7 (July 1837): 242–43; "Need of an Itinerant Missionary," *African Repository* 13, no. 7 (July 1837): 246–47; quote from *Literary and Theological Review* 4, no. 14 (June 1837): 145.

62. *African Repository* 13, no. 7 (July 1837): 242–43. Liberian pidgin is documented to have developed through missionaries. See John W. Frazier and Eugene L. Tettey-Fio, *Race, Ethnicity, and Place in a Changing America* (Binghampton, N.Y.: Global Academic

Publishing, 2006), 146–47; also see Ian F. Hancock, "English in Liberia," *American Speech* 49, no. 3–4 (Autumn–Winter 1974): 225–26.

63. David A. Wilson to Leighton Wilson, January 14, 1857, Records of the Presbyterian Board of Foreign Missions, microfilm reel 65, Schomburg Center for Research in Black Culture, New York. Also see Susan Wilds McArver, "'The Salvation of Souls' and the 'Salvation of the Republic of Liberia': Denominational Conflict and Racial Diversity in Antebellum Presbyterian Foreign Missions," in Wilbert R. Shenk, ed., *North American Foreign Missions, 1810–1914: Theology, Theory, and Policy* (Grand Rapids, Mich.: Wm. B. Eerdmans, 2004), 156.

64. Edward T. Williams to Leighton Wilson, July 15, 1857, Records of the Presbyterian Board of Foreign Missions, microfilm reel 65, Schomburg Center for Research in Black Culture, New York; also see Shenk, ed., *North American Foreign Missions*, 159–60.

65. Alexander Crummell, "God and Nature," in *The Future of Africa: Being Addresses, Sermons, etc., etc. Delivered in the Republic of Liberia* (New York: Charles Scribner, 1862), 151; also Wilson Jeremiah Moses, *Alexander Crummell: A Study of Civilization and Discontent* (New York: Oxford University Press, 1989), 93–94.

66. Crummell, *Future of Africa*, 154–63; Moses, *Crummell*, 94–95.

67. Edward Wilmot Blyden, "Hope for Africa," in *Liberia's Offering, Being Addresses, Sermons, etc.* (New York: John A. Gray, 1862), 24; also see Hollis R. Lynch, *Edward Wilmot Blyden: Pan-Negro Patriot, 1832–1912* (London: Oxford University Press, 1967), 73.

68. Edward W. Blyden, *Christianity, Islam and the Negro Race* (1888; rpt. Baltimore: Black Classic Press, 1994), 66, 277–78.

69. Blyden, qtd. in Dunn, *Episcopal Church in Liberia*, 112.

70. Blyden, *Christianity, Islam, and the Negro Race*, 280. Blyden explained that secular values cause one to "seek material aggrandizement at any cost," and relegate the "human soul—the immaterial—[to] secondary and subordinate importance."

71. Blyden, "A Chapter in the History of the African Slave Trade," in *Liberia's Offering*, 164–65.

72. William Powers, *Blue Clay People: Seasons on Africa's Fragile Edge* (New York: Bloomsbury, 2005), 43; Gershoni, *Black Colonialism*, 33–35; M. B. Akpan, "Black Imperialism: Americo-Liberian Rule over the African Peoples of Liberia, 1841–1964," *Canadian Journal of African Studies* 7, no. 2 (1973): 227–30.

73. David Lindenfeld, "Indigenous Encounters with Christian Missionaries in China and West Africa, 1800–1920: A Comparative Study," *Journal of World History* 16, no. 3 (September 2005): 354. According to *The World Factbook 2013–2014* (Washington, D.C.: Central Intelligence Agency, 2013), 85.6 percent of Liberia's population, in 2016, was Christian in one form or another.

74. Thomas C. Hendrix, "A Half-Century of Americo-Liberian Christianity: With Special Focus on Methodism, 1822–1872," *Liberian Studies Journal* 19, no. 2 (1994): 243–74. Hendrix mentions the existence of Jacksonian ideas in Americo-Liberian society, and religion; however, he fails to mention Crummell or Blyden at any length. Katherine Harris's *African and American Values: Liberia and West Africa* (Lanham, Md.: University Press of America, 1985) makes a strikingly similar claim.

4

"Teaching Them to Observe All Things"

African American Women, the Great Commission, and Liberia in the Nineteenth Century

DEBRA NEWMAN HAM

> The Great Commission:
> Go ye therefore, and teach all nations,
> baptizing them in the name of the Father,
> and of the Son, and of the Holy Ghost:
> Teaching them to observe all things
> whatsoever I have commanded you:
> and, lo, I am with you always,
> even unto the end of the world. Amen.
>
> Matthew 28:18–20, King James Version

The interaction between over eight thousand black female emigrants from the United States, a small group of women from Barbados, fifteen hundred recaptive females (African women rescued from slave ships), and females from many ethnic groups on the West African coast is integral to our understanding of nineteenth-century Liberian history, and it adds a new perspective to the focus on the missionary dimension of African colonization.[1] White men and women talked and wrote about the missionary benefits of the endeavor, and black men like Lott Cary, Daniel Coker, and Alexander Crummell tried to bring that vision to life on the ground in Liberia. Equally important, though often overlooked, was the work of female settlers who ventured to the colony in hopes of helping create a new society.

Much to the surprise of the white male founders of the American Colonization Society (ACS), more women than men sought passage to the colony, and once the women arrived they contributed immensely to the growth and development of Liberia, especially in matters of education and religion. These women from divergent cultures and backgrounds interacted, supported each other, and became distinctly Liberian women. Both freeborn and freed slave women relied on this interdependence to survive on the West African coast, and they took seriously the task of the Great Commission, putting their talents and dedication to use in Liberia, where they helped establish schools, benevolent organizations, and churches.

Free women of color formed many kinds of organizations and benevolent societies when they arrived in Liberia, often collaborating with white women's missionary and literary organizations in the United States or replicating organizations they were a part of in America. The Ladies Liberia School Association of Philadelphia, for example, was responsible for sponsoring the education of some Liberian girls. This group was originally called the Ladies Association Auxiliary to the ACS, but by 1835, the organization's name was changed to the Ladies Liberia School Association. The group was founded in 1831 when a white Philadelphia woman, Beulah Sansom, and some of her friends donated funds for the establishment of two girls' schools in Liberia, one in Monrovia and the other in Caldwell. By the end of the year a larger group of white Philadelphia women had organized for the purposes of continuing Sansom's girls' schools and establishing other schools. Their avowed object was the "promotion of education in Liberia by means of the establishment of schools and the support of competent teachers." The first teacher at the Ladies Association girls' school in Monrovia was a settler named Elizabeth Mars Thompson, who became one of the most important educators in nineteenth-century Liberia. She was born in Connecticut in 1807 and was educated at the expense of friends in Philadelphia. She emigrated to Liberia with her first husband, William Johnson, in 1833, but he died soon after their arrival. She later married James Thompson, an immigrant from the West Indies.[2]

Not all female immigrants to Liberia were married. The number of women traveling to Liberia without men was so great that every ACS agent during the first few decades of the colony's existence wrote to the ACS asking them to modify their emigration policy. One of the ACS agents complained about the number of poor widows and single women who were "too destitute of spirit and industry to set themselves profitably at work."[3] So many women and female-led families were being sent to the colonies that ACS agents claimed that females outnumbered men in both Liberia and Maryland-in-Africa during the first few decades. In 1835 agent Ezekiel Skinner said that women outnumbered men two to one in Liberia. Even as late as 1868 the Liberian newspaper *African Republic* reported, "We now have a female population exceeding the male portion of the people." An 1843 census of Maryland-in-Africa showed that women did actually outnumber men by small margin in that region also.[4]

The female emigrants' first challenge was making preparations for the thirty- to fifty-day journey across the Atlantic Ocean. The missionary spirit was evident in every parting reported in the *African Repository* and newspaper accounts, as revealed by an unofficial theme song sung by emigrants in churches and embarkation ports:

> From Greenland's icy mountains, from India's coral strand:
> Where Afric's sunny fountains roll down their golden sand:
> From many an ancient river, from many a palmy plain,
> They call us to deliver their land from error's chain.[5]

Many emigrants were given heartwarming send-offs. A minister from Montgomery, Alabama, reported the 1885 departure of two families with a total of fourteen members from his church. He stated that the families were "in very good circumstances, industrious and well-respected," and explained that their decision to go to Liberia was "the result of long meditation, beginning even in the days of slavery." He said that their "object seems to be to make a permanent home for themselves and their children, combined with much of a missionary spirit."[6] There were often farewell ceremonies and speeches immediately before the embarkation of the ship. These festivities were usually organized by the local members of the Colonization Society and by black churches in the area. They were attended by friends, relatives, and well-wishers.

On the voyage, scenes were very much like those among African Americans after the American Civil War: couples wanted to legalize their marriages, individuals wanted to form churches and Bible studies, and the untutored wanted to learn reading, writing, and arithmetic. Once settlers arrived in Liberia, survived acclimation, and moved to permanent settlements, they affiliated themselves with church and community groups. Most of those who hoped to bring the light of the gospel to West Africa had only vague ideas what they were about to encounter.

American settlers began arriving in Liberia in 1822 with the hope of establishing a country where they could be truly free to exercise the benefits of citizenship and to hold meaningful leadership roles. Denied rights and privileges in the United States on account of the color of their skin, these black emigrants were determined to prove they were capable of forming and governing a state and to show that Africans could be taught to live in that state with them. Because American blacks were strongly influenced by Western culture, they generally agreed with the Western view that Africans were "uncivilized" and "heathen." However, the settlers believed that, with the benefits of education and Christianity, Africans could demonstrate to the world that they were as capable of intellectual attainments as whites. Many of the settlers, as well as the U.S. government and the ACS agents, also hoped that the establishment of the colony would help bring the Atlantic slave trade to an end. In 1827 a group of colonists wrote an address to the free people of color in the United States. After a lengthy description of life in Liberia and the blessings of liberty, the statement ends with an optimistic view that colonization would lead to "the sound of Christian instruction, scenes of Christian worship, and the founding of a new "Christian empire."[7]

The Education of African and Receptive Women

In every settlement the language barrier posed a major problem to the early Christian missionaries—black and white, male and female. Until the teachers were able to learn the local languages, the students had to be taught through interpreters (usually Africans who lived with the settlers and learned English) or be taught English before they could be tutored in any other subject. There was another problem of significance. Although natives near the Liberian coast were eager to send their sons for training, they were reluctant to allow their daughters to do so. Thus, from the outset, finding native women who were willing and able to be trained in English was extremely difficult. One of the teachers in Liberia went from village to village encouraging native men to allow their daughters to come to her school at Millsburg, but few ever agreed. There were also very few recaptive females in Liberia prior to the 1860s.[8]

In the early years of the Liberian settlement, only a few recaptive girls were educated and Christianized. These girls were willing to relinquish most of their former cultural training and adopt many aspects of the Liberian culture because they were far from their homes and would be unlikely to return. However, most native girls were generally not allowed to attend school because they played important roles in the culture and economy of their ethnic groups. They represented wealth in their communities because a man's greatness depended, to a large extent, on the number of his wives. These women were also a valuable part of the labor force because they performed most of the agricultural work.[9] Virtually all of the people with missionary aspirations for the African women near the Liberia settlements, however, felt that the best way to win them to the faith was to train the women in Christianity and Western culture.

In spite of the natives' resistance, a small number of girls attended school in the early years of the Liberian settlements. During the course of the century their numbers grew as it gradually became easier to persuade them to see the usefulness of Western education in their interaction with the settlers. In 1834 Elizabeth Mars Thompson wrote: "I have some native girls that learn very fast. All of them are spelling—three of them are writing—and one of them is quite fond of composing letters. Some of them, I think, are more intelligent than the Americans. I sometimes wish that my school consisted entirely of them—but you cannot get them from the country unless you pay something for them, and their parents will often come and take them away. I had two little girls living with me, who I took so much pride in, but as soon as they began to learn to talk English and sew, they took them away."[10]

Because native parents received a bride price for their daughters from their child's prospective husbands, they were reluctant to part with the girls before they received this payment. Many of the girls were betrothed from their birth and their husbands-to-be sometimes subsidized the cost of their rearing. It was considered a great shame for a girl to be unmarried after puberty. Consequently, when African girls reached puberty, many of their parents took them out of school to be married, for other initiation rites, or, often, to help plant or harvest the crops.

Despite difficulties, various schools served native girls, though their numbers remained small for most of the century. In 1840 Thompson reported that there were about twenty-two girls in her school; some were colonists' children while others were African girls. In addition to Thompson, other settler women became deeply involved with the education of African females. Matilda VonBrunn, the sister of the third Liberian president, Daniel B. Warner, married Jacob VonBrunn, the son of a Bassa chief. Jacob was educated in Sierra Leone and became a Methodist minister. He and his wife worked among the Bassa people. Early in 1860 Matilda opened a school in Grand Bassa County and continued her work there for many years. In 1882 she reported that she had established two additional schools, both of which were taught by natives. By this time Matilda was working for the U.S.-based

Women's Baptist Missionary Society. She wrote that the Bassas were calling for books and instructors. "There are three women," she wrote, "who would gladly go out among these people if they could be supported."[11]

Mary Garnet Barbazo, the daughter of African American minister and abolitionist Henry Highland Garnet, came to Liberia in 1880 to establish a school for African girls. She came with her husband and children and settled in Brewerville. The Ladies Board Missions of the Presbyterian Church of America supported Barbazo. After being welcomed at a reception given in her honor by the mayor of Monrovia, Barbazo traveled to Brewerville, where she was given a public reception at the Baptist church. Barbazo's father followed her in 1880 after he was appointed U.S. minister resident and consul general to Liberia. However, Garnet lived only a few months in Monrovia before he died, and his daughter passed away soon after he did.[12]

Education was one of the most important areas of cultural assimilation in Liberia, and settlers, recaptives, and native women were all drawn into similar lifestyles. The settler women who came to Liberia with the idea of being missionary teachers probably had a more far-reaching impact on that developing nation than any other settler women because they were willing to dedicate themselves to their work. They sometimes endured the hardships of living outside of the settler communities in situations where there were few luxuries. Their primary interest was to train Liberian children to take a part in the development of their nation by helping them to become well educated and firmly grounded in the Christian faith. These women used their homes and their substance in their zeal for the task.

White and black teachers who worked with African women and who encouraged the development of local Christian villages helped provide an opportunity for the education and evangelization of the indigenous people in and around the Liberian settlements. When natives taught and preached, they could reach far more indigenous people than white missionaries or settlers ever could. They knew the language and the culture of the people they wanted to reach. They could approach their own extended family members and lifelong friends on terms of equality rather than cultural superiority. Trained natives could determine which aspects of the Western culture they wanted to accept. They could explain to their families and friends the benefits of being able to handle themselves in settler society and in the "white man's world."

Although there were several statutes passed by the ACS, other colonization societies, and the Liberian government to finance and regulate education in Liberia, the laws were rarely systematically observed, and benevolent groups in the United States most often sponsored the educational opportunity that did exist in the country. Elementary schools were sporadically established by the ACS and by the Liberian government during the nineteenth century.

Even when those colonists in various settlements earnestly desired schools, they sometimes met great difficulty in finding willing teachers with solid educational backgrounds. Many settler women who were specially prepared for the task of teaching succumbed to the African fever. Often the school died with its teacher. Some elite women who were qualified to teach preferred to refrain from regular employment. Others who accepted teaching positions were barely literate, so the quality of education they were able to impart was limited.[13]

However, there were some extremely well qualified women who helped shape the minds of many young people in the Liberian nation. These women felt that the best preparation for potential young Christians was a sound education in Western letters and values. Eunice Sharpe Moore, a "highly respectable and well-educated" settler from New York City, typified the attitudes of most of the nineteenth-century female teachers. She wrote from Monrovia in 1839 to the members of a female missionary society in New York, explaining that she had "a goodly number" of pupils ranging in age from three to twenty who "were not as advanced in learning" as they were in years. Moore's desire to evangelize her students as well as teach them comes out clearly in this letter. Writing of her love and aspirations for her students, she stated that she had some interesting girls

> who have endeared themselves to me by a thousand tender ties. I have watched them from the alphabet to more interesting things, I have seen them trying to point out the different countries on the map, I have heard them tell me the nature of a noun, conjugate a verb, and tell how many times one number is contained in another; but all this was not half so entertaining to me as when I saw them crowding to the altar of God.... I have heard the wild native of Africa testify that God hath power on earth to forgive sin.... Surely, oh, God! out of the mouths of babes and sucklings thou hast perfected praise. This is the Lord's doing and it is marvelous in our eyes. Rejoice, then, ye daughters of benevolence. The way is opening for the poor native who is now worshipping devils to become acquainted with the worship of the true and living God.[14]

Moore's Christian expressions and those of others like her were probably more likely than any other sentiments to win the praise and support of her contemporaries in the United States and Liberia.

Another woman was so disappointed that she had not utilized the opportunities that her former master had allowed her for her education that she wrote to him encouraging him to administer "a little punishing" to those of his slaves who avoided the schoolroom. As for herself, she lamented that she had often missed school and noted that, as punishment, her master would put her into the barn. She wrote to the master saying, "instead of putting me in the barn, you should have taken me out and given me a severe flogging." She said the primary reason she regretted missing the educational opportunities she had had in Louisiana was that she knew she could have used them and shared them with others in Liberia.[15]

The educational level in Liberia suffered due to the lack of formal education available to most African American women in the United States. For example, a settler woman from Virginia expressed her opinion about the quality of education in Liberia, saying frankly that all four of the schools in the vicinity of Clay-Ashland were "very badly taught." Other evidence seems to support her view. In one letter, Peyton Skipwith wrote that his daughters were both in school and that one of them, Diana, taught night school and Sunday school. Letters from Peyton, Diana, and her sister Matilda indicate that they were all only functionally literate and often spelled words phonetically, like many other nineteenth-century Americans.[16]

Benevolent Organizations

In addition to their teaching, Liberian Christian women wanted to help those in distress. This took no special training and required only a kind, charitable heart. Female settlers were actively concerned about the plight of new immigrants, the aged and the infirm, and poor women and children who were struggling to take care of themselves. Motivated by this concern, these women formed several charitable societies whose purpose was to alleviate the sufferings of their neighbors. Female settlers from various backgrounds became part of these groups. Many of the women were poor themselves, but they were willing to share the little they had with their neighbors. Sometimes settler women of means either led or joined in order to aid their less fortunate sisters. There were members who were former slaves and others who were free women who had been members of such organizations in the United States. Educated and illiterate women were usually found working together in church groups, whose members often expected the educated women to take leadership roles.

The Union Sisters of Charity, formed in 1833 in Monrovia, was a respected organization and was considered to be "the oldest charitable association in Liberia." Female charitable societies like this one were especially concerned with helping new immigrants to feel welcome and comfortable during the sickness they usually suffered soon after their arrival in the country. If newcomers could survive for a year or two, their constitutions generally adjusted to their new environment. The object of the organization was "to assist to the utmost of their ability all subjects of charity, by helping the widow and relieving the orphan and needy, clothe, feed, educate, and otherwise provide."[17]

The Ladies Benevolent Society, formed in 1835 in Monrovia, directed its activities to the relief of "poor and disconsolate" women and attempted "to sustain and countenance virtue" among Liberian females. Some of the members who joined the society were former slaves who were "using their liberty in going on errands of mercy." In 1841 a committee of the Ladies Benevolent Society visited two towns near Monrovia by boat. At New Georgia they presented clothes, uncut cloth, provisions, and soap to seven persons, and at Lower Caldwell they provided similar goods to nine individuals.[18]

The Ladies Dorcas Society of the Methodist Episcopal Church was founded in 1840. This society sought donations of money, clothing, and "any other useful articles" for the purpose of giving them to the poor and to make an effort to "clothe converted natives."[19] When the Barbados immigrants came to Liberia in 1865, they received only two months of support (U.S. settlers traditionally received six months of support), and many of them suffered greatly because they were not able to take care of themselves for the duration of the fever or immediately thereafter. These immigrants were helped by many Liberians, but the Union Sisters of Charity gave the Ladies Benevolent Society and "the newly-arrived and necessitous immigrants . . . every considerable assistance and unremitting attention during their illness."[20]

In 1855, when the Ladies Dorcas Society celebrated its fifteenth anniversary, the speaker commented that, although the expenditures of the society had exceeded its receipts, as a result of the quiet generosity of its members, there remained a "good amount" in the treasury. Another speaker at the anniversary noted that, although the Dorcas Society's activities had not been ostentatious, they had been "eminently beneficial to the community." The speaker stated that the first asylum for the poor to be located in Monrovia had been completely built and maintained by the Ladies Dorcas Society and that the asylum had never been "destitute of inmates." The speaker lamented, however, the building's state of dilapidation, which left the inhabitants—beneficiaries of the society—subject to great exposures. The society planned a tea to raise enough money to put the asylum in a livable condition."[21]

Although the ACS, the Liberian government, and charitable societies made efforts to help women to be successful as settlers, many who came with no money remained extremely poor during their lifetime. A white female missionary commented in the late 1850s that the poverty of the people was great after the six months of rations ended because most were sick during the entire six-month period and were unable to plant crops. Most of the poor settlers had no money, little furniture, and few clothes. The missionary believed that some of the children she taught in Cape Palmas had not had a new dress for years but noted that they were always clean and neat.[22]

Women and the Local Churches

Women in all of the Liberian settlements became deeply involved in the life and work of the church. The Bible was usually their guide, and the preacher or local deacons were often their community leaders. In the church, much cultural assimilation took place as settler, native, and recaptive women demonstrated their organizational abilities, even if the three groups did not always worship together.

Most of the Liberian settlers joined local churches, and much of their social life consisted of church-related activities. Many of the settlers had been members of Baptist or Methodist churches in the United States, although there were also Episcopalians, Presbyterians, and a small number of other denominations, such as Catholics and Moravians. In the Cape Palmas region, where the Protestant Episcopal mission was dominant, some settlers who were not traditionally Episcopalians began to worship with that denomination. Because of the Protestant Episcopal mission's extensive work among the Greboes, hundreds of them became Episcopalians during the nineteenth century. In other parts of Liberia, where churches were sparse, the people tended to worship with whatever church was nearby.[23]

Women continued as an important force in the establishment of Liberian churches. There was a report in 1873 about an elderly woman named Doris Levin who was concerned that there was no house of worship in her neighborhood at Bexley. On her own initiative, Levin began visiting neighbors, friends, and churches to collect money to construct a building. Her efforts were successful, and by December 1873 there was a small frame building dedicated to worship near her home.[24]

In 1869–70 the community of Arthington was formed on the St. Paul's River. The settlers, who were mostly from the southern United States, established a Baptist church in the settlement. The members had no money, but each contributed labor by cutting wood and making shingles until they had adequate materials to build the church and enough products to exchange for nails and hinges. The men dedicated a few days' labor each week, and the women cooked for them. One member reported that the membership of the church grew quickly after its completion. The minister came to preach twice a month, but Sunday school was held each week, and prayer meeting took place each Sunday morning at six.[25]

Women also formed missionary and charity societies. On September 29, 1886, the females of Zion Grove Baptist Church in Brewerville organized a Women's Home Mission Society for the purposes of evangelization and charity. As an incentive to the formation of groups of this type, Rev. J. J. Cheeseman, "a man of some means," promised to give ten dollars to every women's missionary society organized during a one-year period. The women of the Episcopal mission in Sinoe formed a female sewing society. With their creative efforts, the women supplied the children in the area with "appropriate dress for Sundays." A captain in the British Navy reported in 1840 that Liberians had formed various societies, including a ladies' society for clothing the poor.[26]

The most important church program supported by women was the Sunday school. Through regular attendance on Sundays, thousands of Liberian children learned the principles of the Christian faith. For many, the teaching in Sunday school was the only education they received. Sometimes Sunday schools began on a small scale. In 1859 in Caldwell, Martha Harris (probably Martha Ann Harris Ricks) held a Sabbath school with 65 regular attendees. The school was described in 1842 as "very flourishing and highly interesting."[27]

A report on Sunday schools in Monrovia, given in 1864, indicated that the efforts of the churches in this city crossed cultural boundaries. The report stated that the Methodist Episcopal Sunday School, which was founded in 1823, was composed of native and settler students, of which an average of 125 pupils were the former and 50 were the latter. About 100 of the youths were males and 75 were females. Of the twenty-two Sunday school teachers, more than half were women. The report also indicated that there were three other Sunday schools in Monrovia: a Presbyterian school with 60 scholars and nine teachers, a Baptist one with 100 students and twenty teachers, and an Episcopal school with 140 pupils and fourteen instructors.[28]

Periodically, the Sunday schools would band together to have parades, picnics, or Christmas celebrations. These festivities were an important part of the social life of Liberia in that they involved all classes of the society. Rev. James Hayes of Brewerville, a graduate of Shaw Collegiate Institute (later Shaw University), wrote a letter describing an April 1884 picnic jointly sponsored by the Sunday schools and congregations of the four churches in Brewerville and attended by visitors from nearby settlements. The picnic, hosted by the Zion Grove Sunday School, was held at a nearby recreation area. To get there the groups joined with the other members from their Sunday school and marched together to the picnic grounds, carrying six banners with scriptures and temperance slogans. After the picnic, at about five in the evening, a procession was formed again and the groups marched together back to the host church.[29]

A similar event occurred in Monrovia. When one of the Sunday schools united to form a parade, they could find "no church large enough to hold them all." The group, called the Sunday School Army, decided to meet in Government Square opposite the president's house. Bells were rung, and the children proceeded from their Sunday schools to the square with each group carrying a banner with scriptures and exhortations such as "Suffer the little children to come unto me." The Presbyterians formed the smallest group and the Methodists the largest. Episcopalians and Baptists were between the two in size. Each group, led by their officers, dressed in uniform colors to distinguish themselves from one another.[30]

After the children arrived in the Square, a line of still-emaciated recaptives led by about ten settler women came to the celebration. Many of the women of Monrovia were devoting a part of their spare time on Sundays or other days to instruct these recaptives. In the parade the recaptive men and boys were dressed in checkered shirts and trousers with straw hats, and the women in ill-fitting second-hand dresses of every kind with straw bonnets on their heads. The U.S. government had sent their dresses and shoes to them. Most of the recaptives carried their shoes as ornaments because of the pain and difficulty of wearing them.[31]

After the recaptives came the Krus to the Sunday-school gala with the motto "Ethiopia shall stretch forth her hands to God" on their banner. A company of Vai men, women, and children from a town "across the river" where a small church was being built made up the last group. Their banner read, "Come over and help us."[32]

The Sunday-school groups included 898 people at the final tabulation. Speakers at the occasion included President Benson, ex-president Roberts, and numerous clergymen. After further addresses, little cakes were served to the children, and then the Baptist minister gave a short speech to the recaptives which was translated by a recaptive interpreter who had embraced Christianity. Finally, there were short speeches to the Krus and Vais. Then the group formed a procession again and paraded through the town before they disbanded.[33]

Revivals were another major aspect of church life. These were usually week-long events during which a guest preacher would come each night to deliver a sermon designed to revitalize the spiritual life of the church members and to bring non-members to Christ. Monrovia, Bassa, Sinoe, Cape Palmas, and other settlements were, according to one account, "having seasons of refreshing. Sinners old and young, and half-civilized are being converted to God. Backsliders are being reclaimed, and the heathen are becoming more and more interested about the salvation of their souls."[34]

Women organized other social activities connected with the church. For example, they formed prayer and Bible-study groups for the purpose of increasing their piety and their knowledge of the scriptures. In 1833 a settler woman from Charleston said that a prayer meeting for women was held each Monday afternoon and on the first Thursday of each month. She said that the women were also planning to form a charitable society. Church participation was so important that baptisms and conversions were considered special events and often reported in the newspaper. Generally, the settlers were poor and it was cheaper for them to preach to Africans and recaptives periodically than to provide regular teachers for them. Sunday schools were easier to finance than day schools. Thus, Christianity was taught far more often and more widely than reading, and many African and recaptive people were drawn into their community's local church.

A few settler women felt the calling to preach, but there is little information about their activities. There is some mention of "Miss Sharpe's chapel" in Monrovia's "Krootown" section but not many details about her work there. Amanda Smith, an African American missionary who visited Liberia in the early 1880s, mentioned Sharp. Smith wrote in her autobiography that she stayed with Sharp for three weeks and three days. Bishop Taylor of the Methodist Episcopal Church stated that he preached twice to "Miss Sharp's Kroomen" in 1885. After Sharpe's death, a missionary wrote that she had worked in Liberia for thirty years. He stated that she had given "all within her" for the salvation of the Bassa and Kru people.[35]

Although these records do not indicate positively that Sharp was a preacher, Amanda Smith wrote about her own preaching activities, stating that she regularly spoke in Liberian churches at the invitation of their pastors. In January 1882, on her first Sunday in Liberia, the pastor of the Methodist church invited her to preach and then invited her to speak there on Tuesday, Wednesday, and Thursday nights. During her stay of several years in Liberia, she preached and spoke in many settlements.[36]

Amanda Smith spoke out repeatedly against Christians engaged in the liquor trade. There had been many complaints by Christians during the history of Liberia that too many of their number were actively engaged in trading liquor with settlers and Africans. Bishop Taylor reported in 1888 on the effectiveness of Smith's preaching, stating that a "leading merchant in Grand Bassa" assured him "that the rum and gin imported by Liberia during the past year did not amount to one-fourth of the annual importation six years ago. This change was brought about mainly through the agency of our Sister Amanda Smith."[37]

The church was one of the greatest influences on the several hundred recaptive women in Liberia. It was the church that stressed the need for Western dress and the abandonment of polygamy, thereby influencing two important areas of the lives of these women. Church workers were active among the recaptives. During the 1840s Ellen Walberg, along with several other women, organized a Sunday school in New Georgia, a recaptive settlement. By that time the recaptive women who had settled there earlier already dressed in the same fashion as the settler women and had houses, furniture, and other conveniences like those of the colonists. By 1871 many of the recaptives who had been settled in Liberia during the years of the U.S. Civil War were already Christians and were requesting preachers and teachers for their churches. By that year most of the members of the church in Marshall were recaptives, and recaptives formed churches in some of the other settlements on their own.[38]

Nothing caused missionaries, missionary supporters in the United States, and evangelistic settlers more delight than the conversion of natives to Christianity. These conversions were often related with great detail. Elizabeth Mars Thompson wrote in 1840 about a revival that began in her adoptive family and spread to both the girls' and the boys' schools in Mt. Vaughn. After almost ten years, when her adopted African girl was fourteen, she began to inquire what she might do to be saved from hell. When the orphan trusted Christ as her savior, other children in the schools also sought salvation. Thompson reported that, at the end of one week, seventeen young people had professed belief in Christ. On Easter Sunday, five settlers and three African girls were baptized and others were awaiting further trial before they could be baptized. Thompson was so gratified by these events that she said, "I think I have been doubly repaid for what I have done and suffered in Africa." She wrote that she had had the joy of seeing four African boys and two girls, "and my adopted child that I had in my family when the school was first established, come over to the Lord's side."[39]

In all aspects of life, the Great Commission and Christian ideals tended to govern the African American settler women in Liberia. The ideal female was the one described in Proverbs 31 as the "virtuous woman." This woman was industrious, well-dressed, clever, an able economic and domestic manager, a kind and loving wife, a devoted mother, a friend to the poor, a gracious mistress to servants, and, most importantly, a woman who loved the Lord. The concept of the virtuous woman was not just rhetoric for Liberian women; it was an ideal to which many actively aspired.

Some of the educated women became the day- and Sunday-school teachers in Liberia. They taught children from all of the cultures that converged on the Liberian coast. They basically served as elementary education teachers who emphasized reading, writing, and arithmetic and who always included Christian principles and biblical instruction as an essential part of the curriculum. Most of the female educators emigrated to Liberia to teach Christianity as their main purpose. The number of settler women who became day-school teachers during the nineteenth century was probably not greater than one hundred. A greater number of them, however, were involved in Sunday schools or sponsoring native youths in their homes. In the nineteenth century the Sunday-school curriculum generally included reading and writing as well as religious training. Both day and Sunday schools were valuable in the process of cultural assimilation.

Of all of the contributions made by settler women, their role in providing Christian education to the youth of Liberia was probably the most important. Some settler women lived sacrificially so that they could share their knowledge with the children of the growing republic. True, the settler women were sometimes guilty of cultural biases and of feelings of superiority toward the natives they taught, but that did not usually hinder them from acting as dedicated and conscientious teachers.

The educated settler women also filled important leadership roles in the formation of literary, benevolent, and charitable societies. Educated women formed mutual aid societies, sewing circles, missionary societies, temperance clubs, savings and burial organizations, and societies formed for the purpose of aiding the needy.

The contributions of settler women through these organizations were vital for the development of Liberia. The societies helped to provide a warm reception for new immigrants to Liberia and aided them in the process of acclimation. They were also significant because women of different classes and cultures were occasionally encouraged to join. Thus, these groups became effective agents of assimilation because educated or Christianized native women formed similar groups of their own to minister to the members' needs, to help support native churches or missions, and to aid local villagers who were poor or sick. Sewing circles, missionary groups, and mutual aid societies composed entirely of native women, particularly those females who lived in Christian villages, were instrumental in solidifying and encouraging Christian values among their neighbors. Thus the African women took up the Great Commission in their evolving nation.

Notes

1. Numerous ethnic groups lived in the area that came to be known as Liberia. The Dey lived in the region of Cape Mesurado where Monrovia was founded. The area to the north of the cape was populated by the Vai, and the southern coastal strip was occupied by the Bassa, Kru (Kroo), and Grebo. The most populous group in the interior was the Kpelle, and the strongest groups politically were the Vai, the Gola, and the Mandingo. The Mandingo, who specialized in trade, were interspersed among the Gola, the Vai, and other ethnic groups. Moreover, sizeable Mandingo communities were located in towns that dotted the trade routes. Other ethnic groups such as the Kissi, Gbandi, Dan (Gio), Krahn, Loma (Buzzi), Mano, Belle, and Mende lived in the Liberian interior. These indigenous peoples spoke more than twenty local languages and dialects of the Niger-Congo language group, primarily West Atlantic, Kru, Mande-fu, and Mande-tan. To differentiate among the several groups of women who composed Liberian society, "African" or "native" will be used as the designation for indigenous women and "settler," or "immigrant" for the women from the United States and Barbados and their descendants. The African women taken from aboard slave ships will be specifically referred to as "recaptive women" but generally will be classed with the settlers. "Liberian" will be used to refer to all of the women collectively. "Liberia" refers to the territory under the control of the colonists from the earliest period of their history. See William E. Allen, "Liberia and the Atlantic World in the Nineteenth Century: Convergence and Effects," *History in Africa* 37 (2010), 23–25, and Debra L. Newman, "The Emergence of Liberian Women in the Nineteenth Century," PhD diss., Howard University, 1984, 106–11.

2. *African Repository* 38 (October 1862): 317; *African Repository* 1 (January 1826): 352; Gerda Lerner, *Black Women in White America: A Documentary History* (New York: Vintage

Books, 1972), 40; Suzanne Lebsock, "Free Black Women and the Question of Matriarchy, Petersburg, Virginia, 1784–1820," *Feminist Studies* 8 (Summer 1982): 271–92; *First Annual Report of the Ladies Liberia School Association* (Printed by Lydia R. Bailey, 1833), 1–8; *African Repository* 40 (November 1864): 334–35. For Liberian mortality and demographic information, see Tom W. Shick, *Behold the Promised Land* (Baltimore: Johns Hopkins University Press, 1980), and Shick, *Emigrants to Liberia, An Alphabetical Listing* (Newark, N.J.: Department of Anthropology, University of Delaware, 1971). Marie Tyler-McGraw, *An African Republic: Black and White Virginians in the Making of Liberia* (Chapel Hill: University of North Carolina Press, 2014), 92, also mentions the formation in Virginia of the Ladies' Society for Promoting Female Education in the Colony of Liberia.

3. *African Repository* 3 (October 1827): 235; *African Repository* 4 (April 1828): 48–49; Penelope Campbell, *Maryland in Africa* (Urbana: University of Illinois Press, 1971), 23.

4. *African Repository* 3 (October 1827): 235; *African Repository* 4 (April 1828): 48; *African Repository* 11 (January 1835): 5; and *African Repository* 44 (February 1868): 48–49; Campbell, *Maryland in Africa*, 123.

5. Words, Reginald Heber, 1819; music, Lowell Mason 1823, www.cyberhymnal.org/htm/f/r/fromgrim.htm (accessed January 12, 2016).

6. *Sixty-Ninth ACS Annual Report, 1886* (rpt. New York: Negro Universities Press, 1969), 7.

7. *Eleventh ACS Annual Report, 1828* (rpt. New York: Negro Universities Press, 1960), 88–89, 94.

8. Henry John Drewal, "Methodist Education in Liberia, 1833–1856," *Essays in the History of African Education,* ed. Vincent M. Battle and Charles H. Lyons (New York: Teacher's College Press, 1970), 33–60, 45–46; *African Repository* 10 (August 1834): 188–89; *African Repository* 22 (May 1846): 149–50.

9. The importance of women in Liberian society was noted by observers. For example, see Alexander Cowan, *Liberia As I Found It, in 1858* (Frankfort, Ky.: A. G. Hodges, 1958), 48–48, and *African Repository* 31 (August 1855): 246–47.

10. *African Repository* 10 (August 1834): 188–89.

11. *African Repository* 16 (October 1840): 313; *African Repository* 58 (July, October 1882): 95, 127; A. Doris Banks Henries, *Heroes and Heroines of Liberia* (New York: Macmillan Co., 1962), 42; *African Repository* 47 (July 1871): 217.

12. *African Repository* 57 (February, May, July 1881): 22, 57–58, 88; *African Repository* 58 (July 1882): 87.

13. Mary A. G. Brown, "Education and National Development in Liberia, 1800–1900," PhD diss., Cornell University, 1967, 86–120.

14. *African Repository* 14 (March 1838): 73.

15. *African Repository* 23 (September 1847): 264–65.

16. See *Sixteenth MCS Annual Report, 1857* (rpt. New York: Negro Universities Press, 1969), 7; Tom W. Shick and Beverly Gray, "Elites in Twentieth Century Liberia," private library of Tom W. Shick.

17. *African Repository* 31 (April 1855): 122; Charles H. Huberich, *The Political and Legislative History of Liberia* (New York: Central Book Co., 1947), 1510–12.

18. *African Repository* 13 (May 1837): 162; *African Repository* 16 (May 1840): 140; and *African Repository* 17 (October 1841): 312.

19. Huberich, *Political and Legislative History,* 1510–12.

20. *African Repository* 31 (April 1866): 98.

21. *African Repository* 31 (August 1855): 249–50.

22. Harriette Brittan, *Scenes and Incidents of Every-Day Life in Africa* (New York: Pudney and Russell, 1860), 309–11.

23. See Liberian Census of 1843; Samuel D. Ferguson, *An Historical Sketch of the African Mission of the Protestant Episcopal Church* (New York: Foreign Committee, 1884); and Anna M. Scott, *Day Dawn in Africa or Progress of the Protestant Episcopal Mission at Cape Palmas, West Africa* (New York: Protestant Episcopal Society, 1858).

24. *African Repository* 49 (September 1873): 267.

25. Ibid., 31 (April 1866): 98.

26. Ibid., 63 (April 1887): 43; *African Repository* 39 (October 1863): 300; *African Repository* 41 (April 1865): 98; *African Repository* 16 (October 1840): 310.

27. Ibid., 35 (September 1859): 277; *African Repository* 19 (April 1843): 122.

28. Ibid., 40 (May 1864): 148.

29. Ibid., 60 (January 1884): 16.

30. Brittan, *Scenes and Incidents of Every-Day Life,* 286–93.

31. Ibid. This group of receptives had been taken from the slave ship *Putnam* and transported to Liberia on the *Niagara.*

32. Brittan, *Scenes and Incidents of Every-Day Life,* 286–93.

33. Ibid.

34. *African Repository* 53 (January 1877): 29.

35. *African Repository* 61 (July 1885): 86; Amanda Smith, *An Autobiography* (Chicago: Meyer and Brother, 1893), 333; Clinton B. Boone, *Liberia As I Know It* (Westport, Conn.: Negro Universities Press, 1970), 123.

36. Smith, *Autobiography,* 333–58.

37. Ibid., 355; *African Repository* 64 (July 1888): 93–94.

38. *African Repository* 16 (October 1840): 289–91.

39. Ibid., 313.

II

RECONSIDERING THE POLITICAL AND DIPLOMATIC DIMENSIONS OF COLONIZATION

5

The American Colonization Society's Not-So-Private Colonization Project

DAVID F. ERICSON

The American Colonization Society (ACS) may have been a private organization, but its African colonial enterprise was not a private project. Almost from its inception, the society enjoyed the financial support of the federal government. The public-private partnership established to pursue African colonization was not only one of the first of its kind on the federal level; it was also the most enduring such partnership prior to the Civil War. Without federal support, the society probably would never have founded Liberia, nor, once founded, would the colony have survived.[1]

From 1819 to 1865, the ACS received a total of $763,198 in federal assistance. That sum represented 37 percent of the society's receipts of $2,057,133 over those forty-seven years. The ACS case differed qualitatively from other early cases of the federal subsidization of private organizations because of its extension over nearly five decades, through Liberian independence in 1847 and even through U.S. recognition of its independence in 1862. During this time, the federal government also provided disaster relief, cash grants to missionary societies working with Native Americans, land grants to charitable institutions, and stock purchases as well as land grants to canal and railroad enterprises. None of these cases, however, resulted in an enduring public-private partnership as occurred in the case of the ACS.[2]

The primary reason that the ACS-U.S. partnership lasted so long was that from the beginning of its existence the society associated African colonization with the suppression of the slave trade. When President James Monroe diverted an 1819 appropriation for slave-trade suppression to the society to provide it with the start-up costs to establish a colony, he stressed the slave-trade connection on the logic that the colony would serve as a repository for "recaptured Africans."[3] Over time, the connection between African colonization and slave-trade suppression remained strong as the ACS became the conduit for transporting recaptured Africans to the new colony, with the federal government defraying its costs. President James Buchanan formalized this financial relationship in 1858 by signing a contract with the society to cover not only its transportation costs but also the "settling in" costs of the recaptured Africans who were transported to Liberia. At the same time, Buchanan significantly increased the size of the African Squadron, which had been stationed off the Liberian coast to deter the slave trade in 1843.

Although suppressing the slave trade proved to be a useful justification for federal funding, the ACS promulgated quite a few rationales for African colonization, including the existence of ineradicable white prejudice, the promise of an all-white society, the protection of racial slavery, and the encouragement of gradual abolition.[4] The internal consistency and practical feasibility of these multiple rationales were almost beside the point. The founding members of the ACS were determined that the society remain a proverbial "big tent" that could attract support from European Americans with a wide range of attitudes toward African Americans and slavery.

At its inception, the ACS attracted a number of prominent supporters of different political parties and persuasions. Congress did not object to Monroe's diversion of slave-trade-suppression funds because many members of Congress were also members of the society. Some, such as Henry Clay, John Randolph, and Daniel Webster, had signed its original 1816 constitution. Attorney General Richard Rush and Supreme Court Justice Bushrod Washington were also ACS members. Both had helped draft the 1816 constitution, and the latter became its first president. General Andrew Jackson was among its first thirteen vice-presidents. These early supporters included Federalists (Washington, Webster) and Democratic Republicans (Clay, Jackson, Randolph, Rush), future Whigs (Clay, Webster) and Democrats (Jackson), southerners (Clay, Jackson, Randolph, Washington) and northerners (Webster, Rush), as well as those who were fairly staunchly proslavery (Randolph) and antislavery (Rush).[5]

Unfortunately for the ACS, its "big tent" shrunk over time. First, proslavery audiences grew more suspicious of the society because of its efforts to appeal to antislavery audiences. Then, antislavery audiences grew more suspicious of the society because of its efforts to appeal to proslavery audiences. On a partisan level, southern Democrats also began to attack the society, especially because two southern Whigs, Clay and Charles F. Mercer, had emerged as its leading congressional spokesmen. After U.S. Treasury auditor Amos Kendall wrote a highly critical 1830 report of the amount of federal funds that the society had received relative to the number of colonists whom it had settled in Liberia, President Jackson, by this time a former ACS vice-president, pulled the plug.[6] Except, Jackson did not completely pull the plug. The federal government continued to compensate the ACS for the recaptured Africans whom it resettled in Liberia and to offer the colony in-kind subsidies and naval protection.

International factors played a major role in the survival of the ACS-U.S. partnership. A British propaganda war on the United States for not enforcing its own slave-trade laws encouraged federal officials to revisit the original slave-trade-suppression promise of African colonization. A growing British economic presence in western Africa prompted them to reassess its commercial possibilities.[7] These two "national interest" rationales persuaded even federal officials who were otherwise antagonistic to the ACS to continue to assist its colonization project.

On a more concrete level, the two "national interest" rationales inspired the creation of the African Squadron. While the United States agreed to establish such a squadron in response to the British demands to more effectively enforce its own slave-trade laws, the squadron was launched in the 1840s with the dual mission of suppressing American participation in the slave trade and protecting American commerce.[8] Then, in the late 1850s and early 1860s, the slave-trade-suppression rationale, in particular, led to an exponential increase in the ACS's federal funding because of a sharp rise in the number of Africans whom the U.S. Navy seized from slave ships.

The Beginning of a Long Partnership

At first, the ACS seemed to enjoy broad-based support for its goal of settling African Americans, both free blacks and slaves emancipated on the condition of emigration, in a colony to be established on the west coast of Africa. This goal was attractive on multiple grounds to multiple audiences, as it appealed to both benevolent and racist sentiments. Believing that federal funding was the *sine qua non* to the success of their colonization project, ACS officials regularly memorialized Congress in the early years of the society requesting financial support.[9]

Initially, Congress responded positively. When it passed a new slave-trade law in 1819, it not only funded federal slave-trade-suppression efforts for the first time, but it also authorized the resettlement of recaptured

Africans outside the territorial limits of the United States rather than leaving their fate to the discretion of state authorities. In fact, the ACS's rescue of a group of thirty-four recaptured Africans before the state of Georgia sold them into slavery was a major catalyst for the new law.[10] Clearly, Monroe had cogent reasons for placing the $100,000 slave-trade appropriation at the disposal of the society to help it found a colony on the west coast of Africa for resettling recaptured Africans as well as any African American emigrants whom it might recruit.

When the first two groups of colonists sailed to the west coast of Africa, the federal government was literally at their side. The first group of eighty-six colonists sailed to Africa in 1820 aboard the *Elizabeth*, a ship chartered by federal officials. They were accompanied by two U.S. agents and an ACS agent who was carrying a $33,000 draft on the U.S. Treasury upon which he could draw for the needs of the prospective colony. The next year, federal officials chartered the *Nautilus* to transport a second expedition of thirty-three colonists, along with two new ACS agents and two new federal agents to replace those who had died of tropical diseases. Later that same year the ACS Board of Managers sent another agent, Eli Ayres, to Africa aboard the USS *Shark* to secure a colonial site. When he was unable to accomplish that mission on his own, Secretary of Navy Smith Thompson sent Lieutenant Robert T. Stockton to Africa abroad the USS *Alligator* to assist him. Together, they were able to purchase land in what is now Liberia in exchange for goods valued at a mere $300. The deal was consummated at the point of Stockton's gun.[11]

During the early years of the colony, U.S. Navy vessels remained active in the area, protecting the colony from attack and supplying it with goods from the ACS's federal endowment because the society had little money to supply the colony itself. Within a few years, this naval presence dwindled to the occasional visits of vessels en route to and from the Indian Ocean, but even those occasional visits were indicative of the colony's special status in the eyes of federal officials. In 1822, several of the African leaders who had agreed to the treaty of acquisition seized the opportunity presented by the absence of navy ships to attack the colony. Colonial agent Jehudi Ashmun appealed to both the British and American navies for assistance. As the British Navy had a ship in the vicinity, British naval personnel defended the colony. Arriving later, American naval personnel built fortifications in Liberia at an estimated cost of $27,211 in labor and materials.[12]

Ashmun was the first joint ACS-U.S. colonial agent. As a federal employee, he supervised the settlement of recaptured Africans in Liberia, reporting to the secretary of navy. As an ACS employee, he supervised the settlement of the other colonists and was *de facto* governor of the colony, reporting to the society's board of managers and overseeing a locally elected colonial assembly. For performing these roles, he received $1,600 per year from the federal government and $800 from the ACS.[13]

For the remainder of Monroe's two administrations and into the John Quincy Adams administration, Congress did not attempt to block the ACS's federal funding. To the contrary, the House Select Committee on the Colonization of Free People of Colour, chaired by Virginia Congressman and ACS Vice-President Mercer, commended Monroe's "just and liberal construction" of the 1819 slave-trade law in its highly laudatory 1827 report on African colonization.[14] Nevertheless, by the time of the Mercer report, the congressional climate had turned against the ACS.

The allegations of a corrupt bargain between Adams and Clay to gain office fanned the partisan flames. Given that Clay had made colonization an important part of his political agenda, the emerging Democratic coalition adopted a more oppositional stance toward the society. This coalition was anchored in the South, and southern congressmen had become suspicious of the ACS because of its emancipationist rhetoric, however muted that rhetoric may have been. Growing fears for the future of slavery also prompted many southern congressmen to adopt federal retrenchment as their political lodestar. The ACS's federal funding proved to be an easy target because the society's record in recruiting colonists and in raising money from private sources was underwhelming. Meanwhile, in this increasingly hostile political environment, the Adams administration continued to fund its Liberian venture.[15]

With the opposition firmly in control of Congress following the 1826 midterm elections, the Senate Committee on Foreign Relations, chaired by Virginia Senator Littleton Waller Tazewell, wrote a decidedly more negative report on African colonization than Mercer's select committee had. Sounding the watchwords of limited government, enumerated powers, and states' rights, this 1828 report insisted that "the framers of the Constitution most wisely abstained from bestowing upon the government . . . any power whatever over the coloured population of the United States . . . whether this population was bond or free." In its conclusion, the report drew attention to the apparent conflict of interest created by the overlapping memberships of Congress and the ACS.[16]

Soon thereafter, Jackson succeeded Adams as president of the United States. He cut off the ACS's federal funding in 1830 on the basis of Kendall's audit, which found that the federal government had spent $264,710 over the previous decade to assist the society in resettling 260 recaptured Africans in Liberia. Kendall also explicitly criticized Monroe for his diversion of slave-trade appropriations to the society. He praised the society's benevolent purposes in attempting to lessen the evils of slavery and suppress the slave trade, but he believed that it should have pursued those purposes by strictly private means. Kendall then listed the many other ways that the federal government had assisted the society's colonization project, including "to *colonize them* [recaptured Africans], *to build houses for them, to furnish them with farming utensils, to pay instructers* [sic] *to teach them, to purchase ships for their convenience, to build forts for their protection, to supply them with arms and munitions of war, to enlist troops to guard them, or to employ the army or navy in their defense.*" He concluded that "the terms of the [1819 slave-trade] act were hardly sufficient to authorize the *establishment of a colony,* owing allegiance to the United States, and entitled to protection." To Kendall, Liberia was clearly, and inappropriately, a U.S. colony.[17]

After Jackson cut off the ACS's federal funding, Clay and Mercer, now members of the emerging anti-Jackson Whig coalition in Congress, continued to introduce bills to indirectly assist the society. In 1833, with the Whigs holding a congressional majority, Congress approved a Clay-sponsored bill that would have linked state funding of African colonization to the redistribution of the surplus revenues from public-land sales. Jackson vetoed the bill.[18]

By the mid-1830s, the ACS had decided to stop asking for federal funds because it seemed so futile. When Clay became the society's president in 1836, he could not even convince Congress to grant it a federal charter. North Carolina Senator Robert Strange opposed Clay's motion to refer a memorial to that effect to the Committee on the District of Columbia because it would "hold out to the slave population a desire to become free." The Senate voted, twenty-five to sixteen, against Clay's referral motion. It was a highly partisan, sectional vote. Whigs voted ten to three in favor of the motion and Democrats, twenty-two to six in opposition; northern senators voted twelve to nine in favor and southern senators, sixteen to four in opposition. All four of the southern senators who voted in the affirmative represented upper-South states, and three of the four were Whigs.[19]

The rapidly expanding list of ACS vice-presidents had also taken on a more partisan cast. In addition to Clay, Mercer, and Webster, several other prominent Whig members of Congress were now on the list, including Theodore Frelinghuysen, William C. Rives, and Samuel Southard, who had been Monroe's secretary of navy when the navy had offered the society's Liberian colony critical assistance during the early years of its existence.[20]

ACS officials began to lament the fact that the society was under attack from both proslavery and antislavery extremes and to emphasize its neutrality between them. The ACS also tempered its already temperate antislavery rhetoric, which, by its own admission, undercut its appeal in the North without necessarily increasing it in the South. In 1837, the society's board of managers despaired of the future of an organization that "is assaulted by the concentrated power of the Abolitionists on the one side, and very inadequately defended and sustained by its southern friends on the other." By the mid-1830s, then, with a loss of federal funding, declining public support, and heavy debts, the ACS seemed a moribund organization.[21]

A Partnership on Life Support

Indirect federal assistance helped Liberia through these troubled times. The United States had a stake in the survival of the colony because it provided a commercial foothold in western Africa to counteract British influence in the area. Potentially, it could also serve as a point of attack on the slave trade, if federal officials ever decided to make the suppression of the trade a higher priority. A concern for national reputation also probably carried some weight with federal officials in deciding to support a struggling colony of former American slaves. For a number of reasons, then, Jackson did not follow Kendall's advice and sever all ties with the ACS and its Liberian colony.[22]

The Jackson and Van Buren administrations continued the practice of partially paying the salary of a colonial agent in Liberia, though at a somewhat reduced rate. This practice ended, however, in 1841 with the death of Thomas Buchanan. To replace him, the ACS appointed an African American émigré to the position for the first time, Joseph Jenkins Roberts. At that point, the Tyler administration decided to stop supplementing the agent's salary, ostensibly because Liberian independence was imminent.[23]

While Liberia continued to receive naval protection during this period, without a permanent African Squadron that protection remained sporadic. The U.S. Navy also found it difficult to capture slave ships off the west coast of Africa without such a squadron. Nonetheless, two sets of Africans seized elsewhere were resettled in Liberia. In 1835, the ACS received $4,400 for thirty-six Africans who had been seized from the *Fenix* in Cuban waters and resettled in Liberia—slightly more than $120 per capita. The other case involved two African children whom a navy captain, Caleb Miller, had attempted to smuggle into the United States, apparently for his own personal use. In 1836, the ACS received $200 to resettle them in Liberia.[24]

When the U.S. Navy finally established a permanent African Squadron under the terms of the Webster-Ashburton Treaty, the ACS was especially well connected. Both Secretary of State and treaty negotiator Daniel Webster and Secretary of the Navy Abner Upshur were ACS vice-presidents. President John Tyler had been active in the organization as a delegate from the Virginia Colonization Society. The African Squadron enjoyed an early success in 1845 when it captured the *Pons* with approximately 900 Africans abroad. In this case, the ACS had to repeatedly petition Congress to be reimbursed the costs of the care of the 756 *Pons* Africans who were resettled in Liberia. The society finally received $37,800 in 1852, only $50 per capita.[25]

In-kind federal subsidies also continued. The colony received shipments of arms and naval stores in 1839 and 1840 during the Van Buren administration. In 1843, the Tyler administration shipped $1,500 worth of goods for the benefit of the recaptured Africans who lived in their own separate settlement in Liberia.[26] This type of indirect assistance demonstrated that federal officials, both Democrats and Whigs, had defined the survival of the colony as a national interest, however low a priority they may have given that interest.

With the Whigs again in control of Congress, the ACS renewed its appeals for federal assistance in 1842, ending a twelve-year hiatus. These new appeals placed a greater emphasis on the way the colony was an effective tool in suppressing the slave trade. They also placed a new emphasis on the way the colony offered a point of entry to Africa's growing commerce, which, in the ACS's view, the benighted policies of the federal government had allowed British merchants to engross at the expense of their American competitors. Minimally, the society urged federal officials to appoint a commercial agent to Liberia.[27]

The ACS's new appeals to Congress netted $5,000 in supplemental appropriations for the support of recaptured Africans in Liberia. They also prompted a very sympathetic House report. The 1843 report of the House Committee on Commerce, chaired by Maryland Congressman John Pendleton Kennedy, stressed the diplomatic value of the ACS's Liberian colony in countering British (and French) influence in the area and in deterring the slave trade. The report also portrayed the colony as a mixed enterprise, "founded partly by the private enterprise of American citizens and partly by the aid of the Federal and State authorities." Kennedy acknowledged that "the idea of an American colony is a new one" but, unlike Kendall and Tazewell, he saw "nothing in our Constitution to forbid it." He cited Native American removals as a precedent, noting that "Indian tribes had already been placed beyond the limits of the States, on the purchased territory of the Union." In conclusion, the Kennedy report recommended that federal officials should at least establish a commercial agency in Liberia.[28]

From the ACS's perspective, Liberia's 1847 Declaration of Independence merely signified the difference between a colony and a client state. On behalf of its "client," the society implored federal officials not only to recognize Liberian independence but to grant it special trading privileges. In 1848, the Polk administration appointed a commercial agent to Liberia but refused to recognize its independence. This agent served unofficially as the U.S. minister to Liberia until President Abraham Lincoln finally recognized its independence in 1862. In the meantime, both the ACS and the federal government remained heavily involved in Liberian affairs, presumably to ensure that "their" colonists were well treated.[29]

The early 1850s were the society's halcyon days. The Fugitive Slave Law of 1850 produced a spike in free black emigration, and revenues also began to rise. President Millard Fillmore, Secretary of State Edward Everett, Supreme Court Justice James Wayne, and Senators Clay and Stephen A. Douglas were among the dignitaries who attended its annual meetings. Secretary of Treasury Thomas Corwin and Attorney General John Crittenden were also active in the society. Kennedy was the new secretary of navy.[30]

When Franklin Pierce succeeded Fillmore as president of the United States in 1853, the new Democratic administration remained supportive. Pierce himself became a life director of the ACS in 1854 when $1,000 was donated to the society on his behalf. Secretary of State William Marcy was a long-time ACS vice-president. Revenues and emigrant applications continued to rise. More state governments actively supported African colonization. By the end of the Pierce administration, a total of eight state governments—Connecticut, Indiana, Kentucky, Maryland, Missouri, New Jersey, Pennsylvania, and Virginia—had appropriated funds either to establish a settlement in Liberia or to defray the costs of colonizing African Americans from their own states. Six of those initiatives were launched during the Fillmore and Pierce administrations.[31]

In his valedictory address at the 1853 annual meeting of the society, former Virginia congressman and ACS Vice-President Mercer chronicled its long partnership with the federal government. One of the targets of his address was Kendall's 1830 audit. In response to Kendall's charge of the misuse of federal funds to finance African colonization, Mercer argued that the practice was entirely appropriate under Monroe's interpretation of the 1819 slave-trade law and that Congress had acquiesced in that interpretation of the law for more than a decade prior to Kendall's audit. In response to Kendall's suggestion that the Liberian enterprise should have been pursued solely by private means, Mercer insisted that the colony would never have been established nor continued to survive without federal support. He was almost certainly correct on both counts.[32]

At the next annual meeting of the society, Supreme Court Justice and ACS Vice-President Wayne delivered a full-blown constitutional defense of African colonization. In the course of this defense, Wayne referred to a number of constitutional warrants for the project, including the treaty- and war-making powers to acquire territory for an overseas colony and the slave-trade and interstate-commerce powers to populate it. He also invoked the general welfare clause as the broadest constitutional warrant for African colonization. Voicing assumptions widely shared among the ACS membership, he explained that "there is a great constitutional conservative obligation upon the National Government to remove a national evil [free blacks], when it presses upon the general welfare of the United States, and when it can be done without interfering with . . . those institutions which were meant to be guarded by the constitution of the United States." Repeating a well-tested analogy, Wayne concluded that the federal government had exactly the same authority to colonize African Americans as it had to remove Native Americans.[33]

Still, the ACS and its Liberian colony confronted some perennial problems. Even more than Haiti, the other black republic which the United States refused to recognize, Liberia remained in official limbo. In 1852, Liberian President Roberts acknowledged that official recognition of his nation was unlikely as long as slavery continued to exist in the United States, though he had once hoped that, "notwithstanding the peculiar institution of that country, that it would have been among the first . . . to welcome Liberia among the family of nations."[34]

The ACS attempted to inoculate itself from the divisive effects of the slavery issue by officially excluding "all suggestions and discussions of schemes of emancipation" from its publications and proceedings. Such efforts were pyrrhic. When Congress passed the Kansas-Nebraska Act in 1854, the ensuing political realignment sent the society into another tailspin.[35]

By 1858, the ACS had hit rock bottom. The society no longer had any active agents in the South. Only seven state societies were represented at its 1858 annual meeting, and only one of them, Virginia, was from the South. Both free blacks and white slaveholders were proving increasingly reluctant to employ its "services."[36] Whatever future prospects the society had, they now seemed even more dependent on federal support.

The Revival of a Long Partnership

The ACS's fortunes began to rebound again in August 1858, when the USS *Dolphin* captured the *Echo* in Cuban waters with 318 Africans abroad and placed them in the custody of federal authorities at Charleston to await transport to Liberia. By the close of the year, President Buchanan had entered into a formal arrangement with the ACS to reimburse the society $150 for each recaptured African whom it resettled in Liberia. He also appointed its colonial agent, John Seys, the new U.S. agent for recaptured Africans.[37]

When Congress approved this arrangement in 1860, it was the first time the body had expressly authorized the disbursement of federal funds to the ACS. Even though the Senate reduced Buchanan's $150 per capita figure to $100, a surge in slave-ship seizures sent federal money flowing through the society's treasury at an unprecedented rate. This surge was the result of another decision Buchanan made in late 1858, when he authorized Navy Secretary Isaac Toucey to reinforce both the Home and African squadrons for slave-trade suppression. Toucey at least doubled the size of each squadron.[38]

Buchanan had multiple motives for these decisions. Facing a vocal group of southern fire-eaters who favored rescinding the federal slave-import ban, Buchanan was determined not to allow any slippage on the ban. The infamous *Wanderer* case, when Savannah businessman Charles Lamar brazenly smuggled 407 Africans into the United States in November 1858, strengthened that determination. Buchanan's tenures as secretary of state and U.S. minister to England had also personally exposed him to persistent British complaints about the relative lack of American slave-trade-suppression efforts. British diplomatic pressure on the State Department to expand those efforts was now coupled with a threat to unilaterally search and seize American ships suspected of engaging in the slave trade. Regardless of his motives, the effects of Buchanan's decisions were almost immediate. Within a one-year period, from April 26, 1860, to April 21, 1861, navy vessels assigned to the Home and African squadrons captured eight slave ships with a total of more than 5,300 Africans aboard.[39]

Although the onset of the Civil War ended this activity as abruptly as it began, the Africans who had been seized from those eight ships and resettled in Liberia were a financial boon to the ACS because of the federal contracts it received for their first year's care. In fact, Liberian officials thought the arrangement was so profitable that they pressured the society into transferring the responsibility for fulfilling the contracts to their own government. Under this new arrangement, the ACS became, in effect, a third-party auditor of the contracts, transmitting the money it received from the federal government to the Liberian government on satisfaction that the recaptured Africans were receiving adequate care. In return, the ACS received 2.5 percent of the transferred funds in fees.[40]

The federal government owed the ACS $150 per capita for the first year's care of the *Echo* captives under the original agreement with Buchanan. Although Congress had reduced that sum to $100 per capita for the subsequent captures, the Home Squadron seizures proved more expensive because U.S. Navy vessels first landed the recaptured Africans on Key West to await transport to Liberia. To cover the costs associated with the *Echo* capture, Congress appropriated $75,000 in 1859. After the first Home Squadron seizure, Congress appropriated another $250,000 in 1860. It also mandated that in the future the navy should directly transport recaptured Africans to Liberia in order to save money. Home Squadron vessels had, however, already seized two more slave-laden ships in Cuban waters and landed the recaptured Africans on Key West. The African Squadron then began seizing a number of slave-laden ships, a total of five with more than 3,900 Africans aboard by mid-April 1861. Congress made two appropriations of $900,000 each in 1861 to cover the costs of these later seizures. In 1861, $1,800,000 was a significant amount of money, 2.7 percent of total federal expenditures of $66,547,000 in that fiscal year.[41]

Given that the number of recaptured Africans who died between when they were captured and what would have been the end of their first year in Liberia is unknown, it is unclear how much money the federal government actually owed the ACS. Tragically, an estimated 1,000 of the recaptured Africans died before they even reached Liberia. Ultimately, the ACS received $32,500 for the *Echo* Africans and $349,813 for the eight 1860–61 seizures. The society received an additional $54,358 for transporting the Africans temporarily sheltered on Key West to Liberia.[42]

In total, the ACS received $436,671 in federal funds from 1859 to 1865, which would represent 60 percent of its receipts of $721,746 over those seven years. From the standpoint of society officials, recaptured Africans became an unexpectedly large source of colonists, surpassing the number of free black colonists and almost equaling the number of African Americans who emigrated to Liberia as a condition of their emancipation. The society's fiftieth anniversary figures were 5,722 recaptured Africans, 4,541 free blacks, and 5,957 liberated slaves.[43]

Conclusion

Monroe's interpretation of the 1819 slave-trade law initiated the special relationship that developed between the federal government and the ACS's colonization project. Unofficially, Liberia became the nation's first overseas colony. Early in the history of the colony, former South Carolina senator and ACS Vice-President Robert Goodloe Harper explained its special status. He insisted that "I do not wish to see in Africa a colonial government, permanently attached to the United States . . . but I wish to see the paternal arm of authority stretched out for the protection of this colony, until it shall be able to manage its own affairs." According to Harper, the final result was to be independence, not statehood, but in 1825 the paternal model applied with even more force in the Liberian case than it did in the case of official domestic territories.[44]

Prior to independence, supportive federal officials funded the ACS as their colonial mechanism, just as supportive European officials funded private companies as their colonial mechanisms. This "mixed enterprise" model offered federal officials a means to pursue an increasingly controversial project. The least controversial rationale for African colonization was slave-trade suppression, which was why society officials increasingly stressed that rationale. After ACS President Clay declared at the society's 1851 annual meeting that "all hearts are united . . . on the propriety of suppressing that odious traffic in slaves with Africa," he congratulated the membership on finding "the most effectual and complete method by which there can be an end put to that abominable traffic, and that is by Colonization."[45] Indeed, without the slave-trade connection, the ACS's colonization project would have received no federal support and, without federal support, the project would have had a very short shelf-life.

Appendix

Federal Subsidization of African Colonization

Item	Date	Amount
Kendall audit	1819–30	$264,710
Colonial agent[a]	1831–September 1841	$12,925
Fenix captives	1835	$4,400
Two smuggled children	1836	$200
In-kind subsidy	1843	$1,500
Supplemental appropriation	1843	$5,000
Pons captives	1845	$37,800
Echo captives	1858	$32,500
1860–61 seizures	1860–61	$404,173
Total		$763,198

Note: a. Assuming $1,600 per year 1831–33; $1,000 per year 1834–40; $1,125 for the first three quarters of 1841 at $1,500 per year. Through 1830, the federal portion of the colonial agent's salary was included in the Kendall audit figure.

Notes

1. This essay revises the third chapter of my book, *Slavery in the American Republic: Building the Federal Government, 1791–1861* (Lawrence: University Press of Kansas, 2011). I am grateful to the University Press of Kansas for permission to reuse that material.

2. I calculated the society's 1819–65 receipts by subtracting the 1866 receipts from its 1867 fiftieth-anniversary total. See *Annual Reports of the American Colonization Society* (1818–1910; rpt., New York: Negro Universities Press, 1969), vol. 49 (1866): 25; vol. 50 (1867): 21, 24. All financial data have been rounded to the nearest dollar. On these other early cases of federal assistance, see Michelle Landis Dauber, *The Sympathetic States: Disaster Relief and the Origins of the American Welfare State* (Chicago: University of Chicago Press, 2013), 17–23; Carter Goodrich, *Government Promotion of American Canals and Railroads, 1800–1890* (New York: Columbia University Press, 1960), 39–41, 169–70; Stephen J. Rockwell, *Indian Affairs and the Administrative State in the Nineteenth Century* (New York: Cambridge University Press, 2010), 29, 59–60, 150–51, 167; Walter I. Trattner, "The Federal Government and Social Welfare in Early Nineteenth-Century America," *Social Science Review* 50, no. 2 (1976): 243–55.

3. H. Doc. No. 11, 16th Cong., 1st Sess., 1819. "Recaptured Africans" were Africans seized from slave ships operating in violation of American slave-trade laws or while being smuggled into the United States in violation of its slave-import ban.

4. ACS, *Annual Reports* 6 (1823): 23; 7 (1824): 70–71; 10 (1827): 30; 14 (1831): 24; 15 (1832): 16–21; 17 (1834): 27; 31 (1848): 26–27; 32 (1849): 18; 41 (1858): 31–37.

5. Henry Noble Sherwood, "The Formation of the American Colonization Society," *Journal of Negro History* 2, no. 3 (1917): 226-27.

6. P. J. Staudenraus, *The African Colonization Movement, 1816-1865* (New York: Columbia University Press, 1961), 169-78.

7. The British presence began with the establishment of a free black colony at Sierra Leone in the 1790s, which then became a precedent for the ACS's own colonial project. See ACS, *Annual Reports* 3 (1820): 22; 4 (1821): 26; 5 (1822): 18; and Staudenraus, *African Colonization Movement*, 8-11, 20-21, 28. On the British propaganda war, see Matthew E. Mason, "The Battle of the Slaveholding Liberators: Great Britain, the United States, and Slavery in the Early Nineteenth Century," *William and Mary Quarterly*, 3rd ser., vol. 59, no. 3 (2002): 671.

8. The eighth article of the Webster-Ashburton Treaty (1842) obligated the United States to establish a separate African squadron. See *Statutes at Large* 8 (1842): 576. On the squadron's dual mission, see ACS, *Annual Reports* 26 (1843): 28-30; H. Ex. Doc. No. 104, 35th Cong., 2nd Sess., 1859, 3.

9. *Annals of Congress*, 14th Cong., 2nd Sess., 1817, 481-83; ACS, *Annual Reports* 4 (1821): 23-30; 5 (1822): 41-48; 10 (1827): 77-79; H. Doc. No. 277, 21st Cong., 1st Sess., 1830. Despite the spectrum of opinion on slavery within the society, a moderate "necessary evil" position seems to have been the dominant position, at least in its early years. See ACS, *Annual Reports* 14 (1831): 26-27; Eric Burin, *Slavery and the Peculiar Solution: A History of the American Colonization Society* (Gainesville: University Press of Florida, 2005), 14, 22; Alisse Portnoy, *Their Right to Speak: Women's Activism in the Indian and Slave Debates* (Cambridge, Mass.: Harvard University Press, 2005), 102, 174-75; Staudenraus, *African Colonization Movement*, vii; Marie Tyler-McGraw, *An African Republic: Black & White Virginians in the Making of Liberia* (Chapel Hill: University of North Carolina Press, 2007), 4. But see also Douglas R. Egerton, "'Its Origin Is Not a Little Curious': A New Look at the American Colonization Society," *Journal of the American Republic* 5, no. 4 (1985): 479-80.

10. ACS, *Annual Reports* 2 (1819): 15; 3 (1820): 10-11, 15-16; *Statutes at Large* 3 (1819): 532-34. Alabama, Louisiana, and South Carolina had also sold recaptured Africans into slavery. See ACS, *Annual Reports* 3 (1820): 16.

11. ACS, *Annual Reports* 4 (1821): 7-13; 5 (1822): 8-17, 64-66. Staudenraus, *African Colonization Movement*, 59-65.

12. ACS, *Annual Reports* 6 (1823): 257 (1824): 19-20, 26-27; 8 (1825): 32. H. Doc. No. 193, 20th Cong., 1st Sess., 1828, 7, 11. "Letter from Treasury Department," December 1, 1843, Box 622, SG–Illegal Service, including blockade running, piracy, smuggling, and filibustering, Subject File, U.S. Navy, 1775-1901; 0-1910, Office of Naval Records and Library, Record Group 45; National Archives, Washington, D.C. S. Doc. No. 3, 20th Cong., 1st Sess., 1827, 10-29; S. Doc. No. 1, 20th Cong., 2nd Sess., 1828, 139-40. Staudenraus, *African Colonization Movement*, 89-90.

13. "Letter from Treasury Department," 1843. The ACS established the local assembly in 1825, following a series of colonist protests against Ashmun's leadership. See ACS, *Annual Reports* 9 (1826): 15-16; Staudenraus, *African Colonization Movement*, 91-92, 95-96.

14. H. Rep. No. 101, 19th Cong., 2nd Sess., 1827, 4.

15. ACS, *Annual Reports* 11 (1828): 32; Burin, *Slavery and the Peculiar Solution*, 17.

16. S. Rep. No. 178, 20th Cong., 1st Sess., 1828, 11, 14-15; quote at 11.

17. *H. Rep.* No. 283, 27th Cong., 3rd Sess., 1843, 457, 462–63; quotes at 457. All emphases are in the original.

18. ACS, *Annual Reports* 16 (1833): 37; John R. Van Atta, "Western Lands the Political Economy of Henry Clay's American System, 1819–1832," *Journal of the Early Republic* 21, no. 4 (2001): 633–65. Clay's bill listed African colonization as one of the three purposes for which states could use the money, along with education and internal improvements. In 1827, Maryland became the first state to appropriate funds for African colonization. It later established a separate colony at Cape Palmas. See ACS, *Annual Reports* 11 (1828): 48, 78–79; 17 (1834): 16–17; and Penelope Campbell, *Maryland in Africa: The Maryland State Colonization Society, 1831–1857* (Urbana: University of Illinois Press, 1971), 11, 35–36, 53, 55.

19. ACS, *Annual Reports* 19 (1835): 7, 12–13; 20 (1836): 48; 21 (1837): 35–36, 42; *Register of Debates*, 24th Cong., 2nd Sess., 1837, 564–68, 636; quote at 565. On the ACS's upper-South bias, see Douglas R. Egerton, "Averting a Crisis: The Proslavery Critique of the American Colonization Society," *Civil War History* 43, no. 2 (1997): 143, 148. On the society's Whiggish nature, see Daniel Walker Howe, *The Political Culture of the American Whigs* (Chicago: University of Chicago Press, 1978), 18.

20. ACS, *Annual Reports* 13 (1830): xvi; 17 (1834): xxvi; 22 (1838): 32. Southard had also served as Adams's navy secretary.

21. ACS, *Annual Reports* 19 (1836): 10; 21 (1837): 17, 23, quote at 17. Burin, *Slavery and the Peculiar Solution*, 24, 33; Portnoy, *Their Right to Speak*, 100–102; Staudenraus, *African Colonization Movement*, 187, 205–6, 224–27, 236–37; Tyler-McGraw, *African Republic*, 27, 53–54.

22. Staudenraus, *African Colonization Movement*, 178, 186.

23. ACS, *Annual Reports* 26 (1843): 10; Staudenraus, *African Colonization Movement*, 241. In 1834, the federal government reduced its contribution to $1,000 and the ACS raised its contribution to $1,400. See ACS, *Annual Reports* 17 (1834): 23; Staudenraus, *African Colonization Movement*, 186. The Department of Treasury, however, reported that Buchanan's annual (federal) salary was $1,500 at the time of his death in September 1841. See "Letter from Treasury Department," 1843. Buchanan was the brother of the future president. Roberts later became the first president of an independent Liberia.

24. ACS, *Annual Reports* 19 (1835): 16, 28; 20 (1836): 5, 33. From 1823 to 1844, the U.S. Navy seized only one slave ship, with no Africans aboard, off the west coast of Africa. See Judd Scott Harmon, "Suppress and Protest: The United States Navy, the African Slave Trade, and Maritime Commerce, 1794–1862," PhD diss., College of William and Mary, 1977, 239 (appendix E).

25. ACS, *Annual Reports* 26 (1843): 7, 28; 30 (1847): 35, 38; 31 (1848): 13–14; 32 (1849): 11; 35 (1852): 6–7, 36; 45 (1862): 6.

26. ACS, *Annual Reports* 23 (1840): 3–4; 24 (1841): 7; 27 (1844): 34. Unfortunately, the ship carrying the goods was wrecked at Cape de Verde, where it had first landed to deliver supplies to the African Squadron. Liberia also received one in-kind shipment of supplies for the *Pons* captives in 1846. See ACS, *Annual Reports* 30 (1847): 6.

27. ACS, *Annual Reports* 23 (1843): 6–12 (appendix).

28. *H. Rep.* No. 283, 27th Cong., 3rd Sess., 1843, 4–7; quotes at 5, 6; *H. Doc.* No. 162, 28th Cong., 1st Sess., 1844; "Letter from Treasury Department," 1843. By 1843, two state governments had funded colonization endeavors—Maryland and Virginia—and four state

auxiliaries had established their own separate settlements or colonies—Maryland, Mississippi, New York, and Pennsylvania. See ACS, *Annual Reports* 34 (1851): 82.

29. ACS, *Annual Reports* 34 (1851): 27, 31, 69–71; 35 (1852): 31; 36 (1853): 17; 37 (1854): 11–12, 19; 38 (1855): 43, 49; 42 (1859): 51; 43 (1860): 12, 50; 44 (1861): 21, 44; 45 (1862): 7, 15, 26. The commercial agent drew a $1,000 annual salary and, in 1856, added counsel general to his title. See ACS, *Annual Reports* 32 (1849): 15; 39 (1856): 7; 40 (1857): 19; 46 (1863): 12. The ACS retained a colonial agent in Liberia and a building to temporarily house "its" emigrants. See ACS, *Annual Reports* 29 (1846): 39; 31 (1848): 19; 32 (1849): 12.

30. ACS, *Annual Reports* 31 (1848): 17–18, 28; 32 (1849): 20, 21; 34 (1851): 8, 34, 84; 35 (1852): 6, 30; 36 (1853): 12–13; 37 (1854): 4, 15–16. Burin, *Slavery and the Peculiar Solution*, 29–30. Staudenraus, *African Colonization Movement*, 242–45. Tyler-McGraw, *African Republic*, 79, 128. These men all were or were to become ACS vice-presidents, except for Fillmore, who became a life director in 1853. Fillmore inserted an endorsement of African colonization in the draft of his 1852 annual message to Congress but at the last minute deleted the passage on the advice of his cabinet. See Burin, *Slavery and the Peculiar Solution*, 28.

31. ACS, *Annual Reports* 20 (1836): 60; 34 (1851): 84; 35 (1852): 52; 36 (1853): 5, 9–10, 18; 37 (1854): 8; 38 (1855): 39; 39 (1856): 6; 40 (1857): 8, 32. Maryland and Virginia were the early exceptions.

32. ACS, *Annual Reports* 36 (1853): 47–48. Mercer noted that the society had only $746 in cash at the time of its first expedition to Africa.

33. ACS, *Annual Reports* 37 (1854): 38–41; quote at 40. On the analogy between Native American removals and African colonization, see Nicholas Guyatt, "'The Outskirts of Our Happiness': Race and the Lure of Colonization in the Early Republic," *Journal of American History* 95, no. 4 (2009): 986–1011.

34. ACS, *Annual Reports* 36 (1853): 8. On U.S. relations with Haiti, see Tim Matthewson, *A Proslavery Foreign Policy: Haitian-American Relations During the Early Republic* (Westport, Conn.: Praeger, 2003).

35. ACS, *Annual Reports* 35 (1852): 35; 38 (1855): 26–27, 42, quote at 42. Burin, *Slavery and the Peculiar Solution*, 31.

36. ACS, *Annual Reports* 41 (1858): 19, 47; 43 (1860): 45. Tyler-McGraw, *African Republic*, 128–29. Three years earlier, thirteen states had been represented at the society's annual meeting, including Virginia, Georgia, Louisiana, Mississippi, and Missouri. By 1860, only four northern states were represented. See ACS, *Annual Reports* 38 (1855): 13–15; 43 (1860): 36.

37. ACS, *Annual Reports* 42 (1859): 18–20, 46. Seys's appointment resurrected the colonial agent's dual role.

38. ACS, *Annual Reports* 44 (1861): 19; Harmon, "Suppress and Protest," 140, 192, 236–37 (appendix D). For children, the Senate reduced the rate to $50 per capita. Toucey had been active in the ACS as a delegate from the Connecticut auxiliary as well as a member of its board of managers. See ACS, *Annual Reports* 42 (1859): 42.

39. *Mr. Buchanan's Administration on the Eve of the Rebellion* (New York: D. Appleton, 1866), 262; Robert Ralph Davis Jr., "James Buchanan and the Suppression of the Slave Trade, 1858–1861," *Pennsylvania History* 33, no. 4 (1966): 457–59; *H. Ex. Doc. No. 7*, 36th Cong., 3rd Sess., 1860; Warren S. Howard, *American Slavers and the Federal Law, 1837–1862*

(1963; rpt., Westport, Conn.: Greenwood, 1976), 220–23 (appendix A); *S. Ex. Doc.* No. 39, 35th Cong., 1st Sess., 1858; Ronald T. Takaki, *A Pro-Slavery Crusade: The Agitation to Reopen the African Slave Trade* (New York: Free Press, 1971); Tom Henderson Wells, *The Slave Ship Wanderer* (Athens: University of Georgia Press, 1967); Karen Fisher Younger, "Liberia and the Last Slave Ships," *Civil War History* 54, no. 4 (2008): 431–32.

40. ACS, *Annual Reports* 44 (1861): 12–15, 47–48; 45 (1862): 46. Willis D. Boyd, "The American Colonization Society and the Slave Recaptives of 1860–1861: An Early Example of United States–African Relations," *Journal of Negro History* 47, no. 2 (1962): 119. Liberian officials also justified the contract transfer on grounds of national sovereignty. See Younger, "Liberia and the Last Slave Ships," 436. The ACS denied the profitability of the arrangement, claiming that its costs were higher than even the $150 per capita in the initial agreement with Buchanan. See ACS, *Annual Reports* 42 (1861): 18.

41. ACS, *Annual Reports* 44 (1861): 11. Boyd, "American Colonization Society and the Slave Recaptives," 126. *H. Ex. Doc.* No. 7, 36th Cong., 2nd Sess., 1860, 647. *H. Rep.* No. 602, 36th Cong., 1st Sess., 1860; *Historical Statistics of the United States Millennial Edition Online*, Table Ea636-643, hsus.cambridge.org. Howard, *American Slavers*, 221–23 (appendix A). *S. Ex. Doc.* No. 1, 36th Cong., 2nd Sess., 1860, 42. *Statutes at Large* 11 (1859): 404; 12 (1860): 40–41; 12 (1861): 132, 219. Younger, "Liberia and the Last Slave Ships," 433.

42. *The Records of the American Colonization Society,* ser. 4: *Financial Papers, 1818–1963* (Washington, D.C.: Library of Congress), Ledger G (1859–76), roll 276, 74, 77. These totals include the costs of three African children who were found in the hold of the *W. R. Kibby* after it was captured in Cuban waters and taken to New York to be libeled. See *New York Times,* "The Slavers in Port," August 17, 1860. Many of the deaths were due to the gross negligence of ACS and federal officials in arranging for the care of the recaptured Africans and their transportation to Liberia. See ACS, *Annual Reports* 42 (1859): 19; 44 (1861): 11; and Boyd, "American Colonization Society and the Slave Recaptives," 114–16.

43. ACS, *Annual Reports* 50 (1867): 64. The society reported three other categories of colonists: 68 status unknown, 346 from Barbados (who emigrated as a group during the Civil War), and 753 freedmen (who were liberated during or after the war). ACS officials were extremely disappointed with the low number in the latter category because they had expected the abolition of slavery in the United States to spark a sharp increase in colonists. See ACS, *Annual Reports* 48 (1865): 18, 25, 33–34; 49 (1866): 14–15; 50 (1867): 12–13, 51. I calculated the society's total receipts for 1859–65 by adding the receipts from its annual financial statements during those years. See ACS, *Annual Reports* 43 (1860): 51; 44 (1861): 50; 45 (1862): 59; 46 (1863): 52; 47 (1864): 18; 48 (1865): 27; 49 (1866): 25.

44. ACS, *Annual Reports* 7 (1825): 16. On this paternal model and the evolution of territorial governance in the United States, see Jack E. Eblen, *The First and Second United States Empires: Governors and Territorial Government, 1784–1912* (Pittsburgh, Pa.: University of Pittsburgh Press, 1968).

45. ACS, *Annual Reports* 34 (1851): 41–42. In comparing Liberian colonization to the Dutch colonization of South Africa, Tom Schick discounted the extent to which Liberian colonization was also a mixed enterprise. See Tom W. Schick, *Behold the Promised Land: A History of Afro-American Settler Society in Nineteenth Century Liberia* (Baltimore: Johns Hopkins University Press, 1977), 136.

6

James Monroe and the Practicalities of Emancipation and Colonization

DANIEL PRESTON

The age of revolutions of the late eighteenth and early nineteenth centuries spawned an era of reform that received widespread support both among the general population and among political leaders but, as always, the sticking point came in the details. The question was not so much "What do we want to reform?" but rather "How exactly do we go about it?" This quandary was particularly evident in the United States at the turn of the nineteenth century on the question of slavery. Many Americans agreed that slavery should be abolished, but the question was how to do it. This essay proposes to look at this question through the eyes of James Monroe.

Monroe, like others of the founding generation, sought to implement the ideals of the American Revolution. But, as an experienced politician and as chief executive at both the state and federal level, Monroe well understood the difficulty of attaining these goals. Like many of his contemporaries, Monroe believed that slavery was both unjust and a detriment to the United States, and that it should be eradicated, not by acts of individual manumission but by comprehensive state or even national emancipation. But emancipation raised a host of questions about its implementation: What would be the incentive for slave owners to agree to free their slaves? Would the process be immediate or gradual? What would be the economic impact? Would there be a place for free blacks in American society? And who would bear the enormous expense of the undertaking? Monroe believed that the colonization of freed slaves outside the United States was the solution to the problem, and as president he marshaled the resources of the federal government to achieve that end.

James Monroe was born into a slave-owning family in Westmoreland County, Virginia, in 1758; he became a slave owner in his own right when he inherited land and slaves from his father in 1774. Throughout the rest of his life he participated fully in the slave economy—buying, selling, renting, and mortgaging slaves, as well as using them as labor on his Virginia farms. And yet, Monroe, like many of his friends and neighbors, was uncomfortable with the institution. As a young officer in the Continental Army, Monroe imbibed the ideals of the American Revolution and professed allegiance to those ideals, "the sacred cause of liberty," as he termed it, throughout his life.[1] He surely understood the contradiction between those ideals and the practice of holding other human beings in bondage. But slavery was a source of wealth and status, and slave owners like Monroe, whatever their qualms, were reluctant to surrender that status.[2]

Monroe never made a commitment to emancipate his slaves, but at some point in his life he decided that the United States needed to shed itself of slavery. Not only did slavery as an institution contradict the ideals of the Revolution, but it also created sectional tensions that threatened the Union. Monroe fervently believed that the union of the states was essential to the independence, indeed to the very existence, of the nation. He saw the preservation of the Union as tantamount to all other concerns: if slavery threatened the Union, then slavery must end.

It is not known when Monroe first reached this conclusion, but it is known when he first confronted the problem of slavery. Monroe became governor of Virginia in December 1799; nine months later, Gabriel's conspiracy was uncovered. As governor, Monroe was responsible for the suppression of the planned revolt and the punishment of the conspirators. Trials and executions began almost immediately. On September 15—a scant fifteen days after the discovery of the conspiracy—Monroe, sickened by the mass executions, was wondering "Where to arrest the hand of the Executioner." In a letter to Thomas Jefferson of that date he pondered the question of whether "mercy or severity is the better policy."[3] Transportation—selling the condemned conspirators to slave traders who agreed to carry them out of country—seemed to be a more humane solution. Monroe suggested this alternate form of punishment, and the Virginia assembly enacted the measure, along with other laws for controlling the slave population. The debate in the assembly over these measures led to a broader consideration of the problem. It was generally agreed that the threat of slave insurrection would continue as long as slavery existed; in a message to the assembly regarding the rebellion, Governor Monroe had warned: "Unhappily while this class of people exists among us we can never count with certainty on its tranquil submission."[4] The ultimate solution to this threat was obvious—the abolition of slavery.

This solution, however, posed another problem: What would become of the freed slaves? Slavery was first and foremost a labor system, but it was also a system of control of what the dominant white population considered an alien people. If blacks were no longer enslaved, what place would they have in Virginia society? The racism perpetuated by two centuries of slavery forbade that they would be become citizens possessing the same rights as whites. Political demographics underscored this attitude. The governing elite was not about to jeopardize its hold on power by enfranchising a large number of new citizens, particularly in counties where blacks comprised a majority of the residents. Employment also entered into the problem. It could be assumed that some of the freed slaves would be hired as wage employees by their former masters, but what of those who, either by their own choice or by the limited labor needs of the planters, did not? The specter of a large number of unemployed nonwhite noncitizens clearly barred any plan that allowed the freed people to remain in Virginia. The only choice, if Virginia did decide to pursue emancipation, was the removal of the freed blacks from the state. But this also raised a question. If the freed slaves were to be sent out of the state, where would they go?

The idea of colonization was not new. Monroe himself became familiar with it at least as early as 1785, when he read Thomas Jefferson's *Notes on the State of Virginia*, which presented a plan of compensated emancipation and colonization of the freedmen outside the United States, a proposal that Monroe thought would have a "very favorable effect" in Virginia. In fact, colonization was debated in print in Virginia just prior to the conspiracy. Ferdinando Fairfax, a Virginia planter, published a pamphlet in 1790 calling for the emancipation of slaves in Virginia and their resettlement in Africa.[5] St. George Tucker, a prominent Virginia jurist, presented an alternate plan in 1796. Tucker began with the premise that colonization was impractical for two reasons: first, general emancipation would bankrupt Virginia, and second, the state did not have the means to transport over 200,000 people from America to Africa. Instead, Tucker proposed a plan of gradual emancipation that would ease the economic losses incurred by freeing the slaves. But, while the plan eased the burden on the planters, it offered nothing to the freed blacks besides freedom. They would not become citizens, they would be denied all civil rights, and there was no provision for their economic livelihood. Tucker argued that these disadvantages would compel the freed slaves to voluntarily leave the state for more hospitable grounds. Where this would be, or how the freedmen would get there, Tucker did not say.[6]

George Tucker, Judge Tucker's cousin, presented another plan in 1801, hard on the heels of the conspiracy. This plan, like Jefferson's and Fairfax's, provided for general emancipation in Virginia and the colonization of the freed slaves outside the state. The timing of this proposal earned it a little more attention but no better success. Instead, the assembly merely passed a vaguely worded resolution calling on the governor to query the president on the possibility of the national government acquiring a site outside the United States "whither persons obnoxious to the laws, or dangerous to the peace of society may be removed." Monroe drew attention to the vagaries of the resolution in his letter to Jefferson asking him to investigate the possibilities of establishing a colony. The governor noted that, if one gave the resolution a "more enlarged construction" beyond the mere transportation of the conspirators, then "vast and interesting objects present themselves to view." Jefferson concurred in this interpretation and asked for clarification of the assembly's intention. The assembly responded in February 1802 by passing two resolutions. The first affirmed that their previous resolution had referred only to the conspirators. The second resolution went further, calling on the governor and the president to find a site for an "asylum" where "free negroes or mulattoes, and such negroes and mulattoes as may be emancipated, may be sent, or choose to remove."[7]

Some advocates of colonization, including George Tucker, suggested that a refuge be established west of the Mississippi River, but Jefferson rejected the idea of establishing such a colony in North America, instead fixing upon Sierra Leone, the privately owned British colony for freed blacks on the West Coast of Africa, as the only viable destination. The president wrote to Rufus King, the U.S. minister to Great Britain, and instructed him to make inquiries on the possibility of settling American blacks in Sierra Leone. King did so, but the British were not receptive. The management of the colony had become more expensive and more difficult than expected, and the prospect of the influx of thousands of American blacks was unwelcome, especially since recent unrest in the colony had been led by former American slaves who had fled to British protection during the Revolutionary War. The Virginia assembly passed resolutions annually up to 1805 calling for the establishment of a colony, but having no alternative to Sierra Leone at hand, the contemplation of emancipation and colonization in Virginia came to an end.[8]

The Virginia assembly's primary concern was the prevention of slave insurrection rather than emancipation and colonization, so when the overtures to the British failed, the assembly returned to more conventional methods and enacted more severe measures for regulating the movement and behavior of both slaves and free blacks. Paramount among this legislation was a law passed in 1806 restricting the ability of owners to manumit their slaves.[9] Gabriel's conspiracy did, however, leave its mark on Monroe, and the quandary of slavery became a matter of concern to him. Surviving evidence from prior to the conspiracy suggests that Monroe gave little thought to the institution in either moral or political terms; but afterwards it is clear that he wrestled with his personal culpability as a slave owner and with the broader question of dealing with slavery as a state and national problem.

Monroe never went as far as to consider freeing his own slaves; on the contrary, he bought more: between 1807 and 1810 he acquired thirty-three slaves, raising the number he owned from sixteen to forty-nine. But the evidence suggests that he had become more sensitive to the inhumanity of slavery. The clearest example of this came in 1812 when Monroe won a lawsuit against two neighbors who had whipped one of Monroe's slaves with "sticks switches & cowhides." Monroe had filed the suit not for the sake of compensation but to obtain a public condemnation of such behavior. "The God who made us made the black people," he wrote to his agent, "& they ought not to be treated with barbarity."[10]

Monroe also apparently sanctioned marriage among his slaves, even though there was no legal provision for it, and sought to preserve the unity of slave families. In the two documented cases of the sale of slaves after 1802, Monroe took care to keep husbands and wives together and also consulted with the slaves on their willingness to be sold. In 1810 he sent a slave named Roger to his friend Fulwar Skipwith as payment for a debt, informing Skipwith that "his wife having been sold to some one to the South at the same time, he has been desirous of going that way in the hope they might finally meet again. On proposing to sell him to you, & explaining your character residence &c, he was perfectly willing to go to you." In 1816, he wrote to his neighbor, Charles Fenton Mercer (also regarding payment of a debt): "It has occurrd to me, as probable, knowing that you contemplated the establishment of a farm, that it would be agreeable to you to take Ralph & his wife. . . . They belong'd to your father's estate, are known to you, and would I presume, as Ralph has connections here, be unwilling to remove." And when he sold his Albemarle County farm in 1828 he sold the slaves to a Colonel White of Florida, who "will take them in families, to that territory."[11]

At one point Monroe experimented with employing indentured white servants, but the availability of cheap land undermined the business. After some of the servants ran away, he admitted the failure of the endeavor and released the rest from their contracts. Whether Monroe hoped to eventually replace his slaves with indentured labor or simply saw the servants as an additional source of farm labor is not known.[12]

Monroe, like many of his contemporaries, developed a strong aversion to the Atlantic slave trade. His first known expression of opposition to the trade came in early 1801 when a U.S. Navy vessel brought a captured slaver into port at Norfolk. Monroe condemned the trade as not only illegal but as "disgraceful" and hoped that an example would be made of the culprits. When Monroe was in London in 1806 and 1807 as U.S. minister to Great Britain, he became friends with William Wilberforce and his circle of English abolitionists, and they looked upon Monroe as an ally in their fight to end the transatlantic slave trade. Monroe provided them with information on slavery in the United States and the steps taken by his country to outlaw the importation of slaves. He "sincerely" congratulated Wilberforce in February 1807 on the passage of an English law banning the trade, telling him: "It is a very honorable trait in the character of both countries, to have combined their efforts for the accomplishment of so benevolent and humane an object." The United States enacted a law almost simultaneously with the British measure forbidding the importation of slaves after January 1, 1808.[13] Monroe, being absent from the United States, had no hand in its passage, but enthusiastically approved both the American and the English effort.

It could be argued that slave owners supported the abolition of the transatlantic slave trade because it benefited them. The number of slaves already in the United States was more than ample to meet labor needs, and planters who wanted more slaves could easily acquire them through the domestic slave trade, which flourished. Indeed, the ban on imports increased the value of slaves in the domestic market. Furthermore, smuggling and lax enforcement of the ban curtailed the effectiveness of the law and made newly imported slaves available to those who wished to buy them. While all this true, it is also true that the horrors of the African slave trade were well known, and even slave owners like Monroe, who considered themselves benevolent men, were disgusted by it. It was an easy target for them, since they were not dependent on the trade, but that does not detract from their antipathy toward it.

Given these attitudes on slavery, the question once again arises, why didn't Monroe free any of his slaves? Since he never answered the question himself, one can only speculate on the reasons. One may have been the already-mentioned status attached to owning slaves. Another may have been their monetary value. Monroe, like most Virginia farmers of his era, was cash poor. Ownership of land and slaves gave him access to credit; the loss of his slaves would have curtailed this much-needed resource. More important may have been the details of manumission, specifically, what would become of the slaves once they were free, and who would provide labor for the farms? The major impediment here was the 1806 manumission law that required freed slaves to leave the state within twelve months of their emancipation. Monroe and others like him would have understandingly been reluctant to cast their slaves adrift in an unknown and hostile world. Furthermore, it would have deprived them of labor, for it would have been impossible for them to keep their former slaves as paid workers even if they had so chosen. What Monroe needed was a comprehensive plan that offered some level of security to the freed slaves and protected the owners from economic ruin. That plan proved to be gradual compensated emancipation linked to colonization.

The opportunity for Monroe to help implement such a plan occurred almost simultaneously with his assumption of the presidency. In December 1816 a group of men met in Washington and formed the American Colonization Society. Charles Fenton Mercer, a newly elected member of Congress from Virginia, was a central figure in the founding of the ACS. While a member of the Virginia assembly in 1815, Mercer learned of the Monroe-Jefferson correspondence regarding colonization. He attempted to have the assembly revive its earlier resolutions in favor of colonization, but without success. Mercer began to talk to friends in Virginia and elsewhere about the need for an organized effort in support of colonization, and these conversations led to the creation of the ACS.[14]

Although Monroe was not among those who organized the ACS, he was privy to all that was happening through his friendship with Mercer. Monroe had strong ties to the Mercer family and with Charles Fenton, in particular. Monroe and Mercer owned adjoining farms in Loudoun County, Virginia, and Monroe sent his wheat to Mercer's mill for grinding. And, even though Mercer was a Federalist, the two men respected each other and shared an interest in agriculture, educational reform, and internal improvements. They conferred frequently and formed an almost perfect working relationship. Mercer, for his part, found a strong ally in the president, and Monroe found a way out of a dilemma. Both political considerations and ideological restrictions on the power of the presidency prevented Monroe from taking any initiative on colonization, but under this arrangement he did not need to act overtly. Mercer introduced measures and shepherded them through Congress, and Monroe, as president, merely executed the law.

Mercer's first move came in early 1819 when he introduced a bill to amend the 1807 law banning American participation in the African slave trade. After some debate and changes, the bill was enacted in early March with the following provisions: the U.S. Navy would patrol the African coast and intercept slave ships; the president would have the responsibility of returning Africans taken from slave ships to Africa; and the navy would keep agents on the coast of Africa to assist in the resettlement of freed slaves. Monroe signed the bill on March 3, 1819, the day after it passed; almost immediately a delegation from the ACS called on the president, offering the society's cooperation in the execution of the law. It was understood that the ACS would choose the agents appointed to serve in Africa. But the delegation went even further and suggested that part of the money appropriated by Congress be used to buy land in Africa that would serve as a nucleus for a settlement. Monroe at first doubted that the law authorized such an expenditure. He gradually warmed to the idea, and by October 1819 he was fully committed to it. He and Secretary of the Navy Smith Thompson cooperated with the ACS in making arrangements to establish a station for the repatriation of freed slaves in Africa. On December 17 he sent a message to Congress stating that, although the law on the slave trade was not precise on the question, implementation of the law required the establishment of a base in Africa. He had, therefore, appointed agents to oversee the resettlement of the freed blacks and authorized them to "select the most suitable place on the coast of Africa at which all persons who may be taken under this act shall be delivered to them." The agents "hired" eighty-three free American blacks as laborers to build the station, chartered a ship, and, three days after Monroe's message to Congress, set sail for Africa, escorted by an American warship. In short, the government, under Monroe's direction, financed the establishment of Liberia, the ACS colony in Africa, although everyone took care not to call it a colony.[15]

As the establishment of the African station indicates, the colonization movement was integrally connected to the suppression of the slave trade.

Indeed, Monroe, Mercer, and others realized that colonization could not succeed until the traffic in Africans, either illegally into the United States or legally to foreign ports in the Caribbean and South America, ended. Mercer, in an effort to broaden the net for interdicting the trade, attached an amendment to an anti-piracy bill that was before the House of Representatives in May 1820 declaring the slave trade to be an act of piracy. This was not much of stretch, for many of the slavers, who by the nature of trade were smugglers, were also pirates. The bill passed easily. Monroe, who was already waging a vigorous war against the corsairs, was a willing partner in this attack on the slave trade.[16]

The American declaration of the slave trade as an act of piracy in 1820 was the first move in a broader strategy, for Mercer was talking at that time with newly arrived British minister Stratford Canning, who was charged with negotiating a treaty for the suppression of the slave trade. Great Britain had long sought such a treaty with the United States. The unratified 1806 treaty that Monroe had negotiated and the 1814 treaty ending the War of 1812 both contained clauses promoting cooperation.[17] Mercer's strategy was for both nations to enact laws making engagement in the slave trade an act of piracy and then for them to sign a compact pledging cooperation.

The day after he introduced his amendment to the piracy act, Mercer introduced a series of resolutions regarding the slave trade and colonization. The first, calling on the president to negotiate a treaty with friendly powers for the suppression of the slave trade, passed the House of Representatives but died in the Senate. The proposed treaty would have allowed the warships of each nation to search the ships of the other, a proposition that President Monroe and Secretary of State Adams found unacceptable. The British search and seizure of American ships and the impressment of seamen in the years leading up to the War of 1812 was still too raw a wound for the Americans to make any concessions. Mercer and Canning persisted in their efforts, which finally yielded fruit in early 1823. Adams remained reluctant, but the president had decided that relations with Great Britain had improved to the point where he was comfortable with the proposed arrangement.

The very fact that Monroe would agree to allow the British to stop and search American ships indicates the extent of his hostility to the slave trade. He conferred with Mercer on the reintroduction of his resolution and marshaled support for it Congress. When it passed, he instructed Adams to draft a compact that would allow warships of both nations to stop and search vessels of the other suspected of being slavers, taking care to include provisions that would protect merchant vessels and seamen from unwarranted seizures. The British agreed to it immediately, but to Monroe's extreme mortification, the treaty met with opposition in the Senate when he submitted it for ratification.

By the summer of 1823 the campaign to succeed Monroe as president was in full and bitter force. Supporters of William H. Crawford, seeking to deny Adams any diplomatic triumph and thus diminish his image as a candidate, attacked the treaty. Although not strong enough to block ratification, they were able to amend the treaty in such manner as to make it unacceptable to the British, who refused to ratify the amended compact when it was presented to them in August 1823.[18] Mercer tried to revive support for the measure in the House of Representatives, but without success. Monroe, for his part, defied Congress in his annual message of December 1823 by reminding the legislators that the negotiations with Great Britain had originated with a resolution of the House of Representatives and by telling them that he still considered such a treaty as a diplomatic goal. "Instructions have been given," he wrote, "to all the ministers of the United States accredited to the powers of Europe and America, to propose the proscription of the African slave trade by classing it under the denomination, and inflicting on its perpetrators the punishment, of piracy." He went on to say that, "should this proposal be acceded to, it is not doubted that this odious and criminal practice will be promptly and entirely suppressed." He concluded by saying he "earnestly hoped" that such arrangements could be made, since they would be the "most effectual expedient" for ending the slave trade.[19]

Monroe's apprehension about slavery received a jolt in the midst of the legislation and negotiations to suppress the slave trade by the Missouri controversy. Monroe was a confirmed nationalist dedicated to the preservation of the Union. He believed that the states had the responsibility to protect the liberty of the people but that the separate states were not strong enough to do it on their own. The liberty of the people and the independence, indeed the very existence, of the nation depended on the union of the states. Anything that threatened to undermine the Union threatened liberty and independence. He was particularly sensitive to this threat in the aftermath of the War of 1812, and during his tour of New England in 1817 trumpeted the need for the renewal of national unity. "Nothing could give me greater satisfaction than to behold a perfect union among ourselves," he said in a speech in Kennebunk, Maine, on July 15, 1817; a union that would not only make the United States "powerful and respected," but would also "restore to social intercourse its former charms" and "render our happiness, as a nation, unmixed and complete."[20]

The opening of the debate on the admission of Missouri in 1819 rekindled his concern. The president believed that any restriction on the admission of Missouri was unconstitutional, and he threatened to veto any legislation that enacted restrictions. He also suspected that the Missouri controversy was a ploy by the Federalists to revitalize their party and regain their national stature. But Monroe also had faith that a patriotic commitment to the good of the nation would prevail and that Congress would find a viable solution to the problem. "I have never known a question so menacing to the tranquility and even the continuance of our Union as the present one," he wrote to Thomas Jefferson in February 1820. "As however there is a vast portion of intelligence & virtue in the body of the people, & the bond of Union has heretofore prov'd sufficiently strong to triumph over all attempts against it, I have great confidence that this effort will not be less unavailing."[21] Even so, he was not willing to stand by idly and let events take their course.

Although the standard historical literature on the controversy focuses on the debates in Congress and in the press, the real solution to the crisis came through private conversations and deal making.[22] As president, Monroe was barred both constitutionally and traditionally from public involvement in matters before Congress. But like all presidents from Washington onward he used his power and influence to further legislation that he favored. Monroe believed that the proposed compromise that would admit Missouri as a slave state, Maine as a free state, and divide the western territory into free and slave sections would resolve the crisis. He threw his support solidly behind the compromise, writing newspaper essays, cajoling congressmen, and dispensing patronage.[23] The debate on Missouri underscored what everyone knew but had been unwilling to say: that slavery had the potential to destroy the Union. This was intolerable for Monroe and helped confirm his belief that slavery was detrimental to the country.

Monroe made very real contributions to the establishment of the colony in Africa, both through the financial support he provided and through his efforts to suppress the slave trade. The ACS acknowledged this support at its 1824 meeting when it passed a resolution naming the main town of the settlement Monrovia in the president's honor. In offering this resolution, Robert Goodloe Harper, one of the founders of the ACS, remarked that his purpose was not only to provide a name for the town, but to "mark our gratitude to the venerable and distinguished man to whom it is more indebted than to any other single man. It is perfectly well known that but for the wise and liberal use he has been pleased to make of the great power confided to him, all our efforts would have been unavailing."[24] Even so, much remained to be done. The navy had carried Africans freed from slave ships to the colony, and a few free blacks from the United States went, but little progress had been made in moving large numbers of blacks from the United States to Africa.

Critics of the ACS from the time of its founding claimed that its purpose was not to end slavery but merely to remove free blacks from the United States. This is certainly true for many of its members. Charles Fenton Mercer, for example, stated explicitly that he opposed emancipation. His goal, which he considered altruistic, was to remove a disadvantaged underclass from the country and relocate it to a location where it could possibly thrive and rise out of its underprivileged condition.[25] Others supported colonization because they considered free blacks to be a threat to the value and security of their slaves. Monroe agreed with Mercer to a certain extent. He agreed that free blacks did constitute an undesirable underclass; but unlike Mercer he viewed slavery as undesirable and thought all blacks, slave and free, should be removed.[26] But it was not race that informed this opinion.

Monroe's views on race can perhaps be best understood by looking at his beliefs regarding Indians as well as blacks. Monroe, like Jefferson and others of his generation, had a fairly benign view of Indians. The source of conflict was not race but land. The Indians had it and the whites wanted it. Monroe and the others thought that amalgamation was both an acceptable and practical solution to the problem. They did not think that Indians were innately inferior to whites; rather it was their culture. A hunter-gatherer society was inferior to an agricultural mercantile one. Indians could easily amalgamate if they accepted and adopted Anglo-American agricultural practices. Critics of Jeffersonian Indian policy claim that it aimed at the destruction of tribal culture. This was true, and the Jeffersonians, including Monroe, readily admitted it. In their eyes this policy served a multiple purpose: It undermined Indian claims to vast tracts of land desired by the Americans. It eliminated a potentially dangerous alien population by integrating it into white American society. It preserved the Indian people from destruction, and in the paternalistic view of white Americans, it benefited the Indians by their integration into a superior socioeconomic culture. "Experience has clearly demonstrated that independent savage communities can not long exist within the limits of a civilized population," Monroe wrote in his second annual message to Congress. "To civilize them, and even to prevent their extinction, it seems to be indispensable that their independence as communities should cease.... The hunter state will then be more easily abandoned, and recourse will be had to the acquisition and culture of land and to other pursuits tending to desolve the ties which connect them together as a savage community and to give a new character to every individual."[27]

This sense among the whites of their cultural superiority applied to blacks as well. Europeans generally considered African culture as primitive and inferior to their own, but in America there was a deeper division. Monroe and others saw daily proof of their slaves' aptitude as farmers and as craftsmen; black intellectual aptitude was also evident. Despite this, slavery had ingrained whites with a sense of their own superiority and of black inferiority. Two hundred years of slavery had created a divide that was deemed unbridgeable; even if the slaves were free, Monroe believed that the most whites would never accept them as equals. And whereas the differences in racial traits between whites and Indians were slight, those between whites and blacks were great enough to mark a distinction. Whites and Indians could integrate, Monroe thought, but history and race prevented the amalgamation of whites and blacks.

Slavery provided a means of keeping the black population, which many whites considered undesirable and almost all whites considered potentially dangerous, under control. It gave blacks, at least in the eyes of whites, a defined place in American society. Furthermore, the history of classical Greece and Rome had taught Americans that slavery was compatible with republicanism. But there was no precedent for a republic accommodating a large alien population within its bounds. What, therefore, would be the place of blacks in America if they were free? What place could a large permanent underclass of noncitizens have in a republic? There being none, the only options were that blacks remain enslaved or, upon being freed, that they be sent out of the country. Thus, in Monroe's mind, history, race, and political theory linked emancipation to colonization.

Freed from the political restraints of public office following his retirement from the presidency in 1825, Monroe began to be more open in his interest in colonization. He was elected president of the auxiliary chapter of the ACS in Loudoun County, Virginia, and vice-president of the Colonization Society of Virginia, when it was founded in 1828. These were honorary positions in organizations that were largely inactive.[28] Even so, Monroe's interest was real, and he corresponded with friends regarding the desirability and practicality of colonization. In a notable exchange with General John Mason of Maryland, a vice-president of the national organization, Monroe posed those very questions: "Can slavery ever be extirpated ... in our union, in our state, or in any of the southern and western states, where it exists? If free, in this state, for example, where the number is reported officially by the auditor, to be 425,148 could they be transported to Africa, or elsewhere ... either voluntarily or by compulsion? Would the funds of the state ... be equal to the object? If free, & not removed from the country ... should they be allowed equal priviledges & rights with the white population, or be held in an inferior grade, and what would be the consequences, in either case?"[29]

Mason replied that slaves throughout the United States should be emancipated and repatriated to Africa, for reasons of policy as well as humanity. This would necessarily be a gradual process, since it would be impractical in terms of both logistics and expense to try to settle two million people in a foreign land in a short amount of time, but it should begin immediately. He suggested that the national government take responsibility for the administration of Liberia, promoting the security and viability of the colony. The individual states would bear the expense of compensation to owners and the transportation of the freed slaves, an expense that would be made affordable by extending it over a number of years. Mason estimated that the program could be completed in fifty or sixty years and cost less than the War of 1812.[30]

Monroe sent his query to Mason shortly before the meeting of a convention in Richmond to consider revising the Virginia state constitution. Monroe anticipated that the question of emancipation might arise, and he told Mason that he wanted the information so that he could "make up my own mind on the subject, for my own satisfaction," and so that it could serve "as a guide, in any occurrence, in which my opinion may be sought." But Monroe remained uneasy, despite Mason's lengthy argument. He felt that the northern states and the national government would need to support any decision to emancipate and colonize slaves—presumably by helping to finance the undertaking. The animosity of the debate over Missouri, however, made him doubtful about allowing the northerners a role in emancipation, a role that he knew many of his fellow southerners would flatly oppose. He was also aware that an increasing number of southerners were opposed to emancipation in any form. In any case, the abolition of slavery was not a major concern of the convention, which focused more on universal suffrage and tax policy. Emancipation entered the debates only as an adjunct to these other questions. Monroe spoke twice when slavery was being discussed. He never openly advocated emancipation or colonization, but limited his remarks to the general observation that, if Virginia did decide to emancipate its slaves, then they must be sent out of the United States, and that Virginia would need the support of the other states, presumably through the agency of the national government, to do it.[31]

James Monroe died in 1831 without having resolved the question of slavery and emancipation. He maintained his perception of himself as a beneficent patriarch, but he never took the ultimate step of freeing any slaves or arranging for their migration to Liberia, as some of his neighbors did. Economic considerations appear to have remained paramount. Monroe wished to leave his daughters a creditable inheritance, and all he owned was land and slaves. Farms in Virginia were greatly devalued as they were; without slave labor his farm in Loudoun County would have been worthless.

Nor did the nation resolve the question. Quite the contrary, as the proslavery and antislavery advocates became more entrenched in their opinions. Those who sought a middle ground remained perplexed on the matter of how to achieve their goals. Abraham Lincoln wrestled with the same questions regarding the place of freed blacks in American society and the practicality of colonization in the 1850s that Monroe did in the 1820s. Colonization itself, as is well known, never took hold. Some slave owners manumitted their slaves and provided for their passage to Africa, but a large-scale national movement never occurred, as slave owners became increasingly opposed to any form of national or state emancipation. And very few free blacks were willing to leave their homes and communities to resettle in Africa. Monroe's worst fear came to pass when slavery divided his beloved Union into warring sections. And as he possibly foresaw, abolition came only when, the slave owners having failed to act for themselves, the national government imposed emancipation on a recalcitrant South.

Notes

1. Speech to the Society of the Cincinnati, July 4, 1817, in Daniel Preston, ed., *The Papers of James Monroe* (Santa Barbara, Calif.: ABC-CLO, 2011), vol. 1: 204.

2. Robert McColley, *Slavery and Jeffersonian Virginia* (Urbana: University of Illinois Press, 1964); Peter S. Onuf, *The Mind of Thomas Jefferson* (Richmond: University of Virginia Press, 2007); David Brion Davis, *The Problem of Slavery in the Age of Revolution* (New York: Oxford University Press, 1999).

3. Monroe to Thomas Jefferson, September 15, 1800, *Papers of James Monroe* 4: 410.

4. Ibid.; Monroe to Larkin Smith and Richard Kennon, December 5, 1800, *Papers of*

James Monroe 4: 450; Douglas R. Egerton, *Gabriel's Rebellion: The Virginia Slave Conspiracies of 1800 and 1802* (Chapel Hill: University of North Carolina Press, 1993), 147–50.

5. Thomas Jefferson, *Notes on the State of Virginia,* ed. William Peden (rpt. New York: W. W. Norton, 1996) 137–38; Monroe to Jefferson, January 19, 1786, *Papers of James Monroe* 2: 265; Ferdinando Fairfax, "Plan for Liberating the Negroes within the United States," *American Museum,* December 1790, 285–87.

6. St. George Tucker, *A Dissertation on Slavery: With a Proposal for the Gradual Abolition of It, in the State of Virginia* (Philadelphia: Mathew Cary, 1796). Tucker submitted his plan to the Virginia assembly, but the legislators rejected it. Phillip Hamilton, *The Making and Unmaking of a Revolutionary Family: The Tuckers of Virginia, 1752–1830* (Charlottesville: University Press of Virginia, 2008), 80–83.

7. Egerton, *Gabriel's Rebellion,* 151–55. Monroe to Jefferson, June 15, 1801; Jefferson to Monroe, November 24, 1810; Monroe to Larkin Smith and Richard Kennon, December 21, 1801, *Papers of James Monroe* 4: 522–23, 542–44, 556; see also 552–53, 555, 575.

8. Egerton, *Gabriel's Rebellion,* 154–61. Egerton argues that Monroe and Jefferson lost faith in the project and abandoned it.

9. Egerton, *Gabriel's Rebellion,* 163–67.

10. James Monroe, Bill of Complaint, October 31, 1810, Charlottesville, Va., Circuit Court Record; Monroe to Charles Everett, April 25, 1812, *Tyler's Quarterly Historical and Genealogical Magazine* 4 (1923): 107.

11. Monroe to Fulwar Skipwith, October 9, 1810, James Monroe Papers, Manuscript Division, New York Public Library; Monroe to Charles Fenton Mercer, July 15, 1816, James Monroe Papers, Special Collections, College of William & Mary; Monroe to James Madison, March 28, 1828, James Madison Papers, Manuscript Division, Library of Congress.

12. Thomas Slaughter to Monroe, February 19 and April 10, 1817, James Monroe Museum, Fredericksburg, Va.

13. Monroe to Thomas Newton, February 11, 1801, *Papers of James Monroe* 4: 477; Monroe to William Wilberforce, February 13, 1807, Wilberforce Collection, Bodleian Library, Oxford University. The British law for the permanent abolition of the transatlantic slave trade within the British Empire received the king's assent on March 25, 1807. The American law was enacted on March 2, 1807.

14. Douglas Egerton, *Charles Fenton Mercer and the Trial of National Conservatism* (Jackson: University Press of Mississippi, 1989), 105–12; Eric Burin, *Slavery and the Peculiar Solution: A History of the American Colonization Society* (Gainesville: University Press of Florida, 2005), 13–15; Robert Pierce Forbes, *The Missouri Compromise and Its Aftermath: Slavery and the Meaning of America* (Chapel Hill: University of North Carolina Press, 2007), 26–32.

15. Egerton, *Charles Fenton Mercer,* 164–73; Benjamin Homans to Monroe, October 9, 1819, Monroe Papers, Manuscript Division, Library of Congress; John Mason, Francis Scott Key, and Elias Caldwell, to Monroe, October 23, 1819, and Caldwell to Monroe, December 13, 1819, Monroe Papers, New York Public Library; Monroe to the Senate and the House of Representatives, December 17, 1819, in James D. Richardson, ed., *A Compilation of the Messages and Papers of the Presidents, 1789–1897* (Washington, D.C.: Published by Authority of Congress), vol. 2: 63–65.

16. Egerton, *Charles Fenton Mercer,* 179–81.

17. Article 24 of the 1806 treaty reads: "The high contracting parties engage to communicate to each other, without delay, all such laws as have been or shall be hereafter enacted by their respective Legislatures, as also all measures which shall have been taken for the abolition or limitation of the African slave trade; and they further agree to use their best endeavors to procure the co-operation of other Powers for the final and complete abolition of a trade so repugnant to the principles of justice and humanity." Article 10 of the 1814 treaty is similar: "Whereas the traffic in slaves is irreconcilable with the principles of humanity and justice; and whereas both his Majesty and the United States are desirous of continuing their efforts to promote its entire abolition, it is hereby agreed that both contracting parties shall use their best endeavors to accomplish so desirable an object" (*American State Papers: Foreign Affairs* 3: 151, 748, https://memory.loc.gov/ammem/amlaw/lwsplink.html).

18. Egerton, *Charles Fenton Mercer*, 179–92; Harry Ammon, *James Monroe: The Quest for National Identity* (Charlottesville: University of Virginia Press, 1990), 520–27; Samuel Flagg Bemis, *John Quincy Adams and the Foundations of American Foreign Policy* (New York: Random House, 1949), 423–35.

19. Monroe to the Senate and the House of Representatives, December 2, 1823, in Richardson, ed., *Messages and Papers of the Presidents* 2: 210.

20. *Papers of James Monroe* 1: 281.

21. Monroe to Jefferson, February 19, 1820, Thomas Jefferson Papers, Manuscript Division, Library of Congress.

22. See, for example, Glover Moore, *The Missouri Controversy, 1819–1821* (Lexington: University of Kentucky Press, 1966).

23. Forbes, *The Missouri Compromise and Its Aftermath*, 33–120; Ammon, *James Monroe*, 449–58. Monroe wrote a two-part letter, dated February 12 and 13, 1820, that was published in the Richmond, Virginia, *Enquirer* on February 17, 1820, under the heading "A Gentleman in Washington." For an overview of Monroe's correspondence on the controversy and compromise, see Daniel Preston, *A Comprehensive Catalogue of the Correspondence and Papers of James Monroe* (Westport, Conn.: Greenwood Press, 2000), vol. 2: 773, 775, 777–781.

24. Philip Slaughter, *The Virginian History of African Colonization* (Miami: Hard Press Publishing, 1989), 10.

25. Egerton, *Charles Fenton Mercer*, 107–8.

26. Monroe remarked to John Quincy Adams in March 1819 that the free blacks in the United States were a "very dangerous people" and that many of them lived by "pilfering" (qtd. in Egerton, *Charles Fenton Mercer*, 169).

27. Bernard W. Sheehan, *Seeds of Extinction: Jeffersonian Philanthropy and the American Indian* (Chapel Hill: University of North Carolina Press, 1973; rpt. 2011); Ammon, *James Monroe*, 536–37; Monroe to the Senate and the House of Representatives, November 16, 1818, in Richardson, ed., *Messages and Papers of the President* 2: 46.

28. Slaughter, *The Virginian History of African Colonization*, 13, 19.

29. Monroe to John Mason, August 31, 1829, Monroe Papers, New York Public Library.

30. Mason to Monroe, September 24, 1829, Monroe Papers, New York Public Library.

31. Monroe addressed the convention on November 2 and 4, 1829 (*Proceedings of the Virginia State Convention of 1829-30* [Richmond, 1830], 148–51, 172–74).

7

The Missouri Crisis and the "Changed Object" of the American Colonization Society

NICHOLAS P. WOOD

The political influence of the American Colonization Society (ACS) peaked in March 1819, with the passage of a new slave-trade law providing funding for settling "recaptured" Africans, confiscated from slave smugglers, on the West Coast of Africa. The leaders of the ACS saw the 1819 law as merely the initial step in making colonization a national program, anticipating that in time the federal government would fund the voluntary expatriation of many free black Americans and manumitted slaves as well. However, African colonization never became a government program to the extent the ACS leadership had hoped.

In the 1820s and 1830s, the ACS program became increasingly controversial and Congress rejected colonizationists' future appeals for greater federal aid. Some scholars have suggested that Congress passed the 1819 Slave Trade Act only because southerners were unaware of its connection to the ACS.[1] However, it is likely that this interpretation exaggerates the level of initial southern hostility to the ACS without appreciating the extent to which other events in 1819—especially the Missouri Crisis—destroyed the cross-sectional trust essential for a federal colonization program.

Like many compromises, the Missouri Compromise left both sides feeling bitter and believing the other had gotten the better deal. Discontented northerners and southerners imputed the worst possible motives to the other side. The fact that southern members of the ACS had defended slavery in Missouri seemed to confirm the suspicions held by some abolitionists and free people of color that the ACS had always been a scheme to strengthen slavery. By contrast, many white southerners dismissed northern professions of antislavery sentiment during the Missouri debates as cover for an economic agenda that sought to restrict slavery for self-interested rather than humanitarian motives. Others concluded that the ACS had been hijacked by fanatical abolitionists and could no longer be trusted. Thus in the ensuing years, the ACS was attacked on all sides, charged with being proslavery by some and abolitionist by others.

In this altered political climate, cross-sectional support for the ACS in Congress collapsed. During the rest of the antebellum period, colonizationists were unable to mobilize a congressional majority in favor of greater federal support. Outside of Congress, colonization retained some of its popularity, but the ACS came to function in a very different way than initially intended. Instead of becoming a large federally backed program, the ACS remained dependent on private funds and was superseded in importance by a decentralized network of auxiliary societies. Operating with a great deal of independence, sometimes even running separate African colonies, the auxiliary societies were able to avoid much of the political tension that hindered the ACS's initial plan.

The ACS Agenda

In the 1810s the vast majority of white Americans were not galvanized into proslavery and antislavery positions, and the chief supporters of the ACS viewed the seemingly paradoxical goals of strengthening slavery in the short term and promoting eventual emancipation as not only compatible but inseparable. Furthermore, while few ACS leaders desired or expected the rapid eradication of slavery, they believed that colonization would help ameliorate the conditions of slavery and reduce slave trading.

John Randolph of Roanoke, a Virginia congressman and founding member of the society, was fairly representative of the ACS position, eluding classification as proslavery or abolitionist. At the formation of the ACS, Randolph asserted that the society would "not in any wise affect the question of negro slavery, but, as far as it goes, must materially tend to secure the property of every master in the United States over his slaves." He explained that he went to such length to disavow abolitionism in order to "obtain the co-operation of all the citizens of the United States." Yet Randolph also endorsed the "higher and nobler motives" of atoning for the evils of the slave trade by spreading Christianity in Africa, and claimed there were "thousands of citizens" who would manumit their slaves if they could be sent to Africa.[2]

Charles Fenton Mercer, the Virginian who inspired the creation of the ACS, held similar views. He complained about the influence free black "banditti" had on slaves, promising that colonization would "render the slave who remains in America more obedient, more fruitful, more honest, and, consequently, more useful to his master." But Mercer also believed colonization would "afford every facility to emancipation, when the colonization of the slave will be the consequence of his liberation."[3] The promise of freedom in Africa would encourage good behavior among slaves in the meantime.

Furthermore, ACS members argued that colonization would help reduce the domestic slave trade within the nation and help suppress the Atlantic slave trade. Congress had banned the Atlantic slave trade as of 1808, though Americans remained involved in the illicit trade, especially to Cuba and Brazil. Moreover, each year slaveholders and slave traders sold tens of thousands of slaves domestically, generally transporting them from the older slave states to the Southwest. Americans widely recognized this traffic as the most reprehensible component of slavery for the way it tore families apart. In 1816, John Randolph led a congressional investigation into the conditions of the domestic slave trade in Washington, D.C. He denounced the trade as "a crying sin before God and man" but also vowed not to interfere "in the very delicate subject of the relation between the slave and his owner." In 1818 he wrote to an abolitionist correspondent: "If any thing would reconcile me to a consolidation of the States it would be the placing of a power where it might be exercised of stifling the Slave trade domestic as well as foreign."[4] Recognizing the ways that African colonization promised to reduce slave trading—rather than directly promoting emancipation—helps explain the support that many slaveholders initially extended to the society.

Colonization presented a method for reducing both the domestic and Atlantic slave trades without infringing on states' rights or individual property rights. Slaveholders who wanted to extricate themselves from the institution could manumit and colonize their slaves without undermining the social order or resorting to the domestic slave trade. Meanwhile an American colony in Africa could serve as a base for naval ships suppressing the Atlantic slave trade and could also help "civilize" the continent and encourage peaceful forms of legitimate commerce. Indeed, this was how the British used their Sierra Leone colony. As one early ACS publication explained, "the connexion of this subject with the object of the American [Colonization] Society is very intimate. If Africa is ever civilized, the slave trade must cease. If Africa is ever colonized, the slave trade *will* cease, at least in the vicinity of the colonies." In sum, colonizationists promised "the more complete abolition of the slave trade, the elevation of the free people of colour in this country, and the improvement of the condition of the African tribes who may come within our influence."[5] These goals had broad appeal across partisan and sectional lines, seeking to ameliorate many of the worst features of slavery without threatening radical social change or violating property rights.

From the start, ACS members recognized that the vast costs involved would make colonization dependent on federal funding. As Elias B. Caldwell stated at the first meeting, "it is a great national object, and ought to be supported by a national purse." Less than a month later, John Randolph delivered the first ACS petition to Congress on January 14, 1817. Introducing the petition, Randolph "pray[ed] that Congress will aid with the power, the patronage, and the resources of the country, the great and beneficial object of their institution." The petition described the problems created by "the existence of distinct and separate castes" of free people of color, which in turn forced slaveholding states "to impose restraints upon the practice of emancipation." Praising Congress for abolishing the "abominable traffic" in slaves from Africa, the petitioners portrayed colonization as a panacea that would benefit white Americans, slaves, free people of color, and the inhabitants of Africa. The House of Representatives voted to refer the petition to its Slave Trade Committee, which also received petitions from abolitionists and Quakers callings for laws to protect free African Americans from being kidnapped and sold in the domestic slave trade as well as for revisions to the 1807 Slave Trade Act.[6]

The Slave Trade Committee endorsed the concept of colonization in its report issued on February 11, 1817. The report and resolution, authored by Federalist Timothy Pickering of Massachusetts, advised that the most cost effective method would be an arrangement with the British to permit the transportation of willing African Americans to Sierra Leone. However, the report suggested that, if the British declined, "the design of a separate colony might be announced, by the American ministers, to the maritime powers, and their guarantee of neutrality of the colony obtained." The House passed a resolution instructing President James Monroe to pursue such an agreement with Great Britain. In response, the ACS organized an expedition to meet with British officials and colonizationists and then visit Sierra Leone and the African coast. The ACS also established auxiliary societies to demonstrate public support for colonization. Published ACS correspondence predicted "that the general government would soon take up the measure, and that it was only required of individuals and societies to make a commencement—to give an impulse to public feeling."[7]

Some of the largest demonstrations of support for the ACS came from the state of Georgia. In May 1817, an editorial in the *Savannah Republican* defended colonization against charges that the scheme was impractical, while making it clear the goal was getting rid of free people of color and not slavery. Refuting the opinion that sending African Americans to Sierra Leone would strengthen the British Empire, the writer responded: "In fact, it disburthens us of the non-productive part of our population—affords a receptacle for the filth and offals of society."[8]

Support for the ACS in Georgia was not confined to removing free blacks; Georgians also connected African colonization to the suppression of the Atlantic slave trade. Under the federal Slave Trade Act of 1807, states were given control over the "disposal" of recaptured Africans, and most southern states chose to sell them as they would other contraband goods. In November 1817, the Georgia legislature modified its corresponding statute. The new law still allowed the state to sell such recaptured Africans as slaves but also included a provision authorizing the governor to turn them over to the ACS if the society would assume the cost to "transport them to Africa, or any other foreign place."[9] This was a major demonstration of support, especially coming from the Lower South.

The ACS and the 1819 Slave Trade Law

The 1819 Slave Trade Law was the culmination of ACS lobbying, which had begun with their petition in January 1817. Throughout this time, congressmen who were also ACS members, such as Charles Fenton Mercer and Henry Clay, made no effort to hide the extent of their efforts to achieve federal funding. During the congressional session of 1817–18, Mercer headed a House committee that received petitions from auxiliary colonization societies in Kentucky, Virginia, North Carolina, and Tennessee.[10]

Meanwhile, the ACS held its January 1818 meeting in the House of Representatives and published accounts of the speeches by Mercer and Clay and others in newspapers and in pamphlet form.[11] Three months later, Mercer issued a congressional report encouraging new legislation to combine the suppression of the Atlantic slave trade with a program for colonizing free African Americans. He denounced the slave trade as "the scourge of Africa, and the affliction and disgrace of America." He also complained of the mechanism for disposing of recaptured Africans under the 1807 Slave Trade law, and indicated that the federal government should instead send them to an African colony. In addition to establishing an African colony, Mercer proposed sending additional naval vessels to patrol the African coast. The report concluded with a resolution requesting the president "to ascertain whether a suitable territory can be procured on the coast of Africa, for colonizing such of the free people of the United States as may be willing to avail themselves of such an asylum."[12] Mercer's congressional committee report made it explicitly clear that he hoped the federal government would directly embrace the ACS's project of establishing an African colony in order to suppress the Atlantic slave trade and provide an asylum for free African Americans. Mercer delayed presenting his report because Congress had recently passed the 1818 Slave Trade Act, in response to smuggling off the coast of Spanish Florida, and passing a second slave trade law that session was unlikely.

When Congress considered colonization in the following session, the connections between Mercer, the ACS, and the new slave trade bill were clear for all to see. On November 26, 1818, the colonization report was printed for the House of Representatives at the request of South Carolinian Henry Middleton, head of the House's Slave Trade Committee.[13] On January 4, 1819, the House of Representatives passed two resolutions authored by Mercer, requesting information about slave trade violations and calling for a new slave trade bill that would prevent recaptured Africans from being "condemned to hereditary slavery" as permitted by the laws of 1807 and 1818. Five days later, at the annual ACS meeting, Mercer told his fellow colonizationists of his confidence that their society would soon be "nourished by the resources, as well as countenanced by the authority of the Federal Government." At the same ACS meeting, Henry Clay, acting in his role as a vice-president of the ACS, oversaw the creation of a colonizationist petition addressed to himself in his role as the Speaker of the House of Representatives. Far from attempting to keep the incestuous relationship of the ACS and Congress secret, the colonizationists published an account of their proceedings in the *National Intelligencer,* the mouthpiece of the Monroe administration.[14]

The public connection between the slave trade bill and the ACS was further reinforced on January 23 when Clay presented the ACS's petition and its *Second Annual Report* to the House of Representatives. The petition expressed the colonizationists' hopes that their program would be "adopted and patronized by the Government, so as to become essentially national in its means and its objects." The ACS's *Second Annual Report* clearly referred to the pending slave trade bill, arguing that the best method of dealing with recaptured Africans would be "their colonization upon the western Coast of Africa, in conjunction with the free people of colour of the United States, who may voluntarily seek the same asylum." The report also recounted the expedition of ACS agents to London and West Africa, praising the way the Sierra Leone colony facilitated British efforts to suppress the slave trade. The ACS reported that territory in West Africa could be cheaply acquired, but that an American colony could only be successful if "nourished by the resources, as well as countenanced by the authority of the Federal Government."[15]

Congressional consideration of the slave trade bill and ACS materials were delayed, in part because of other pressing matters, including James Tallmadge's proposals to restrict slavery in Missouri. On February 13, Tallmadge proposed requiring the Missouri Territory to enact a program of gradual emancipation before entering the Union as a state. After three days of debate the House passed the Tallmadge amendment, but the Senate rejected it, leaving the issue unresolved until the next session.[16]

During the first round of the Missouri debates, Henry Clay's defense of slavery in Missouri opened the ACS up to charges of hypocrisy. Whereas Clay and other slave-state representatives emphasized that Missourians had a constitutional right to enter the Union with slavery intact, northern "restrictionists" framed the question in moral terms. They equated the defense of slavery in Missouri with support for the domestic slave trade, a position that appeared antithetical to colonization. Timothy Fuller, a Massachusetts Republican, observed that the ACS was the "favorite of the humane gentlemen in the slave-holding states," but argued that the domestic slave trade to Missouri would "tempt the cupidity of those who otherwise perhaps might gradually emancipate their slaves" and thus "render abortive the generous and philanthropic views of this most worthy and laudable society."[17]

Arthur Livermore, a Republican from New Hampshire, said that defending slavery's expansion belied slaveholders' alleged regret for slavery: "Let us no longer tell idle tales about the gradual abolition of slavery; away with colonization societies, if their design is only to rid us of free blacks and turbulent slaves." In this view, southern support for colonization and suppressing the Atlantic slave trade were cynical ploys calculated to boost the security and profits of slavery and domestic slave trading. Livermore even suggested that the true purpose of the 1819 slave trade bill was "to prevent the glutting of a prodigious market for the flesh and blood of man, which we are about to establish in the west, and to enhance the price of sturdy wenches, reared like black cattle and horses for sale on our own plantations."[18] Such characterizations were extreme and did not seriously threaten the prospects of the new slave trade bill.

In fact, the overall effect of the initial Missouri debates may have been to increase support for the slave trade bill. Southerners who defended Missouri's right to enter as a slave state claimed they were motivated by constitutional concerns, not a commitment to slavery. Supporting the new slave trade law allowed southerners to demonstrate their willingness to use proper constitutional powers against slavery. In any event, Mercer reported that by March 1 the bill "had made so many friends, that a motion was prevailed, to postpone all prior orders of the day" and discuss the bill.[19]

When the House debated the 1819 slave trade bill, there could have been little doubt about its connection with Mercer and the ACS. Although Henry Middleton formally presented the bill as head of the Slave Trade Committee, the reporters in Congress stated: "Mr. Mercer supported the bill throughout, explaining and defending its provisions against all objections." Little of the surrounding debate was recorded, but it appears that the main objections concerned the loss of revenue and financial incentives to suppress the slave trade resulting from the colonization of recaptured Africans rather than their sale by state authorities. Reporters characterized the objections as based on "various reasons of expediency, and not from an unwillingness to destroy the traffic and kidnapping, &c., of slaves." The final version of the law passed by the House and Senate was nearly identical to the initial bill drafted by Mercer and the Slave Trade Committee.[20]

Immediately after the law's passage, Mercer and others from the ACS lobbied President James Monroe, encouraging him to interpret the law as liberally as possible in terms of its connection to colonization. Mercer later reported that Monroe was willing to go "to any length to aid us, in forming a colony of our free people of colour, short of an immediate purchase of territory." Not all of Monroe's cabinet was enthusiastic about the prospect of federal support for colonization. Secretary of State John Quincy Adams of Massachusetts expressed the greatest opposition, whereas Treasury Secretary William Crawford of Georgia—a vice-president of the ACS—was the most enthusiastic. Adams recorded in his diary that Crawford had privately admitted "he has no faith in the practicality" of colonization, and concluded that the Georgian's involvement was "one of his traps for popularity."[21]

Crawford was a shrewd politician with presidential ambitions, and his support for the ACS may have been calculated to appeal to northern critics of slavery. However, he would not have supported the ACS and the broad construction of the 1819 Slave Trade Act if he believed such a position would alienate his southern base. Indeed, when President Monroe visited Athens, Georgia, as part of a southern tour in May, locals feted him with toasts, including "*The Colonization Society*—Planned by the wisest heads and purest hearts. May it eventuate in the happiness of millions" and "*The Slave Trade*—The scourge of Africa; the disgrace of humanity. May it cease forever, and may the voice of peace, of Christianity and of civilization, be heard on the savage shores."[22] Developments over the rest of 1819, however, rendered African colonization decidedly less popular in Crawford's native state and throughout the South.

The Decline of ACS Support in the South

When the Fifteenth Congress disbanded in March 1819, it had left the "Missouri question" unresolved, but newspapers and public meetings kept the issue alive throughout the summer. Increased northern antislavery agitation heightened white southerners' sensitivity in matters relating to slavery and the expansion of federal power. In addition, the economic Panic of 1819 and the nationalistic Supreme Court ruling in *McCulloch v. Maryland* further increased southern agriculturalists' concern about federal consolidation.[23] In the midst of this intensifying atmosphere, the ACS undertook a controversial mission in Georgia.

After the passage of the 1819 Slave Trade Act, ACS members hoped the federal government would use some of its appropriation to colonize the recaptured Africans who had been confiscated in Georgia the year before. When Monroe's cabinet determined the law could not be applied retroactively, the ACS decided to act on its own, sending one of its board members, the Reverend William Meade, to Georgia.[24] As per the 1817 state law, the slaves were to be sold at auction unless the ACS could coordinate and fund their transportation out of the United States.

Meade, an evangelical Virginian slaveholder, met a decidedly mixed response as he traveled to Georgia. In some places he successfully increased awareness and support for colonization by establishing auxiliary societies and raising funds, but he also provoked some concerns by showing too much sympathy for the slaves. In May of 1819, in a letter reprinted by the ACS, Meade wrote that on the faces of the Africans he "could see written these memorable words: 'Am I not a man and a brother?'" This standard slogan of British abolitionism and Meade's sympathy for "this unfortunate race" would have raised eyebrows among slaveholders at any time, but following the Tallmadge amendment debates, Meade's words could appear as part of a growing assault on slavery.[25]

Slaveholders soon began accusing the ACS of switching from an acceptable purpose—ridding the nation of free people of color—to an unacceptable one—ridding the nation of slaves. The pages of the *National Intelligencer* reveal the contours of this debate, and the increasingly unavoidable connections between colonization and the restrictionist effort in Congress. Early in July 1819, "Limner," from Georgia, charged that the Reverend Meade's actions demonstrated "the *changed* object of the Society." The ACS had apparently switched from "at first contemplating the colonization of the *free* people of color only" to "premeditating the emancipation of all blacks."[26] While "Limner" complained that the ACS was becoming abolitionist, "Benjamin Rush" celebrated the ACS's emancipationist potential.

"Benjamin Rush"—actually abolitionist Robert J. Evans of Philadelphia—hoped that the federal government would fund a national program of colonization to an extent "sufficient to induce the master, as well as the slave to concur in it." He also promised that because slavery was a national problem, the North would be happy to contribute to its solution. Evans suggested that the sale of public lands in the West could finance the estimated $600 million required for compensated emancipation and colonization. He acknowledged that the constitutionality of such an act could be questionable, but he optimistically noted that constitutional amendments could supply "whatever may be the defect of the existing powers of Congress." In response, "Limner" concluded: "It is now sufficiently developed by the everlasting writing of Benjamin Rush, and other modern advocates of the Colonization Society, that its founders have been abused by the changing of their object to the abolition of slavery."[27] The editors of the *National Intelligencer* supported the ACS but not abolitionism and felt obligated to clarify that they disavowed the opinions of both "Limner" and "Benjamin Rush," but allowed them the use of their pages as a public forum.

Although the ACS did seek federal patronage and spoke of facilitating eventual emancipation, support from people like Evans proved counterproductive. Evans viewed colonization as an active form of gradual abolition, whereas the ACS founders envisioned it only as a precursor to possible gradual abolition in an unspecified future. The editors of the *National Intelligencer* clarified that the ACS's "incidental operations" might promote the "mitigation" of slavery and "make the manumission of slaves less objectionable," but the "direct object of the Society is to separate the casts [*sic*] of

Black and White" rather than promote abolition. Meanwhile, Evans raised the fear, foreshadowed by "Limner," of a loss of slaveholder control over federally supported colonization. Proposing a constitutional amendment expanding the federal government's power over slavery would be controversial at any time, but especially during the Missouri Crisis, when many southerners felt northerners were "using slavery as an instrument for effecting a balance of power," as John Taylor of Carolina argued.[28]

Furthermore, in November Evans began to connect colonization directly to the Missouri question. He called on all northern congressmen to act in unison to prevent the spread of slavery, and hoped southerners would support restriction as well.[29] This was the opposite of the view held by the founders of the ACS, who recognized slaveholders would tolerate federally run colonization only if they felt confident it would not be used by non-slaveholders as a political tool. Evans's talk of "inducing" masters to free their slaves and connecting colonization to restriction was sure to alarm slaveholders during this time of heightened sectional tension. Even though Evans was not officially connected to the ACS (as he acknowledged in his essays), he presented the specter of what colonization could become if backed by a federal government controlled by a free-state majority.

The Missouri Crisis and African Colonization

Just as the Missouri Crisis shaped public debates over the ACS, ideas about African colonization also influenced how Congress debated the proposed restriction of slavery in Missouri and other federal territories. At one level, the dispute was all the more jarring because the initial popularity of the ACS had heightened expectations of sectional cooperation in regard to slavery. In the midst of the controversy, the ACS continued petitioning for federal funding and advocating colonization as the most responsible and pragmatic method of dealing with the problem of slavery; but congressmen unaffiliated with the ACS drew on the rhetoric of colonization in ways that eroded support for the society. Northern congressmen's use of broad construction and sectional majorities provoked a resurgence of states' rights sentiment in the South. All of these developments undermined the foundations necessary for increased federal support of the ACS.

Some southern congressmen invoked colonization in ways that could only increase suspicions among African Americans and white northerners sympathetic to abolitionism. Alexander Smyth of Virginia took an extreme stance against any restriction on slavery's expansion, whereas Clay and Mercer defended slavery in Missouri while supporting a compromise restricting slavery in parts of the remaining federal territories. Nonetheless Smyth was unwilling to abandon a symbolically antislavery posture, praising the "diffusion" of slavery as well as colonization: "Let the enslaved blacks be dispersed as much as possible; their situation will become more comfortable, and their chances of being emancipated will become greater; and, as they are emancipated, let them immediately be sent to the colony. For these purposes, let there be a rich colonization fund." Whereas the ACS always emphasized the importance of black consent, Smyth implied that he was unconcerned with such niceties.[30] Although Smyth was unaffiliated with the ACS, such sentiments conformed to northern suspicions that colonization was merely a scheme to strengthen slavery.

The position of the ACS leadership remained largely consistent throughout this time. At the annual meeting in January 1820, ACS president and Supreme Court Justice Bushrod Washington oversaw the creation of another petition requesting federal funding. Referring to the 1819 Slave Trade Law, the petition argued that the best way to establish a settlement for recaptured Africans would be the creation of an American colony in Africa, which would also provide a refuge for free people of color who chose to emigrate there. ACS member John Randolph submitted the petition to Congress on February 3, 1820, the day after giving a three-hour speech against the restriction of slavery, which he viewed as unconstitutional.[31]

Whereas the ACS petition essentially reiterated the type of moderate requests they had been making since 1817, a much more expansive program of colonization was proposed by Henry Meigs, a New York Republican unaffiliated with the ACS. Meigs was one of the small minority of northerners, subsequently known as "doughfaces," who ultimately voted with the South against restricting slavery in Missouri. On January 26, 1820, Meigs explained his unpopular decision to break with the instructions from the New York legislature and vote against restriction in Missouri. Observing that "reason and logic" in Congress appeared to divide starkly along the geographical division of slave and free states, Meigs eschewed constitutional hermeneutics and abstract arguments, focusing instead on practical considerations. He argued that concentrating on slavery in Missouri would do little to undermine slavery as an institution and warned that sectional discord imperiled the Union. Instead of squabbling over a single state, Meigs hoped a program of federal funding for the "emancipation and colonization of the unfortunate slaves" could unite the people in "the redemption of a nation."[32] On February 7, Meigs described slavery as "an enormous evil" and hoped that colonization would restore enslaved blacks to "that equal grade in the scale of beings for which Providence had formed them." But he made it clear that he was even more concerned with slavery's negative political impact. Sectional controversy posed a grave threat to the future of the republic, and by ending slavery they could "remove the subject of complaint." He told Congress that he had "become convinced that the Colonization Society had pointed to the only method of accomplishing this grand object." He hoped Congress would use the proceeds of federal land sales to finance the compensated emancipation and colonization of the nation's slaves, and thus remove the nation's greatest source of political conflict. However, the House rejected his motion by a vote of seventy-eight to sixty-six.[33]

The votes on Meigs's resolutions were not roll-call votes, so the sectional breakdown cannot be determined, and the reactions of Clay, Mercer, and other ACS members are unknown. Most of them almost certainly feared Meigs's plan was too ambitious and provocative. The ACS petition which John Randolph had submitted was much more cautious in its reference to the potential for the "gradual, and almost imperceptible, removal of a national evil."[34] Like Robert Evans's "Benjamin Rush" writings, Meigs's resolutions likely fueled white southerners' concerns that colonization was too potentially dangerous to be entrusted to the federal government.

The Missouri Crisis debates over constitutional interpretation were at least as damaging to the ACS's desire for increased federal support as the specific references to colonization in the course of debates. Northern restrictionists embraced a doctrine of broad construction that was anathema to the cross-sectional trust needed for a national program of African colonization. Throughout the debates, southerners emphasized constitutional concerns in their opposition to the proposed ban on slavery in Missouri.

The final version of the Missouri Compromise permitted slavery in Missouri while banning it in most of the remaining Louisiana Purchase Territory (north of latitude 36°30'). Even then nearly all northerners voted to ban slavery in Missouri.[35] Many white southerners perceived this example of northern intransigence as disregard for the U.S. Constitution and a willingness to cynically exploit antislavery sentiment among the northern public in pursuit of a power grab and a sectional economic agenda. The states' rights reaction against restriction and broad construction foreclosed the possibility of increased congressional support for the ACS, at least for the time being, as Brandon Mills will illustrate in the next chapter.

Conclusion

By 1820, colonizationists found themselves attacked from all sides. As one from Virginia complained: "some have falsely charged us with wishing to rivet more strongly the fetters of slavery by removing the free persons of colour; while others, with no less absurdity, have accused us of an intention to emancipate all the slaves by a compulsory process equally repugnant to our wishes and transcending our authority."[36] The Missouri Crisis created or confirmed opposition to the ACS from a diverse range of Americans.

Black Philadelphians had protested against the ACS in 1817, and the Missouri Crisis increased their suspicion of the organization. In a published statement they asserted: "the recent attempt to introduce slavery, in all its objectionable features, into the new states . . . confirms us in the belief, that any plan of colonization without the American continent or islands, will completely and permanently fix slavery in our common country." White abolitionist Roberts Vaux drew the same lesson, pointing to the Missouri Crisis as proof "that the plan of colonizing the blacks in Africa, was a hypocritical measure, proceeding from a quarter utterly destitute of any *good feelings* toward that abused race."[37]

Meanwhile, some prominent early supporters of the ACS turned against it. John Randolph believed that the restrictionist effort in Congress had been led by "unprincipled . . . ambitious men, availing themselves a good as well as fanatical spirit in the nation." Although he continued to sympathize with antislavery as an ideal, he believed that the federal government could not be trusted with such delicate matters, and he refused to submit ACS petitions to Congress in the future. Timothy Pickering, who had authored the 1817 congressional report endorsing colonization also turned against the ACS. In response to the Missouri Crisis, he wrote that the only inference that could be drawn from slaveholder support for the ACS was "that they considered it as the best and perhaps only means of ridding themselves of troublesome and dangerous inmates. . . . After which, *the chains of their slaves would be forever invincibly riveted.*" He noted that this had been the fear expressed by the "people of color in Philadelphia, in protesting against the colonization plan," and concluded that they had been correct.[38]

The ACS had never been about perpetuating slavery, nor had it changed its goals; its annual reports continued stressing its commitment to improving the conditions of free people of color and the continent of Africa, curtailing the slave trades, and promoting the eventual extinction of slavery without violating the rights of states or slaveholders. But the changing political circumstances changed the means by which the ACS pursued its goals. Although the ACS continued to receive aid and subsidies in connection with the 1819 Slave Trade Act, the hope of greater federal funding was repeatedly rebuffed by Congress.[39]

After failing to gain more federal support in 1820, the ACS focused on building up its auxiliary societies for a number of years, but the desire for federal funds did not end. In 1823, Mercer wrote, "In the next Congress we shall try our strength in an effort to obtain further aid from the Federal Government." Yet, at the ACS meeting the following year, Mercer discouraged petitioning the federal government. He suggested that those advocating another petition "overrate the amount of our moral influence in society," and predicted they would "be met with the charge of enthusiasm." Mercer was correct; the next year witnessed an organized newspaper assault on the ACS in the *Richmond Enquirer*. Beginning in August of 1825, John White Nash, writing as "Caius Gracchus," denounced colonization in a series of letters addressed to the local ACS auxiliary, the national ACS, and the ACS president, Bushrod Washington. Echoing the earlier accusation of "Limner," Nash charged that the ACS had changed into an abolitionist society. ACS board member William Fitzhugh responded as "Opimius," defending colonization.[40]

The battle which ensued in the pages of the *Richmond Enquirer* over the coming year demonstrates how much of the ACS's perspective had become outdated and politically untenable by the mid-1820s. Attempting to prove "that the original objects of your Association have been changed," Nash emphasized the ACS's initial proslavery bona fides and contrasted them with a speech from the 1820 ACS meeting that mentioned one benefit of colonization as tending "to rid us gradually and entirely in the United States of slaves and slavery." This abstract support for distant abolition had once been typical among slaveholders, but by 1825 such previously mild rhetoric appeared rabidly antislavery. Nash defended slavery as something approaching a positive good. He informed readers that American slaves were better off than European laborers, and that all white people were equal in the South whereas the North had established a form of white slavery based on wealth. Nash described the ACS as inseparably connected to the "wicked" and "unconstitutional" attempts to limit slavery in Missouri, although he did "not have the means of establishing a clear concert and connection between these political movements, and the operations of your Society." In the post–Missouri Crisis era, one was either for slavery or against it in the minds of a growing number of Americans.[41]

Fitzhugh's writings as "Opimius" demonstrate his failure to comprehend the extent to which states' rights fervor and sectional jealousy were ascendant at the time. Although denying any interest in abolition and emphasizing the ACS's commitment to protecting the property of slaveholders, Fitzhugh linked colonization to a host of other galvanizing issues. He gave examples of precedents for broad construction, such as internal improvements, and dismissed constitutional objections to federally funded colonization as "existing only in the imagination of those who suggested them." Furthermore, he cited a recent proposal by Rufus King to use federal land sales to support colonization and compensated emancipation. Although he heaped scorn on free people of color, Fitzhugh also described slavery as "an evil of the darkest character," and expressed outdated optimism about southerners' willingness to abandon the institution. Stating that the negative effects of slavery were "almost universally acknowledged," he naively asserted there was "no riveted attachment to slavery prevailing extensively in any portion of our country." In sum, he linked the ACS to broad construction, a northern politician accused of exploiting slavery for sectional gain, and a desire to abolish the evil institution, even if only gradually and without infringing on property rights.[42] In the charged atmosphere of the 1820s, this must have seemed an admission of guilt rather than a defense. Although Fitzhugh was correct in insisting the ACS's position had remained consistent, he also demonstrated that this stance was no longer politically viable in the South.

In the midst of the *Richmond Enquirer* controversy, ACS member Francis Scott Key asked John Randolph to present another petition to Congress. Randolph gave him a "firm and positive refusal." Like the ACS, Randolph had remained largely consistent during the previous decade. Randolph said he still "wished all the free negroes removed, with their own consent, out of the slave States especially," but dismissed the practicality of colonization. Comparing it to the exodus of the Jews, he said it would require the "miraculous interposition of the hand of God."[43] In the aftermath of sectional and constitutional struggles, Randolph felt colonization was too dangerous, even though he still sympathized with the idea.

In 1828, Virginia's ACS auxiliaries broke with the parent organization to form the independent Virginia Colonization Society (VCS). In 1855 a VCS historian explained their reasons: "There was growing jealousy in the

South of all interference with any question touching the colored race by any person or association without the territory of Virginia, and not identified in principles, interest and sympathy with our people."⁴⁴ Southerners had become convinced that, just like slavery, colonization also had to be protected from outside interference. Under local control, colonization auxiliaries continued to receive significant support in the Upper South.

Somewhat paradoxically, the failure of a national program of colonization may have increased support for colonization among antislavery northerners. Although the first Philadelphia Colonization Society had dissolved shortly after its creation in 1819, white Philadelphians established a new Pennsylvania Colonization Society (PCS) in 1826. Supporters of the PCS even included some, like abolitionist Roberts Vaux, who had previously denounced the ACS as a scheme to strengthen slavery. With greater local control, the PCS was able to direct its efforts to facilitating southern slave manumissions rather than colonizing African Americans who were already free.⁴⁵ Whereas the ACS leaders had initially viewed local auxiliaries' private donations as a temporary measure before receiving federal funding, the colonization movement instead remained largely locally organized and privately funded and could pursue colonization only on a small scale. In the federal government, colonizationists like Charles Fenton Mercer used congressional committees to continue some funding for colonization under the 1819 Slave Trade Law.⁴⁶ But they never convinced a congressional majority to endorse a more active federal program of colonizing black Americans. Of course, whether greater federal support for the ACS would have been good for the nation and American race relations is a separate set of questions.

Notes

1. Douglas R. Egerton, *Charles Fenton Mercer and the Trials of National Conservatism* (Jackson: University Press of Mississippi, 1989), 164; Eric Burin, "The Slave Trade Act of 1819: A New Look at Colonization and the Politics of Slavery," *American Nineteenth Century History* 13 (March 2012): 1–14, esp. 2. While differing with Egerton on aspects of the creation of the 1819 Slave Trade Act and the role of the Missouri Crisis, this essay supports the broader arguments of his "Averting a Crisis: The Proslavery Critique of the American Colonization Society," *Civil War History* 43 (June 1997): 142–56.

2. Nicholas Wood, "John Randolph of Roanoke and the Politics of Slavery," *Virginia Magazine of History and Biography* 120 (Summer 2012): 106–43. The speeches from the first ACS meeting, on December 21, 1816, can be found in: *National Intelligencer* (Washington, D.C.), December 24, 1816; ACS, *A View of Exertions Lately Made for the Purpose*

of Colonizing the Free People of Colour, in the United States, in Africa, or Elsewhere (Washington, D.C.: Jonathon Elliot, 1817).

3. ACS, *Second Annual Report* (Washington, D.C.: Davis and Force, 1819), 9; ACS, *First Annual Report* (Washington, D.C.: D. Rapine, 1818), 16.

4. John Randolph to Thomas P. Cope, September 28, 1818, Society Collection 1816–1830, John Randolph folder, Historical Society of Pennsylvania (HSP). Wood, "John Randolph and the Politics of Slavery," 118–24.

5. Ebenezer Burgess, *Address to the American Society for Colonizing the Free People of Colour of the United States* (Washington, D.C.: Davis and Force, 1818), 12–13.

6. *National Intelligencer,* December 25, 1816; *Annals of Congress, 14th Congress–2nd Session* (hereafter, *AC,* followed by Congress and Session numbers), 481–83; *AC 14-2,* 234–35 (December 4, 1816), 311–12 (December 18, 1816), 442 (January 9, 1817), 639 (January 20, 1817), 769 (January 29, 1817), 842–43 (February 3, 1817).

7. *AC 14-2,* 939–41; Report of Rev. Meade, in *National Intelligencer,* June 24, 1819.

8. Rpt. in *National Intelligencer,* May 5, 1817.

9. Hazel Akehurst, "Sectional Crisis and the Fate of Africans Illegally Imported into the United States, 1806–1860," *American Nineteenth Century History* 9 (June 2008): 97–122; Egerton, *Charles Fenton Mercer,* 163–64.

10. *AC 15-1,* 488 (December 19, 1817), 517–18 (December 30, 1817), 529 (December 31, 1817), 532–33 (January 2, 1818), 799 (January 22, 1818).

11. *National Intelligencer,* January 16, 1818; ACS, *First Annual Report.*

12. *AC 15-1,* 1771–74 (April 18, 1818).

13. Charles Fenton Mercer to John Hartwell Cocke, April 19, 1818, Papers of the Cocke Family, box 26, University of Virginia Special Collections Library; *AC 15-2,* 320 (November 26, 1818).

14. *AC 15-2,* 442 (January 4, 1819); "Second Annual Meeting," Records of the American Colonization Society, Library of Congress (RACS), 67, 77 (January 9, 1819); *National Intelligencer,* January 13, 1819.

15. *AC 15-2,* 721 (January 23, 1819); "Second Annual Meeting" (1819), RACS, 79–80.

16. Robert Pierce Forbes, *The Missouri Compromise and Its Aftermath: Slavery and the Meaning of America* (Chapel Hill: University of North Carolina Press, 2007), 34–49.

17. *AC 15-2,* 1183 (February 15, 1819).

18. *AC 15-2,* 1192 (February 15, 1819).

19. Charles Fenton Mercer, *An Address to the American Colonization Society at their 36th Annual Meeting* (Geneva, Switzerland: 1854), 6; Egerton, *Charles Fenton Mercer,* 166–68; Burin, "Slave Trade Act of 1819," 7–8; W. E. B. Du Bois, *The Suppression of the African Slave-Trade to the United States, 1638–1870* (1896; rpt., Mineola, N.Y.: Dover Publications, Inc., 1970), 120–22.

20. *AC 15-2,* 1430 (March 1, 1819).

21. Charles Fenton Mercer to Cocke, April 2, 1819, Papers of the Cocke Family, box 28; John Quincy Adams, *Memoirs of John Quincy Adams: Comprising Portions of his Diary from 1795 to 1848,* ed. Charles Francis Adams (Philadelphia: J. B. Lippincott & Co., 1875), vol. 4: 298–99.

22. *American Beacon,* June 18, 1819; *The American,* June 19, 1819; *Providence Patriot,* June 19, 1819; *Columbian Centinel,* June 19, 1819.

23. Duncan Macleod, "The Triple Crisis," in *The Growth of Federal Power in American History*, ed. Rhodi Jeffrey-Jones and Bruce Collins (DeKalb: Northern Illinois University Press, 1983), 13–24.

24. P. J. Staudenraus, *African Colonization Movement, 1816–1865* (New York: Columbia University Press, 1961), 53–54.

25. *Address of the Board of Managers of the ACS* ([Washington D.C.,] 1819), [9–10].

26. From the *Georgia Journal*, rpt. with a new introduction by "Limner" in the *National Intelligencer*, July 9, 1819.

27. Robert J. Evans to James Madison, June 3, 1819; James Madison to Robert J. Evans, Montpellier, June 15, 1819, *Founders Online* (founders.archives.gov/).

28. *National Intelligencer*, September 30, 1819; John Taylor, *Construction Construed, and Constitutions Vindicated* (Richmond, Va.: Shepherd & Pollard, 1820), 298.

29. *National Intelligencer*, November 4, 1819; November 24, 1819.

30. *AC 16-1*, 1018 (January 28, 1820).

31. *National Intelligencer*, January 14, 1820; *AC 16-1*, 1047–51 (February 3, 1820).

32. *Speech of Mr. Meigs, of New York, on the Restriction of Slavery in Missouri* ([Washington, D.C., 1820]), 2, 4.

33. *National Messenger* (D.C.) February 9, 1820. The *Annals* do not include Meigs's speech or indicate that a vote was taken. *AC 16-1*, 1113–14 (February 5, 1820), 1136 (February 7, 1820).

34. *AC 16-1*, 1048.

35. In the House of Representatives, northerners voted sixty-six to ten in favor of banning slavery in Missouri on February 16, 1819, and eighty-seven to fourteen on the second vote on March 2, 1820 (*AC 15-2*, 1214; *AC 16-1*, 1586–87).

36. Auxiliary Society of Frederick County, *The Annual Report of the Auxiliary Society of Frederick County, Va., for Colonizing the Free People of Colour in the United States* (Winchester, Va., 1820), 14.

37. "Protest and Remonstrance of the Free People of Colour," New York *Commercial Advertiser*, November 20, 1819; Vaux to Thomas Clarkson, Philadelphia [May] 1, 1820, Vaux Family Papers, HSP.

38. Randolph to Dr. John Brockenbrough, qtd. in Wood, "John Randolph and the Politics of Slavery," 127; Pickering to Randolph, Wrenham, December 24, 1819, Pickering Papers, Massachusetts Historical Society, reel 15, 188; Pickering to Charles Fenton Mercer, January 15, 1820, Pickering Papers, reel 15, 199–200.

39. *AC 16-1*, 2207–11 (May 8, 1820), 2215–16 (May 9, 1820), 2236–37 (May 12, 1820); Staudenraus, *African Colonization Movement*, 57–79.

40. Mercer to John H. Cocke, January 13, 1827, Papers of the Cocke Family; ACS, *Seventh Annual Report* (Washington, D.C.: Davis and Force, 1824), 10–11; Staudenraus, *African Colonization*, 183–85. The essays were republished as *Controversy between Caius Gracchus and Opimius in Reference to the American Society for Colonizing the Free People of Colour of the United States, First Published in the Richmond Enquirer* (Georgetown, D.C.: James C. Dunn, 1827).

41. *Controversy between Caius Gracchus and Opimius*, 13–14, 18–20; 24, 28–29, 57–58.

42. Ibid., 39, 52, 46–48.

43. Randolph to Dr. Brockenbrough, February 20, 1826, in Kenneth Shorey, ed., *Collected Letters of John Randolph of Roanoke to Dr. John Brockenbrough* (New Brunswick, N.J.: Transaction Publishers, 1988), 67–68.

44. Philip Slaughter, *The Virginian History of African Colonization* (Richmond, Va.: Macfarlane & Fergusson, 1855), 19.

45. Beverly Tomek, "Seeking 'An Immutable Pledge from the Slave Holding States': The Pennsylvania Abolition Society and Black Settlement," *Pennsylvania History* 75 (Winter 2008): 26–53, 42–48; Beverly Tomek, *Colonization and Its Discontents: Emancipation, Emigration, and Antislavery in Antebellum Pennsylvania* (New York: New York University Press, 2011); Eric Burin, "Rethinking Northern White Support for the African Colonization Movement: The Pennsylvania Colonization Society as an Agent of Emancipation," *Pennsylvania Magazine of History and Biography* 127 (April 2003): 197–229.

46. David F. Ericson, *Slavery in the American Republic: Developing the Federal Government, 1791–1861* (Lawrence: University of Kansas Press, 2011), 53–79.

8

Situating African Colonization within the History of U.S. Expansion

BRANDON MILLS

The creation of Liberia was one of the United States' first attempts to engineer democracy abroad. While there is no clear path from Liberia to contemporary efforts at nation-building, debates over African colonization consistently raised questions about whether the ethos of U.S. expansionism conformed with ideas of planting a colony outside the nation's borders. Even so, it would be difficult to argue that the United States actively pursued an expansionist agenda in Liberia. Throughout much of the nineteenth century the U.S. government largely kept the colony at arm's length, and white colonization supporters were primarily concerned with how it could be used to address issues within the United States. Nevertheless, it is striking that historians have been seemingly reluctant to place the colonization movement within the United States' long history of nation-building. This oversight illustrates the domestic preoccupations of the literature on African colonization, as well as the difficulty of integrating such a distinct and multifaceted movement into traditional narratives of U.S. expansion. Despite these complicating factors, historians should fundamentally reconsider the movement's impact on early U.S. politics by examining how it connected domestic racial policies to the United States' practices of both continental and overseas expansion.

A number of interrelated factors account for the difficulty of situating African colonization within the history of U.S. expansion. First and foremost is the fact that most white Americans supported the movement for ostensibly domestic considerations and believed that the colony could help bring a gradual end to slavery or eliminate the social problems they projected onto the free black populations. While these concerns largely drove the movement, colonizationists also vocally promoted the idea that an

American colony would bring "Christianity, civilization, and commerce" to Africa, even if the commitment to these objectives was often secondary. So, while some colonization supporters occasionally attempted to make Liberia more directly serve U.S. foreign policy interests, in the end the United States did not significantly pursue the colony as a commercial or strategic outpost. In contrast to the contemporaneous settler colony in Texas or the missionary colonization of Hawaii, Americans' efforts in Liberia did not lead to informal domination of the nation or eventual annexation of the territory by the United States. However, while there is little evidence to suggest that supporters of African colonization were primarily interested in Liberia for the direct material benefits it offered to the United States, grappling with the movement reshapes the ideological landscape of early U.S. expansionism.

In the last two decades, literary and cultural-studies approaches to the topic have begun to shift the horizons of scholarship by placing the colonization movement within the culture of early U.S. imperialism. While these valuable departures have challenged the dominant trends within the historiography of the colonization movement, even the strongest examples of this work have primarily been limited to shorter pieces that deeply analyze a selection of literary texts. Generally the historical study of African colonization has remained largely separate from the study of U.S. foreign relations.[1]

The ideas articulated by colonizationists intersect with various ideologies of U.S. expansion, which makes the movement particularly difficult to categorize but also ripe for deeper exploration. Considering the colonization movement in this context sheds light on an issue that has long vexed U.S. historians: how the United States transitioned from a collection of settler colonies into a global superpower. Scholars studying the history of the early U.S. empire have typically focused on a familiar narrative of westward expansion that resulted in the creation of a white settler state. However, such histories often don't account for the fact that the United States' exercise of power overseas was often very different from its exercise of power as a settler state in North America. By reexamining the African colonization movement, historians can begin to bridge this divide and show how it served as a crucial link between the United States' initial territorial expansion strategies and later approaches to empire that emphasized the spread of U.S. institutions.

In order to resituate African colonization within this context it is important to consider how the concept of creating black colonies developed at a critical moment when the United States was just beginning to define the character and scope of its territorial expansion. While many historians have emphasized the colonization movement's connections to the British colony of Sierra Leone and the efforts of African Americans such as Paul Cuffe, before the formation of the American Colonization Society (ACS), white proponents of black colonies generally looked to the West rather than across the Atlantic. Indeed, the earliest proposals for black colonies were, in many ways, an extension of the United States' plans to colonize the North American continent, even as they were designed to contain the continuing threat of rebellion by enslaved African Americans. Many of these proposals explicitly reacted to the escalating revolution in Saint Domingue or to Gabriel's thwarted rebellion in Virginia, which were both viewed by whites as disturbingly local and increasingly radical manifestations of the contagion of liberty sweeping the globe. Within this context, antislavery activists and anxious slaveholders tentatively proposed that colonies in western North America could circumvent the seemingly inevitable tide of racial revolution in the United States.[2]

Many of the proposals suggested that black settlements could participate in the United States' efforts to colonize the continent, thus turning a potentially threatening population into an ostensible agent of U.S. expansion. While one of the first such proposals, by a Virginian lawyer, St. George Tucker, speculated that African Americans could "become Spanish subjects" by being transplanted to Louisiana, most of the other plans articulated during this era envisioned an ongoing and clearly hierarchical relationship between black colonists and the U.S. government. Moses Fisk imagined that his proposed colony would be a kind of training ground for liberty, complete with "temporary guardians, governours, and instructors" that would prepare black settlers to ultimately have "a voice in Congress." However, Fisk also suggested that any black colony in the West would be an unequal partner in expansion who would need to be "defended, if any should invade them; and awed by soldiery, if they should rebel."[3]

Other early proponents of such colonies imagined them in similar terms of subordination. St. George Tucker's cousin, George Tucker, said of the United States' relationship to his proposed colony: "We may be to them a haughty and domineering neighbor [but] they never could be terrible to us." Both Thomas Branagan and John Parrish envisioned colonies within the newly acquired Louisiana Territory that could be set apart from the United States' typical processes of colonization but which would nevertheless afford African Americans the opportunity to, in Parrish's words, "enjoy liberty and the rights of citizenship." By either implicitly or explicitly seeking to displace native populations, all of these proposed colonies echoed the emerging logic of the U.S. settler state. At the same time, they tentatively proposed a new model of colonial relations by offering differentiated political status for black colonies within the broader framework of U.S. colonization.[4]

It is not surprising that white leaders would look to settler colonies to resolve the contradictions created by the presence of African Americans in the early republic. Americans had long viewed expansion onto territory occupied by indigenous people as a solution to the political, economic, and cultural crises that had been created by earlier waves of colonization. American colonists' desire for unrestrained expansion had been a major component of the revolutionary grievances they raised against the British Empire. However, unlike the framework for U.S. colonization established by the Northwest Ordinances in the 1780s, these proposals all suggested that black colonies would be afforded terms of sovereignty, statehood, and political integration different from the rest of the states in the union. Although the plans did not situate African Americans as equal partners in empire, they did suggest that black and white settlers might loosely cooperate in colonizing North America. This prospect would seem unthinkable only a few years later, when the idea of white settler expansion and the institution of slavery had become so firmly entrenched.[5]

The common assumption that undergirded this diverse set of proposals was that the resulting colonies would be subsumed within the United States' settler state and yet would remain distinctly separate from it. In this respect, the colonies imagined by these early proposals resembled the emerging status of Indian nations under U.S. law, which would soon become considered, in Chief Justice Marshall's famous phrase, as "domestic dependent nations." While some proposals vaguely promised eventual "independence" for the colony or some form of political incorporation through Congress, they suggested that any such settlement would never acquire full sovereignty over their territory just like the native groups they were intended to displace.[6]

Ultimately, it is this overlap between western black colonies and Indian nations that suggests a major reason why the colonization movement decisively turned its attention from North America to Africa in the mid-1810s. If large-scale slave revolts remained a looming, but largely unrealized, threat to whites in the early republic, then indigenous resistance movements were a fundamental reality facing an expanding settler state. The various attempts by some Indian nations to resist U.S. settler encroachment peaked with the pan-Indian political confederacies that formed around the War of 1812. These movements threatened far more than mere violence against frontier populations because they raised the prospect of a permanent boundary to U.S. settlement as well as competing national sovereignties within domestic space claimed by the United States.[7]

In some instances, the threat of Native American and African American revolt overlapped, as was the case in the various alliances between escaped slaves and the Seminoles, Choctaws, and Creeks during the first decades of the nineteenth century. Just months before the ACS first convened in 1816, U.S. military forces destroyed the so-called "Negro Fort" in the Panhandle region of then-Spanish Florida. The encampment was targeted because it was occupied by nearly eight hundred fugitive slaves, as well as a handful of Choctaw and Seminole Indians. The existence of an ostensibly sovereign settlement of heavily armed African Americans near the border was deemed intolerable by both the U.S. military and southern slaveholders; however, the settlement's connection to surrounding native communities made them all the more disconcerting to whites.[8]

The fort was part of a longer tradition of black-Indian collaboration in the Southeast. Several African Americans were soldiers in the Red Stick War amongst dissident Creeks, and some of the refugees from this defeat were responsible for the construction of the fort. Also, the Seminoles had often provided sanctuary for fugitive slaves by adopting them into their communities and, as a result, African Americans had played an important role in several Seminole-led conflicts with the United States during this era, such as "Payne's War" from 1812 to 1814 in Northern Florida. Such military and political alliances of African Americans and Indians were even more threatening than mere slave revolt or pan-Indian confederations because these suggested the possibility of a broader coalition against white settler expansion.[9]

This concern about interracial revolt helped shift the early colonization movement's focus away from North America. The early proponents of black colonies had assumed that any settlements would displace indigenous peoples and become secondary partners in U.S. expansion, even as they would resemble the subordinate status of Indian nations. However, the early literature of the ACS and the writings by some of its founders, such as Robert Finley and Samuel Mills, pushed back against earlier colonization proposals by arguing that black colonies in the West were just as likely to align with Indian nations or other foreign powers.[10]

So, while the plans for western colonies would foreshadow the form and concept of the colony that was ultimately implemented in Liberia, such colonies could never be reconciled with emerging plans for a white settler state in North America. The western colonization plans failed to achieve mass support, in part, because white leaders were threatened by the prospect of multiple racialized political states under the umbrella of an American continental empire, particularly as the United States renewed its commitment to the expansion of slavery in the first decades of the nineteenth century. This early series of proposals reveals that, while the colonization movement would always remain focused on responding to the interrelated issues of race and slavery, it also raised fundamental questions about the form and limitations of U.S. expansion.[11]

Although the American Colonization Society's definitive move towards Africa reinforced racial boundaries within the United States, the early African colonization movement would be forced to further define the place of an African colony within the nation's identity as an expanding empire. In the late 1810s, some advocates of colonization briefly considered directing their efforts toward supporting the already existing British colony in Sierra Leone, a possibility that Paul Cuffe previously explored with some success. However, the disruption of Cuffe's efforts during the War of 1812 had demonstrated that the fragility of diplomatic relations between Britain and the United States could threaten to undermine any cooperation within such a colony.[12]

While the instability of relations with Britain may have dissuaded colonization advocates from pursuing such a path, for many U.S. colonizationists the existence of a separate, and uniquely American, colony was as much ideological as it was practical. On the eve of the first ACS meeting, in 1816, the *National Advocate* published an editorial that echoed the anticolonial sentiments of the Revolutionary Era. It contended that Sierra Leone would not be a suitable settlement because it "exists like various other of the *humane* establishments of England, calculated to make rich a few hungry parasites who must be provided for." Instead, the writer argued that a U.S.-supported colony in Africa should be distinctly American and "as different, in every respect, from Sierra Leone as the government of the states is from Great Britain."[13]

However, other observers, such as the influential newspaper editor Hezekiah Niles, were concerned that even an "independent" colony modeled on U.S. republicanism would inevitably lead the United States to become too much like Britain by saddling the nation with the corrupting burdens of an empire. In response, one of Niles's readers pushed back against these claims by asserting that any colony devised by the United States would be an exception to previous imperial projects. The writer noted that the "*establishment* or *acquisition* of colonies" was a fundamental fact of human history, but insisted that the United States did not need to adopt "such a policy, *as it has generally been pursued by other nations.*"[14]

While many early American proponents of a U.S. colony in Africa spoke of Sierra Leone as an inspiration for their efforts, these early debates reveal a crucial distinction over how these colonies were situated in relation to their respective mother countries. As Sierra Leone transitioned from a "Province of Freedom" to a crown colony in the early nineteenth century, it was integrated into Britain's established network of diverse colonies which ranged from settler to strategic to commercial in character. While Americans were zealous proponents of a settler empire in North America, they had a less established protocol for overseas expansion than Britain and were generally skeptical of the colonial system, from which they had recently fought to free themselves. Therefore, just as proponents of colonization began to abandon the West as a potential site for black colonies, they were careful to frame Liberia as both distinct from settler expansion in North America and as an opportunity for African Americans to reproduce their own republican empire in Africa. This framework became crucial to the ideology of the movement, which situated Liberia as a rejection of expansionist models that bred "dependence," thus aligning the colony's trajectory with the United States' history of anticolonial struggle.[15]

Throughout the 1820s and 1830s the colonization movement frequently situated Liberia as a reproduction, rather than an extension of, the United States' "empire for liberty." However, the ACS's attempts to get financial support from the federal government would continue to raise issues about how the colony related to the United States' practices of expansion. Colonization supporters tentatively secured partial federal funding for the movement through the passage of the 1819 Slave Trade Law, which empowered the United States to return recaptured slaves to Africa, as David Ericson explained in a previous chapter of this collection.

While President Monroe believed that the act empowered the federal government to purchase land for a colony in Africa, he faced resistance from his secretary of state, John Quincy Adams. Adams argued that it was unconstitutional for the federal government to assume this authority because it would amount to the "establishment of a colonial system of government subordinate and dependent upon that of the United States" which, he believed, was wholly distinct from "contiguous" purchases of territory such as Louisiana. In doing so, Secretary Adams raised a persistent objection to federal support for colonization by asserting the integrity of continental boundaries for U.S. expansion and warning that the colony would lead to the United States developing an overseas empire on the European model. While Secretary Adams did not prevail in dissuading President Monroe from supporting the colony through the Slave Trade Act, his basic view that an African colony pushed the limits of U.S. expansionism persisted and, consequently, Liberia would always maintain a fraught relationship with the federal government despite its attraction as a key tool in fighting the slave trade.[16]

These early objections made it necessary for colonizationists to walk a fine line by asserting that federal support for an African colony was continuous with prior U.S. expansion yet exceptional enough that it would not lead the United States down the path to an overseas empire. Throughout the 1820s the colonization movement attempted to build on this tentative government support, and the legislatures of some northern states sent memorials to Congress urging it to take an even more direct role in building the fledgling colony. These calls for expanding federal involvement in African colonization occasionally rekindled questions about the boundaries of U.S. expansion as a part of broader discussions that ostensibly concerned the limits of federal interference with slavery.

For instance, in 1824 and 1825 the Richmond *Enquirer* ran a series of editorials debating the merits of federal support for colonization, in part by discussing an African colony's precedence within the history of U.S. expansion. The opponent of colonization argued that the ACS was a dangerous vehicle being used by politicians to expand the powers of the federal government, as in creating colonies abroad. He argued that "distant colonies" were "at war with the interests of a republic," that the federal constitution provided no authority to "hold any people or any country as a *permanent colony*"; such a policy would cause the United States to make Liberia a directly administered colony, just as Britain had done with Sierra Leone. His opponent countered that an African colony did have precedent in the purchase of Louisiana and Florida as well as in the United States' existing relations with Indian nations. An African colony would not result in a "colonial system" because the settlement would eventually become a republic with a "separate and independent government." In the next few years, debates over federal intervention in colonization would repeat similar arguments over Liberia's place within the landscape of U.S. expansion.[17]

Proponents of federal support for African colonization often cited the United States' relationships with Indian nations as a precedent, as it pertained to both the acquisition of territory and U.S. policies of removal and "civilization." This comparison is particularly instructive when considered in relation to ideologies of U.S. expansion. In many ways, the debates over Indian removal and African colonization ran on mirrored trajectories and resulted in divergent outcomes, which reflected both the United States' commitment to territorial expansion and persistent concerns about extending the nation's entanglements abroad. The early "Indian colonization" plans proposed by the Baptist missionary Isaac McCoy were partially inspired by the African colonization movement. His proposals also influenced the benevolent justifications for removal policies which were employed cynically by President Andrew Jackson, even as the government's policy moved further away from civilizationist reform and closer to forced displacement.[18]

At the same time, most Jacksonians were staunchly opposed to the idea of expanding federal support for an African colony, and they often took pains to distinguish Indian and African colonization as distinct varieties of U.S. expansionism. Senator Littleton Tazewell, a Jacksonian from Virginia, penned a report for the Senate Committee on Foreign Relations which argued that African colonies were fundamentally different from the colonization of "contiguous" Indian lands because "holding distant colonies" or "creating new empires" was opposed to the "the genius and spirit of all our institutions."[19]

Thus, Jackson's supporters perceived no contradiction between the president's support for what amounted to Indian "colonies" west of the Mississippi and his veto of an 1833 bill championed by Henry Clay that would have provided greater federal funding for an African colonization. Within this logic, they viewed the creation of a federally administered Indian territory as a legitimate extension of U.S. territorial expansion while contending that Liberia would set the nation on a dangerous path to overseas empire. Although such arguments were only a small part of the worsening climate for the ACS in the early 1830s, they reveal the tenuous place of the colonization movement within the politics of expansionism. While the early colonization movement attempted to situate the embryonic African colony against other models of empire, the failure of ACS efforts to secure direct federal support throughout the 1820s and 1830s ensured that the United States would continue to have a deeply ambivalent relationship with Liberia.[20]

Throughout these years of tenuous federal support for colonization, the United States' primary relationship with the colony was through the U.S. Navy. The United States dispatched agents to Liberia under the auspices of policing the slave trade, but the navy had limited effectiveness because it possessed no regular squadron in the region. U.S. officials were keen to avoid entanglements with both African populations and European merchants in the region. As a result, any meaningful action against the slave trade was frequently undermined by indifferent presidential administrations and bureaucratic disputes over the scope of authority given to federal agents in Africa.

The ineffectiveness of the U.S naval presence speaks to the fragile nature of colonial authority in the region. The displaced and neighboring indigenous peoples, such as the Dey, Grebo, Bassa, and Kru, generally had little regard for the American settlers. These groups occasionally tolerated, or sought to benefit from, the presence of the settlements. However, the American colonists maintained their small territorial position through a series of military conflicts during the first decades of settlement. While many settlers had come to West Africa steeped in an ethos of benevolent civilizationism, more often than not, their practices mirrored the patterns of violence and dispossession which also characterized the United States' settler empire in North America.

In 1842 the United States signed the Webster-Ashburton Treaty with Britain, which led the U.S. Navy to create an Africa Squadron. It would patrol the West African coast for slave traders and protect American interests in the region. Greater naval reinforcement was something that colonizationists had long lobbied for, and the new squadron did lead to a brief period of increased U.S. intervention to protect the settlements. However, the fact that the colony was settled and administered by private citizens from the United States, yet informally protected by the U.S. military, led the British government to increasingly question whether the settlements were independent in nature or if the United States had begun to assume some degree of authority over them.[21]

In a sense, this diplomatic situation pressed the U.S. government to do what it had been reluctant to do since the beginning of the movement: define the precise nature of the colonial relationship between the United States and Liberia. In 1843, the Committee on Commerce in the U.S. House of Representatives looked into this question and issued a joint resolution accompanied by a lengthy report recommending that the United States expand its presence in Liberia through the appointment of additional agents.

The committee argued that the United States should move beyond its traditional mandate of suppressing the slave trade and work to "protect and advance the interest of American trade in the region." By endorsing this course of action, the committee suggested that establishing a more formal colonial relationship with Liberia would better protect the colony while providing the United States with a commercial and strategic advantage. The report noted that "the idea of an American colony is a new one" but pointed out that it had a precedent in U.S. relations with "Indian tribes which have been placed beyond the limits of the States, on the purchased territory of the Union." In doing so, the report essentially upended the Jacksonian distinction between Indian policy and African colonization and revisited a traditional argument for federal intervention in colonization by asserting the continuity between other forms of U.S. expansion, while still maintaining that the colony was exceptional.[22]

Although the beleaguered ACS of the early 1840s clearly welcomed any expansion of federal support, the organization's official journal, the *African Repository and Colonial Journal,* published an article that took issue with some of the Commerce Committee's recommendations. It argued that the "American Government [should] become the ally and protector of these colonies" and "avail themselves of the advantages" of their "valuable commerce, which is now opening to the world." However, the article expressed concern about the committee's suggestion that Liberia become a formal U.S. colony and argued its "character would be changed" and, as a result, colonists "would no longer be actuated by the same spirit of enterprise and independence."[23]

In the end, Liberia was not destined to become a U.S. colony. Secretary of State Daniel Webster rejected the advice of both the House Committee on Commerce and the secretary of the navy and decided not to pursue an expanded commercial and military agenda in Liberia. Following this policy directive, the U.S. diplomat Edward Everett wrote to the British government in 1843 to declare that "extra-continental possessions" were not extended the protections "to which colonies are entitled from the mother country by which they are established." Having briefly flirted with an official colonial policy in West Africa, the U.S. government reverted to its traditionally ambiguous position by informing British authorities that they would continue to limit their intervention in colonial disputes to policing the slave trade, albeit with a bolstered naval presence in the region.[24]

While the Commerce Committee's report made a compelling argument that any distinction between continental and extra-continental colonialism was somewhat arbitrary, the ACS was also correct in noting that a move toward formal colonial policy in Liberia would have undermined the ethos of the movement and the colony's settlers. Colonizationists had long attempted to define Liberia against both U.S. continental expansion and European colonial models by arguing that the colony was destined to become a free and independent republic and thus ultimately separate from the United States. This ideology would be on full display shortly after the United States resumed its agnostic stance towards the colony after 1843. The colonists formally declared themselves an independent republic in 1847, partially in order to resolve the ongoing disputes over Liberian sovereignty among European powers, indigenous Africans, and the United States. By declaring political sovereignty, Liberian settlers attempted to cleverly resolve the colony's diplomatic disputes, but independence also worked as a splendid performance of republican nationhood that conveniently validated the long-standing ideology of the movement.[25]

Although ACS officials had initially been somewhat concerned about the prospect of diminished control over an independent Liberia, the organization quickly worked to turn what could have been perceived as a rebuke of the society's authority into a public relations campaign to reframe the case for colonization. Colonizationists argued that Americans should support and celebrate the independence of a black republic modeled after the United States. Such an argument offered the possibility for sympathetic white Americans to feel that their own exclusionary racial settler state was justified even as they proclaimed support for the spread of universal liberty in Africa.

The United States' brief consideration of making Liberia a U.S. colony in the early 1840s had been the most straightforward attempt to integrate the settlement into the ideology of U.S. expansionism, even as it offered the possibility for a new type of "American colony." However, the government's rapid abandonment of this idea and the eventual independence of Liberia reveal the endurance of the republican language behind the movement. By symbolically severing its ambiguous colonial ties with the United States and asserting its right to self-government, Liberia validated the anticolonial rhetoric that had animated the colonization movement from the beginning and demonstrated a purportedly benevolent method by which the United States could reshape the world in its image. Ironically, the African colonization movement revealed perhaps its most powerful relationship to the ideology of U.S. expansion at the moment when both the United States and Liberia rejected formal U.S. colonialism.[26]

While the independence of Liberia can be considered an endpoint in the debate over the place of African colonization within the boundaries of U.S. expansion, the way in which the event was framed in U.S. discourse foreshadowed how the United States would increasingly project its power as it expanded beyond North America. The United States' attempts to create both formal colonies and proxy states in the late nineteenth and early twentieth centuries would often be justified as attempts to liberate racialized populations by helping to build their societies into versions of the U.S. republic.

Following Liberia's independence, colonizationism maintained considerable appeal and began to show growing convergence with the United States' broader strategic and economic considerations. For instance, shortly after independence, colonization advocates in Congress pursued a line of steamships that would facilitate direct commerce in West Africa, transport black emigrants to Liberia, and serve as an auxiliary to the U.S. Navy. The *African Repository* enthusiastically endorsed this legislation and argued that building the United States' relationship with an independent Liberia would be the nation's first step to accessing West African markets for "the articles manufactured in the United States, and for the surplus productions of our soil," which would bring "the inexhaustible treasures of that immense continent" and "increase our wealth and our glory." This was an argument for U.S. commercial expansion that would become commonplace by the second half of the nineteenth century. By the late 1850s, several prominent Republicans were also using the well-established conceptual framework of the colonization movement to advocate for independent black colonies in Central America that could help produce like-minded republics as a bulwark against British commercial dominance within the region.[27]

While neither Liberia nor any of the other colonies proposed during this period would come to realize the heady commercial ambitions envisioned by their advocates, the manner in which they were discussed offers a glimpse of the United States' eventual pursuit of an informal empire which relied on an abstract commitment to the spread of U.S. political ideals by creating politically aligned, yet subordinate, proxy states. If the ideologies of an "empire for liberty" and "Manifest Destiny" were fundamentally about asserting the United States' determination to establish an expansive settler state within North America, the African colonization movement illustrates the ways that Americans began to envision new modes of expansion that were somewhat distinct from their previous practices of territorial acquisition or the implementation of a European-modeled colonial system.

The colonization movement articulated a worldview in which the United States would work to foster nation-states that could ascend to nominal equality on the world stage even as they remained hierarchically differentiated through race. In this way, the movement to create Liberia is awkwardly positioned between the United States' practice of settler colonialism in the early nineteenth century and the nation's eventual pursuit of a global empire which relied on less direct forms of control over territories and populations. While African colonization does not easily conform to the territorial or economic motivations behind the dominant forms of expansion during the era, situating African colonization within the context of U.S. expansionism is useful precisely because its contemporaries consistently framed it as an exceptional project. The colonization movement grew from the practices of U.S. colonialism, and yet it existed in constant tension with it, a tension still evident in American rhetoric and global realities.[28]

Notes

1. Amy Kaplan, "Manifest Domesticity," *American Literature* 70, no. 3 (September 1998): 581–606; Susan M. Ryan, "Errand into Africa: Colonization and Nation Building in Sarah J. Hale's Liberia," *New England Quarterly* 68, no. 4 (December 1995): 558–83; David Kazanjian, "Racial Governmentality: The African Colonization Movement," in *The Colonizing Trick: National Culture and Imperial Citizenship in Early America* (Minneapolis: University of Minnesota Press, 2003); Etsuko Taketani, "Postcolonial Liberia: Sarah Hale's Africa," in *U.S. Women Writers and the Discourses of Colonialism, 1825–1861* (Knoxville: University of Tennessee Press, 2003). For recent historical work on the topic, see: Eugene S. Van Sickle, "Reluctant Imperialists: The U.S. Navy and Liberia, 1819–1845," *Journal of the Early Republic* 31, no. 1 (Spring 2011): 107–34; Bronwen Everill, "'Destiny Seems to Point Me to That Country': Early Nineteenth-century African American Migration, Emigration, and Expansion," *Journal of Global History* 7, no. 1 (2012): 53–77; Bronwen Everill, *Abolition and Empire in Sierra Leone and Liberia* (London: Palgrave Macmillan, 2012); Nicholas Guyatt, "'The Outskirts of Our Happiness': Race and the Lure of Colonization in the Early Republic," *Journal of American History* 95, no. 4 (March 2009).

2. On the radicalizing impact of revolutionary Haiti, see: Robin Blackburn, "Haiti, Slavery, and the Age of the Democratic Revolution," *William and Mary Quarterly* 63, no. 4 (October 2006): 643–74; Alfred N. Hunt, *Haiti's Influence on Antebellum America: Slumbering Volcano in the Caribbean* (Baton Rouge: Louisiana State University Press, 1988). For references to the revolutionary context among proponents of western colonies, see: Moses Fisk, *Tyrannical Libertymen a Discourse Upon Negro-Slavery in the United States: Composed at—in New Hampshire, on the Late Federal Thanksgiving-Day* (Hanover, N.H.: Eagle Office, 1795), 9; St. George Tucker to Jeremy Belknap, June 29, 1795, Jeremy Belknap Papers, Massachusetts Historical Society; St. George Tucker, *Letter to a Member of the General Assembly of Virginia on the Subject of the Late Conspiracy of the Slaves; with a*

Proposal for Their Colonization (Baltimore: Bonsal & Niles, 1801), 6–7; Thomas Branagan, *Serious Remonstrances, Addressed to the Citizens of the Northern States, and Their Representatives; Being an Appeal to Their Natural Feelings & Common Sense* (Philadelphia: Thomas T. Stiles, 1805), 43–54; John Parrish, *Remarks on the Slavery of Black People; Addressed to the Citizens of the United States Particularly to Those Who Are in Legislative of Executive Stations in the General or State Governments; and Also to Such Individuals as Hold Them in Bondage* (Philadelphia: Kimber, Conrad, & Co., 1806), 8–9, 41. On how the various proposals from Virginia were informed by the threat of revolution, see: James Sidbury, *Ploughshares into Swords: Race, Rebellion, and Identity in Gabriel's Virginia, 1730–1810* (Cambridge, U.K.: Cambridge University Press, 1997); Douglas R. Egerton, *Gabriel's Rebellion: The Virginia Slave Conspiracies of 1800 and 1802* (Chapel Hill: University of North Carolina Press, 1993).

3. St. George Tucker, *Dissertation on Slavery: With a Proposal for the Gradual Abolition of It, in the State of Virginia* (Philadelphia, 1796), 94–95; Fisk, *Tyrannical Libertymen*, 9–11.

4. Tucker, *Letter to a Member of the General Assembly of Virginia on the Subject of the Late Conspiracy of the Slaves*, 21. For more on the early western colonization plans, see: Guyatt, "The Outskirts of Our Happiness"; Beverly Tomek, "'From Motives of Generosity, as Well as Self-preservation': Thomas Branagan, Colonization, and the Gradual Emancipation Movement," *American Nineteenth Century History* 6, no. 2 (June 2005).

5. On how American colonists developed a sense of themselves as a white settler community with unrestrained right to expansion, see Peter Silver, *Our Savage Neighbors: How Indian War Transformed Early America* (New York: W. W. Norton & Co., 2009).

6. On "domestic dependent nationhood" and the legal contingency of Native Americans and African Americans, see: Priscilla Wald, "Terms of Assimilation: Legislating Subjectivity in the Emerging Nation," in *Cultures of United States Imperialism*, ed. Donald E. Pease and Amy Kaplan (Durham, N.C.: Duke University Press, 1993), 672; Robert A. Williams, *Like a Loaded Weapon: The Rehnquist Court, Indian Rights, and the Legal History of Racism in America* (Minneapolis: University of Minnesota Press, 2005), 47–70. On the United States as an imperial space of differentiated sovereignties organized through race, see: Aziz Rana, *The Two Faces of American Freedom* (Cambridge, Mass.: Harvard University Press, 2010); Left Quarter Collective, "White Supremacist Constitution of the U.S. Empire-State: A Short Conceptual Look at the Long First Century," in *Political Power and Social Theory* (Bingley, U.K.: Emerald Group Publishing, 2009), vol. 20: 167–200.

7. On the counter-nationalist threat of pan-Indianism, see John Sugden, "Early Pan-Indianism: Tecumseh's Tour of the Indian Country, 1811–1812," *American Indian Quarterly* 10, no. 4 (Autumn 1986): 273–304.

8. Kevin Mulroy, *Freedom on the Border: The Seminole Maroons in Florida: The Indian Territory–Coahuila and Texas* (Lubbock: Texas Tech University Press, 1993), 13–15; Kenneth Wiggins Porter, *The Black Seminoles: History of a Freedom-Seeking People* (Gainesville: University Press of Florida, 1996), 13–24.

9. Claudio Saunt, *A New Order of Things: Property, Power, and the Transformation of the Creek Indians, 1733–1816* (Cambridge, U.K.: Cambridge University Press, 1999), 235–40, 269–70. For an example of this concern about interracial collaboration among white leaders, see Kenneth Wiggins Porter, "Negroes and the East Florida Annexation Plot, 1811–1813," *Journal of Negro History* 30 (1945): 24.

10. On the early colonizationists' concerns about the threat posed by planting black colonies on the lands of indigenous peoples, see: Robert S. Finley, *Thoughts on the Colonization of Free Blacks* (Washington, D.C., 1816), 6; Samuel Mills, qtd. in George Washington Edwards Phillips, "Diary of George Washington Edwards Phillips," 1817, pp. 110–11, George Washington Edwards Phillips Papers, Special Collections, Duke University Library; American Colonization Society, *A View of Exertions Lately Made for the Purpose of Colonizing the Free People of Colour, in the United States, in Africa, or Elsewhere* (Washington D.C., 1817), 7; report cited in "Report on Colonizing the Free People of Color of the United States," *Daily National Intelligencer,* March 28, 1817; "Colonization of Free People of Color," *National Register,* April 5, 1817.

11. On the transformation of western borderland spaces into "slave country," see: Stephen Aron, *American Confluence: The Missouri Frontier from Borderland to Border State, A History of the trans-Appalachian Frontier* (Bloomington: Indiana University Press, 2006); Adam Rothman, *Slave Country: American Expansion and the Origins of the Deep South* (Cambridge, Mass.: Harvard University Press, 2007). Long before black western colonies had been abandoned, Thomas Jefferson had already expressed his opposition to western colonies because he felt that it would place a "blot" on the white settler empire he envisioned. See Jefferson to James Monroe, November 24, 1801, in Paul Leicester Ford, ed., *The Works of Thomas Jefferson* (New York: G. P. Putnam's Sons, 1905), vol. 9: 315–19. By the late 1810s the prospects for a western colony had so rapidly diminished that the American Convention for Promoting the Abolition of Slavery (ACPAS) withdrew its support for a western colony that it had advocated only a year earlier. See: *Minutes of the Sixteenth American Convention for Promoting the Abolition of Slavery, and Improving the Condition of the African Race* (Philadelphia: William Fry, 1819), 51; *Minutes of the Seventeenth Session of the American Convention for Promoting the Abolition of Slavery, and Improving the Condition of the African Race* (Philadelphia: Atkinson & Alexander, 1821), 44.

12. Lamont D. Thomas, *Paul Cuffe: Black Entrepreneur and Pan-Africanist* (Urbana: University of Illinois Press, 1986). During this early phase of the African colonization movement, several newspapers reprinted an 1811 letter by Thomas Jefferson which recommended Sierra Leone as a destination for African Americans. For examples, see: "Colonization of Free Blacks," *National Advocate,* December 20, 1816; "Colonization of Free Blacks," *Daily National Intelligencer,* April 14, 1817; *National Advocate,* April 16, 1817; "African Colonization," *Niles' Weekly Register,* April 19, 1817; "Colonization of Free Blacks," *Boston Recorder,* April 29, 1817.

13. *National Advocate,* December 20, 1816.

14. "The Colonization Scheme," *Niles' Weekly Register,* October 4, 1817; "To H. Niles," *Niles' Weekly Register,* November 8, 1817.

15. On the U.S. tradition of "anti-imperial" nationalism, see: Mary Ann Heiss, "The Evolution of the Imperial Idea and U.S. National Identity," *Diplomatic History* 26, no. 4 (Fall 2002): 511–40; Walter LaFeber, "The American View of Decolonization, 1776–1920: An Ironic Legacy," in *The United States and Decolonization: Power and Freedom,* ed. David Ryan and Victor Pungong (Basingstoke, U.K.: Macmillan, 2000). The colonization movement's use of republican language was evident early in the movement. The ACS's first memorial to Congress argued that colonists would build "the glorious edifice of well ordered and polished society," which was based on "the deep and sure foundations of equal laws"

and the "prevailing power of liberty." See American Society for Colonizing the Free People of Colour of the United States, *Memorial of the President and Board of Managers of the American Society for Colonizing the Free People of Colour of the United States: January 14, 1817: Read and Ordered to Lie Upon the Table* (Washington D.C.: William A. Davis, 1817), 3.

16. Eric Burin, "The Slave Trade Act of 1819: A New Look at Colonization and the Politics of Slavery," *American Nineteenth Century History* 13, no. 1 (2012): 1–14; Charles Francis Adams, ed., *Memoirs of John Quincy Adams, Comprising Portions of His Diary from 1795 to 1848* (Philadelphia: J. B. Lippincott & Co., 1875), vol. 4: 292–94; P. J. Staudenraus, *The African Colonization Movement, 1816–1865* (New York: Columbia University Press, 1961), 53–57.

17. These editorials were eventually compiled into a pamphlet in 1827. The anonymous colonization advocate "Opimius" was determined to be William Henry Fitzhugh, a vice-president of the ACS. See *Controversy Between Caius Gracchus and Opimius: In Reference to the American Society for Colonizing the Free People of Colour of the United States: First Published in the Richmond Enquirer* (Washington, D.C.: Georgetown, 1827), 11, 40–41, 52. For a more detailed examination of this debate, see the preceding essay in the present book. Other examples of arguments for and against African colonization based on the precedent of U.S. expansion can be found in: Sen. Robert Hayne, "The Colonization Society," *Register of Debates*, 19th Cong., 2nd Sess. (1827): 289–90; *Report of the Senate Committee on Foreign Relations, April 28, 1828*, 20th Cong., 1st Sess., Senate Document no. 178, serial 167 (Washington D.C., 1828); Kentucky Colonization Society, "Memorial of the Kentucky Colonization Society," *African Repository and Colonial Journal* 5, no. 11 (January 1830): 347–48; "Petitions of Congress," *Daily National Intelligencer*, February 12, 1831.

18. Guyatt, "The Outskirts of Our Happiness"; Susan M. Ryan, *The Grammar of Good Intentions: Race and the Antebellum Culture of Benevolence* (Ithaca, N.Y.: Cornell University Press, 2003), 25–45. For earlier explorations of the relationship between removal and colonization, see: Mary Young, "Racism in Red and Black: Indians and Other Free People of Color in Georgia, Law, Politics, and Removal Policy," *Georgia Historical Quarterly* 73, no. 3 (1989): 492–518; Lawrence Jacob Friedman, *Inventors of the Promised Land* (New York: Knopf, 1975), 199–215. On Isaac McCoy's relationship to the politics of removal, see: James P. Ronda, "'We Have a Country': Race, Geography, and the Invention of Indian Territory," *Journal of the Early Republic* 19, no. 4 (Winter 1999): 739–55; George A. Schultz, *An Indian Canaan: Isaac McCoy and the Vision of an Indian State* (Norman: University of Oklahoma Press, 1972), 120–33; *Report of the Senate Committee on Foreign Relations, April 28, 1828*, 5–6.

19. For a Jacksonian pamphlet on how African colonization reflected a pattern of federal overreach, see Robert James Turnbull, *The Crisis: Or, Essays on the Usurpations of the Federal Government* (Charleston, S.C.: A. E. Miller, 1827).

20. On how the anti-slavery activist began to recognize the contradiction between support for colonization and opposition to removal policy, see: Mary Hershberger, "Mobilizing Women, Anticipating Abolition: The Struggle Against Indian Removal in the 1830s," *Journal of American History* 86, no. 1 (June 1999): 39; Alisse Portnoy, *Their Right to Speak: Women's Activism in the Indian and Slave Debates* (Cambridge, Mass.: Harvard University Press, 2005). On Jackson's veto of the distribution bill, see Staudenraus, *African Colonization Movement*, 184–87.

21. Van Sickle, "Reluctant Imperialists"; see also: Amy Van Natter, "The Mary Carver Affair: United States Foreign Policy and the Africa Squadron, 1841–1845," PhD diss., City University of New York, 2010; Donald L. Canney, *Africa Squadron: The U.S. Navy and the Slave Trade, 1842–1861* (Washington, D.C: Potomac Books, 2006).

22. House Committee on Commerce, *African Colonization*, 27th Cong., 3rd Sess., 1843, H. Rep. 283, 6; *Joint Resolution for Advancing and Protecting the Commercial Relations of the United States with the Western Coast of Africa*, H.R. Res. 44, 27th Cong., 3rd Sess., *Congressional Globe* 12, no. 1, February 28, 1843, 366.

23. "Reviews," *African Repository and Colonial Journal* 20, no. 3 (March 1844).

24. *Colony of Liberia, in Africa*, 28th Cong., 1st Sess., 1844, H. Rep 162, 5.

25. On the ambivalent role of the ACS in the process of independence, see Robert T. Brown, "Simon Greenleaf and the Liberian Constitution of 1847," *Liberian Studies Journal* 9, no. 2 (1980); on Liberia's performance of postcolonial nationhood, see Taketani, "Postcolonial Liberia."

26. On the reception of independence in the United States, see Brandon Mills, "'The United States of Africa': Liberian Independence and the Contested Meaning of a Black Republic," *Journal of the Early Republic* 33, no. 1 (Spring 2014): 79–107.

27. United States Congress House Committee on Naval Affairs, *Report of the Naval Committee to the House of Representatives, August, 1850, in Favor of the Establishment of a Line of Mail Steamships to the Western Coast of Africa* (Washington, D.C.: Gideon and Co., 1850); "Great Scheme for Carrying on Colonization," *African Repository* 26, no. 5 (May 1850). On the post-independence commercial interest in Liberia, see Everill, *Abolition and Empire in Sierra Leone and Liberia*. On arguments for U.S. expansion based on "surplus production," see Matthew Frye Jacobson, *Barbarian Virtues: The United States Encounters Foreign Peoples at Home and Abroad, 1876–1917* (New York: Macmillan, 2001), 15–57. On colonization plans for Central and South America, see: Gerald Horne, *The Deepest South: The United States, Brazil, and the African Slave Trade* (New York: New York University Press, 2007), 172–197; James D. Bilotta, *Race and the Rise of the Republican Party, 1848–1865* (New York: Peter Lang, 1992); Eric Foner, *Free Soil, Free Labor, Free Men: The Ideology of the Republican Party Before the Civil War.* (New York: Oxford University Press, 1970), 267–80.

28. Reginald Horsman, *Race and Manifest Destiny: The Origins of American Racial Anglo-Saxonism* (Cambridge, Mass.: Harvard University Press, 1981). The mode of expansion modeled by the African colonization movement is distinct from the martial ethos of "Manifest Destiny" in many ways and more clearly aligns with the "restrained manhood" Amy Greenberg has observed among missionaries. See Amy S. Greenberg, *Manifest Manhood and the Antebellum American Empire* (Cambridge, U.K.: Cambridge University Press, 2005).

9

Experiments in Colonial Citizenship in Sierra Leone and Liberia

BRONWEN EVERILL

In 1786, the British humanitarian Granville Sharp set out a new model of self-governance for the establishment of a settlement of free black Britons at Sierra Leone: "Most of the following regulations are mere *temporary* expedients, devised, indeed, with sincere intention to promote the happiness of the new settlement in its infant state; but subject, nevertheless, either to be entirely set aside, rejected in part, or altered on revision, according to the prevailing sentiment, from time to time, of the majority of the settlers, after mature deliberation in their *common Council*; because they themselves will certainly be the most competent judges of their own situation and affairs."[1] Liberia—the settlement established in 1816 for freed slaves by the American Colonization Society (ACS)—was granted similar allowances for representative decision-making in the early nineteenth century. The Atlantic-wide projects of defining citizenship and subjecthood within newly emerging political forms in the late eighteenth century spawned numerous innovations in self-representation and constitutionalism. Experimenting with ideas of colonial citizenship and representation, empires sought to retain and expand their influence in the wake of the American, Haitian, and Latin American revolutions for independence.[2] Equally, polities that did not consider themselves empires had to navigate ideas of citizenship, representation, and independence as they expanded beyond their original borders.

I will argue that structures of colonial governance in early Sierra Leone and Liberia were reflective of and constitutive of the emergence of two competing models of far-reaching constitutional colonial government. Attempting to codify the relationship between citizen or subject and the state, these new constitutional forms were experiments in ruling territories and subjects while granting elements of self-representation.

Sierra Leone and Liberia have similar founding stories. Both grew out of the late eighteenth-century interest in ameliorating slavery, ending the slave trade, and solving the problem of a growing free black poor population. Both were established on the same part of the West African coast in a fit of utopian enthusiasm that was quickly followed by disease, disappointment, and decline. Most interestingly for the growth of colonialism in the late eighteenth and nineteenth centuries, both gave rise to influential and largely successful black settler populations. Looking at these two colonies together, it becomes clear that, in the wake of the American, Haitian, and Latin American revolutions, territorial expansion would require adapting the existing models of imperial rule through some form of compromise whereby negotiation between colonial settlers and metropolitan governments could serve the interests of both.

The American Colonization Society's project in Liberia was representative of an American model that combined the British colonial governance example with a new approach that saw territories gradually accumulating a population, institutions, economic growth, and ultimately (in the case of the western states), representation at the federal level. Sierra Leoneans[3] negotiated governance with different local and metropolitan actors as the colony was run successively by a benevolent organization, a company, and the British government. In both cases, the settler or "pioneer" status of the colonists was in tension with ideas about racial characteristics and benevolent (and heavy-handed) humanitarian utopianism.

Historiography

The historiography of Sierra Leone and Liberia has rarely brought the two colonies' experiences into comparison, and this omission is due in large part to the very nature of their representative institutions. With both colonies founded by similar organizations, for similar groups of settlers, in similar parts of the world, the differences in their governance—and particularly the historiography's insistence on the lack of "imperial" oversight in Liberia—has created entirely divergent historiographical interests. Equally important in shaping this lacuna has been the emphasis of the historiography on the motivations of the ACS and its domestic role in the antislavery movement.

More recently, however, historians have begun to explore America's forays into "imperialism" with more enthusiasm, making great strides in incorporating American expansionism and its politics into a broader picture of nineteenth-century imperial expansion.[4] The role of settlers in particular has helped in drawing the American experience into broader global trends of the nineteenth century. Recent work on Liberia has also begun to see that project as part of the older "manifest destiny" literature on American westward settlement.[5] This historiographical shift raises new questions about the role of the United States within the realm of global empires in the nineteenth century. Although its forms of expansion differed from British imperialism, Cooper and Burbank's concept of imperial "rule of difference" clearly brings the nineteenth-century United States into the scope of imperial history.[6]

Studying the expanding United States through the perspective of imperial history raises questions about the role of representative government in imperial history. America's written constitution was self-consciously a reaction against what the founders deemed a lack of representation within the British Empire, and similar written constitutions emerged as founding documents of self-representation and self-governance as New World colonies broke away from imperial rule. While scholars such as George Athan Billias present an argument for the role of American constitutionalism in granting wide acceptance of the idea that self-representation and rights must be codified and written down (in contrast to Britain's unwritten constitution), Liberia and Sierra Leone, examined together, reveal a different influence of American independence: the attempt to create a represented citizenship *within* an imperial frame in the wake of the failures of Britain to do the same in the new United States.[7]

British constitutional history has long had strains suggesting that a global, comparative, and fluid frame is necessary for viewing the evolution of written constitutions and charters.[8] A. F. Madden suggests a comparative approach to the spread of imperial constitutions and a more nuanced understanding of the negotiated process through which representative models were imported and adapted over time. He writes that "it was not just a matter of the realm's intentions in charter, statute or instruction, but of how men regarded the instruments they received and how they worked them."[9] This vantage point seems especially pertinent in the cases of Liberia and Sierra Leone, where experiments in citizenship were expressly written into their design. These two experiments challenge the commonly held understanding of constitutions as the foundation for representative self-rule, and instead bring together the real variety of representative types that could have emerged in the 1800s. While the constitutions are an important aspect of the story, the rise of modern representative institutions stretches beyond those documents themselves into the negotiation of power, the process of representation, and the development of exclusionary national— or imperial—identities.

Rather than working back from the nation-states and self-governance of the twenty-first century, this chapter follows a line of historical reasoning proposed by Frederick Cooper.[10] In his discussion of the different fates of French colonial West Africa during the mid-twentieth century, his analysis focuses on the strong possibility that the entities would negotiate a non-territorial, representative government, keeping intact the French West African polity and the union—although in a different form—between France and its African possessions. Cooper's clear insight into the processes through which independence, and not representation, became the rallying cry could be translated to the situation in Liberia a century earlier. In other words, while representation was important for most post–American Revolution settler societies, independence or self-rule were often less important—an opt-out clause, rather than a desired state. Representation could occur within the empire; self-rule and independence demanded an exit from empire.

Citizenship and "subjecthood" were the crucial issues under debate throughout the post-enlightenment, humanitarian-tinged imperial period of the eighteenth to the twentieth century. Both the American and British empires sought to expand while maintaining control over citizenship, representation, and the internal values that made up a British or American identity. Sierra Leone and Liberia present revelatory case studies in the comparison of these Atlantic imperial expansions. Sierra Leone, as the first British colony established after American independence, reveals the ideological developments taking place in the metropole in this crucial period for settler and antislavery claims on British values.[11] Liberia, growing up in the heyday of American expansion, reveals the expansiveness of American imperial ambition, but also the limits imposed by racial ideology. These colonies were unusual in these respects, but they were also representative of broader trends, and should therefore be seen as part of a larger picture of experimental citizenship, constitution-writing, and expansion taking place from the late eighteenth century through the mid-nineteenth.

Sierra Leone and British Imperial Representation

As the first of the post–American Revolution utopian societies, Sierra Leone—or the "Province of Freedom" as it was known—experienced a number of growing pains as settlers and their governments negotiated power. Between the founding in 1787 and the establishment of Crown control in 1808, the colony went through a series of changes that both characterized and helped to shape the ideas of colonial representation. From the establishment of British rule in the colony in 1808, changes took place more slowly and reflected the settlers' awareness of their role in the wider empire, their symbolic value in the metropole, and the spreading examples of representation within expansionist polities in the broader Atlantic milieu.

At the time of the settlement of Sierra Leone, wider changes in the British Empire's notion of representation and citizenship were being formed in places like Canada and the West Indies, as well as increasingly in Britain itself. Under British East India Company military rule, even India was experiencing a moment of negotiated governance in the period before the military machine and corresponding Raj bureaucracy had expanded enough to effectively control from the top down.[12] In the settler colonies, after American independence, the American call for representation in dealings with Parliament was repeatedly invoked by the elite.[13] The "doctrine of parliamentary supremacy" was challenged, and secession threats were made, particularly by West Indian planters who felt they were under siege by the new abolition lobby in Britain.[14] But as Andrew Jackson O'Shaughnessy points out, "the white colonial elite wanted autonomy and self-government but within the British Empire."[15]

Within Britain itself, it was predominantly the abolitionists who were concerned with reforming the constitutional system. As Christopher Brown notes, "those who had hoped that the loss of the American colonies would result in the remodelling of the British constitution participated in large numbers" in the early antislavery movement.[16] Their focus on reforming the empire helped to create the movement out of which the Sierra Leone experiment emerged.

Granville Sharp, heavily involved in both antislavery and constitutional reform, proposed the colony in Sierra Leone to provide a place of refuge for the "Black Poor" of London, and also to help demonstrate a new system of representative democracy. Sharp's plan for the "Province of Freedom" built on mythical English heritage, creating a system of elected "Tythingmen" and "Hundredors" meant to mirror ancient Anglo-Saxon representation or "Frankpleadge." The rudimentary constitution bound the settlers to protect each other, and all settlers were provided with proof of their free status—in case they encountered slave traders. While the charter was written with English precedent in mind, and the settlers declared their allegiance to King George before they departed, they were not intended to be a settlement within the British Empire once they landed, but to rule themselves and promote British values in the region.[17]

The colony faced many of the problems of all early settlements: high mortality, abandonment of the colony, difficulty establishing agriculture, and disputes between the elected governors. These were compounded by aggressive neighbors—mostly uncooperative European and African slave traders who objected to the colony. By 1790, Sharp proposed a new trading company—the St George's Bay Company—to provide capital for the settlers to trade in the region. This developed into the Sierra Leone Company, which, given its expenditure in investment, desired a role in the governance of the colony. The Sierra Leone Act, which granted the Crown's land purchase to the company, created a group of thirteen directors responsible for legislating for the colony. The colony ceased being a self-governing settlement established by, but operating outside the remit of, the British government.[18]

After the Sierra Leone Company took charge of the colony, it was clear that new governance structures were needed in order to regulate the relationship between the company's governor and the settlers.[19] Zachary Macaulay, governor from 1794 to 1799, continued to deal with the hundredors and tythingmen of Sharp's model community, but suggested that some form of constitution that took into account his own role would benefit the colony. In October 1796, Macaulay wrote back to the company's director, Henry Thornton, advising him that "I have been drawing out the outlines of a Constitution which I hope we shall be able to put into activity when the new Tythingmen enter on their office on the 1st of January." Although he worked primarily with the suggestions "received from you, Messrs. W. Elliot, Grant, Gibson, and Babington with respect to the outlines and with respect to the Detail," he noted that "I shall endeavour as far as I can to suit it to local circumstances."[20]

In Macaulay's constitution, representation was based on landholding, or income, as well as consent to the laws of the colony: "The legal possession of an acre of land in the Colony for twelve months is *for the present* to constitute a right to vote for representatives &c. Posession is not legal unless the Consent of the Government hath been obtained by a stranger coming among us to his settlement and the declaration of submission to the laws of the Colony signed. A vote is also allowed those who tho they have no Land have a salary from the Company of not less than £40 a year."[21] The provision for income rather than landholding was intended to include European

Company officers in the voting, thereby ensuring that "the proceedings at public meetings might be a little better regulated than at present."[22] Therefore, while representative, the provisions of the constitution were intended to place paternalistic controls on the settlers, both in terms of their behavior at meetings, and their ability to be recognized as having the right to vote.

In the terms of the constitution itself, the requirements for voting were more explicit: "none but Citizens are entitled to vote," the second article declared, and "their qualifications are, 21 years of Age; acknowledgement of the belief of one God & of the divine Authority of the Bible; Subscribing the act of Submission to the Laws of the Colony, and the payment of a direct tax of at least Twenty Cents yearly." The qualifications for citizenship excluded many indigenous Africans who entered, traded with, and lived in the colony, effectively enshrining cultural assimilation—as well as taxation—into the model of representative colonialism in Sierra Leone. The model was not wholly dissimilar from that practiced in colonial North America, particularly given that the right to vote only applied to the House of Commons, with the upper house chosen by the tythingmen and the governor and council appointed by London and retaining "not only a negative but a power of originating Resolutions on every matter."[23]

The governor's and council's roles expanded yet again in the next incarnation of Sierra Leone's constitutional governance. Although the handover to the Crown in 1808 did not immediately change the governance of the colony—military rule was not imposed, trial by jury was retained, and the company's provisions were mostly kept intact—a gradual change occurred as individual governors sought to increase their authority over the settlers and the growing liberated African population.[24]

Thomas Perronet Thompson, the first royal governor, preferred a more martial rule and disliked the democratic initiatives of company rule: he changed Freetown to "Georgetown," did away with the dollar currency, chose military personnel for civilian positions, and imposed the established church.[25] This reflected his dislike for "Republican institutions" and his preference for the martial Maroon settlers over the (perceived) democratic tendencies of the Nova Scotians, who had been steeped in American revolutionary ideas. While Thompson was fairly quickly removed from his position, until 1815 the settlers experienced harsher rule and less representation at the whim of a string of more military-minded governors.

With the arrival of Governor Charles MacCarthy in 1815, the settlers finally resumed some of their older rights and responsibilities. However, the governor and council maintained legislative and executive authority. It was not until 1862 that the legislative council achieved its earlier representative function, and even then, elected representatives were not a part of the new constitution. In the interim, the paternalistic nature of the early colony redoubled with the arrival, settlement, and assimilation of the "liberated Africans" freed from the now-illegal slave trade. The arrival of these new settlers who had not come from other parts of the British Empire—as the Black Poor, Nova Scotians, and Maroons had—shifted the center of political gravity away from these "British" settlers and toward a more acculturated African creole community.

Fundamental to the changing nature of colonial representation were the Sierra Leoneans' claims of "Britishness," through which they articulated their "citizenship" in a broader imperial community. In 1829, settler and liberated African petitioners requested of the colonial and metropolitan governments that available government roles "would be open only to merit and good conduct without reference to the color of the individual."[26] Sierra Leoneans hoped to advance in the colonial hierarchy, getting the higher-salaried jobs suited to those with educations provided by the colony. Citing their contributions toward the "civilization" of Africa, the Sierra Leoneans confessed that they had been cheered "by the hope that they would at some no distant period, be permitted to participate in those favors, so exclusively bestowed on their European, British fellow subjects."[27]

The petitioners reminded the governor of "their loyalty and devotion to His Majesty in the performance of the duties of such offices as the Public Service may require in this Colony." Sierra Leoneans did not only want to receive from the government; they wanted an active participatory role. While this did not include representation in a legislative body, they did hope the government would not see it as too onerous to "permit the African British subjects the full opportunity to become a useful member of the community, create in him a laudable, and virtuous ambition."[28]

There was in fact an ongoing discussion from the 1810s about the virtues of virtual versus real representation with regard to Sierra Leone, a result of the confusing nature of Sierra Leonean citizenship. Colonial government correspondence regularly warned indigenous peoples against interfering with the "British subjects" of Sierra Leone.[29] With the focus on assimilation of liberated Africans into British culture, combined with the high level of education available to all Sierra Leonean children, it is not surprising that, even without official avenues for representation, a thriving political community developed within the society. Like other settler colonies, Sierra

Leone believed that British political life should be representative at some level, even as much of the clamor for representation in the post-revolutionary Atlantic world had begun to change the nature of Canadian and West Indian rule in the 1840s.[30]

In 1847, the Colonial Office had to decide whether to make the Sierra Leone Council—established in 1821 to promote harmony between the governor and the Sierra Leonean community—a true legislative assembly with the power to legislate beyond the authority of the governor and his council. The conclusion of the Colonial Office was that any decision that clarified whether the body was actually legislative would raise broader imperial concerns. The Colonial Office commented that "it wd. be necessary to apply to Parliamt. & to tell a story better kept out of sight" in case other colonies demanded similar representative bodies.[31] This debate continued in the 1850s, especially as Liberia became an independent state and representation was debated in Canada and Australia.[32]

In 1858, believing that they had "progressed" to the state of real rather than virtual representation, Sierra Leoneans petitioned for elective government. This campaign was led by the Mercantile Association, and the group agitated for a legislature in the model of the Canadian or West Indian settlements, again highlighting their connections to the rest of the Atlantic empire and their continued desire to be recognized as equals within imperial governance. However, Governor Stephan Hill (1854–55, 1855–59, and 1860–61) rejected the petition, arguing that it represented only the desires of the small minority—194 Sierra Leoneans—who would be enfranchised under the English £10 property rule.[33] With no prospects of representative government, the creation of associations linking Sierra Leoneans to broader African diaspora networks and the maintenance of links to allies in Britain remained important tools for furthering the colony's economic and political interests in the face of recalcitrant governors, strategies that would become increasingly important in the decades to follow.

Sierra Leoneans attempted throughout the first fifty years of the settlement to negotiate their own "citizenship" within the British Empire in the same way that the West Indian planters and Canadian settlers attempted to negotiate theirs. Representation at the local level was a major concern for all of these groups, and was generally conceded at some level by the metropolitan government and humanitarian organizations involved in governance. But representation and recognition of citizenship—at the level of "global Britishness"—was more complicated for those settlers residing in foreign settlements. As Madden notes, colonies were always "dependencies," and the British government allowed local autonomy only within the bounds of parliamentary authority.[34] Sierra Leoneans, like their West Indian counterparts, could appeal to the British Parliament, but they had no representative there. Instead, they relied on a lobby to make their case for them in the metropole. In the case of Sierra Leone, this meant balancing the assertion of rights with the acceptance of the paternalistic condescension of that same lobby. While race was not a determining factor in imperial citizenship, it did play a role in the way that "citizenship" was represented in the metropole.

Ultimately, however, it became clear that some kind of guarantee of citizenship was necessary, especially as Sierra Leoneans moved elsewhere in Africa and demanded continued British protection. With an increasing number of Sierra Leoneans leaving for Lagos, Abeokuta, and Badagry to seek their fortunes elsewhere, the application of British laws beyond the boundaries of Sierra Leone came into question as well. Finally, after more than a decade of uncertainty about Sierra Leoneans' status as British subjects, in 1853 a Parliamentary Act declared that "all liberated Africans domiciled or resident, or who hereafter may be domiciled or resident, in the colony of Sierra Leone or its dependencies, shall be deemed to be and to have been for all purposes as, from the date of their being brought into or of their arrival in said colony, natural-born subjects of Her Majesty."[35]

However, while this changed the status of Sierra Leoneans within the empire, it did not grant them representation beyond their normal methods of petition at the local and metropolitan levels. Even the establishment of the Legislative Council in 1862 did not grant elected representation to the various groups of settlers, receptives, and their descendants in Sierra Leone. Ultimately, to keep the merchant community happy, one elected member of that community was given a seat on the council—outnumbered by the Executive Council and four councillors appointed by the governor from among the ranks of the Europeans in the colony. The experiment in colonial citizenship and self-representation that had begun in the post–American Revolution moment with Granville Sharp's "Province of Freedom" had culminated in imperial citizenship and one representative member of a Westminster-style legislative body.

Liberia and the Territorial Model

Meanwhile, Liberia was moving on a different trajectory. Although the idea for American expansionary representation did not begin with Liberia, or necessarily reflect the experiments taking place in Sierra Leone and around the British world in the 1780s and 1790s, it shared a number of features that were later amalgamated with those models in the establishment of Liberian constitutionalism. Representation was not immediately linked to citizenship in the American model of expansionary rule, but settlers who moved outside of the established states were seen to be on a path toward representation. This model differed from the British attempts at colonial representational governance because it assumed a "progression" that, perhaps unsurprisingly, followed America's own historical "progression" from colonies ruled by appointed governors, to increasingly representative legislatures, to the formation of, and incorporation into, a national legislature.

The post-revolutionary United States accounted for territorial expansion with the Northwest Ordinance. In 1784 and 1785, the Continental Congress passed this legislation, signed into law by President George Washington and ratified by the new Congress in 1789, which developed the method by which new states would be added to the Union. The process followed a series of stages: settlers would arrive; a territorial government—run by a congressionally appointed governor, treasurer, and judge—would be established; and when the free male population of voting age reached five thousand, they could vote for a legislature. The Enabling Act of 1802 then laid out the steps for achieving statehood. Territories did not have to be contiguous to earlier territories or states, and they did not have to enter the Union consecutively. By 1821, Michigan, Missouri, Arkansas, and Oregon territory were being administered and settled while eight new states had already been added to the Union. There was little controversy about the lack of representation for early settlers in the territories because there was an assumption that this was merely a step on the way toward full recognition and representation within the Union.[36]

Throughout the process of territorial expansion and incorporation, the indigenous American population was increasingly marginalized. Like the proslavery white elites in the West Indies who claimed British constitutional rights at the expense of their enslaved workers, American settlers who gained representation in the federal union also defended their constitutional rights at the expense of indigenous rights. In fact, throughout the Atlantic world, in the wake of the post-revolutionary moment, citizenship and representation were being recast continually as an exclusionary exercise.[37]

It was in this context, then, that Liberia's settlements were established in West Africa. Susan Ryan argues that colonizationists believed that, through the establishment of these settlements, they were improving the opportunities available to free African Americans, giving them a chance for economic self-sufficiency and a place to operate their own limited representative institutions.[38] But this was also part of the wider Atlantic reimagining of expansion and imperial governance: nation-building and expansionism were not limited to the British experiment in Sierra Leone, but contributed significantly to the ACS's ideas of African colonization. When the aggressive antislavery activist and expansionist Jehudi Ashmun was appointed as agent of the colony in the 1820s, Staudenraus writes that his approach was extremely popular among American colonizationists, who "hailed it as the first step in building an American empire."[39]

In fact, in 1828, a committee of colonizationists, "asking for the patronage of the General Government to be extended to the colony at Liberia," noted that they "entertain no doubt, whatever, but that the Government of the United States has the constitutional power to acquire territory; and that the people of every inhabited country, so acquired, must be regarded as standing, towards the Federal Government, in the relation of colonial dependencies till admitted as co-ordinate States with the common Union."[40]

The ACS sent out an agent with the first colonists, who would be responsible for making treaties for land, defending the territory against slave traders, and governing the territory. Many settlers participated because they felt they had a better chance at obtaining the rights and responsibilities of citizenship in Liberia than in the continental United States.[41] John Brown Russwurm, a graduate of Maine's Bowdoin College and editor of *Freedom's Journal*, argued that "full citizenship in the United States is utterly impossible in the nature of things, and that those who pant for it must cast their eyes elsewhere."[42]

The first viable Liberian settlement—in Monrovia—was quickly followed by state-authorized offshoots along the coast. The Maryland, Virginia, Pennsylvania, and New York colonization societies all set up their own settlements, with their own local agents, responsible to the state colonization societies. The Liberian agent's duty was to provide for new settlers, as well as liberated Africans arriving in the colony. Each of the state colonies established along the coast had a dual-governance structure, responsible to the state colonization society in addition to the ACS agent, creating a double-layered bureaucracy. This was not the most efficient model for funding the colonies, as individual or state auxiliaries funded projects in their own colonies.

The Maryland State Colonization Society drafted its constitution for its colony in Cape Palmas, roughly 250 miles down the coast from Monrovia, in 1835. The first article gave the state society the full power to decide laws and regulations for the colony "until the state society shall withdraw their agents, and yield the government wholly into the hands of the people of the territory."[43]

As with the provisions for incorporating territories into the United States, this document made provision for the gradual hand-over of authority to the American settler population. The election of representation within the colony would be "by ballot, the qualifications of voters to be fixed by the state society." Although article seven gave the citizens of Maryland in Liberia the same protections of the U.S. Bill of Rights, their ability to vote and legislate was to be determined by the metropolitan authority. They were forbidden from altering the constitution, which included paternalistic and utopian provisions that commanded all those wishing to move into the colony to "bind themselves to refrain from the use of ardent spirits" and preventing those wishing to hold office in the colony from using or trafficking in the same.[44] As with Granville Sharp's idealistic vision for Sierra Leone, the founders of Maryland in Liberia were attempting to establish a paternalistic model of settler colonialism. Morality would be regulated in order to "improve" the population, with citizenship and representation dependent on adherence to a set of values meant to represent the best of the metropole.

As in the United States, Liberian expansion often came at the expense of indigenous Liberians. Equally, "Liberian" identification and citizenship came to be defined by connections to America, even as the new Liberians advertised the benefits of the settlements to Americans back home. Svend Holsoe has shown that the settlers' relationships with indigenous Africans depended on the ease of manipulating conflicts between the Dei, Gola, and Condo tribes in their need for trading partners and security for the settlement. Claude Clegg describes the settlers creating employment by apprenticeship and networks of trade with these indigenous groups and, through them, "spread[ing] both colonial culture among indigenous people and African cultures among immigrants and provided a bit of security for the latter."[45] Throughout the early years of the settlement, military force was the preferred method for enforcing Liberian settlement and violent encounters were frequent, but as the years progressed, treaty-making became increasingly sophisticated and negotiators became increasingly conscious of the reciprocal trading needs of the Liberians and their neighbors. Trade was the predominant form of interaction, as was the taking on of wards, and the increasing use of local foods and materials.⁴⁶ But despite interaction with the settlement and even certain amounts of cultural integration between the Americo-Liberians and the Gola, Dei, Vai, Kru, and Kpelle, the indigenous groups were largely excluded from any form of citizenship in the colonial framework, even as they were relied on for trade and economic development.

Reflecting their uneasy coexistence with indigenous Liberians, the settlers often made use of them for rhetorical point-scoring in the metropole. Writing back to the ACS, state colonization societies, and former owners, Liberian settlers noted that they shared more in common culturally with America than with Africa. Settler Peyton Skipwith wrote that "it is something strange to think that those people of Africa are called our ancestors."⁴⁷ Another settler, Samson Ceasar, noted his discomfort "when I first Saw the nativs naked I thought that I never could get ust to it" but acknowledged that "it is an old saing use is second nature I do not mind to see them now."⁴⁸

Settlers also objected to the enfranchisement of recaptive Africans settled in the colony by the naval squadron.⁴⁹ They extolled the virtues of the colony in promoting American "civilization" in West Africa. The *Liberia Herald* noted in 1832, "Our recaptives of the Congo tribe, have progressed so far in civilization, that several frames (some of which are up) are preparing to be erected during the present season. Their meeting house is so far finished, that they hold regular meetings therein, and through the whole village, there reins so much neatness and comfort, that we have seen few spots to surpass it."⁵⁰ Aside from these feelings of civilizational superiority, the growth of civil society meant that Liberians were increasingly interested in taking charge of the governance of the colony. As in Sierra Leone, religious and civil society leaders, as well as merchants, emerged as the elite Americo-Liberians who hoped to play some role in their own government. The new agitation for a change in governance coincided with ACS statements supporting the eventual self-government of the colony by its settlers.

In 1838, the settlers in Monrovia wrote to the ACS asking that the original Plan of Government be amended to account for the growth of the colony and its preparedness for self-government. However, even in 1838, the ACS hoped to maintain Liberia within the broader structure of their governance. The settlers were allowed to draft a new constitution while the governor of Bassa Cove, Thomas Buchanan, was asked by the ACS to write an alternative draft. In neither constitution was there a call for the ACS government to be dismantled nor independence given. Both documents did suggest more executive power for a governor of all the territories who would still be paid and appointed by the ACS for the immediate future but might at some point be appointed by settlers. The new composite constitution aimed to satisfy settlers' demands for a more efficient government, consolidating the settlements and representing their interests and providing security.[51]

The new commonwealth constitution demonstrated that the ACS government—like the U.S. government more broadly in interactions with the territories it governed—was responsive to the demands of the settlers, even while ruling without representation. The document also marked a large step towards self-rule for the Americo-Liberians, given the implication of a settler-appointed governor in the future and their participation in the process of drafting the constitution, a fact that did not go unrecognized by Sierra Leoneans as they sought their own form of representation.

Despite the success of the commonwealth constitution in unifying the settlements and providing a common government, common protection, and common revenue collection, what became increasingly important in the Liberian situation was recognition of its legitimacy on the West Coast of Africa. Challenged by Sierra Leonean and British traders in a variety of coastal towns, Liberians required the support of the federal government. Similar challenges in the contested areas of North America saw the federal government step in to protect settlers. In this period the federal government faced down Mexico, Britain, and the Cherokee nation over territorial rights. But in Liberia, this was not an option. Federal recognition of Liberia would require a decision about its role within the federal system. Liberians themselves became increasingly frustrated in these engagements as they vainly called on the support of the ACS. Finally, Liberia's assembly declared its independence in 1847, modeling its declaration of independence and constitution on the American documents, although differing in its attitudes towards race and slavery.[52]

After holding a constitutional convention and voting on the draft in October, the new constitution of the Republic of Liberia was made the law of the land in November 1847. Despite the outcome of the Liberian experiment in colonial citizenship, the ACS was unperturbed, declaring in resolutions delivered at its 1849 annual meeting that the independence of Liberia had succeeded in "founding a new republican empire on the shores of Africa, introducing there civilization and Christianity."[53]

The Liberian situation was clearly part of a wider American project in experimenting with "territorial" government and citizenship. Between the 1780s and the 1830s, the Liberian territories were part of a broader expansionary project that saw "American" peoples ruled by governments appointed in Washington. Liberia was not an outlier; nor was it wholly in the model of the Northwest Ordinance. The ACS experiment in Liberia was representative of the American model that combined British colonial governance, which many of the older ACS members had experienced firsthand, with the new approach that saw territories gradually accumulating a population, institutions, economic growth, and finally representation at the federal level. But it was a private organization, and its appointed governors—although frequently overlapping with congressionally appointed U.S. Navy agents—were privately chosen. There was no expectation that the Liberian territories would achieve statehood. Rather, this was a sort of representative compromise whereby the metropolitan authority would allow the development of representative institutions, but with indefinite metropolitan oversight.

Race was an integral issue in the formation of these ideas of gradual representation. In the Northwest Territories and in the Liberian territories, slavery was illegal. In neither, however, were black settlers considered full citizens. In the Northwest Territories they would be "governed" by the territorial government, then the legislature, and ultimately by the state and federal government. In Liberia, representative institutions were developed in response to settler demands, but the paternalistic rule of the ACS was expected to continue indefinitely. The representative institutions that emerged in Liberia over the course of the late 1830s and 1840s increasingly saw the territories moving away from their connection to the Union, rather than toward it, as the legislatures in the various new continental territories heralded. While race was a consideration throughout the period, it gradually became an exclusionary factor.

Finally, in 1847, Liberia declared independence from the ACS and elected Governor Joseph Jenkins Roberts its first president. The new constitution mirrored that of the United States, with a president, Supreme Court, House of Representatives, and Senate responsible for representing the Liberian settlers. The right to vote was based on Liberian citizenship, but indigenous Liberians were not given the franchise as they were, in M. B. Akpan's words, "*de facto* subjects of the Americo-Liberians."[54] Self-rule and independence became the default form of constitutional citizenship for Liberians because the Americans and Americo-Liberians involved in the project could not conceive of a United States that included fully equal black citizens, even as they could conceive of a black republic sharing equality on the world stage. As in America, and in settler colonies around the world, citizenship and representation continued to be limited, the settler population always separating itself from indigenous civilizations through a constitutional link to the metropole.

Conclusion

Sierra Leone and Liberia were both part of a wider movement to establish models of extraterritorial representative citizenship in the period following American independence. Fearing the demands of self-government by other colonies, Britain adapted its approach to settler demands. Local representation of some kind was almost guaranteed for those claiming British identity. Working within local representative structures, however limited, Sierra Leoneans were also able to go over the head of the governor. Imperial representation was achieved through a balance of lobbying power and the right to petition. In the eighteenth and early nineteenth centuries, although paternalism was a significant factor in attitudes toward Sierra Leonean settlers, race had little role to play in the ability to claim a British imperial identity. While it was a different kind of post-revolution angst that led to the establishment of Sierra Leone's constitution, West Indian plantation owners and freed slave settlers in Freetown could equally demand representation in the imperial system.

On the other hand, Liberia fit uncomfortably into an American model of settler expansion. The pattern of Western territorial government matched the ACS's plan for Liberian rule up to a point, but the natural evolution from territory to state was never a real option for the Liberian settlements. Here, race played a much more influential role in definitions of citizenship and representation, even as it failed to preclude the establishment of an American-style democracy (similarly unconcerned for indigenous rights) made up entirely of African Americans excluded from U.S. citizenship. Liberian settlers did, however, make a claim for their own "Americanness" throughout much of the 1830s as they sought aid from the United States in establishing their authority over the Dei, Gola, slave traders, European traders, and other neighboring groups.

Liberia's own experience with representative government differed significantly from Sierra Leone's, in large part because of this context. With paternalistic colonial rule present in each colony, race became a more important factor in the American setting because it effectively, ultimately, precluded Liberia from participation in the Union. Sierra Leone, with fewer representative institutions and constant battle between settlers, colonial government, and imperial government, actually spent much of the nineteenth century operating in exactly the same extraterritorial context as other British settler societies.

For both British and American philanthropists and government agents involved in the project, the new colonies were an opportunity to re-center national values at the heart of constitutional forms of government. Because the settlers were from a dependent class, the paternalistic encroachments on their liberty in the name of "self-improvement" or "rehabilitation" were deemed to be appropriate. But these utopian or reform models were also represented in other settler movements in the same period, with Mormons emigrating west in the 1830s or Australian penal colonies being established in the same year as Sierra Leone. Race may have been influential in the treatment of Sierra Leone and Liberia by the metropoles, but "civilization" and the ability to adhere to British or American values were articulated by both the settlers and the institutions that supported them as equally influential. In the late eighteenth and early nineteenth century, settlers were able to use these other goals—temperance, antislavery, education, Christian mission, commerce—to occasionally overcome those who attempted to exclude them from imperial citizenship on the basis of race.

A comparative frame makes clear that, in both colonies, these antislavery projects attempted to construct a dependent, but free, black citizenry. Sierra Leonean and Liberian colonists strove for a government that represented their interests against the interests of European slave traders, indigenous Africans, and often, the colonial agents sent to govern them. In their frames of colonial empire, wherein black citizenry had limited rights and a continued dependent relationship with the state, the colonial agents, metropolitan organizations, and colonists themselves tried to work out a new form of modern settler society. Ultimately, neither system achieved that perfect balance: Sierra Leone was ruled increasingly autocratically while Liberia became fully independent. By the end of the nineteenth century, both groups of settlers had their independence severely restricted by the new imperial world order. However, the experiences of these two colonies represented a moment in settler colonialism when "modernity" and "civilization" were given more weight than race in the determination of citizenship and representation.

Notes

1. Granville Sharp, *Short Sketch of Temporary Regulations (until better shall be proposed) for the Intended Settlement on the Grain Coast of Africa, near Sierra Leone* (London, 1786), iii; see also Christopher Fyfe, *A History of Sierra Leone* (Oxford, U.K.: Oxford University Press, 1962), 16, on the early founding of the settlement.

2. Maya Jasanoff refers to this as the "spirit of 1783," which was characterized by global expansion of the British Empire, a commitment to humanitarianism and liberty, and an increase in centralization and hierarchical governance (*Liberty's Exiles: American Loyalists in the Revolutionary World* [New York: Random House, 2011], 12–13).

3. I will be using the term "Sierra Leoneans" to refer to the people who came to live in the Sierra Leone colony itself, people made up of the original settlers, the Nova Scotians, the Maroons, liberated African slaves, and people from the Susu, Temne, and other African groups who were absorbed into the colony or who chose to move there and live permanently in the settlement. Since the area beyond the Freetown peninsula was not yet part of the colony of Sierra Leone, people who were living and operating beyond the remit of the colony will be referred to by their ethnic identities. For more on the debate over whether "Sierra Leoneans" should be called "Krios" in this period, see David Skinner and Barbara E. Harrell-Bond, "Misunderstandings Arising from the Use of the Term 'Creole' in the Literature on Sierra Leone," *Africa: Journal of the International African Institute* 47, no. 3 (1977): 305–20; Akintola J. G. Wyse, "On Misunderstandings Arising from the Use of the Term 'Creole' in the Literature on Sierra Leone: A Rejoinder," *Africa: Journal of the International African Institute* 49, no. 4 (1979): 408–17; Christopher Fyfe, "The Term 'Creole': A Footnote to a Footnote," *Africa: Journal of the International African Institute* 50, no. 4 (1980): 422; David Skinner and Barbara E. Harrell-Bond, "Creoles: A Final Comment," *Africa: Journal of the International African Institute* 51, no. 3 (1981): 787; Odile George, "Sierra Leonais, Creoles, Krio: La Dialectique De L'identité" *Africa: Journal of the International African Institute* 65, no. 1 (1995): 114–32.

4. Ian Tyrrell, *Transnational Nation: United States History in Global Perspective since 1789* (Hampshire, U.K.: Palgrave Macmillan, 2007); Jay Sexton, *Debtor Diplomacy: Finance and American Foreign Relations in the Civil War Era 1837–1873* (Oxford, U.K.: Oxford University Press, 2005); James Belich, *Replenishing the Earth: The Settler Revolution and the Rise of the Anglo-World, 1783–1939* (Oxford, U.K.: Oxford University Press, 2009); Andrew Thompson and Gary Magee, *Empire and Globalisation* (Cambridge, U.K.: Cambridge University Press, 2010); Sven Beckert, *Empire of Cotton: A New History of Global Capitalism* (New York: Alfred A. Knopf, 2014); Brian Schoen, *The Fragile Fabric of Union: Cotton, Federal Politics, and the Global Origins of the Civil War* (Baltimore: Johns Hopkins University Press, 2009).

5. Nicholas Guyatt, "'The Outskirts of Our Happiness': Race and the Lure of Colonization in the Early Republic," *Journal of American History* 95, no. 4 (2009): 986–1011; William E. Allen, "Liberia and the Atlantic World in the Nineteenth Century: Convergence and Effects," *History in Africa* 37 (2010): 7–49; Richard Douglass-Chin, "Liberia as American Diaspora: The Transnational Scope of American Identity in the Mid-Nineteenth Century," *Canadian Review of American Studies* 40, no. 2 (2010): 213–34; Bronwen Everill, "'Destiny

Seems to Point Me to That Country': Early Nineteenth-Century African American Migration, Emigration and Expansion," *Journal of Global History* 7, no. 1 (2012): 53–77.

6. Jane Burbank and Frederick Cooper, *Empires in World History: Power and the Politics of Difference* (Princeton, N.J.: Princeton University Press, 2010), chap. 9.

7. George Athan Billias, *American Constitutionalism Heard Round the World, 1776–1989: A Global Perspective* (New York: New York University Press, 2009); Jasanoff, *Liberty's Exiles*, 14.

8. Linda Colley, *Britons: Forging the Nation, 1707–1837* (New Haven: Yale University Press, 1992); Jonathan Fulcher, "The English People and Their Constitution after Waterloo: Parliamentary Reform, 1815–1817," in James Vernon, ed., *Re-reading the Constitution: New Narratives of the Political History of England's Long Nineteenth Century* (Cambridge, U.K.: Cambridge University Press, 1996); M. C. Mirow, "The Age of Constitutions in the Americas," *Law and History Review*, 32:2 (2014), 229–35.

9. A. F. Madden, "'Not for Export': The Westminster Model of Government and British Colonial Practice," *Journal of Imperial and Commonwealth History* 8, no. 1 (1979): 11.

10. Frederick Cooper, *Decolonization and African Society: The Labor Question in French and British Africa* (Cambridge, U.K.: Cambridge University Press, 1996), 177–78; Frederick Cooper, *Citizenship Between Empire and Nation: Remaking France and French Africa, 1945–60* (Princeton, N.J.: Princeton University Press, 2014).

11. Jasanoff, *Liberty's Exiles*, 307.

12. James Lees, "A 'Tranquil Spectator': The District Official and the Practice of Local Government in Late Eighteenth-Century Bengal," *Journal of Imperial and Commonwealth History*, 38, no. 1 (2010), 1–19; Jon Wilson, *The Domination of Strangers: Modern Governance in Colonial India, 1780–1835* (Basingstoke, U.K.: Palgrave Macmillan, 2008).

13. Jasanoff, *Liberty's Exiles*, 347; Andrew Jackson O'Shaughnessy, *An Empire Divided: The American Revolution and the British Caribbean* (Philadelphia: University of Pennsylvania Press, 2000), 245.

14. Christer Petley, "'Devoted Islands' and 'That Madman Wilberforce': British Pro-slavery Patriotism During the Age of Abolition," *Journal of Imperial and Commonwealth History* 39, no. 3 (2011): 393–415.

15. O'Shaughnessy, *An Empire Divided*, 248.

16. Christopher Leslie Brown, *Moral Capital* (Chapel Hill: University of North Carolina Press, 2007), 445.

17. Fyfe, *History of Sierra Leone*, 16.

18. Ibid., 26–27.

19. For more on MacCarthy, see Padraic Scanlan, "The Rewards of their Exertions: Prize Money and British Abolitionism in Sierra Leone, 1808–1823," *Past and Present* 225, no. 1 (2014): 113–42; Suzanne Schwarz, ed., *Zachary Macaulay and the Development of the Sierra Leone Company, c. 1793–4* (Leipzig: Institut fur Afrikanistik, 2000).

20. Zachary Macaulay to Henry Thornton, October 6, 1796, Huntington Library, MY 635.

21. Ibid.

22. Ibid.

23. Macaulay's Journal, November 30, 1796, Huntington Library, MY 418; Zachary Macaulay to Henry Thornton, October 6, 1796.

24. Fyfe, *History of Sierra Leone*, 97–98.

25. Ibid., 107–8; Michael Turner, "The Limits of Abolition: Government, Saints and the 'African Question,' c. 1780–1820," *English Historical Review* 112, no. 446 (1997): 319–57.

26. Received January 29, 1830, The National Archives, U.K. (TNA), CO 267/99.

27. Ibid.

28. Ibid.

29. See, for instance: B. C. Pine to Tom Coubak Bonthe, April 1848; B. C. Pine to Fourry Bundo, June 27, 1848; B. C. Pine to R. A. Oldfield and W. Saukey, July 17, 1848, all in Sierra Leone Archives, Fourah Bay College, Freetown (SLA), Governor's Local Letters 1846–48.

30. David Cannadine, *Ornamentalism: How the British Saw Their Empire* (London: Oxford University Press, 2002), 12; Ged Martin, "Confederation Rejected: The British Debate on Canada, 1837–1840," *Journal of Imperial and Commonwealth History* 11, no. 1 (1982): 33–57; Peter Burroughs, "State Formation and the Imperial Factor in Nineteenth-Century Canada," *Journal of Imperial and Commonwealth History* 24, no. 1 (1996): 118–31.

31. James Stephen, Minute on Sierra Leone Legislative Council, April 12, 1847, TNA, CO 267/197.

32. Bruce A. Knox, "The British Government, Sir Edmund Head, and British North American Confederation, 1858," *Journal of Imperial and Commonwealth History* 4, no. 2 (1976): 206–17; Jasanoff, *Liberty's Exiles*, 346–50.

33. Mary Louise Clifford, *The Land and People of Sierra Leone* (Philadelphia: J. B. Lippincott, 1974), 58; Fyfe, *History of Sierra Leone*, 282.

34. Madden, "'Not for Export,'" 11.

35. Parliamentary Papers, 1855, vol. 37 (383): 36.

36. The appointment of territorial governments by Congress was controversial at various points in the antebellum period, notably in the Kansas-Nebraska debates, because Congress was seen to be interfering in the "popular sovereignty" debate. See Cathy D. Matson and Peter S. Onuf, *A Union of Interests: Political and Economic Thought in Revolutionary America* (Lawrence: University Press of Kansas, 1990), 61–62.

37. See Jack P. Greene, *Exclusionary Empire: English Liberty Overseas, 1600–1900* (Cambridge, U.K.: Cambridge University Press, 2010). For more on Liberia and ideas of citizenship, see Brandon Mills, "'The United States of Africa': Liberian Independence and the Contested Meaning of a Black Republic," *Journal of the Early Republic* 34, no. 1 (2014): 79–107.

38. Susan M. Ryan, "Errand into Africa: Colonization and Nation Building in Sarah J. Hale's Liberia," *New England Quarterly* 68, no. 4 (1995): 565.

39. P. J. Staudenraus, *The African Colonization Movement, 1816–1865* (New York: Columbia University Press, 1961), 157.

40. Benjamin Lundy, ed., *Genius of Universal Emancipation*, May 24, 1828, 118.

41. See Phil S. Sigler, "The Attitudes of Free Black Americans Towards Emigration to Liberia, 1817–1865," PhD diss., Boston University, 1969; Bronwen Everill, "'Destiny Seems to Point Me to That Country,'" 53–77; Christine Whyte, "Between Empire and Colony: American Imperialism and Pan-African Colonialism in Liberia, 1810–2003," *National Identities*, dx.doi.org/10.1080/14608944.2016.1095493, October 29, 2015; Mills, "'The United States of Africa,'" 79–107.

42. Lamin Sanneh, *Abolitionists Abroad: American Blacks and the Making of Modern West Africa* (Cambridge, Mass.: Harvard University Press, 1999), 221.

43. Constitution of Maryland in Liberia, Liberian Collections Project, Indiana University Archives, archive.org/details/constitutionand00libegoog.

44. Ibid.

45. Claude Andrew Clegg III, *The Price of Liberty: African Americans and the Making of Liberia* (Chapel Hill: University of North Carolina Press, 2004), 95.

46. Svend E. Holsoe, "A Study of Relations between Settlers and Indigenous Peoples in Western Liberia, 1821–1847," *African Historical Studies* 4, no. 2 (1971), 331–62; William E. Allen, "Rethinking the History of Settler Agriculture in Nineteenth-Century Liberia," *International Journal of African Historical Studies* 37, no. 3 (2004): 435–62.

47. Peyton Skipwith, April 22, 1840, Skipwith Family Letters, in *Dear Master: Letters of a Slave Family,* ed. Randall Miller (Athens: University of Georgia Press, 1990).

48. Samson Ceasar to Henry Westfall, April 1, 1834, University of Virginia Archives, ead.lib.virginia.edu/vivaxtf/view?docId=uva-sc/viu02800.xml.

49. Charles Henry Huberich, ed., *The Political and Legislative History of Liberia* (New York: Central Book Co., 1947), 636.

50. *Liberia Herald*, vol. 3, no. 3 (June 7, 1832).

51. Huberich, ed., *Political and Legislative History of Liberia*, 654.

52. Billias, *American Constitutionalism Heard Round the World,* 346–47; Bronwen Everill, *Abolition and Empire in Sierra Leone and Liberia* (Basingstoke, U.K.: Palgrave Macmillan, 2013), 140–47.

53. *Liberia Herald*, vol. 15, no. 24 (November 5, 1847); *Report of the Naval Committee to the House of Representatives, August, 1850, in favor of the establishment of a line of Mail Steamships to the Western Coast of Africa, and thence via the Mediterranean to London; Designed to promote the emigration of free persons of color from the United States to Liberia: Also to increase the steam navy, and to extend the commerce of the United States. With An Appendix by the American Colonization Society* (Washington, D.C., 1850), 67.

54. M. B. Akpan, "Black Imperialism: Americo-Liberian Rule over the African Peoples of Liberia, 1841–1964," *Revue Canadienne des Etudes Africaines* 7, no. 2 (1973): 226.

10

The American Colonization Society and the Civil War

SEBASTIAN N. PAGE

One area that has fallen through the cracks between scholarship on the African colonization movement and on federal resettlement policy is the study of the American Colonization Society (ACS) during the Civil War. Such an account would cover not only a period in which an essentially northern-managed ACS suffered an abrupt severance from its associates in the South, but also one in which the U.S. government enacted emancipation, recognized Liberia, and officially endorsed colonization for the first and only time. If ever there were a moment when the ACS redefined itself, this would surely be it. An all-too-familiar failure to initiate African American exodus notwithstanding, the wartime society's significance lies in what its activities tell us about its leaders' understanding of their mission, as well as in bearing witness to Washington's other attempts at colonization, which, it is now clear, have not been as thoroughly uncovered as historians had assumed.

Despite some differences of attitude among the key officers of the ACS and its remaining state auxiliaries, the overall picture that emerges is one of surprising reticence about crucial developments such as emancipation and the federal government's "political" colonization. This reserve stemmed from both specific misgivings and the broader proclivity for caution that was inherent in an established organization with official stances to respect as well as an otherwise unmanageable range of opinions among its administrators.

Naturally, the mixed fortunes of the 1850s influenced any consideration of engaging with government. The decade was one of what Allan Nevins aptly termed "race-adjustment," with a widespread renewal of state-level black exclusion and colonization provisions, but in the absence of careful legislative coordination, sustained white coercion, or adequate black voluntarism, the ACS derived little direct benefit. Largely unusable, often miserly appropriations and short-lived local auxiliaries alike lapsed by the eve of war, while the screws of racial proscription latterly tightened so much as to produce absolute bans on manumission and an expulsion-or-enslavement mania throughout the South, which cut off the ACS from its major source of emigrants.[1]

At the federal level, various politicians put out feelers to colonization in the early 1850s, but any emancipationist tilt ultimately came too close to disturbing the peace after the Compromise of 1850. In a parallel development, in 1852 and again in 1855, the ACS banned itself from making any public allusion to the end of slavery, though the move preserved its flexibility on the operational definition of "free" African Americans. Subsequently, against a backdrop of changing political alignments, elements of the new Republican Party adopted colonization as a means to emancipation, their preference for Latin America over Liberia making them even less conceivable as potential allies of the ACS than they already were as a partisan and sectional grouping.[2]

Yet approaches to Washington on matters that could unite the disparate colonizationists still yielded precious little success. If the ACS channeled its most enthusiastic efforts into fruitlessly lobbying for a subsidized line of steamers to the colony, its most persistent objective was that of securing U.S. recognition of Liberia, which had declared its independence in 1847. Such an act entailed acknowledging black nationhood, a sensitive precedent that pointed to the recognition of Haiti and evoked black diplomats strolling the halls of Washington. Even with quiet confessions from President Fillmore and President Buchanan that they were personally favorable to the deed, and a tied Senate vote for recognition in 1853, on its own the ACS could do little more than hope that U.S. interactions with Liberia might build up a case for claiming inadvertent acknowledgment of the African republic after the fact.[3]

Indeed, it was business with the federal government that provided the ACS with its closest thing to an endorsement on the eve of war. In reality, that support was more a traditional response along the line of least resistance to a spate of captured slave ships, which had saddled Washington with the familiar problem of dealing with "recaptives," those Africans freed from their traffickers on the high seas. Despite carping from some slave-state congressmen, even implicit approval of the illegal international trade remained anathema to most southerners, and Congress accepted President Buchanan's application of the Slave Trade Act of 1819.

Placed under renewed domestic scrutiny, the ACS also found itself in an awkward position with respect to a now-independent Liberia, which successfully demanded a transfer of the contracts that the society had unilaterally made with the U.S. government. Taken as a whole, this latest round of involvement in federal receptive policy conferred mixed blessings on the ACS. On the one hand, the business allowed it an opportunity to remind Washington of its existence at what would turn out to be a most timely juncture, but, on the other hand, it had drawn unwanted attention to Liberia's distance and duly obvious limitations in coping with a large influx of settlers.[4]

In institutional terms, the ACS retained a national structure despite being driven primarily by state action. The dominance of state-level leaders, however, left it without clear goals. During the secession winter of 1860–61, the divergent propensities of the auxiliaries were already apparent in private. John B. Pinney, corresponding secretary of the New York State Colonization Society and a Republican, looked forward to an administration backed by several known supporters of colonization on Capitol Hill, who would save the ACS from having to "crawl along on private beneficence" much longer.[5] Meanwhile, Joseph Tracy, Pinney's counterpart at the Massachusetts society and a conservative who rued all dealings with government for making the ACS "an object of suspicion at the South," hoped that a confederacy of the Lower North and Upper South would emerge and force both intransigent latitudes of the nation into making concessions.[6] Several officers of the Pennsylvania society, where colonization's breach with abolition had never been firmly in evidence, issued an early call for a national colonization policy.[7]

Such talk was premature, however. Like the federal government, the ACS faced existential concerns in early 1861: with its head office in Washington and routine port of embarkation in Baltimore, encirclement by secession and Confederate invasion both loomed large, the latter again in summer 1862. Under the circumstances, the society canceled the spring expedition, and shipping agent James Hall dispatched the *Mary Caroline Stevens* on an unprofitable charter to spare it "attack by the mob as a Black Republican ship."[8] Meanwhile, James Redpath's rival emigration scheme, for Haiti, drew those African Americans who were keen to flee the country.[9]

Once the initial crisis had passed, the ACS received its first call to action in Abraham Lincoln's annual message of December 3, 1861. Although an avowed colonizationist, the president's modest national reputation prior to his nomination and his tactful silence in its wake meant that his views were not as well known as those of the Blair family or Sen. James R. Doolittle (R-WI), the Republican Party's most prominent advocates of black resettlement. Nevertheless, in a May 1860 interview in Springfield, Illinois, Lincoln had firmly conveyed his willingness to recognize Liberia so long as he could do so without offending southern congressmen, most of whom had now withdrawn from the government.[10] The ACS received hints in late November 1861 that something was in the offing when its financial secretary, William McLain, met Lincoln, who "almost promised to recommend Congress to make us an appropriation."[11]

In fact, true to his burgeoning behind-the-scenes interest in colonizing the Chiriquí region of what is now Panamá (then a part of Colombia), Lincoln did not explicitly endorse the ACS. Calling for financial provision for the resettlement of those slaves covered by the First Confiscation Act of August, the president also asked Capitol Hill to include the free black population of all parts of the United States in any such scheme. Elsewhere in his address, Lincoln recommended the appointment of chargés d'affaires to Haiti and Liberia, but promised to leave such a "novel policy" to Congress.[12] He gave no more specific explanation than that recognition was overdue and commercially advantageous, but, unbeknown to his audience, he had made the suggestion on the advice of Montgomery Blair, postmaster general and the cabinet's preeminent proponent of racial separation, which hints at colonizationist intent.[13]

Despite spurring some adherents of the ACS into lobbying Congress, Lincoln's appeal for the recognition of Liberia never needed their assistance to become reality. Favorable congressmen, especially Sen. Charles Sumner (R-MA) of the Committee on Foreign Relations, were already eager to press ahead with the president's proposal. Just as Haiti rather than Liberia had always been the real object of lurid southern fears, though, it was likewise the prospect of recognizing the former rather than the latter that represented the real coup from the perspective of abolitionists, who mostly did not conjoin the measure with talk of colonization. Subsequently faced with racial invective and obstructionism from border-state senators, however, Sumner would allow recognition of the two black republics to pass as late as June 1862 so that the emancipation bill for the District of Columbia might draw any attempted colonization riders instead.[14]

The recognition of Liberia aside, the president's first annual message left many questions unanswered for the ACS. Did Lincoln mean colonization to proceed in Liberia, somewhere else in Africa, or on another continent altogether? Did he mean to employ the society's services, and if so, to force it to violate its constitution and cause an outcry by shipping settlers without their consent? Or did he mean to bypass the ACS, which would probably suffer a fatal collapse in private donations, especially with so many war-related causes clamoring for charity, if the government levied taxes to pay for black resettlement?[15]

As colonization worked its way through congressional committee in early 1862, alongside harsher confiscation measures that seemed poised to make it all the more necessary, Tracy reviewed the alarming "heresies" of the policy's newfound friends in Washington. One was internal colonization in peripheral territories of the United States, in violation of the law of races that destined the entire American continent for whites and Africa for blacks, an ACS article of faith that the Republican colonizationists had already challenged by placing the American tropics in the black zone. Furthermore, with an old hand's knowledge of how frustrating voluntary recruitment would prove for enthusiastic converts to colonization, Tracy feared that legislation blithely framed "as if the 'emigrants' had no 'consent' to give or withhold" would place government policy on the slippery slope to coercion.[16] Given some of the remarks issued from the floor of Congress that spring, Tracy's concerns were not as overblown as they seemed. Moreover, he correctly predicted an administration role for James Mitchell, the former secretary of Indiana's state colonization board and a man prone to mixed sounds on the issue of compulsion.[17]

As always where the legal proscription of African Americans was concerned, members of the ACS lacked sufficient perspective to consider that manumission on condition of emigration, a formula from which they had gained so many settlers, also fell under a gray area of consent at best. Yet their antipathy toward deportation was earnest in its own blinkered way, even when talk of coercion apparently originated with Liberians. Despite feeling the loss of missionary funds and emigrants from the South, especially while trying to sustain its own "civil war" with native Africans, Monrovia's sympathies in the American contest were never in doubt, and it swiftly decided to exploit its newfound recognition and the Union's colonizationist mood by appointing Pinney as its consul general and sending over a commission to canvass emigrants independently of the ACS.[18] Much to the society's vicarious embarrassment, however, rumors appeared in the press that the commissioners, J. D. Johnson and Alexander Crummell, had appeared before Lincoln in mid-April 1862 advocating the "compulsory transportation" of "contraband" escapees from Confederate slavery.[19] While the president readily put his signature to a statement that they had not touched on compulsion in their interview, Johnson suffered physical assault that summer at the hands of anti-emigration forces within Washington's African American population, who extended similar shows of hostility to Redpath and other recruiters.[20]

If a strict aversion to deportation marked one of the ACS's self-imposed limitations on exploiting current events, the more restrictive one was its unwillingness to accept settlers not free "by the law of the land," or even to modify its official stance of neutrality on the desirability of ultimate emancipation.[21] Buoyed by Lincoln's March 1862 message on compensation and gradualism, traditionally part of the same package of moderate antislavery as colonization, corresponding secretary Ralph R. Gurley, who privately felt that "the day will be glorious indeed when the institution of slavery shall no longer be recognized in our National Constitution," started to let emancipationist notes emanate from the *African Repository*.[22] His colleagues responded with a range of mild to severe censure, however, and Gurley thereafter acted with more restraint.[23]

In May 1862, recollecting years of entanglement in the slave states with manumission laws of unpredictable enforcement and with contested wills, the executive committee voted against accepting "contrabands" as emigrants, since their freedom was legally uncertain. Crucially, the ACS would not interpret the Second Confiscation Act of that July, or even the Emancipation Proclamation of January 1863, as sufficiently watertight to overturn its decision. Such caution did not go unchallenged: several officers would request updates and further clarification at regular intervals, or make the case to headquarters for broad construction of the "free people of color" specified in the society's constitution. Indeed, per the federal structure of the ACS, the executive committee's resolution could not stop Pinney, working in conjunction with Johnson, from prevailing upon the New York auxiliary to canvass "contrabands" from any location. But for now, the parent organization could only look to the former slaves of Washington, D.C., freed in April under legally sound congressional jurisdiction, and to the $100,000 earmarked for their colonization. At first, the district was not fertile ground for the ACS: having gained Lincoln's ear over a potential contract, a sheepish McLain was then able to name only one would-be emigrant to Secretary of the Interior Caleb B. Smith, whose department had assumed the task of colonization.[24]

The middle months of 1862 brought further frustration for the ACS. It watched with dismay as the vacant post in Liberia went to an unknown, Abraham Hanson of Wisconsin (through Doolittle's patronage), rather than to its own man, John Seys, who had been the U.S. agent for recaptives in Monrovia. Moreover, the ACS could only fume when it belatedly discovered that Congress had quietly passed measures to direct any slave ships thereafter intercepted in the western Atlantic to the labor-hungry plantations of the Danish West Indies, an action in keeping with Lincoln and Secretary of State William H. Seward's desire to save money.[25]

As to domestic emigration business, the ACS could hardly take solace in the growing black opposition to Redpath's Haiti scheme when, since at least the spring, it had been forced to observe the shady Chiriquí project's ever tighter hold on Washington officialdom. In mid-August, McLain introduced former Liberian president Joseph J. Roberts, on a lecture tour of eastern colleges to raise money for education back home, to Lincoln, who conceded that, while the current generation of African Americans might do as well for themselves in Central America as in Liberia, their best prospects ultimately lay in Africa.[26] Shortly afterward, Lincoln met a delegation of free black Washingtonians to espouse colonization in an address that has gained lasting notoriety for its profoundly pessimistic analysis of race relations. While the president's broad rationale for colonization could have easily appeared in the pages of the *Repository*, his thoughts on the best location for black resettlement did not exactly chime with those of the ACS. "The colony of Liberia has been in existence a long time. In a certain sense it is a success," Lincoln admitted, before moving swiftly on to the comparative advantages of Central America, especially its proximity to the United States.[27] While the ACS seethed at what it regarded as an act of betrayal and another cynical attempt, like the Danish arrangement, to remove black people on the cheap, Roberts wondered whether Lincoln's support for the principle of emigration might turn discerning minds to Liberia in the end.[28]

The ACS's sense of exclusion from federal policy ran deeper still: reports confirmed that it was the newly created "commissioner of emigration," James Mitchell, who had arranged Lincoln's meeting with the black delegation. Veteran colonizationists groaned at the memory of one of their former colleagues, a man who had placed the official colonization policy of the state of Indiana on a needlessly independent basis from the ACS during the 1850s, even negotiating with Roberts for a Hoosier *imperium in imperio* within Liberia, and who had tried to draw much of the Midwest into his orbit, in which capacity he had indeed met Lincoln.[29] For his part, Mitchell bitterly recalled a promising trip to Washington during the upheaval following the Kansas-Nebraska Act (1854), in the course of which President Pierce had intimated that his entire cabinet would support colonization as a measure to stop the slave trade, being thwarted by collusion between the executive committee of the ACS and the Whigs John M. Clayton and Seward, who wanted to deny Mitchell's Democratic Party the "strong card" of colonization.[30] Mitchell had then cut his ties with the parent society except for attending annual meetings to demand concessions to the states. Opinionated and prone to sweeping, conspiracy-laden assertions about many other topics as well as race relations, Mitchell was also hardworking, keen to ignore partisan differences whenever he could reach out to kindred colonizationists, incorruptible around the wartime appropriations where his superiors at the Department of the Interior faltered, and perfectly capable of securing allies even as he alienated many people.[31] "James Mitchell . . . I know, and like," recorded Lincoln in 1861.[32]

Taken together, the administration's actions left the ACS bemused by the late summer of 1862, no surprise where official policy remained genuinely embryonic and where Lincoln already shared others' inklings that the Chiriquí scheme was likely to throw up diplomatic complications and a public stench of graft. In volunteering to become leader of that expedition, the abolitionist Sen. Samuel C. Pomeroy (R-KS) placed yet another, wholly unexpected, pair of hands on the reins of colonization policy, and openly appealed for free black recruits from the northern states, covered by neither the $100,000 appropriations for the black population of Washington, D.C., nor the $500,000 recently apportioned to those slaves who came under the Second Confiscation Act. Having already asked Lincoln "point blank if that money could be used to colonize the free," McLain had received only the noncommittal answer from the president that he was not sure that it could, but that he had not closely examined the legislation.[33] The financial secretary then requested written clarification, which Smith and Mitchell both stalled off. The latter eventually confirmed that Lincoln currently envisaged only the Chiriquí scheme, and disingenuously added that he could not assist those African Americans not encompassed by the recent acts.[34]

Nevertheless, the ACS swooped when, shortly after Lincoln reaffirmed colonization in his preliminary Emancipation Proclamation, the administration suspended the Chiriquí expedition against a background of Central American protest at something akin to filibustering on behalf of an undesirable race of immigrants. In reality, the postponement had more to do with recent civil war in Colombia having left two regimes purporting to represent that country, an obstacle that Lincoln hoped to overcome with the emigration treaty policy that he would present in his second annual message that December. Indeed, the fall of 1862 was one of those rare moments in the history of the colonization movement when black demand suddenly outstripped white supply: Pomeroy had received thousands of applications from intending emigrants, and so the executive committee of the ACS decided to try to get Lincoln to redirect the movement to Liberia. Despite some nonbinding reservations from the lawyerly ACS president, John H. B. Latrobe, complicity in misusing government appropriations for the sake of free African Americans did not evoke the same litigious horrors as taking "contraband" Confederate property, and in any case, the society now had several names from the aboveboard District of Columbia.[35]

In a couple of cordial meetings with ACS officers in the middle of October, Lincoln stressed that he was perfectly keen to send a "cargo" to Liberia, admitting a preference for that destination over Central America, as well as for dispatching the free over "contrabands," at least until his Emancipation Proclamation came into effect.[36] He added that he understood that black Americans simply would not go to Africa, however. Addressing Lincoln's concerns, on November 1, an agent of the ACS introduced him to Chauncey Leonard, pastor of Washington's First Baptist Church and would-be missionary to Liberia. The president was inclined to award Leonard four hundred or five hundred dollars, and even left his guests with the impression that he would sign off on one hundred dollars per capita passage for the fifty emigrants that Leonard planned, a generous offer where rival, western-Atlantic colonization schemes invariably undercut ACS rates. Leonard's initial party did not manage to gather itself before the early November sailing of the *Stevens*, but the minister anticipated an even larger group early the next year.[37]

Perhaps more surprisingly, Mitchell entered the picture once more, helping Leonard in conjunction with a clerk in the Department of the Interior, the black emigrationist John W. Menard. Mitchell had never soured on African colonization, ranking Liberia below only the British West Indies in a late 1862 review of resettlement locations. He also entertained a burgeoning skepticism about American concessionaires who showed up clutching dubious leases from foreign governments, a point on which the ACS heartily agreed. Yet Mitchell did not return to the fold smoothly, accurately citing black opposition to the ACS proper, as distinct from support for emigration to Liberia, to justify his initial attempts to bypass the central organization in favor of Pinney and Johnson's independent efforts.[38]

For its part, the ACS did little to preempt splinter initiatives so long as its executive committee adopted stances such as commemorating the Emancipation Proclamation by ruling that the "contrabands" were still off-limits, not to say unlikely to emigrate anyway if their legal standing did improve. While McLain briefly approached the Senate Judiciary Committee at the end of January 1863 to sound it out on a congressional resolution to open up the appropriations for the benefit of African Americans nationwide, that plan incurred the disapproval of the society's board of directors and essentially ended up in the hands of Mitchell and Pinney, the latter of whom alleged that McLain's purpose had actually been to dissuade congressmen and scupper the idea.[39]

Yet it was hardly new for colonizationists to entertain respectful differences of opinion about means, and all could agree on the validity of the main upcoming project, the slated emigration from the District of Columbia. Secretary Gurley and Thomas S. Malcom of the Pennsylvania society collected two hundred dollars for Leonard in a January 30 meeting with Lincoln, choosing to take less than the president had offered, and the minister sailed out early the next month as an advance scout for his church.[40]

It is little wonder that Lincoln continued to take an interest in Liberia when he kept burning his fingers so badly, repeatedly, and yet knowingly, on "contract" colonization schemes in the Caribbean. Having realized that Ambrose W. Thompson, the leaseholder for the Chiriquí site, could hardly speak for the privileges that a foreign government would allow immigrants, in his second annual message the president had proposed first reaching treaties with host states, or with metropolitan governments where the European colonies of the American tropics were concerned. Such arrangements were to incorporate the same minimum living standards for settlers that Seward had outlined in a diplomatic circular of September 30. Lacking a viable colonization project even as he issued the Emancipation Proclamation, however, Lincoln immediately broke his own rules. On the morning of January 1, 1863, he hurriedly signed another contract with a domestic businessman, Bernard Kock, for the Île à Vache, off Haiti, only to suspend and later rescind it when warnings reached the White House of Kock's low reputation.[41]

With such questionable rivals, the ACS and Liberia had much to recommend them, as did the European empires to which the administration increasingly turned. They alike offered established systems for introducing immigrant laborers under enumerated rights and obligations, a minimal interest in profiteering from one-time contracts at the expense of cultivating a steady influx of settlers, and a refreshing lack of troublesome middlemen claiming rights that did not fall within their purview. Admittedly, Liberia's independence had brought some tensions of dual control with the ACS, which even after 1847 retained the right to approve new locations for U.S. immigrants, but during the 1850s arguments on such matters had unfolded as much *within* the ACS as between Monrovia and the same.[42]

In practice, early 1863 marked the best chances of agreement between the administration, the ACS, and the Liberian government, visible fault lines notwithstanding. Commissioner Johnson approached Lincoln in early March and reminded him of the White House's previous offer to fund anyone who wanted to go to Liberia, citing the support of Pinney, Blair (despite his preference for Central America), and the new secretary of the interior, John P. Usher (despite his secret stake in the Chiriquí project). The president sent Johnson to Mitchell, who was keen to make a contract with the ACS to take roughly 160 emigrants from Washington on the regular May sailing of the *Stevens,* as long as the venture addressed the problem of black opposition to the ACS by remaining under the nominal auspices of the federal government.[43]

There was some confusion about whether the arrangements would include one of Seward's most recent innovations, a guarantee from the host state that, black emigration treaty with the United States or no, it would at least underwrite the terms of his circular against contractors' failure to meet the stipulations of that document. Johnson argued that his commission allowed him to speak for the relevant host government, uniquely among all colonization proposals then in circulation; Gurley found Mitchell and Usher at odds over whether Seward meant the new template contract to extend to the ACS at all; and McLain feared that competitors or Pinney's own enthusiasm would alert the administration to the lack of up-to-date consent from Liberia, a precondition that had just mothballed the Haitian venture of James De Long, a rival scheme to that of Kock and heretofore another option that had tempted Menard and his emigration-minded associates.[44]

From early April, however, an all-too-familiar experience beckoned for the ACS. It realized that the list of 160 emigrants, mostly based on expressions of interest from late 1862, was likely to fall through, partly owing to discontent at Leonard's church against its absent minister. By this point,

Pinney was not alone in suggesting resort to "contrabands" from the Washington area and Fort Monroe, a proposal that the administration offered to neither fund nor impede. For in an analogous development—namely, that of an organization departing from its self-imposed rules—the Lincoln White House now signed a revamped agreement for Île à Vache, rashly asking that the new contractors merely secure retroactive Haitian approval of Seward's guarantee, rather than sticking to its demands for prior approval from the host state.

Curiously, the president's stated purpose was to bring relief to the inhabitants of the very refugee camps that the ACS had offered to canvass. It seems that Lincoln entertained second thoughts about the expense of passage to Liberia, even if he maintained that, theoretically, it remained the most suitable location for African Americans. No sooner had the executive committee decided once more against changing its stance, though, than Secretary of War Edwin M. Stanton denied Pinney the requisite military pass for the camps.[45] "So ends the contrabandity," mused Hall.[46] In fact, the notoriously insubordinate Stanton did not speak for the president, who would personally countermand an identical ban on recruiters from the British colonies that June and explain that it was his "honest desire" that their efforts proceed.[47]

Rather, such developments indicated that it took champions within the administration such as Mitchell and Blair, who both rallied to the British option for its hitherto elusive combination of diplomatic reliability and geographical proximity, to overcome the obstruction of well-placed opponents. By this point, the latter comprised Stanton, Usher (who turned against the entire policy through frustration with Mitchell and with the diminished prospects of the Chiriquí scheme), and Seward, a quiet foe of colonization who dragged his feet on executing the president's will whenever he could. So perhaps the ACS missed its last chance in spring 1863, when timely success in securing an adequate number of emigrants just might have seen its own supporters of a broader definition of "free people of color" persuade their skeptical colleagues. As it was, only three settlers sailed to Liberia that May. Symbolically, having missed the ship for want of a travel pass to Baltimore, Menard immediately threw himself wholeheartedly into the British scheme.[48]

From mid-1863, the ACS settled down to a more routine existence. It watched the rebel-leaning Maryland society cease all vestiges of active operations, while inquiries in the Midwest confirmed that the region still struggled to match its taste for racial separation with adequate institutional provision. Changes of hands in the political swing state of Indiana had reduced Mitchell's former office to a sinecure on a list of partisan spoils, and correspondents in Ohio, Iowa, and Illinois all reckoned that their respective state societies had become defunct by 1860. Although the ACS had long argued for the logistical importance of running predictable biannual sailings to Liberia, it cited low emigrant numbers to sell the *Stevens* at a considerable loss in 1864. By the end of the war, the society could boost its morale only by taking a party from the overcrowded island of Barbados to Liberia, quite in breach of its own constitutional restriction to assisting emigrants from the United States. As to its domestic mission, the ACS providentially looked to the day when African Americans would realize the worthlessness of nominal freedom.[49]

In fairness, the ACS kept its eyes on affairs in Washington. It watched from the sidelines when representatives of Henry Highland Garnet's African Civilization Society met Lincoln and Mitchell in November 1863 to request funding for their own African emigration projects. The Civilization Society spurned concurrent offers of cooperation from the loathed ACS, except to push for an unconditional award of money. Despite a common scholarly emphasis on the public relations dimension to Lincoln's colonization plans, even the Pennsylvania Avenue–based ACS knew little about the Île à Vache expedition other than the basics of its departure in April 1863 and its whimpering return the next March. Ironically, the guarantee clause that had been supposed to protect the emigrants actually secured their maltreatment when Haiti refused to underwrite it, thus setting in motion the administration's refusal to pay the contractors, and thereby the contractors' effective abandonment of the settlers.[50]

Some ACS officers feared that an uninformed public would conflate the fiasco with the noble, Christian endeavors of the society, but others relished the chance to lay into "political" colonization. Likewise, as the resultant motion to repeal the resettlement appropriations worked its way through Congress, some colonizationists rued how little of that fund the ACS had secured, while others were happy to see rival agencies starved, or gleefully spotted that legislators had forgotten to include an obscure 1862 tax law setting aside considerable sums for colonization.[51] In a pleasant surprise, Lincoln recommended selling a gunboat to Liberia in his annual message of December 1864, also hinting that he had not shed his lifelong interest in colonization with cryptic remarks that that republic "may be expected to derive new vigor from American influence, improved by the rapid disappearance of slavery in the United States."[52] Certainly, the president's suggestion helped provide journalistic copy for the *Repository* when his death sparked fervent internal debate about whether even to take formal notice of emancipation in his obituary.[53]

Like all parties that brought colonization proposals before the federal government, the ACS was only intermittently privy to the innermost workings of an administration that handled the policy on a counterproductively secretive and compartmentalized basis. Nevertheless, the ACS accurately surmised, from the sum of its interactions with Lincoln, executive officers, legislators, and African Americans of various degrees of freedom, that the policy had been squeezed by black recruitment, technical difficulties, and inadequate support in any tangibly useful form, rather than dismissed on the strength of some kind of personal philosophical departure by the president. Indeed, as colonizationists would have been first to ask, how could an individual possibly grow out of a policy premised on others' racism? Like rival purveyors of black resettlement, the ACS also knew all too well the serious complications inherent in the ostensibly promising circumstances of war, be it the doubtful legal status of "contrabands" through 1865, the grim possibility of Confederate privateers intercepting a shipload of black voyagers, or the competition posed by black enlistment from 1863, which not only offered alternative employment in general but also drew on the same clusters of escapees that colonization agencies hoped to exploit.[54]

In its dealings with the executive branch, the ACS bore witness to clashing jurisdictions over colonization, often unfathomable interpretations of the relevant legislation, and a painfully unsteady learning curve regarding domestic contractors' inability to speak for foreign governments. Such incompetence has generally counted as grounds for belittlement of the policy in the eyes of the last half-century of scholarship, which has been eager to read weakness of intent into paucity of results and messiness in the execution, especially where Lincoln is concerned. Yet, as ever, the argument needs turning on its head: it is the fact that supporters of colonization persisted as much as they did, despite knowing as well as modern academics the fundamental ambiguities and continual disappointments that the policy incurred, that imbues their efforts with their true significance. Such perseverance demonstrates the recurrent appeal of escapism in reconciling the founding promises of the United States with the realities of prejudice, exploitation, and the preeminence of states' rights in determining blacks' status.

For a body of literature on wartime colonization dominated by an unnecessarily defensive debate about Lincoln, that escapism provides a major point of extenuation, one usually linked to the president's psychological "avoidance" of the potential fallout of proclaiming emancipation.[55] Yet as students of the wider movement know, such low expectations for race relations were standard colonizationist fare. Easy apologias aside, what does it *really* tell us that Lincoln never wavered from the highly restrictive principle of voluntarism while repeatedly making time for blatantly flawed emigration projects? As abolitionists alleged, such pessimism not only allowed colonizationists to duck all sorts of dilemmas between the rights of the black minority and the demands of the white majority, but, when expressed publicly, it also proved self-fulfilling by stoking the very same prejudices that colonizationists cited in order to justify their work. To put it another way, support for racial separation tended less toward a calculated, transient indulgence of other whites' prejudices, and more toward a fatalistic resignation to the persistence of discrimination, which necessarily impinged on alternative, integrative solutions to the presumed problem of race relations.

By dint of the sheer range of agents that had to come into alignment for colonization to succeed, the major obstacle that the impetus faced was always that of obtaining meaningful and coordinated consent without alienating broad swathes of an unwieldy range of supporters, a problem that the Civil War placed in even sharper relief. Consent was what private contractors could not offer on behalf of Latin American states, the American Colonization Society guarantee on behalf of Liberia, or an African American pro-emigration minority claim on behalf of an anti-emigration majority. Indeed, many of the latter feared that the slightest division in black ranks would allow pro-colonization politicians, who seemed blasé at best on the matter of black volition and unmindful of the heterogeneity of the African American population, to claim tokenistic support as the united voice of a singular community.[56] Yet the Civil War showed that a presumed need for consent could also stifle responses to promising but fast-changing developments, for most administrators of the ACS did not feel empowered to interpret the absence of southern friends as grounds to exploit the very circumstances of mass slave liberation and government sponsorship that they had always been supposed to embrace. Rather, as the society's executive committee resolved, even as Abraham Lincoln issued the Emancipation Proclamation, "a higher mission could not be ours than to stand by and properly touch the helm as the ship drives on amid the fury of the waves and the raging of the storm."[57]

Notes

1. Eric Burin, *Slavery and the Peculiar Solution: A History of the American Colonization Society* (Gainesville: University Press of Florida, 2005), 27–33. Since most arguments in this article are based on several sources, citations will usually appear at the end of each paragraph (or run of paragraphs, if the same sources recur), with the exception of those paragraphs containing a direct quotation.

2. Joseph Tracy to Ralph R. Gurley, March 12, 1862, reel 92, American Colonization Society Records, Library of Congress (hereafter ACS).

3. *Congressional Globe*, 32nd Cong., 2nd Sess. (hereafter *CG* 32-2), 1064–65, and appendix, 231–34; Tracy to Joseph J. Roberts, February 17, 1857, ACS, reel 235; Tracy to Gurley, March 3, 1859, ACS, reel 236; William McLain to John N. Lewis, December 29, 1851, ACS, reel 239; Journal of the Executive Committee, October 18, 1860, ACS, reel 292.

4. Willis D. Boyd, "The American Colonization Society and the Slave Recaptives of 1860–1861: An Early Example of United States-African Relations," *Journal of Negro History* 47 (1962): 108–26.

5. John B. Pinney to Gurley, December 15, 1860, ACS, reel 90.

6. Tracy to Gurley, February 10, 1860, to John H. B. Latrobe, December 17, 1860, ACS, reel 236.

7. Willis D. Boyd, "Negro Colonization in the National Crisis, 1860–1870," PhD diss., University of California, Los Angeles, 1953, 51.

8. James Hall to McLain, August 10, 1861, ACS, reel 92.

9. John Orcutt to McLain, March 20, 1861, ACS, reel 91.

10. G. W. S. Hall to Charles Sumner, November 18, 1861, Charles Sumner Papers, microfilm, reel 23, Chadwyck-Healey Publications.

11. McLain to Alexander Guy, November 26, 1861, ACS, reel 203.

12. Roy P. Basler, ed., *Collected Works of Abraham Lincoln* (New Brunswick, N.J.: Rutgers University Press, 1953–55), vol. 5: 39, 48 (hereafter *CW*).

13. Francis P. Blair Sr. to John A. Andrew, March 11, 1862, reel 12, John A. Andrew Papers, Massachusetts Historical Society.

14. Latrobe to William H. Seward, December 5, 1861, Abraham Lincoln Papers, Library of Congress (hereafter Lincoln Papers). William Coppinger to Gurley, February 4, 1862, ACS, reel 92; April 3, 1862, ACS, reel 93; McLain to Tracy, March 15, 1862, ACS, reel 203. Beverly W. Palmer, ed., *Selected Letters of Charles Sumner* (Boston: Northeastern University Press, 1990), vol. 2: 109–10.

15. Tracy to McLain, December 10, 1861, ACS, reel 92.

16. Tracy to McLain, February 19, 1862, ACS, reel 92.

17. Tracy to Coppinger, March 15, 1862, ACS, reel 236; *CG* 37-2, 1520–21. James Mitchell rejected the use of overtly exclusionary pressures in his *Report of the Secretary of the State Board of Colonization* (Indianapolis: Austin H. Brown, 1853), 9; *Circular to the Friends of African Colonization* (Jeffersonville: n.p., 1855), 1; *Report on Colonization for 1860* (Indianapolis: John C. Walker, 1861), 5–6; and *Educational Claims of the Children of the Non-Slave-Holding Whites of the South* (Atlanta: James P. Harrison, 1891), 11, but entertained them in his *Letter on the Relation of the White and African Races in the United States* (Washington, D.C.: G.P.O., 1862), 25.

18. Boyd, "Negro Colonization," 350–52.

19. Tracy to Gurley, April 18, 1862, ACS, reel 93.

20. McLain to James Hall, July 30, August 6, 1862; to Gurley, Orcutt, and Tracy (respectively), August 4, 1862, ACS, reel 203. *African Repository* 38 (1862): 241–43.

21. Gurley to Pinney, April 24, 1863, ACS, reel 235.

22. Gurley to Franklin Butler, July 1, 1861, ACS, reel 235; *Repository* 38 (1862): 94–95, 103–10.

23. Tracy to Gurley, March 12, 1862, ACS, reel 92. Orcutt to McLain, April 17, 1862; Butler to Gurley, May 7, 1862, ACS, reel 93. McLain to Orcutt, March 10, 1862, ACS, reel 203.

24. Coppinger to McLain, March 7, 1862, ACS, reel 92. Orcutt to McLain, April 7 and 17, 1862; Pinney to Gurley, May 12, October 24, 1862; to McLain, July 14, 1862; Henry Connelly to McLain, June 16, 1862; Maria Bell to McLain, July 20, 1862; Gurley to McLain, August 2, 1862; Tracy to McLain, September 8, 1862, ACS, reel 93. McLain to Orcutt, April 3, May 13, 1862; to Tracy, April 22, 1862; to Caleb B. Smith, April 23, 1862; to Hall, May 3, 1862; to Butler, June 19, 1862; to Bell, August 7, 1862, ACS, reel 203. Gurley to Pinney, October 23, 1862, ACS, reel 235. Journal of the Executive Committee, May 9, 1862, ACS, reel 292. Alexander Crummell and J. D. Johnson to Smith, May 16, 1862, Miscellaneous Letters, reel 8, Records of the Office of the Secretary of the Interior Relating to the Suppression of the African Slave Trade and Negro Colonization, R.G. 48, M-160, National Archives and Records Administration, College Park, MD (hereafter STNC). *Repository* 38 (1862): 243.

25. John Seys to McLain, May 19, June 2 and 23, July 21, 1862; to Gurley, June 7, 1862, ACS, reel 93. McLain to Seys, May 27, June 12, July 1 and 25, August 19, 1862; to Butler, August 18, 1862, ACS, reel 203.

26. Coppinger to McLain, June 20 and 25, 1862; McLain to Gurley, August 26, 1862, ACS, reel 93.

27. *CW* 5: 370–75.

28. Butler to Gurley, August 16, 1862; Samuel Storrs Howe to McLain and Gurley, August 21, 1862; Roberts to McLain, August 30, 1862, ACS, reel 93. McLain to Hall, April 28, 1862; to Coppinger, April 29, 1862; to Butler, August 18, 1862, ACS, reel 203.

29. McLain to Howe, August 25, 1862, ACS, reel 203; Tracy to Latrobe, October 14, 1862, ACS, reel 236; "Lincoln and the Negro," *St. Louis Daily Globe-Democrat*, August 26, 1894.

30. *CG* 33-1, 1604; Mitchell, *Educational Claims*, 11.

31. Mitchell to Lincoln, April 18, 1862, Mitchell Communications, STNC, reel 8; Proceedings of the Board of Managers, January 22, 1857, ACS, reel 290.

32. *CW* 4: 547.

33. McLain to Tracy, September 10, 1862, ACS, reel 204.

34. Mitchell to McLain, September 4, October 3, 1862; Hall to Smith, October 8, 1862; to Lincoln, October 11, 1862; to McLain, October 11 and 13, 1862; John P. Usher to McLain, October 13, 1862, ACS, reel 93. McLain to Lincoln, August 27, 1862; to Hall, October 6, 10, and 13, 1862; to Coppinger, October 6 and 16, 1862; to Smith, October 11, 1862, ACS, reel 204. Journal of the Executive Committee, October 10, 1862, ACS, reel 292.

35. Sebastian N. Page, "Lincoln and Chiriquí Colonization Revisited," *American Nineteenth Century History* 12 (2011): 307–13. Coppinger to Gurley, October 13 and 17, 1862; Hall to Gurley, October 15, 1862; Pinney to McLain, October 16, 1862; Latrobe to Gurley, October 16, 1862; Tracy to McLain, October 16, 1862, ACS, reel 93. McLain to Pinney,

October 11, 1862, ACS, reel 204. Tracy sketched the various ACS officeholders' personal receptiveness to political involvement to Butler, November 3, 1862, ACS, reel 236.

36. Gurley to Coppinger, October 18, 1862, ACS, reel 235.

37. Coppinger to Gurley, October 23, 1862; to McLain, December 4 and 27, 1862; George W. Samson to Gurley, November 1 and 5, 1862; McLain to Gurley, November 1, 1862; Chauncey Leonard to Samson, November 4, 1862; to Gurley, November 8, 1862; Gurley to McLain, November 10, 1862, ACS, reel 93. McLain to Hall, November 1, 1862; to Gurley, November 1, 1862; to Orcutt, November 6, 1862; to Coppinger, December 26, 1862, ACS, reel 204. Gurley to Hall, October 23, 1862; to Pinney, November 7, 1862, ACS, reel 235. Donald MacLeod Diary, October 23, 1862, MacLeod Family Papers, Virginia.

38. James Mitchell, *Report on Colonization and Emigration* (Washington, D.C.: G.P.O., 1862), 19–20, 27. Connelly to Gurley, December 27, 1862, ACS, reel 93. Gurley to Coppinger, November 4, 1862, ACS, reel 235. Mitchell to Hall, February 21 and March 18, 1863, reel 8, Maryland State Colonization Society Papers, microfilm, Maryland Historical Society (hereafter MSCS). Johnson to Usher, April 10, 1863; John W. Menard et al. to Lincoln, May 13, 1863, Miscellaneous Letters, STNC, reel 8.

39. Orcutt to McLain, April 17, 1863, ACS, reel 94. Pinney and Mitchell, Memorial to the Senate of the United States, 1863, ACS, reel 177B. McLain to Hall, January 24, 1863; to John Maclean, January 30, 1863, ACS, reel 204. Gurley to Connelly, January 23, 1863, ACS, reel 235. Statement of the Executive Committee, January 1, 1863, ACS, reel 286. "Forty-Sixth Annual Report of the American Colonization Society," *New-York Colonization Journal*, March 1863.

40. Leonard to Gurley, January 28, 1863; Tracy to McLain, February 7, 1863; Butler to McLain, February 13, 1863, ACS, reel 94. Coppinger to Gurley, November 27, December 29, 1863; Thomas S. Malcom to Hall, January 5, 1864, ACS, reel 95. Malcom, certificate, February 6, 1863, Miscellaneous Letters, STNC, reel 8.

41. Page, "Lincoln and Chiriquí Colonization Revisited," 311–13; Bernard Kock, *Statement of Facts in Relation to the Settlement on the Island of A'Vache* (New York: William C. Bryant, 1864), 4–5.

42. Burin, *Peculiar Solution*, 147–48. *Repository* 24 (1848): 257–59. Tracy to J. H. Snowden, February 13, 1857, ACS, reel 235. Journal of the Executive Committee, June 19, 1855; October 10, 1856, ACS, reel 292.

43. Hall to Gurley, April 13, 1863; Mitchell to Gurley, April 16, 1863, ACS, reel 94. McLain to Mitchell, March 18, 1863; to Hall, March 31, 1863, ACS, reel 204. Gurley to Tracy, March 13 and 31, 1863; to Coppinger, March 17, 1863, ACS, reel 235. Gurley to Hall, March 14, 1863, MSCS, reel 8. Johnson to Lincoln, March 3, 1863; to Seward, April 9, 1863; to Usher, April 10, 1863, Miscellaneous Letters, STNC, reel 8.

44. Hall to McLain, April 1, 1863, ACS, reel 94. McLain to Hall, April 2, 3, 11, and 14, 1863, ACS, reel 204. Menard to Mitchell, April 23, 1863, enclosed in Menard to Usher, May 14, 1863, Miscellaneous Letters, STNC, reel 8. Menard and Charles B. De Long, contract, 1863, Miscellaneous Contracts, STNC, reel 8. Charles K. Tuckerman to Usher, April 18, 1864, Forbes and Tuckerman Correspondence, STNC, reel 9. *Repository* 39 (1863): 89–90.

45. McLain to Gurley, April 6, 1863; Mitchell to Gurley, April 8, 1863; Malcom to Gurley, April 10, 1863; Hall to McLain, April 13 and 14, 1863; Pinney to McLain, April 14, 1863;

to Gurley, April 22, 1863, ACS, reel 94. McLain to Hall, April 7 and 21, 1863; to Pinney, April 13, 1863, ACS, reel 204. Gurley to Coppinger, March 31, 1863; to Pinney, April 24, 1863, ACS, reel 235. Journal of the Executive Committee, April 17 and May 8, 1863, ACS, reel 292. Illegible to Usher, April 28, 1863, War Department Communications, STNC, reel 3. Statement of the Executive Committee, January 1, 1864, ACS, reel 286, hints that officers met with Lincoln around March 20, 1863, and surmised that he thought Liberia best for African Americans but transportation there too costly. On Lincoln's death, Orcutt recalled to Coppinger, April 28, 1865, ACS, reel 97, that the president deemed Liberia "too far off" in an undated final meeting.

46. Hall to McLain, May 1, 1863, ACS, reel 94.

47. Phillip W. Magness and Sebastian N. Page, *Colonization after Emancipation: Lincoln and the Movement for Black Resettlement* (Columbia: University of Missouri Press, 2011), 15–16, 33–42.

48. Orcutt to Gurley, May 25, 1863, ACS, reel 94. Menard to McLain, November 28, 1863, ACS, reel 95. McLain to Pinney, May 4, 1863, ACS, reel 204. Gurley to Orcutt, May 28, 1863, ACS, reel 235. Menard to McLain, May 26, 1863, McLain Communications, STNC, reel 10.

49. Hall to Samuel Miller, May 6, 1879, New Jersey Colonization Society Records, Library of Congress. James M'Kay to Orcutt, February 7, 1863; illegible to Gurley, March 18, 1863; William W. Wick to Gurley, April 5, 1863; W. W. Hibben to Gurley, June 10, 1863, ACS, reel 94. Howe to McLain, October 1, 1863; Hibben to Gurley, November 10, 1863; Guy to McLain, March 28, 1864, ACS, reel 95. Charles P. McIlvaine to Coppinger, March 17, 1865; James C. Conkling to Coppinger, March 21, 1865; Howe to Coppinger, May 3, 1865, ACS, reel 97. Coppinger to Malcom, November 2, 1864, ACS, reel 209. *Repository* 40 (1864): 303, 341–42.

50. African Civilization Society to Lincoln, November 5, 1863; Mitchell to Lincoln, November 5, 1863; to Usher, November 5, 1863, Lincoln Papers. Tracy to Gurley, October 31, 1862, ACS, reel 93. Orcutt to McLain, November 17, 1863; H. M. Wilson to McLain, November 21, 1863, ACS, reel 95. McLain to Hall, November 7 and 13, 1863; to Tracy, November 13, 1863, March 26, 1864; to Butler, April 4, 1864, ACS, reel 204. Coppinger to Butler, April 5, 1864, ACS, reel 209. Tracy to Pinney, November 17, 1863, ACS, reel 236.

51. Malcom to Coppinger, May 16, 1864; Butler to Coppinger, May 16, 1864; Orcutt to Coppinger, May 18, 1864; Tracy to Orcutt, May 19, 1864, ACS, reel 95. Coppinger to James H. Lane, May 12, 1864; to D. S. Gregory, May 13, 1864, ACS, reel 209. Tracy to Butler, May 19, 1864; to Orcutt, May 19, 1864, ACS, reel 236.

52. *CW* 8: 138; Seys to McLain, December 13, 1864, ACS, reel 96; Coppinger to Edward S. Morris, December 12, 1864, ACS, reel 209.

53. Orcutt to Coppinger, April 22 and 28, 1865; Samuel E. Appleton to Coppinger, May 2, 1865, ACS, reel 97. Coppinger to Edward S. Morris, December 12, 1864; May 30, 1865; to Orcutt, April 20 and 25, 1865, ACS, reel 209.

54. Hall to McLain, August 10, 1861; Orcutt to McLain, September 18, 1861, ACS, reel 92. Seys to McLain, April 30, 1862, ACS, reel 93. Pinney to Gurley, March 16, 1863, ACS, reel 94. Tracy to McLain, November 11, 1864, ACS, reel 96. McLain to Hall, June 5, 1861; to Orcutt, September 21, 1861, ACS, reel 203. Coppinger to Samuel H. Perkins, October 3, 1864, ACS, reel 209. Tracy to Hall, September 23, 1861; to Orcutt, October 31, 1863, ACS, reel 236.

55. Gabor S. Boritt, "The Voyage to the Colony of Lincolnia: The Sixteenth President, Black Colonization, and the Defense Mechanism of Avoidance," *Historian* 37 (1975): 619–32.

56. Kate Masur, "The African American Delegation to Abraham Lincoln: A Reappraisal," *Civil War History* 56 (2010): 141–44.

57. Statement of the Executive Committee, January 1, 1863, ACS, reel 286.

III

REDIRECTING THE FIELD AND OFFERING NEW ANSWERS TO OLD QUESTIONS

11

The Cape Mesurado Contract

A Reconsideration

ERIC BURIN

In recent years, scholars have produced a host of works on the American Colonization Society (ACS), the organization that sought to solve America's problems concerning race, slavery, and freedom by sending black Americans to Africa. These works have changed our thinking about the ACS in many ways, but most reinforce the old notion that colonization was a pipe dream that allowed its supporters to sidestep the dilemmas that sprang from the existence of slavery and racism in a nation devoted to freedom and equality. In truth, colonization was not just a form of escapism. Its proponents transformed their ideas into actions, and those actions shaped society in significant ways. Most importantly, they converted their notions about colonization into the founding of Liberia, a colony-turned-country that profoundly affected the debates over slavery, freedom, and race and that still exists today.

Liberia's establishment was much harder than historians have supposed. Among other things, colonizationists had to secure government funding, recruit emigrants, establish a toehold in Africa, resolve internal divisions, thwart external foes, create a viable economy, and maintain a self-reproducing population. This chapter examines one aspect of their far-flung enterprise—contracting for land in Africa.

Scholars who overlook the colonizationists' accomplishments underestimate the difficulties of obtaining a contract. In their accounts, a contract virtually fell into the colonizationists' lap. Or, more precisely, it fell into their lap once a U.S. naval officer, Lt. Robert Stockton, accompanied an ACS agent to Cape Mesurado in December 1821, leveled a pistol at the head of the Dei ruler, King Peter, and made him an offer he could not refuse.

In spotlighting Stockton's gunplay, previous historians imply that extortion, and little else, enabled colonizationists to obtain a contract. While the threat of violence certainly influenced the contract negotiations, other factors complicated matters. Consequently, colonizationists had to play their cards right. Sometimes they erred, but eventually they put together a winning hand. Good thing, too, because securing a contract, while challenging, was easier than the other tasks necessary for creating a colony. Colonizationists ultimately surmounted all of these obstacles, effecting their most significant but often overlooked accomplishment, the founding of Liberia.

The "Mission of Inquiry," Government Aid, and Willing Emigrants

The ACS was founded in December 1816, and within a year the organization sent two evangelicals, Samuel J. Mills and Ebenezer Burgess, to Africa on a "mission of inquiry." The party touched at Freetown, Sierra Leone, where they consulted with British officials and other individuals. Among the latter was John Kizell, an "Atlantic creole" who had previously befriended Paul Cuffe, the black mariner who in the early to mid-1810s had twice visited Sierra Leone with the goal of assessing the possibilities of an African emigration scheme.

Mills and Burgess, along with Kizell, then embarked for Sherbro Island, which lies fifty miles south of Freetown. There, myriad indigenous rulers schooled the white agents in African business tactics. During formal palavers and informal conversations, native leaders coaxed presents from the Americans by expressing interest or indignation, or claiming influence or impotency, as the occasion demanded. Despite the diplomatic travails, Mills thought the ACS could do well at Sherbro. The ACS ought to establish their initial settlement near Jenkins, which was on the north side of the island, opined Mills, while the main settlements would be across the sound, on the mainland, about twenty-five miles up Bagroo River. As for Kizell, Mills adjudged him a "second Paul Cuffee." Mills died on the voyage home, and his partner Burgess delivered the party's findings to the ACS.[1]

The "mission of inquiry" would mean little if colonizationists failed to pry open the national government's coffers. They had tried to do so for decades, usually with abysmal results. That changed in March 1819, when Congress passed the Slave Trade Act, a statute written and championed by Charles Fenton Mercer, a Virginia conservative and ACS founder. This law placed "recaptured Africans"—that is, Africans rescued from slaving vessels—in the hands of the federal government and authorized the president to make arrangements for their "safekeeping, support, and removal" beyond the nation's borders, and to appoint a person "residing on the coast of Africa, as agent," to receive them.

Most of President James Monroe's cabinet favored a strict reading of law, prompting colonizationists to badger a reluctant Attorney General William Wirt into opining that the measure empowered the president to establish an agency in Africa, arrange for the construction of shelters there, protect the station, and even send over free black laborers. Wirt insisted that this is what the law allowed, not necessarily what Congress intended, and counseled caution until that body could clarify its intentions. In response, in December 1819, Monroe delivered to Congress a special address on the subject, a disquisition that so artfully blended conciliation, rationalization, and obfuscation it aroused no opposition from lawmakers. When Congress let the matter slide, colonizationists had cleared the last hurdle to obtaining public aid.[2]

Next, ACS officials needed to find black Americans who were willing to move overseas. In recent years, scholars have highlighted the dynamic debate among the era's African Americans over colonization. According to this research, many black leaders were sympathetic toward colonization, largely because they envisioned it as a hemispheric program of racial uplift. These leaders were taken aback when the black masses denounced colonization, protests which prompted the black elite to either hide their lingering interest in the scheme or to rally to the opposition standard. These studies are surely correct, but it is worth remembering that, even if the vast majority of black folk opposed colonization, some did not. ACS officials always claimed that they had more applications for passage than berths in their vessels. Indeed, without colonists, there would have been no colonization.[3]

Sherbro Island

The first group of eighty-eight emigrants, along with two ACS agents and one U.S. agent, embarked from New York on the *Elizabeth* in February 1820. The party was supposed to be escorted by the USS *Cyane*, but the ships were separated soon after departing New York. After a month at sea, the *Elizabeth* touched at Freetown, Sierra Leone. During their brief stay at Freetown, the agents learned that the three-hundred-ton *Elizabeth* would never be able to navigate the treacherous waters surrounding Sherbro Island, so they purchased a schooner, the *Augusta*. The two vessels then sailed for Sherbro Island. At Sherbro, John Kizell, the man who had befriended

Cuffe and assisted Mills, escorted the party to his village of Campelar. Soon thereafter, a boat from the long-lost *Cyane* showed up, with seven sailors and one officer on board having orders to help with the venture. As the Americans brought their goods ashore, they began talking with indigenous rulers about acquiring land. Several assured the Americans that a deal could be struck. They cautioned, however, that any transaction would have to be sanctioned by King Sherbro and approved at a general palaver. Though frustrated with the slow pace of the negotiations, the Americans were confident that they would eventually purchase territory. They were tragically mistaken.[4]

Why did the Americans fail at Sherbro? Most historians have suggested that the enterprise was doomed from the start because indigenous people had no desire to transfer their land to foreigners. When indigenous rulers indicated that they wanted to sell their land, so the argument goes, they were just trying to bilk more presents from the Americans. There is some truth in this idea. Yet it must be noted that, at the time, land deals were fairly common in the region. Sierra Leone officials had signed several prior to the Americans' arrival at Sherbro, and they would sign three more within the next fifteen months. Moreover, as shall be seen, following the Sherbro debacle in 1820, the Americans signed two land contracts in 1821. And as far as Sherbro is concerned, it is often forgotten that the Americans there *did* strike some sort of bargain for land. In that instance, the Americans' territorial claims were tenuous and soon forfeited, but the transaction suggests that the Sherbro rulers did not automatically dismiss land deals. Indeed, just a few years later, Sierra Leone officials acquired the territory, ostensibly to save the inhabitants "from the destruction threatened by their cruel and implacable enemies." In short, perhaps under different circumstances, the Americans might have obtained a land contract at Sherbro.[5]

If indigenous opposition did not thwart the Americans at Sherbro, what did? The emigrants' presence complicated the quest in several ways. First, from the moment the party had left New York, there had been disputes between the emigrants and the agents, as well as among the emigrants themselves, about the relationship between the U.S. government, the ACS, and the emigrants, and these ongoing quarrels about rights and responsibilities prevented unified action on the Americans' part while in Africa. Second, not long after their arrival at Sherbro, malaria and other maladies raked the Americans' ranks, forcing them to devote resources to medical affairs that could have been used to solidify their bargaining position. Finally, widespread suffering and discontent filled the Americans with a sense of urgency, a desperation that was exploited by African negotiators, who were experts in prolonging business affairs. It was no coincidence that, when the Americans signed land deals at Grand Bassa and Cape Mesurado the following year, they struck the bargains while nearly all the emigrants were temporarily lodged in Sierra Leone.[6]

Britain's actions also contributed to the Americans' failures at Sherbro. Since the days of Cuffe, Sierra Leone officials had evinced mixed attitudes towards the Americans' African enterprise. On one hand, they welcomed it as a means of combating the Atlantic slave trade. On the other hand, they fretted that an American settlement—especially one that was nearby, as would be the case with Sherbro—would lure away American expatriates who were living in Sierra Leone and undermine Britain's geopolitical interests in the region. So when the Sherbro venture began to unravel, the British offered to accommodate the Americans in Sierra Leone, not reinforce them at Sherbro. In effect, the British were willing to help the Americans escape Sherbro, not to establish a toehold there.[7]

Emigrant Daniel Coker must also shoulder blame for the Americans' mishaps at Sherbro. By mid-May, all of the white agents had died. Prior to their demise, they transferred their agencies to Coker. They did so because Coker had convinced the agents that he was an intermediary between themselves and the emigrants. There is some evidence that Coker had been duping the agents all along, that he secretly wanted black people to control the enterprise. Even so, Coker's coziness with the agents had irked many of the other emigrants, and their distrust of him never abated. Indeed, as it turned out, when Coker championed black power he really meant aggrandizing his personal power.[8]

Coker wanted the perks of being an agent, but not the responsibilities. Soon after he took over, he declared that the party's provisions were mostly intended for prospective recaptured Africans. As a man who had been accused of financial improprieties in America, perhaps Coker was especially keen to avoid any taint of malfeasance in Africa. Whatever the reason, Coker was exceedingly tightfisted with the party's supplies, compelling some emigrants to sell their clothes to indigenous people in order to survive. Yet Coker helped himself to the party's goods, and he could justly claim that he was simply following the practices of his predecessors. A month later, at a grand palaver, Coker gave presents to various indigenous leaders, claiming that these items constituted payment for lands on the Bagroo River. The indigenous rulers demanded another puncheon of rum, but Coker refused, insisting that it was a ploy to drag out the negotiations.

As the deal fell apart, Coker asked the adult male emigrants whether the party should settle on the Bargoo River lands, relocate to Sierra Leone, or head for Yonie, where King Sherbro had offered accommodations. Given how much Coker had alienated the other emigrants, the vote said less about his affinity for black self-determination, and more about his aversion to accountability—if things went poorly, he could claim it was others' decision. The group opted for Yonie, but Coker fared no better there. He continued to anger the emigrants and indigenous people, and by late September 1820, he and a handful of supporters left for Freetown, supposedly to await instructions from America. A few weeks later, he briefly returned to Sherbro Island, accompanied by two officers from the USS *John Adams*, an entrance that further alienated him from the emigrants and Africans alike. He left Sherbro for good in late October, his "leadership" having all but eliminated the Americans' chances of obtaining land in the Sherbro region.[9]

Grand Bassa

A few months later, in January 1821, the U.S. government dispatched to Africa another vessel, the *Nautilus*, which had on board two government agents, two ACS agents, and thirty-three emigrants. Once the ship docked at Freetown in early March, the agents asked British officials for permission to establish a temporary residence and to unload their cargo duty-free, measures that would allow the Americans to deal with the debacle at Sherbro. The British were willing to assist the Americans—for a price. Specifically, they demanded that the Americans disavow any claims to the Sherbro region. The American agents quickly conceded the point, whereupon British officials began arranging for the party to rent an estate at nearby Fourah Bay. Given the dreadful state of the Americans' colonial enterprise, Britain's timely aid was essential to their ultimately securing a contract for African land.[10]

While the Americans were negotiating for the Fourah Bay estate, the head ACS agent, Joseph Andrus, and the assistant U.S. agent, Ephraim Bacon, sailed southward aboard the *Augusta*. Greedy, rude, and hypocritical, agent Bacon, who had become fast friends with Coker, represented the enterprise at its worst, which is saying something. Bacon and Andrus cruised past Sherbro, where many of the *Elizabeth* survivors were still stranded, and eventually went ashore at Grand Bassa, 285 miles south of Freetown.[11]

The context in which Bacon and Andrus negotiated at Grand Bassa differed in significant ways from that of their predecessors at Sherbro. For starters, they did not have the pressure of treating for land while simultaneously coping with calamitous sickness and widespread discontent among the emigrants. Moreover, whereas U.S. naval personnel had been involved in the Sherbro affair, there was no military presence at Grand Bassa. Finally, because Coker had blamed Kizell for the disaster at Sherbro, the man once deemed a "second Paul Cuffe" had fallen out of favor among U.S. and ACS officials, and consequently Bacon and Andrus instead relied on two well-traveled "Atlantic creoles" they had met in Sierra Leone, William Tamba and William Davis, both of whom had two years earlier accompanied an English missionary to Grand Bassa. Bacon never acknowledged the advantages of treating while the emigrants were elsewhere, but he later attributed his successes at Grand Bassa to the military's absence and Davis's presence.[12]

At first, it appeared that the Americans would fail to secure a contract at Grand Bassa, just as they had failed at Sherbro, largely because the parties could not agree on whether the prospective colony could interfere with the slave trade. Even so, King Jack Ben and other indigenous leaders were willing to meet repeatedly with the Americans, titillating, but not satisfying, their desire for land, and procuring presents at each encounter. The Americans tried to hold firm on the slave-trade issue, telling their counterparts that the prospective settlement would engage in so-called legitimate commerce, with the result being that indigenous people could abandon slave trading. They had wasted their breath. King Jack Ben would not budge, and so the Americans buckled. The parties signed a contract in which King Jack Ben and his headmen agreed to give the ACS about forty square miles of land in exchange for a yearly payment of $300 in trade goods and a promise that no one living in the Americans' settlement would be "permitted . . . to give notice to ships of war of slave vessels on our coast, so as to cause them to be seized; nor shall they be permitted to use anything but persuasion to cause us to abandon the slave-trade."[13]

When the palaver concluded, the parties went to the shore, where one of King Jack Ben's sons, who was to accompany the Americans to Sierra Leone in order to receive an education, ascended a tree and hung a symbol of the United States. The record is not clear if it was an American pendant, pennant, or flag. From a legal standpoint, this was a meaningless act: The U.S. government had no claims—and made no claims—on Grand Bassa. But the episode begged the question of when the Americans would occupy the land. In Bacon's telling of the story—and his is the only one we have—the indigenous population was "anxious that we should return immediately," or, if not immediately, when the rainy season ended in November—that is, six months hence. Whether King Jack Ben and the others were being sincere is a matter of speculation. Indeed, it is not even clear if the indigenous people were hoping for the return of the two gift-bestowing agents, or the entire American party. In any case, neither agent seemed interested in coming back to Grand Bassa. Andrus soon decided that he would sail for the United States and perhaps return to Africa as a missionary. Bacon was thinking along the same lines. All of which meant that, when Bacon and Andrus returned in Freetown in late April, the most they could say about the enterprise's future was that the emigrants would not be settled at Grand Bassa until the rainy season concluded, and that neither of them would likely be agents when that time came. The agents' risk-adverse, wait-and-see approach exasperated some other colonizationists, including Lt. Robert Stockton, the aggressive, brash commander of the USS *Alligator*.[14]

Stockton and Monroe

When Stockton's *Alligator* docked at Freetown in mid-May 1821, Stockton was not impressed by what he saw. The head U.S. agent, Jonathan Winn, had his virtues, thought Stockton, but the "division . . . [of] feeling" and "multiplicity of . . . counsels" among the agents were undermining the cause. In response, Stockton offered to assist the enterprise, suggesting in particular that one of the agents accompany him to Sherbro, where he would gather up the *Elizabeth* emigrants and take them either to Grand Bassa or Fourah Bay. Confusion reigned among the agents. In typical fashion, Bacon came up with excuses as to why the mission should not be undertaken—or at least why he should not undertake it. Andrus apparently agreed to go, only to renege on his commitment. Andrus even went so far as to tell others that Stockton was the problem, insisting that the naval commander had suddenly declared that he would not transport female evacuees from Sherbro. After sixty hours of such shenanigans, Stockton had had enough. To his "astonishment and disappointment," the agents had failed to take advantage of his services. When Stockton embarked from Freetown, he left "without a very high opinion of their zeal or their abilities."[15]

Stockton had no doubts about his own zeal or abilities, particularly when it came to stifling the slave trade. Although Stockton was authorized to stop only ships flying the U.S. flag, over the next four days, the *Alligator* captured four French vessels, which combined had just two slaves. After assigning prize crews to convey the captured ships to the United States, Stockton sailed westward, arriving in Boston in late July 1821. At the time, many white Bostonians were sympathetic to the ACS. And several hundred miles to the south, Washington, D.C., was abuzz with colonizationist activity.[16]

The bustle was partly caused by the arrival of the Grand Bassa contract in Washington. Upon receiving the contract, the ACS Board of Managers had rejected the deal on account of the controversial slave-trade clause. Considering that the African venture was being pitched, and funded, as an anti–slave-trade crusade, the managers were wise to disavow the Grand Bassa contract. Had they done otherwise, private and public support for colonization likely would have weakened and the African enterprise may have collapsed.[17]

If the managers' abrogation of the Grand Bassa contract constituted a necessary setback for the colonization cause, the Monroe administration was taking small measures to promote the ultimate success of the African enterprise. A week after the ACS Board had nixed the Grand Bassa deal, President Monroe allowed his navy secretary to make Dr. Eli Ayres a navy surgeon, charged with providing medical assistance to the U.S. agents, re-captives, and emigrant "mechanics, labourers, & families" in Africa. In permitting the appointment, Monroe seized new powers under the Slave Trade Act of 1819. Of course, given that the president had already sent warships to help establish an African agency, and that two U.S. agents, a half-dozen naval personnel, and about twenty emigrant "labourers" had died in Africa, it is doubtful that Monroe fretted much over whether to send a physician overseas. In the meantime, ACS officials, who had dialogued with the administration all along and who had previously picked evangelicals as their agents in Africa, quickly relieved Bacon of his duties as head agent and named Ayres as his replacement.[18]

Monroe's decision later that summer to send Lt. Robert F. Stockton back to Africa entailed greater risks but also promised greater rewards. Difficulties stemmed from the four French vessels that Stockton had captured back in mid-May. For starters, three of the French ships, including the *Daphne*, had escaped from Stockton's prize crews. The fourth ship, the *Jeune Eugenie*, already had become a source of conflict in America. The French minister, for example, had complained about Stockton's violation of his nation's maritime rights. In response, Secretary of State John Quincy Adams, who disliked colonization, assured the French that the capture was the act of an overzealous naval commander, not the administration's general policy. Even so, the question of what to do with the *Jeune Eugenie* became a legal dispute. The case ultimately went to the U.S. Supreme Court, where Daniel

Webster, an ACS vice-president, argued that Stockton had not erred in seizing the *Jeune Eugenie* because the "barbarous" traffic in slaves violated the laws of nature and France. In the meantime, Adams—who feared that, if the United States pursued an overly aggressive slave-trade policy against other nations, foreign states might start harassing American ships—suggested that the Navy Department call a court of inquiry against Stockton and relieve him of his command, a course of action rejected by Navy Secretary Smith Thompson. Amid this whirlwind of controversy, the Monroe administration decided to send Stockton back to Africa.[19]

When the *Alligator* embarked from Boston in early October 1821, it was clear that Stockton had not changed one iota. He still embraced the naval élan that exalted individual glory in pursuit of the public good, and tolerated "creative disobedience" when eliding orders advanced one's overall objectives and conformed with natural law. Indeed, on his way to Africa, Stockton once again was involved in a controversial capture of a foreign ship. He arrived in Freetown in early December 1821, about a month after Ayres, the new ACS agent and navy surgeon, had landed there. By this juncture, the *Elizabeth* survivors had finally been brought from Sherbro Island to Fourah Bay, but the Americans still lacked a permanent abode in Africa. Ayres had decided that it was pointless to revisit Grand Bassa, so the party would have to look elsewhere. Thus just days after his arrival at Freetown, Stockton sailed 250 miles south to Cape Mesurado, with Ayres and seven emigrants following suit in the *Augusta*.[20]

Cape Mesurado

Cape Mesurado was a portal through which a considerable amount of trade flowed to and from the hinterland. The coast and its environs were held by the Dei, a loosely affiliated group that had recently named King Peter its principal local leader. The Dei lately had been muscled by the increasingly powerful Gola, whose territory began about thirty miles inland. Beyond the Gola was the Condo Confederacy and its formidable ruler, Sao Boso, an astute man who had turned commercial profits into political and military clout, which he occasionally used to intervene in the affairs of others, including the coastal Dei. In Stockton's estimation, "no spot [was] more eligible" for an American settlement than Cape Mesurado.[21]

The Americans had investigated Cape Mesurado twice before. In mid-April 1820, when the *Elizabeth* expedition was falling apart at Sherbro,

Lieutenant Matthew C. Perry of the *Cyane*, at the request of then–U.S. agent Samuel Bacon, sent a letter of inquiry to three Mesurado residents, including John S. Mill, a mixed-race, English-educated Atlantic creole who lived on Dazoe Island at the mouth of the Mesurado River, which separates the cape from the mainland. Their response was upbeat, but they confessed that, not "being natives of this part of the country we are not capable of returning you an explicit answer." They indicated they would convene "the kings and chiefs of the country" to discuss the matter. Perry replied that, as he himself was not authorized to treat for land, the indigenous rulers' communications ought to be directed to Bacon at Sherbro. Evidently, nothing more came of the matter. In fact, Perry's communications on the subject remained something of a secret for a quarter-century, but colonization insiders knew that Perry regarded Mesurado as the "most eligible situation for a settlement." In fact, he had hoped that its "advantages" would "induce Mr. Bacon to remove his colony hither." In a roundabout way, that is basically what happened.[22]

Agents Joseph Andrus and Ephraim Bacon had also visited Cape Mesurado, stopping there while on their way to Grand Bassa in April 1821. The two had heard favorable things about Cape Mesurado, intelligence that may have come from Lieutenant Perry's semi-secret inquiries. Like Perry, the agents thought highly of Mesurado, and went ashore hoping to meet with King Peter. Their efforts were in vain. King Peter "was not ignorant of the object of our visit," reported Bacon, and consequently refused to meet with the agents. Bacon speculated that, "if we had been mere missionaries, he would have received us readily." If King Peter was truly wary of the unarmed Andrus and Bacon, he must have been even more concerned when the *Augusta* returned to the cape with the warship *Alligator*.[23]

Stockton, Ayres, and their entourage arrived at Cape Mesurado on December 11, 1821, and while their initial attempts at negotiation did not go well, they learned from their experiences. At first, Stockton and Ayres could not even get a meeting with King Peter. When the Americans went ashore at "Bushrod Island" on December 12, the first person of authority with whom they spoke was an unnamed "king" who insisted that King Peter was a "fool" who did not speak English. The unnamed king then declared that he could speak for King Peter. The Americans pitched their project. They began with a disingenuous declaration that they had come to Mesurado first because they had heard favorable things about King Peter. They further explained that they intended to "erect houses" and produce tobacco, sugar, and rum, which they would exchange for rice, yams, beeswax, and other items. They also proclaimed that they would build schools and educate native youth. "This immediately excited their suspicions that we were going to break in upon the customs of their forefathers," observed Ayres. The Americans quickly realized that "the only way in which we could expect to succeed was to touch their interest." In practical terms, this meant stressing the commercial opportunities that an American presence would bring, and refraining from mentioning Christianity and "civilization."[24]

Later that day, King Peter joined the palaver. In their initial meeting with him, the Americans revised their pitch. They continued to believe that they could massage King Peter's ego by claiming that they preferred coming to him first, and they again touted their enterprise's commercial prospects, but they did not mention "houses" or farms, and they said nothing of Christianity and civilization. However, when the Americans indicated that they wanted to purchase Dazoe Island and the cape, King Peter objected, insisting that he would be killed "if any white man was to settle on it." The palaver continued a while longer; no record documents what was said. But when the meeting dispersed for the night, King Peter, according to Ayres, indicated that he would call his headmen together, and that they would "write a book" the next morning. The expectant Americans gave their hosts rum and tobacco and returned to their vessels.[25]

The following day, instead of getting "a book," the Americans got more lessons in African diplomacy. Sundry headmen showed up, but not King Peter, who arrived only after several messages had been sent for him. "After sitting three hours in palaver," wrote Ayres, "the unfortunate subject of the slave-trade was broached, and we again broke up the palaver." After two days of negotiations, the Americans had dispensed gift after gift, only to discover that the things they needed most—an audience with King Peter, a willingness on his part to sell land, and a ban on slave trading—were exactly the things that their African counterparts guarded most jealously.[26]

The next day, December 14, the Americans landed on an empty beach, receiving only a message from King Peter that he would not meet with them, "nor let ... [them] have any land." Ayres and Stockton decided to intrude upon King Peter's town, which was several miles away, in the middle of Bushrod Island, and hired a Krooman to show them the way. After they arrived, they were seated in a palaver house. King Peter made the Americans wait an hour before granting a meeting, and forced them to move to another palaver house; both measures were surely public shows of power on his part. The talks did not go well for the Americans. A Krooman knowledgeable about the Grand Bassa affair told the attendees that the Americans had killed King Jack Ben's son (the youth to be educated in Sierra Leone had in fact died) and that, once the Americans secured land, they "would cut [the indigenous peoples'] throats and bury them." Another identified the party as the people "who had been quarreling so much at Sherbro." Then a man who had worked aboard the *Daphne*, one of the French slavers that had escaped from Stockton's prize crew back in May 1821, "presented" himself to Stockton. "These circumstances accounted for the change of conduct in the king and people," reported Ayres. The confrontations also affected Stockton, exasperating a man who had little patience to spare.[27]

The row was the trigger mechanism for Stockton's infamous gun play. According to Ayres, when the subject of the French slavers came up, Stockton said that his orders had had nothing to do with non-American ships. All he had done was send a boat to investigate the situation, but the French had opened fire on him. Stockton proclaimed that he would not suffer anyone to fool him, and that is why he had "whipped" the French. And now, fumed Stockton, King Peter was trying to fool him. For three days, declared Stockton, King Peter had been telling him that he would sell land, all the while drinking the Americans' rum and smoking their tobacco. In truth, King Peter had thrice expressed strong sentiments against selling land. Such inconvenient facts were incinerated by Stockton's outraged sense of dishonor. In his mind, this public insult had to be answered. Stockton consequently leveled a pistol at King Peter's head. "I believe the old king was afraid of being served as the French vessel was," wrote Ayres, "for he soon ... promised to call some more kings, and meet us on the shore [the] next morning, and make a book, which was to give us the land." King Peter had promised such things before; this time, the parties actually signed a contract.[28]

The contract was "imperfectly executed," Stockton remarked, a rare understatement on his part. According to the contract, "certain ... Citizens" of the United States who desired "to establish themselves on the Western Coast of Africa" had empowered Stockton and Ayres to treat for land. In exchange for what Ayres calculated to be three hundred dollars' worth of trade goods, a portion of which was to be paid immediately, with the balance due at an unspecified time in the future, King Peter and six other indigenous leaders "forever cede[d] and relinquish[ed]" Dazoe Island and an ill-defined portion of the mainland to Stockton and Ayres, "to have and to hold . . . for the use of these said Citizens of America." The indigenous rulers also promised to build for the "Citizens" "six large houses, on any place selected by them within the . . . ceded land." The "contracting Parties" then pledged to live "in peace and friendship for ever," an ironic clause, given Stockton's antics. A document that raised more issues than it resolved, the contract was the sole basis for the Americans' claim to the Mesurado area.[29]

Did duress compel King Peter and the headmen to sign the contract? Stockton's brazen threats of bodily harm on December 14 may have prompted King Peter and the others to sign the contract on December 15. And even if Stockton wasn't brandishing his pistol when the deal was struck, his warship, with its seventy sailors, was nearby, as was the *Augusta*. Indigenous people knew not to take such situations lightly. Only eight years earlier, the British, in an effort to curb slave trading, had attacked an enclave at Mesurado. Within this context, there may have been some truth to Ayres's later claim that King Peter and the other Dei leaders dreaded "the name of captain Stockton and of our shipping." In short, the threat of violence must have had some effect on the negotiations. But most modern historical accounts, failing to note that the gun incident and the contract signing occurred on different days, entirely attribute the latter to the former, and thus overstate the case.[30]

Modern accounts also portray the contract as the product of indigenous ignorance, depicting King Peter and the others as frightened dupes who did not comprehend the nature of Western land transactions. Indeed, the apparent lopsidedness of the contract reinforces this view: Is it reasonable to believe that, for a mere three hundred dollars in trade goods, only half of which was to be paid up front, the Dei would forgo all claims to what Ayres described a million dollars' worth of land and the best harbor between Gibraltar and the Cape of Good Hope? Likewise, a dispute over a sacred site on Cape Mesurado that the Americans called "the devil's bush" calls into question indigenous rulers' understanding of what it meant to "cede" and "relinquish" land. Indigenous people later claimed that the site held such religious significance that they never would have actually sold it. Even by Western legal traditions, the "devil's bush" may have been *res extra commercium*, a "thing outside commerce," that is not the object of private rights and therefore not subject to sale. In short, direct and circumstantial evidence suggests that the Dei did not see themselves as transferring title and sovereignty to the Americans, but rather giving them merely the right to occupy or use the lands. As U.S. naval officer Robert T. Spence later remarked, the indigenous rulers insisted that "they were ignorant of the paper they had signed" and that "they never had sold, and never would consent to give up, Cape Montserado, the abode of one of their ideal beings."[31]

Spence was skeptical about the indigenous people's arguments, and maybe historians should be, too. For starters, as noted previously, several contracts of this sort had been signed by the British and indigenous people in recent years. No such deals had been struck at Mesurado, but given the fact that Europeans and Americans had been trading there for centuries, it seems unlikely that indigenous residents would have been completely unfamiliar with Western ideas about land transactions. And whatever knowledge the Dei had about such matters could have been reinforced by John S. Mill, a local "Atlantic creole" who had been educated in England, served as an interpreter for the two parties, and signed a separate contract with the Americans, exchanging several houses for sundry trade items. Moreover, it is worth remembering that the contracting parties pledged to live together peacefully "for ever," indicating that the kings knew that the Americans intended to reside at Mesurado indefinitely. The Dei's grasp of Western real estate law surely was imperfect; but it seems unlikely that they had no comprehension of Western ideas about land ownership.[32]

Nor did King Peter and his headmen sign because the Americans had outwitted them. Stockton and Ayres naturally believed that their deft diplomacy had made the deal possible. Ayres crowed that, for one hundred years, European powers had been trying to obtain Mesurado, and thus the contract represented "a triumph over savage prejudice ... [and] European negotiation" tactics. To their credit, Stockton and Ayres perceived the advantages of touting commerce and downplaying religion, all while maintaining the threat of force. Otherwise, Stockton and Ayres were not half as clever as they thought themselves. Their flattery had no discernible effect on King Peter, for example. Likewise, their feigned indifference regarding Mesurado was belied by the indigenous people's knowledge of the Americans' misadventures at Sherbro and Grand Bassa, and by Stockton's desperate gunplay. Simply put, King Peter and the others did not sign the contract because they were outfoxed, ignorant, or intimidated. Rather, they signed because they saw advantages in doing so.[33]

By agreeing to the deal, the kings could exact still more gifts from the Americans. By December 15, Stockton and Ayres had spent three days bestowing presents upon the indigenous rulers. Perhaps King Peter and the headmen reckoned that they had obtained from the Americans as much as possible without providing something in return, and the concession they offered—the contract—surely would be the subject of profitable palavers in the future. In fact, that is exactly what happened. In the kings' minds, the contract was a conduit to another round of bargaining, not an end unto itself.

Even in the unlikely event that there were no more palavers, the indigenous rulers may have believed that the potential rewards of signing the contract outweighed the risks. Let us first consider the risks, of which there were two. The first was incurring the wrath of other indigenous peoples, particularly the powerful hinterland ruler Sao Boso of the Condo Confederacy. Sao Boso resided at Bopolu, one hundred miles from Cape Mesurado. The negotiations on the coast took place over three days, meaning there was probably not enough time for news of the affair to reach Sao Boso's village, and for his response to travel back. Indeed, no historical documents concerning the negotiations mention the Condo leader. In short, Sao Boso almost certainly had no direct influence on the Mesurado contract. No one knew what would happen once he learned about the deal. He might welcome it. But if he objected and tried to render it inoperable, the Dei leaders who had signed it would likely feel his displeasure. What that would mean exactly is anyone's guess—Sao Boso recently had executed a coastal king, but that had been for fomenting a rebellion. Ultimately, King Peter and the others must have reckoned that Sao Boso would either accept the contract, or if he disapproved, inflict tolerable punishments on Dei leaders.[34]

The other great risk was that the American settlement might grow strong enough to threaten Dei interests. Consequently, the kings sought to circumscribe the Americans' prospects. In this respect, they scored two major triumphs. First, the contract said nothing about the slave trade, an enterprise that had been reviving lately in the Mesurado region, and a subject that had caused the second day's palaver to break up in failure. Second, the Americans agreed to settle on Dazoe Island instead of the better-situated cape. The Americans preferred the cape, but Ayres thought the island had its merits, believing, for example, that it had "excellent springs of water" near where the Americans intended to erect a "city." The indigenous parties knew far more about the island, including the fact that it had a large, brackish pond, and that many residents had lived there in recent times, with none lasting very long. The information asymmetry that existed between the American and indigenous parties helps explain why, when the kings "peremptorily objected" to the Americans settling on the cape, the latter "yielded and agreed to [build on] . . . Dozoe island." By isolating the Americans on a small, marshy island with a history of rapid residential turnover, and by making no contractual commitments regarding the slave trade, the Dei kings minimized the newcomers' potential influence. Indeed, thus situated, the prospective settlement, in all likelihood, could be easily extinguished, probably without bloodshed.[35]

There was a good chance that the Americans would not even occupy Dazoe Island, and, if they did, they would remain briefly but spend profusely. Recall that the Americans had spent nearly fifteen months at Sherbro Island, where they had run up a sizable bill purchasing desperately needed food, supplies, and shelter from locals, only to abandon the place. Worse still, the Americans, after securing a contract for Grand Bassa, had not even attempted to settle there. Even Sierra Leoneans had profited from the Americans' presence at Fourah Bay. In short, history suggested that the Americans' tenure at Mesurado would be short-lived at best.

And what if the Americans' prospective settlement at Mesurado prospered? American trade would funnel through Mesurado, allowing savvy, well-placed individuals to profit financially and politically. Moreover, the Deis, as a group, might benefit. With the hinterland's Gola and Condo Confederacy weighing down on them, the coastal Dei may have welcomed anything that would lessen their burden. Within this context, King Peter and other Dei leaders could see that the Americans offered something of real value. Their offer was tempting.

The offer might be fleeting, as well. Although the Americans had failed at Sherbro and Grand Bassa, there were other likely sites for their settlement. Indeed, prior to Stockton's embarkation from the United States, Navy Secretary Thompson had instructed him to consider establishing the settlement at Axim, which lies over one thousand miles from Freetown, a site that Stockton dismissed for a variety of reasons, including his opinion that it was too far from British influence. There were plenty of options closer—but not too close—to Freetown. Consider Cape Mount, which is situated fifty miles north of Mesurado. While at Fourah Bay, the Americans had heard mixed reports about whether land could be had at Cape Mount. It was certainly possible that Cape Mount's rulers would welcome an American settlement. Gaje, the Vai chieftain who was Cape Mount's most influential figure, had built his power on commerce. So had the even more formidable Gola leader, Zolu Duma, who lived about sixty circuitous miles inland and was reputed to be among the region's wealthiest individuals. King Peter and his headmen must have wondered whether Gaje and Zolu Duma, to say nothing of indigenous rulers elsewhere along the coast, really would turn away Americans. And if they embraced them, would Cape Mesurado wither as commercial opportunities dried up? From the Mesurado kings' viewpoint, to spurn the Americans was to run the risk of personal, tribal, and regional misfortune.[36]

So the Dei leaders signed the contract. Thereafter, Stockton sailed for the West Indies aboard the *Alligator*. Ayres took the *Augusta* to Fourah Bay, where he gathered up supplies and some of the male emigrants, and then returned to Cape Mesurado on January 7, 1822. Not surprisingly, the Dei challenged the contract the moment the Americans tried to enforce it. If striking a deal with Africans was somewhat difficult, occupying the land and building a viable colony represented even greater challenges. All of which is to say that the founding of Liberia was no mean feat. It was, rather, the colonization movement's most significant and consequential—if underappreciated—accomplishment.[37]

Notes

1. Gardiner Spring, *Memoirs of the Rev. Samuel J. Mills, Late Missionary to the South Western Section of the United States, and Agent of the American Colonization Society* (New York: J. Seymour, 1820), 171–213, quotation on 182.

2. Eric Burin, "The Slave Trade Act of 1819: A New Look at Colonization and the Politics of Slavery," *American Nineteenth Century History* 13, no. 1 (2012): 1–14; Benjamin F. Hall, comp., *Official Opinions of the Attorneys General of the United States* (Washington, D.C.: Farnham, 1852), 317; *Annals of Congress*, 16th Cong., 1st Sess., 30–31.

3. Julie Winch, *A Gentleman of Color: The Life of James Forten* (New York: Oxford University Press, 2002); Richard S. Newman, *Freedom's Prophet: Bishop Richard Allen, the AME Church, and the Black Founding Fathers* (New York: New York University Press, 2008).

4. Daniel Coker, *Journal of Daniel Coker, a Descendant of Africa, from the Time of Leaving New York, in the Ship Elizabeth, Capt. Sebor, on a Voyage for Sherbro, in Africa, in Company with Three Agents, and about Ninety Persons of Color* (Baltimore: Edward J. Coale, 1820), 37; Charles Henry Huberich, *The Political and Legislative History of Liberia* (New York: Central Book Co., 1947), 91, 98; John Crozer Journal, March 23, in Supplement to Christian Wiltberger Journal, Earnest Edward Eells Papers, Amistad Research Center, Tulane University (hereafter ARC, TU); J. Ashmun, *Memoir of the Life and Character of the Rev. Samuel Bacon* (Washington, D.C.: Jacob Gideon Jr., 1822), 262–66.

5. Lewis Hertslet, *A Complete Collection of the Treaties and Conventions, and Reciprocal Regulations, at Present Subsisting Between Great Britain and Foreign Powers, and of the Laws, Decrees, and Orders in Council, Concerning the Same: So Far as They Relate to Commerce and Navigation, to the Repression and Abolition of the Slave Trade, and to the Privileges and Interests of the Subjects of the High Contracting Parties* (London: Henry Butterworth, 1880), vol. 14: 932–51, quotation on 948; John Kizell to Ebenezer Burgess, August 17, 1823, in Ebenezer Burgess Papers, Massachusetts Historical Society (hereafter MHS); American Colonization Society, 4th *Annual Report* (1820), 21, 52.

6. The disputes, illness, and African business practices are evident in Coker, *Journal*;

Elijah Johnson Journal, in Supplement to Wiltberger Journal, Eells Papers, ARC, TU; John Kizell to Ebenezer Burgess, August 17, 1823, in Burgess Papers, MHS; Edmund Wigfall, *The First and Accurate Account of One of the American Colonists who has Returned to the United States of America* (New York: n.p., 1821).

7. Coker, *Journal*, 26; Huberich, *Political and Legislative History* 1: 23; Governor McCarthy to Jno. P. Bankson, May 5, 1820, in Supplement to Wiltberger Journal, Eells Papers, ARC, TU. See also Ashmun, *Memoir of the Rev. Samuel Bacon*, 275-76.

8. Huberich, *Political and Legislative History* 1: 124, 134; Elijah Johnson Journal, May 14, 1820, Supplement to Wiltberger Journal, Eells Papers, ARC, TU; Coker, *Journal*, 19; James Sidbury, *Becoming African in America: Race and Nation in the Early Black Atlantic* (New York: Oxford University Press, 2007), 173-77.

9. John Kizell to Ebenezer Burgess, August 17, 1823, in Burgess Papers, MHS; Sidbury, *Becoming African in America*, 172; Elijah Johnson Journal, in Supplement to Wiltberger Journal, Eells Papers, ARC, TU; Wigfall, *First and Accurate Account*, 6-9; Floyd J. Miller, *The Search for a Black Nationality: Black Emigration and Colonization, 1787-1863* (Urbana: University of Illinois Press, 1975), 65-68.

10. Huberich, *Political and Legislative History* 1: 164-66, 172; Wiltberger Journal, in Eells Papers, ARC, TU, passim; Sidbury, *Becoming African in America*, 182-86.

11. E. Bacon, *Abstract of a Journal of E. Bacon, Assistant Agent of the United States, to Africa* (Philadelphia: S. Potter, 1821), passim; Wiltberger Journal, in Eells Papers, ARC, TU.

12. E. Bacon, *Abstract of a Journal*, 10, 26-27, 67-73.

13. Ibid., 19, 24-25.

14. Ibid., 27, 29, 39; Wiltberger Journal, in Eells Papers, ARC, TU.

15. Huberich, *Political and Legislative History* 1: 177, 181; Wiltberger Journal, 147-53, in Eells Papers, ARC, TU. See also E. Bacon, *Abstract of a Journal*, 49.

16. R. John Brockman, *Commodore Robert F. Stockton: Protean Man for a Protean Nation* (Amherst, N.Y.: Cambria Press, 2009), 44.

17. Huberich, *Political and Legislative History* 1: 161.

18. Ibid., 183; Smith Thompson to James Monroe, July 16, 1821, James Monroe Papers, www.loc.gov/collections/james-monroe-papers/about-this-collection/; March 20, 1821, John Quincy Adams Diary, Massachusetts Historical Society, www.masshist.org/jqadiaries/php/doc?id=jqad31_324; ACS Board of Mangers, Minutes, July 25, 1821, Reel 289, Records of the American Colonization Society, Library of Congress; Smith Thompson to Eli Ayres, July 25, 1821, reel 1, Civil Society Network Against Corruption (CSNAC).

19. Brockman, *Commodore Robert F. Stockton*, 46-50. J. B. Winn to Smith Thompson, August 6, 1821, Reel 1, CSNAC. Hyde de Neuville to John Quincy Adams, August 24, 1821, Reel 1, CSNAC. John Quincy Adams to Daniel Brent, September 6, 1821; Daniel Brent to Smith Thompson, September 11, 1821, in reel 1, CSNAC. John Quincy Adams to Daniel Brent, September 19 and 22, 1821, in Worthington Chauncey Ford, ed., *The Writings of John Quincy Adams* (New York: Macmillan Co., 1917), vol. 3: 178-79.

20. Brockman, *Commodore Robert F. Stockton*, 12-14; Wiltberger Journal, in Eells Papers, ARC, TU; Huberich, *Political and Legislative History* 1: 185-87.

21. Svend E. Holsoe, "A Study of the Relations Between Settlers and Indigenous People in Western Liberia, 1821-1847," *African Historical Studies* 4, no. 2 (1971), 333-62; Huberich, *Political and Legislative History* 1: 192.

22. Huberich, *Political and Legislative History* 1: 215–18.

23. E. Bacon, *Abstract of a Journal*, 14; Huberich, *Political and Legislative History* 1.

24. Brockman, *Commodore Robert F. Stockton*, 44; Huberich, *Political and Legislative History* 1: 185–88.

25. Huberich, *Political and Legislative History* 1: 188.

26. Ibid., 189.

27. Ibid., 189–90.

28. Ibid., 190.

29. The ceded territory was "that portion of Land bounded north and west by the Atlantic Ocean and on the south and east by a line drawn in a south-east direction from the north of Mesurado River," Huberich, *Political and Legislative History* 1: 191–92, 195–96.

30. Holsoe, "Study of the Relations Between Settlers and Indigenous People," 333; Huberich, *Political and Legislative History* 1: 202.

31. Huberich, *Political and Legislative History* 1: 191, 197, 287–88.

32. Ibid., 196–97, 225.

33. Ibid., 191.

34. J. Ashmun, *History of the American Colony in Liberia, from December 1821 to 1823* (Washington, D.C.: Way and Gideon, 1826), 14; Holsoe, "Study of the Relations Between Settlers and Indigenous People," 335.

35. Huberich, *Political and Legislative History* 1: 195–96, 201.

36. Ibid, 192. On Cape Mount, see E. Bacon, *Abstract of a Journal*, 13; Wiltberger Journal in Eells Papers, ARC, TU; Svend E. Holsoe, "The Manipulation of Traditional Political Structures among Coastal Peoples in Western African during the Nineteenth Century," *Ethnohistory* 21, no. 2 (Spring 1974): 158–67.

37. Huberich, *Political and Legislative History* 1: 199–213.

12

"A Desire to Better Their Condition"

European Immigration, African Colonization,
and the Lure of Consensual Emancipation

ANDREW DIEMER

In recent years, historians have come to approach colonization and antislavery in diverse ways. While many historians, following in the tradition of abolitionist William Lloyd Garrison's critique, have depicted colonization as at least functionally proslavery, more recently a revisionist historiography has challenged this interpretation. These historians have depicted African colonization as antislavery in at least two ways. First, colonizationists saw themselves and their efforts as part of a larger antislavery movement. Second, they note that colonization itself led to the emancipation of enslaved people.[1]

Yet even as these revisionists illuminate our understanding of colonization, they raise unanswered questions. It is clear, for example, that colonization led to the emancipation of *some* slaves, yet how should historians weigh this against the possibility that colonization in various ways prevented the emancipation of others? Certainly many northern colonizationists saw themselves as opponents of slavery, yet what are we to make of this antislavery desire? What antislavery opportunities were lost because of the zeal with which colonizationists promoted their movement as the essential means by which emancipation could proceed?

While we should not forget the individual men, women, and children who were emancipated under the auspices of colonization societies, the rhetoric of colonization was just as important, perhaps more important, than these practical consequences. After all, the largest of the colonization societies, the American Colonization Society (ACS), facilitated only six thousand emancipations in the almost fifty years between its founding and the passage of the Thirteenth Amendment abolishing slavery. In the same period colonization played a large role in shaping the discourse of antislavery: pastors delivered pro-colonization sermons; national, state, and local colonization societies published newspapers and pamphlets; and colonization-friendly articles were reprinted in newspapers across the United States. Through these prominent public platforms, colonization promoted itself as a moderate, practical alternative to more radical forms of abolition, and in doing so helped to determine the boundaries of what could be considered moderate antislavery.[2]

One of the most significant ways in which colonizationists depicted the practicality and antislavery implications of their movement was by linking African colonization to the growing European immigration *into* the United States. European immigration, and discussions of its connection to the project of African colonization, served to make colonization seem plausible, and supporters helped portray colonization as a means of promoting emancipation as a part of a natural, consensual process.

While colonizationists saw this parallel as a critical means of depicting their movement as a practical alternative to radical abolition, it ultimately weakened the antislavery potential of the colonization movement. Images of European immigration within the discourse of colonization allowed colonizationists to distance themselves from the contentious politics which had brought about the first round of emancipation in the northern states, enabling colonizationists to imagine an emancipation that did not depend on the coercive power of the state and which did not violate the property rights of slaveholders. Colonizationists' rhetorical use of European immigration helped render antislavery politics all but impotent before the 1850s, by moving away from the gradual but coercive model of emancipation toward an entirely consensual one.

Making Colonization Plausible

The founders of the ACS were in no way united in their views of the ultimate goal of their organization, but what they all agreed upon was that they needed to establish a colony in Africa and to people this colony with free African Americans. In the eyes of many critics, this was utterly impractical, because of the difficulty of securing a suitable location for the colony, because of the cost of maintaining this colony, and, perhaps the greatest problem, because of the cost of transporting free blacks across the Atlantic.

Even supporters of colonization agreed that the obstacles facing African colonization were daunting.³

Colonizationists attempted to counter these doubts about the practicality of their project by comparing it to similarly daunting moments in American history. Early colonizationists in particular pointed to the founding of English colonies in North America as a direct parallel to their plan for a colony in West Africa. "What America *was* when our fathers first landed," insisted one colonization supporter, "Africa *is*." Unsurprisingly, these colonizationists tended to invoke the New England colonies rather than the Chesapeake ones, not only because of the complicating factor of slavery in the Chesapeake but because Plymouth and Massachusetts Bay allowed them to emphasize the providential nature of American colonies. Just as God had planned for Englishmen to illuminate the New World through the establishment of colonies in New England, so would he illuminate Africa through an American colony. The guiding hand of Providence would make the impossible possible. Nor was this simply a matter of public propaganda. "The time will doubtless come," wrote one colonizationist, "when the names of some of these people will be recorded and their memory revered as those of the early Pilgrims to our country."⁴ Even in private correspondence, such parallels helped colonizationists see their project as both practical and divinely ordained.

If colonization was to be a means of removing the free black population of the United States (and then ultimately the enslaved population as well), then colonizationists faced a further, even more daunting problem. In 1820, a few years after the founding of the ACS, the United States contained more than 200,000 free African Americans and more than 1.5 million enslaved.⁵ Was it conceivable for all of these men, women, and children to be transported across the Atlantic to the West Coast of Africa?

According to historian William Freehling, this dilemma has led many historians to dismiss African colonization as "absurd." As Freehling notes, however, nineteenth-century America was ripe with evidence that massive numbers of human beings *could* be moved, even over long distances. Not all of these movements were appealing parallels for colonizationists, though. To take one of the most obvious parallels, the forcible ejection of Native Americans from their homes and the westward movement of these people proved to be a problematic point of comparison. Advocates for colonization, especially those who lived in the Northeast, tended to be *critics* of the policies of Indian Removal. It was William Lloyd Garrison, the most prominent opponent of colonization, who emphasized this parallel, not to defend colonization but to denounce it.[6]

In order to counter broad skepticism about the possibility of transporting huge numbers of individuals to a West African colony, defenders of African colonization turned increasingly to a different historical parallel: they compared the colonization of Liberia with ongoing European immigration to the United States. This parallel was increasingly appealing as the numbers of European immigrants grew dramatically. While a mere 8,385 individuals immigrated to the United States in 1820, just two decades later that number had grown tenfold to 84,066. Two years later that number would top 100,000, and by 1854 it would be 427,833, a number greater than the total free black population of the United States in 1850.[7] Perhaps removal of that population was not so absurd.

Supporters of African colonization worked hard to make sure Americans were thinking about colonization through the prism of European immigration. A Virginia colonizationist insisted in 1827 that, once the colony of Liberia was successfully established, free blacks would "rush to your seaports in droves," and that they would do so "with even more eagerness than the hundred thousand oppressed, toil-worn and poverty stricken children of Europe [who] now fly annually to this country." In reply to critics who doubted that colonization could significantly reduce the free black population of the United States, Charles Fenton Mercer noted that, "from Europe to North America, more than fifty thousand persons have reached this continent in a single year." In 1842, the officers of the Maryland Colonization Society hoped that "emigration from Europe to America and emigration from America to Africa will be on the same footing."[8] For many colonization supporters, European immigration to the United States proved that African colonization was feasible.

Yet this was not the only purpose that European immigration served within the discourse of colonization. If the sheer numbers involved posed one challenge, an equally vexing dilemma soon emerged alongside it: free blacks did not *want* to go to Liberia. Although there had been some interest among free African Americans in the *idea* of emigration, whether to Africa or elsewhere, the vast majority of free blacks rejected colonization under the aegis of the ACS. African Americans were wary of the white leadership of the ACS, especially since significant numbers of slaveholders were counted among the leadership of the society, and they were particularly distressed at depiction of black "degradation" in the rhetoric of colonization.[9]

Initially many colonizationists assumed that once the Liberian colony was successfully established large numbers of free blacks would willingly emigrate. It soon became clear that this was not the case, though colonizationists did not agree on the cause of this reluctance. Some ascribed it to misinformation. Others thought it the result of the malign influence of white abolitionists. Colonizationists sought to counter black reluctance by promoting the colony with glowing prose and by reminding free African Americans of the intractability of white prejudice. For the most part, colonizationists remained convinced that free blacks would eventually be persuaded, and they continued to be committed to the idea that colonization would occur only with the consent of free blacks.[10]

Colonizationists invoked European immigration to try and secure this consent. White colonizationists reassured free African Americans that they were asking of them no more than (white) European immigrants had done themselves. "We welcome to our shores yearly as many emigrants as would rapidly melt away a mass equal to the whole of our colored population," argued Philadelphia colonizationist and Whig politician Joseph Ingersoll, "converted from bondage to liberty, made men instead of chattels," and "changed from outlaws into makers and administrators of law." Just as impoverished and oppressed Europeans had willingly transported themselves to the United States in order to better themselves, so should free African Americans accept the offer of colonization.[11]

Emphasizing this parallel also reminded free blacks of the racial basis of the American nationality.[12] The ease with which white immigrants became a part of the American body politic underscored the fact that African Americans were denied that right in the land of their birth. European immigration, then, offered potential immigrants a positive, optimistic view of the possibilities available to them in Africa, coupled with a pessimistic reminder of what sort of future awaited them in the United States.

If this was not enough inducement for free blacks, colonizationists also presented European immigration as part of a natural, consensual process whereby free blacks were pushed out of the United States. "A few years ago," noted the *Maryland Colonization Journal*, "the labour about Fell's Point [in Baltimore] and the shipping was performed mostly by free coloured men. Now there are but few, comparatively, to be seen there. In their place is a German population, which has gradually, but thoroughly, elbowed them away—and long as Baltimore may exist as a city, labour on Fell's Point will be white labour."[13]

There was no need to employ the coercive power of the state to induce black men and women to emigrate to Liberia; nor was it even necessary for whites to use private force to drive unwanted free blacks out of their communities, though this sometimes happened, to the regret of many "benevolent" colonizationists who genuinely worried about free blacks who remained in the United States. European immigration would gradually, painlessly, show free African Americans that they had no place in the United States and a better future in Liberia. In the rhetoric of colonization, black emigration and white immigration were two parts of the same natural process.

Emancipation without Coercion

European immigration helped colonizationists depict their project as plausible, but if colonization was to be a means of emancipation, rather than simply the removal of free blacks, colonizationists faced another problem. In northern states, emancipation had been accomplished through the coercive power of the state. This "first emancipation" came about gradually, especially in states like New York with significant numbers of slaves, but nowhere was it left to private benevolence. Further south, however, especially in the Lower South states where slaves approached (or even surpassed) 50 percent of the population in 1820, any hint of coercive emancipation met with vehement opposition.[14]

At its founding the leadership of the ACS denied any intention to interfere with slavery, much less any intention to do so in a coercive manner. This emphasis, and the denial of antislavery intentions, should to a certain extent be seen as tactical choices. Leaders of the ACS hoped to cultivate national support, and deemphasizing slavery as the target of their organization might bring into the fold southerners who would be wary of a more vocally antislavery ACS. The leadership of the ACS also soon decided that it would petition the federal government for support. Emphasizing the national nature of the free black "problem," they hoped, furthered their argument for a national solution.[15]

Despite the efforts of leading colonizationists to deny antislavery intentions, Lower South senators saw the ACS, and in particular federal support for colonization, as an imminent threat to slavery despite reassurances by prominent colonizationists that the federal government had no constitutional right to interfere with the system. Although they advocated for federal support for African colonization, supporters insisted this did not mean they believed that the federal government had the power to interfere with slavery. This did not mean that *states* did not have the right to legislate on slavery, but most colonizationists, while hopeful, were evasive when discussing this possibility. Instead, a significant number of leading colonizationists, at least in public, proclaimed their commitment to individual, consensual emancipation.[16]

In the early 1830s, such hopes were given a new imperative when Nat Turner's rebellion led to a renewed discussion of the evils of slavery and a willingness to consider plans of emancipation, which depended upon the coercive power of the state government. Whatever their private hopes, in public many colonizationists denied that emancipatory legislation of any sort would be necessary. Instead, they held that vast numbers of slaveholders *wanted* to emancipate their slaves but were prevented from doing so by concerns about the growing free black population. Removing free blacks from the United States, and providing means for newly emancipated slaves to be transported to Liberia, would liberate benevolent masters to follow the dictates of their conscience.[17]

Through this constant repetition of their commitment to the "consent" of slaveholders, and belief that large numbers of masters sincerely hoped to emancipate their slaves, colonizationists, even those genuinely committed to ending slavery, were sustaining the idea of the reluctant slaveholder. In the late eighteenth and early nineteenth centuries, many slave owners had decried slavery while at the same time proving extremely reluctant to act on their antislavery sentiments.[18]

The rhetoric of colonizationists helped explain how slavery could continue and expand, despite the claims of slave owners to be done with the institution. In large part, colonization accomplished this by shifting the blame for the continuation of slavery off of slaveholders. It was not the fault of the owners of slaves that slavery continued, but rather it was the fault of free blacks whose presence prevented benevolent masters from freeing their slaves. The resistance of free blacks to efforts to colonize them occupied the very heart of colonization discourse. Both in public and in private, colonizationists expressed frustration at the stubbornness of free black opponents of colonization and their abolitionist allies. While white Europeans had sought to better their condition via emigration, free black Americans refused to take similar initiative. As a result, not only did they fail to better themselves, but the emancipatory promise of colonization was thwarted.[19]

Blaming free blacks for the failure of colonization also helped assuage the concerns of benevolent reformers about the oppression of northern free blacks. Historian Beverly Tomek has cautioned against blaming colonizationists for violent acts by those who *invoked* the colonizationist cause. Yet if most colonizationists did not join antiblack mobs, even those who sincerely wished to aid African Americans could see the *practical* usefulness of such violence. "My feelings have been much excited by observing the expulsion of the blacks from Ohio," wrote Philadelphia colonizationist Elliot Cresson in August 1829, following the riot which convulsed the city of Cincinnati, "and yet—by teaching them that this is not the place of their rest, that here they can hope for no continuing—it may be the means of directing the thoughts of these poor people more generally to Africa."[20] Colonizationists did not necessarily advocate the mistreatment of free blacks, but they could not help but notice the utility of such mistreatment.

This particular "moderate" approach toward race, in turn, would prove to be a critical feature of the emerging Whig Party. African colonization, especially as advocated by Henry Clay, was a distinctively Whiggish means of dealing with the political problem of slavery. Like their Democratic opponents, Whigs could only hold together a national coalition by submerging differences over slavery, and the rhetoric of colonization helped them do so. Since slaveholders really wanted to emancipate their slaves, Whigs argued, there was no reason to take vigorous action to bring about emancipation; since free blacks were the true obstacle to emancipation, it was tolerable for them to be the target of mob violence, even if such violence was regrettable.[21]

Similarly, southern advocates of colonization reassured their northern allies that emancipation was within their reach, but only colonization could unleash the antislavery benevolence of southern masters.[22] Surely some Whigs simply sought to keep slavery out of politics for reasons of expedience, but for those who genuinely opposed slavery, colonization allowed them to have their cake and eat it too. For antislavery Whigs, imagining that colonization could unleash a consensual migration of African Americans across the Atlantic permitted them to ignore sectional differences which might have threatened any antislavery plans that relied upon a willingness to wield the coercive power of the state.

European Immigration and "Easy" Emancipation

As time wore on, however, assurances of slaveholder benevolence rang false for many northern opponents of slavery. Between 1820 and 1850, the enslaved population of the United States more than doubled. Even in the

Border South states, where colonizationists assured northern audiences that slavery was doomed, the census told a different story. In Maryland the enslaved population had declined, but only slightly, by 15 percent. In Kentucky, on the other hand, the enslaved population had grown dramatically, by more than 65 percent, and in Missouri (not yet a state at the time of the 1820 census) the enslaved population was eight times what it had been.[23] Colonizationists argued that, if their plans had been put into place more effectively, the nation would not have seen this kind of growth, but certainly slaveholder benevolence was a harder sell in the 1840s than it had been when the ACS was founded in 1816. In these years, European immigration was used not simply as a demonstration that free blacks could be removed from the United States; it also came to be seen as a means of encouraging emancipation in a more direct manner.

In 1846, Judge William Bullock of Kentucky laid out just such a case. To a certain extent, Bullock was simply drawing on what at this point were common colonization arguments concerning the parallels between European immigration and African colonization. "Whilst our Government has afforded an asylum to the nations of the earth, and its glorious immunities and privileges are freely bestowed upon all," Bullock reminded the Colonization Society of Kentucky, "the African brought here against his will, is made to occupy in his best estate, a condition of unqualified inferiority." Unsurprisingly, he counseled his audience to "look at the amount of emigration annually to our shores by the poor of Europe" for evidence that colonization could successfully transport massive numbers of African Americans across the Atlantic.

Bullock went beyond this, however, to develop an argument for the antislavery potential of European immigration. "Besides, there is an external force operating upon the slave States in connection with this subject," he argued, "I mean the spirit of the age. The achievements of science and of art, the improvements in agriculture and the various and wonderful application of labor-saving machinery, with the overflowing and ever increasing tide of emigration to our shores from every country in Europe, are undermining the value of slave labor." It was not just that European immigration proves that African colonization was possible; it also served to undermine the value of slaves, and it therefore made masters more likely to emancipate them. As one contributor to the *Maryland Colonization Journal* wrote in 1847, these immigrants would find "a knowledge of our language, our laws, of true liberty, and a pure Christianity." They would also bring with them a great advantage to their adopted nation, "supplanting our own slaves, rendering their services less and less valuable every year, thereby weakening and cutting the cords that have so long bound them to their masters, thus creating another tide, that is setting back toward Africa."

American culture and religion would transform these white immigrants into Americans, and these new Americans in turn would help undermine the institution of American slavery. Opponents of slavery need not push for legislation to advance their cause; the voluntary movements of people across the Atlantic, African Americans in one direction, Europeans in the other, would bring about the end of slavery in a peaceful, consensual manner.[24]

To a certain extent, this linking of immigration with emancipation is related to the emerging "Free Labor" ideology, which would serve a crucial role in the emergence of the Republican Party.[25] Northerners had long argued that, as an economic system, slavery was backward and unprofitable. Eventually, this notion would become a potent part of antislavery politics. In the hands of colonizationists, though, it explained why antislavery politics was unnecessary, since European immigration was gradually undermining the supposedly backward slave economy of the Border South.

By the start of the 1850s, the notion that natural processes were slowly, peacefully, and inevitably undermining American slavery was appealing to politicians hoping that the Compromise of 1850 had truly settled the political issues of slavery once and for all. At the January 1851 meeting of the ACS, Henry Clay reassured his audience that the organization had never intended to "interfere upon the subject of slavery as it exists in the several states." He hoped, however, that slavery would ultimately be extinguished from the United States, "and it is the operation of natural causes to which I look for its ultimate extinction." According to Clay, "there will be an extinction of slavery whenever the density of the population in the United States shall be so great that free labor can be procured by those who want the command of labor, at a cheaper rate and under less onerous conditions than slave labor can be commanded." The influx of white immigrants, therefore, would bring about the end of slavery, not simply though the benevolence of slave owners but through their shifting evaluation of their own economic interests.[26]

At the same meeting, Baltimore colonizationist and future president of the ACS Benjamin Latrobe delivered an address that echoed Clay's celebration of "natural processes." Latrobe assured his audience that "we will see an emigration from America to Africa like that which now seeks our shores from Europe," a line which drew applause from the crowd. Again and again he reminds his audience of "thousands" of Europeans who come "to make our canals and railroads, to fill our country, to add to its teeming population, and to add to our wealth and prosperity." It is this immigration, he insisted, that is driving colonization. "How simply, how easy Colonization appears in this light."[27] Yet Latrobe's vision of this "easy" process studiously avoids mention of slavery. It is left to his audience's imagination whether the "homogeneous population" Latrobe envisioned would include African Americans slaves.

The Forgotten Lessons of the First Emancipation

Antislavery colonizationists had long been willing to tolerate this sort of ambiguity. In an 1833 letter, for example, Baltimore philanthropist Moses Sheppard acknowledged that some slaveholders supported colonization for the purpose of making their enslaved property more secure. He hoped, however, that in doing so they were unwittingly doing the work of emancipation.[28] Yet, their willingness to tolerate this practice, abetted by their celebration of the inevitability of emancipation and their denigration of legislative efforts, ultimately weakened efforts to challenge slavery in more effective ways. While colonization was used as a tool for emancipation, its promotion of the idea that emancipation would come about through a natural process, a consensual migration across the Atlantic, proved to be a barrier to the growth of antislavery politics.

The founders of the ACS, of course, knew quite well that emancipation had not occurred in the North simply through the consent of benevolent slave owners. It had been the coercive power of the state that guaranteed the end of slavery in the northern states. Beyond this, the passage of gradual abolition laws was not the end of northern legislation on slavery. Northern legislatures continued to fight over and pass bills that closed loopholes in the gradual abolition laws and which expedited the slow process of emancipation. In addition, as historian John Craig Hammond has noted, the exclusion of slavery from the Northwest was a result not of the unsuitability of that land for slavery, but of fierce political battles that ultimately turned state power against slavery. In other words, colonizationists, both North and South, knew quite well that the emergence of a "free" North was a product of state power, not of private benevolence.[29]

Colonization, as an idea, was not necessarily inconsistent with the use of state power to emancipate slaves. Certainly the Virginia advocates of gradual emancipation in 1831 insisted that colonization be coupled with abolition, and in the 1850s Kentucky abolitionists made similar arguments.[30] Yet if the *idea* of colonization might be a part of an effective antislavery politics, *colonizationists* tended to argue that antislavery politics was unnecessary and undesirable. There was broad agreement in the antebellum United States that the federal government had little power over the institution of slavery in the states where it existed, but colonizationist arguments that slavery would disappear naturally as a result of European immigration served as an argument against the importance of state-level antislavery action as well.

While historians once depicted the early American republic as relatively free of political conflict over slavery, recent work has shown instead that this was a period of fierce political conflict over the issue. We can now see that an event like the crisis over the admission of Missouri as a slave state, rather than an anomalous outburst, was just a more prominent moment in a longer struggle over slavery. This political conflict was not simply a prelude to the emergence of radical abolition in the 1830s. As historian Donald Radcliffe has provocatively argued, Garrisonian abolition emerged in reaction to the *decline* of the robust antislavery politics of the early republic.[31]

The reasons for that decline are complex, yet it is clear that the emergence of national political coalitions in the form of the Democratic and Whig parties played a crucial role in this process. In his account of the politics of slavery in the early republic, Matthew Mason has noted that broad antislavery sentiment existed in the North, but that sentiment did not automatically translate into antislavery action. Antislavery sentiment entered politics when "leaders showed them how slavery impinged on their rights and interests." Party leaders, unsurprisingly, generally emphasized these threats when they saw some partisan advantage in doing so; parties which aspired to win votes in all sections needed to downplay the issues associated with slavery.[32]

In the South, both the Whig and Democratic parties sought to portray themselves as the surest defender of slavery, but that sort of reputation might prove costly in the North, so northern politicians found various ways to ameliorate southern concerns while at the same time protecting themselves from potential losses in the northern electorate. Certainly partisanship itself, the desire to defeat one's political opponents, proved to be a powerful centrifugal force, holding together diverse political coalitions. Yet, centripetal forces remained, threatening to pull these coalitions apart; in the North, antislavery sentiment was one of these centripetal forces.[33]

Both parties sought to manage these forces, but did so in somewhat different ways.

Democrats had perhaps the easier task in this regard. They argued that any agitation on the issue of slavery posed an imminent threat to the union, and they tended to depict their opponents as abolitionists, invoking the most extreme and unpopular views of radical critics of slavery. Presidential candidate William Henry Harrison was termed the "Whig Abolitionist" candidate, in one pamphlet. Such accusations were a gross exaggeration of Whig sympathies for abolition, but it is clear that Whigs were no match for their Democratic opponents when it came to suppressing abolitionists. This opened Whigs up to Democratic attacks, in particular accusations that they supported racial amalgamation. Any opposition to slavery by Whigs was depicted as advocacy of social and political equality for African Americans.[34]

Whigs for their part worked hard to evade these charges; colonization, and in particular the image of colonization as European immigration in reverse, proved to be a useful tool for doing so. If colonization was capable of unleashing a consensual, natural process of emancipation, then abolition was not simply dangerous, it was unnecessary. Southern Democrats might depict colonization as the opening wedge of abolition, but for many northerners it was instead the moderate opposition to the radical doctrines of Garrison and others. Certainly they could point to the vitriol aimed at colonization by radical abolitionists to bolster this claim. Whigs kept the antislavery elements of their coalition in line by arguing that radical challenges to slavery were sure to produce disunion and civil war. They could also use colonization, with its insistence that blacks and whites could not live together peacefully on terms of equality, as a means of refuting accusations that they were advocates of racial amalgamation. Celebration of white immigration as the flip side of colonization helped to reassert colonization's distance from the racial egalitarianism of radical abolitionists.[35]

In order to appreciate the consequences of the rhetoric of colonization, its insistence that given the right circumstances slavery would consensually pass away, it is useful to consider some of the ways in which an effective antislavery politics did finally emerge in the 1850s. In broadest terms, the existence of these national political parties themselves served as a deterrent to the emergence of an antislavery political party. Historians have differed in their explanations of the collapse of these intersectional political coalitions, but certainly the belief that slavery was dying of natural causes, a belief promoted by colonization, played some role in keeping potential antislavery voters in line until the early 1850s. Since European immigration was gradually, consensually undermining southern slavery, they argued, there was no need to upset party unity by pushing for specific antislavery policies.

Ultimately, many white voters would be motivated to embrace antislavery politics not out of concern for slaves, but instead because they felt slavery posed a threat to white liberties. In the fight over the expansion of slavery, critics of expansion had often argued this land needed to be saved for white farmers. Slavery, they contended, would make the land unfit for free white men, in many cases the same white immigrants who were supposed to be transforming the slave economy of the South but who instead looked to the West for "free soil." Yet if such contentions had produced brief expressions of northern solidarity, eventually these dissident antislavery voters returned to the party fold. In the 1850s, however, the Republican Party was able to point to dramatic events like the Kansas-Nebraska crisis, the caning of Charles Sumner, and the Dred Scott decision to argue that an aggressive "Slave Power" was threatening white liberties as it sought to expand slavery.[36]

The concept of a "Slave Power" was not a new one, but in previous decades, colonization-promoted notions that slavery was in retreat had helped national parties to contain the outrage over the expansion of slavery or the violation of white liberties. If benevolent slaveholders were simply awaiting their opportunity to emancipate their slaves, then such violations could be accepted in the interest of inter-sectional (and intra-party) comity. By the 1850s, however, such notions had worn thin, and many of those who felt that colonization would be the path to the ultimate extinction of slavery also saw the need for a Republican Party which would prevent the expansion of slavery and undermine the influence of the "Slave Power." Even Republicans who continued to believe that colonization was the key to gradual, consensual emancipation had by the 1850s come to see that the active hand of the federal government was necessary to make this happen. European immigration and its mirror image of African colonization, in other words, were not enough to defeat the "Slave Power."[37]

Furthermore, if Republicans could win elections by appealing only to northern voters, this does not mean that they had given up entirely on the South. In what was perhaps the most disturbing element of the new Republican Party, in the eyes of slaveholders, it held out hope that non-slaveholding whites might flock to its ranks. These hopes were bolstered by the publication of *The Impending Crisis of the South and How to Meet It* by Hinton Rowan Helper of North Carolina. Helper denounced the institution of slavery as antagonistic to the interests of poor whites. Here was evidence that *within* the South there existed a class of white men who might be the key to ending slavery. Helper's plan for the ultimate extinction of slavery included the colonization of emancipated slaves, but it was a clear departure from the image of peaceful, consensual emancipation that colonizationists had done so much to promote in the preceding decades.[38] Whiggish colonizationists had hoped to hold together a sectional coalition by assuring antislavery northerners of the benevolence of southern masters; the Republican Party, instead, hoped to mobilize a class of non-slaveholding whites to end slavery.

Colonizationists had spent decades arguing that slavery was, in fact, a doomed institution, and that there was no need for government action to bring this about, aside from some financial support for the colonization of African Americans. They had done a great deal to claim for their movement the legacy of Revolutionary antislavery, invoking both George Washington and Thomas Jefferson as evidence that slaveholders' genuinely wanted to emancipate their slaves. All that the opponents of slavery needed to do was to create the circumstances in which this could happen; for many, the ongoing, massive immigration of white Europeans into the United States was the most compelling evidence that this could work. They continued to promote this belief long after evidence had proven it to be illusory. In doing so they helped to forestall the willingness of northerners to support a vigorous antislavery politics.

Finally, the Republican Party succeeded in mobilizing an antislavery political coalition by portraying the actions of their political opponents as a betrayal of the Founding Fathers' antislavery vision. Abraham Lincoln and other Republicans argued that they were the conservative defenders of the antislavery consensus of the Founders and that the defenders of slavery were the true radicals. Abolitionists had long sought to portray the Constitution as an antislavery document, with little success. Yet many Americans, especially but not exclusively in the North, believed that the Founders had hoped for the eventual end of slavery. As historian James Oakes has noted, even prior to the 1850s, "there is something almost willfully naïve in this vision of American history," but the events of the 1850s shattered this illusion.[39] Despite the hopes of colonizationists, slavery was not going to disappear via a painless, consensual mirror image of European immigration; it would instead take the coercive power of the state, and unimaginable bloodshed, to bring about the end of American slavery.

Notes

1. Richard S. Newman, *The Transformation of American Abolition: Fighting Slavery in the Early Republic* (Chapel Hill: University of North Carolina Press, 2002), 96–99; Eric Burin, *Slavery and the Peculiar Solution: A History of the American Colonization Society* (Gainesville: University of Florida Press, 2005); Beverly Tomek, *Colonization and Its Discontents: Emancipation, Emigration, and Antislavery in Antebellum Pennsylvania* (New York: New York University Press, 2011).

2. Burin, *Slavery and the Peculiar Solution*, 2, 16. As Marie Tyler-McGraw notes, "the very small percentage of Virginia's African American population that migrated to Liberia is not as significant as the debate among them over their rightful destiny and the roiling of local waters that the discussion of emigration to Africa caused" (*An African Republic: Black and White Virginians in the Making of Liberia* [Chapel Hill: University of North Carolina Press, 2007], 66).

3. *Niles' Weekly Register* (Baltimore), October 4, November 8, and November 15, 1817.

4. Nicholas Guyatt, *Providence and the Invention of the United States, 1607–1876* (New York: Cambridge University Press, 2007), 185–94, quote on 192; Robert Goodloe Harper to R. R. Gurley, January 25, 1829, ACS Papers, reel 5.

5. Historical Census Browser, Geospatial and Statistical Data Center, University of Virginia, mapserver.lib.virginia.edu/collections/ (accessed January 7, 2013).

6. William W. Freehling, "'Absurd' Issues and the Causes of the Civil War: Colonization as a Test Case," in *The Reintegration of American History: Slavery and the Civil War* (New York: Oxford University Press, 1994), 138–57. On abolitionist opposition to Indian Removal, see Guyatt, *Providence*, 211; Mary Hershberger, "Mobilizing Women, Anticipating Abolition: The Struggle Against Indian Removal in the 1830s," *Journal of American History* 86, no. 1 (June 1999): 15–40. For an example of colonizationists' disapproval of Indian Removal, see "Some of the Causes of National Anxiety: An Address by Professor Silliman, of Yale College," *African Repository and Colonial Journal* (Washington, D.C.), vol. 8, no. 6 (August 1832): 165.

7. "Statistical Review of Immigration, 1820–1910," *Reports of the Immigration Commission* (Washington, D.C.: Government Printing Office, 1911), 9–10; mapserver.lib.virginia.edu/collections/

8. *The Seventh Annual Report of the American Society for Colonizing the Free People of Color* (Washington, D.C.: Davis and Force, 1824), 314; "General Mercer and Colonization," *African Repository and Colonial Journal* 9, no. 9 (November 1833): 265–67; "Eleventh Annual Report," *Maryland Colonization Journal* (Baltimore), vol. 1, no. 20 (January 15, 1843): 310.

9. Benjamin Quarles, *Black Abolitionists* (London: Oxford University Press, 1969), 6.

10. Latrobe to RRG, April 9, 1827, ACS Papers, reel 2: 65–66; "Prospects at the North," *African Repository and Colonial Journal* 5, no. 4 (June 1829): 118–22.

11. Joseph Reed Ingersoll, *Address of Joseph R. Ingersoll at the annual meeting of the Pennsylvania Colonization Society, October 25, 1838 . . .* (Philadelphia: William Stavely, 1838), 20.

12. For a variety of approaches to the racial basis of the American nation in this period, see the essays in Michael A. Morrison and James Brewer Stewart, eds., *Race and the Early Republic: Racial Consciousness and Nation-Building in the Early Republic* (Lanham, Md.: Rowman & Littlefield Publishers, Inc.), 2002.

13. *Maryland Colonization Journal* 1, no. 9 (February 1842): 134.

14. Arthur Zilversmit, *The First Emancipation: The Abolition of Slavery in the North* (Chicago: University of Chicago Press, 1967).

15. William W. Freehling, *The Road to Disunion*, vol. 1: *Secessionists at Bay, 1776–1854* (New York: Oxford University Press, 2007), 157–61.

16. *Register of Debates*, Senate, 21st Cong., 1st Sess. (Washington: Gales and Seaton, 1830), 641–46; *Fourteenth Annual Report of the American Society for Colonizing the Free People of Color of the United States* (Washington, D.C.: James C. Dunn, 1831), 23. François Furstenberg has provocatively argued that Americans' struggle over the problem of slavery shaped their understanding of the nature of consent. In the discourse of colonization and slavery considered here, as in the discourses of citizenship and slavery examined by Furstenberg, we can see competing notions of consent in tension with one another. See Furstenberg, *In the Name of the Father: Washington's Legacy, Slavery, and the Making of a Nation* (New York: Penguin Press, 2006), esp. 71–103.

17. Lacy K. Ford, *Deliver Us from Evil: The Slavery Question in the Old South* (New York: Oxford University Press, 2009), 361–89; "Letter of Mr. Gurley," *African Repository and Colonial Journal* 9, no. 2 (April 1833): 51–56, quote on 54; *The Twentieth Annual Report of the American Society for the Colonization of the Free People of Colour* (Washington, D.C.: James C. Dunn, 1837), 43–44.

18. Ford, *Deliver Us from Evil*, 19–48; Matthew Mason, *Slavery and Politics in the Early American Republic* (Chapel Hill: University of North Carolina Press, 2006), 232.

19. Elliot Cresson to R. R. Gurley, August 23, 1828, ACS papers, reel 4: 299–300; Moses Sheppard to Samuel Ford McGill, December 6, 1849, Moses Sheppard Papers, Friends Historical Library, Swarthmore College; "A New Attack on the Colonization Society," *African Repository and Colonial Journal* 9, no. 6 (August 1833): 181–85.

20. Elliot Cresson to R. R. Gurley, August 3, 1829, ACS Papers, reel 6: 334–35.

21. Daniel Walker Howe, *The Political Culture of the American Whigs* (Chicago: University of Chicago Press, 1979), 135–37; James Brewer Stewart, "Modernizing 'Difference': The Political Meanings of Color in the Free States, 1776–1840," in *Abolitionist Politics and the Coming of the Civil War* (Amherst: University of Massachusetts Press, 2008), 35–57, esp. 49–51.

22. "Mr. Key's Letter," *Colonization Herald* (Philadelphia), vol. 1, no. 6 (June 1839): 253–65; Ingersoll quote on 24.

23. Historical Census Browser, Geospatial and Statistical Data Center, University of Virginia, mapserver.lib.virginia.edu/collections/ (accessed January 14, 2013).

24. "Address of Judge Bullock," *African Repository and Colonial Journal* 23, no. 4 (April 1847): 99–110; "Letter No. 4," *Maryland Colonization Journal* 4, no. 6 (December 1847): 100–102. Dale T. Knobel notes that some northern nativists recognized the implicit

connection between colonization and European immigration and therefore denounced African colonization ("'Native Soil': Nativists, Colonizationists, and the Rhetoric of Nationality," *Civil War History* 27, no. 4 [December 1981]: 314–37).

25. Eric Foner, *Free Soil, Free Labor, Free Men: The Ideology of the Republican Party Before the Civil War* (New York: Oxford University Press, 1970).

26. "Speech of the Hon. H. Clay," *Thirty-Fourth Annual Report of the American Colonization Society* (Washington, D.C.: C. Alexander, 1851), 34–43.

27. "Speech of J. H. B. Latrobe," *Thirty-Fourth Annual Report of the American Colonization Society*, 55–61.

28. Moses Sheppard to Robert S. Finley, April 27, 1833, Moses Sheppard Papers, Friends Historical Library, Swarthmore College.

29. Zilversmit, *First Emancipation*, 192–229; John Craig Hammond, *Slavery, Freedom, and Expansion in the Early American West* (Charlottesville: University of Virginia Press, 2007).

30. Alison Goodyear Freehling, *Drift Toward Dissolution: The Virginia Slavery Debate of 1831–1832* (Baton Rouge: Louisiana State University Press, 1982); William W. Freehling, *The Road To Disunion*, vol. 2: *Secessionists Triumphant, 1854–1861* (New York: Oxford University Press, 2007), 227–30.

31. Mason, *Slavery and Politics*; Robert Pierce Forbes, *The Missouri Compromise and Its Aftermath: Slavery and the Making of America* (Chapel Hill: University of North Carolina Press, 2007); Donald J. Radcliffe, "The Decline of Antislavery Politics, 1815–1840," in John Craig Hammond and Matthew Mason, eds., *Contesting Slavery: The Politics of Bondage and Freedom in the New American Nation* (Charlottesville: University of Virginia Press, 2011), 267–90.

32. Mason, *Slavery and Politics*, 1–8, quote on 5.

33. William J. Cooper Jr., *The South and the Politics of Slavery, 1828–1856* (Baton Rouge: Louisiana State University Press, 1978). The language of centrifugal and centripetal forces comes from Michael F. Holt, *The Rise and Fall of the American Whig Party: Jacksonian Politics and the Onset of the Civil War* (New York: Oxford University Press, 1999), xiii.

34. Elizabeth R. Varon, *Disunion! The Coming of the American Civil War, 1789–1859* (Chapel Hill: University of North Carolina Press, 2008), 140–48, quote on 144; Alexander Saxon, *The Rise and Fall of the White Republic: Class Politics and Mass Culture in Nineteenth-Century America* (New York: Verso, 1990), 142–54.

35. Stewart, "Modernizing 'Difference,'" 49–51.

36. Varon, *Disunion!* 235–304.

37. On the late 1850s revival in interest for colonization among Republicans, see Eric Foner, *The Fiery Trial: Abraham Lincoln and American Slavery* (New York: W. W. Norton, 2010), esp. 123–31.

38. Varon, *Disunion!* 311–12.

39. James Oakes, *Freedom National: The Destruction of Slavery in the United States, 1861–1865* (New York: W. W. Norton, 2013), 69–75, quote on 70.

13

The End of Emancipation Street

"Civilization," Race, and Cartography in Colonial Liberia

ROBERT MURRAY

At its heart, colonization is an argument about space. By relocating to Africa and inhabiting the "civilizing" space of Liberia, degraded American blackness would be uplifted and transformed. Charles F. Mercer's address before the first meeting of the American Colonization Society (ACS) described African Americans living within the United States as a "wretched civilization . . . consisting of this degraded, idle, and vicious population." Of course, the ideology propounded in this first meeting of colonizationists also assumed that the same inhabitants of this "wretched civilization" would become the vehicle of African uplift by establishing "colonies, composed of blacks already instructed in the arts of civilized life." There is a duality here that has always perplexed and intrigued scholars of Liberia. How could such an uncivilized and violent class in America form the civilizing backbone of a rejuvenated and Christian Africa? Claude A. Clegg referred to it as "a tortured logic geared more toward effecting their ends than to proving the intellectual cogency of their position." Marie Tyler-McGraw found this transformation more indicative of "alchemy." In his seminal work, *The Black Image in the White Mind,* George M. Frederickson at least attempted to give the colonizationists more ideological cohesion than a reliance on black magic by categorizing them as conservative "social environmentalists." Within this framework, colonizationists dismissed inherent black degeneracy and instead located the root of the "wretched civilization" in the racism of Euro-Americans who would never accept African Americans into society. Their inherent conservatism led colonizationists to assume that the United States could never escape its racist foundations and, thusly, the only means to provide uplift to those people of African descent was to change their social setting to escape white prejudices.[1] Frederickson's "social environmentalism" argument certainly encapsulates a broad swath of colonizationist thinking, but it is incomplete.

Many colonial societies attempt to replicate the home society, and Liberia was no different in its effort to recreate the United States in Africa. Settlements were erected utilizing American-patterned street grids along with the names, farming techniques, churches, civic institutions, clothing, and culture of the United States. William Thornton, architect of the U.S. Capitol, presented a plan in 1821 for the proposed town of Mesurado, the future Monrovia, that curiously combined the realities of a besieged military post with the sweeping avenues and public squares of L'Enfant's vision for Washington, D.C. Thornton foresaw a future Liberian capital with a grid pattern of streets, intersecting diagonal avenues all convening in an enormous circle, including a grand avenue similar to the National Mall but renamed "Emancipation Street." But, whereas L'Enfant's squares and circles were designed as public spaces, the focal point of Liberia's capital was occupied by a twelve-foot-tall tower that would function as an arsenal, complete with a circular defensive wall and battery of cannons. The great space between the fort and streets centered less on the idea of public gatherings and more on providing a clear field of vision for the fort's defenders to fire upon any potential attacker. Thornton very literally envisioned the capital of Monrovia as another District of Columbia, but with the ever-present potential of being overrun. Thornton's effort to drop the District of Columbia into western Africa is indicative of this broader dream to reconstruct the United States in Africa. Situated near the equator, without a nominal national identity beyond the structures of a private benevolent society, and with a local polyglot population, Liberia never fully functioned as a new United States. The transmutation was incomplete, inadequate, and challenged by the locals who did not care for the expansionist trajectory of the Liberian settlers.

Beyond spotlighting the hopes of some colonizationists like Henry Clay, who hoped to spark an African America and "behold a confederation of Republican States, on the Western shores of Africa, like our own, with their Congress and annual legislatures thundering forth in behalf of the rights of man," Thornton's proposal likewise reveals the incompleteness of Frederickson's "social environmentalism" argument and a paradox within colonization thought. If colonizationists saw the social environment of the United States as a hindrance to black capacity, then why did they work diligently to recreate the United States in Africa? Many colonizationists were upfront regarding their opinions of African "civilization" and the changes they hoped the African American settlers would create. Robert J. Breckinridge argued that, because of their American residency, African Americans had learned the "manners, the habits, the wants, and the attainments, of a civilization—low as compared with ours, respectable as compared with the average of the human race, and exalted as compared with the bulk of their own."[2] This certainly is a great deal of intellectual legwork to transform American savagery into African civilization, but the overarching premise was not a rejection of an American social environment as ill suited for either Africans or those of African descent. Indeed, the proclaimed goal of many colonizationists was to recreate the United States in Africa.

A central premise of the colonization movement was the supposed inherent racial similarity between Africans in Africa and people of African descent living within the United States. The idea that this migration of African Americans was actually a "return" or "restoration" undergirded the location of the colony and offered supposed benefits like spreading "civilization" in the form of Western governance and Christianity. "Every colonist transported," Daniel Mayes informed his audience of Kentucky colonizationists in 1831, "may be, literally and strictly, considered a missionary." The African native would embrace the "returning" benighted children of the continent more readily than white missionaries because they were "missionaries of his own race." Frederickson also highlighted these "romantic racialist" beliefs that African Americans were "natural Christians," an assumption most evident in Harriet Beecher Stowe's *Uncle Tom's Cabin*.[3]

And therein lies the paradox at the intersection of Mayes's "romantic racialism," Thornton's tower, and Frederickson's "social environmentalism." If Africans would be more willing to embrace the settlers' cultural practices because they were of the same race and African Americans would flourish in this United States without white prejudice, then why did Thornton not only include a defensive fortification in his city plan, but actually made this projection of military might *the* central feature of the settlement? Even as the colonizationists broadcast that the African inhabitants and neighbors of Liberia desired "the arts of civilized life" and their shared racial identity with the settlers facilitated this conversion, they likewise assured their audiences that Monrovia had been "commenced on a regular plan, comfortable houses constructed, and works thrown up for defence against the Barbarian powers."[4]

The African American settlers were simultaneously one with and set against native Africans—both the celebrated cultural apex of the "African race" imitated by its lesser members and outsiders who buttressed themselves against the oncoming storm of barbarians. Intriguingly, these differences between the settlers and the Africans were codified racially in Liberia. Colonizationists, or really anyone willing to read their publications, were intimately aware of the evolving structures of race in their African colony. For the West African observers of the Liberian settlers, the dress, language, religion, behavior, in short, the culture of the newcomers, resembled more the European and Euro-American traders who had been traveling the western shores of Africa for centuries. These native Africans labeled the African American settlers as whites, a racial transformation the Liberians readily noticed even as many dismissed this categorization as yet another example of their neighbors' lack of "civilization." Peering beyond Liberia's "civilized" areas of settler habitation, the editor of the *Liberia Herald* denounced those natives who "look with suspicion upon the colony, and a word from a 'white man' (a generic term for all classes, colors and conditions enveloped in clothing)." Settler George McGill, progenitor of one of Liberia's most prominent families, informed the white leaders of the Maryland State Colonization Society (MSCS) that the Greboes living at the future site of that organization's creatively named colony, Maryland in Liberia, "express a strong wish to become white men, (i.e. Read & Write)." Thus, whiteness was a shifting cultural category reflecting one's association with the culture, education, literacy, dress, language, and Christianity of the United States or Europe.[5]

Despite their dismissive attitude towards native cultural attainments, the Liberian settlers still found their African whiteness a useful tool in certain situations. Freeborn northerner Samuel Williams served as a missionary to many of the villages surrounding Monrovia. Williams elected to leave his native Pennsylvania in the wake of the vote for the reformed Constitution of 1838, the document that explicitly altered that requirement to vote from "freeman" to "white." Although he had been permitted to vote in previous elections in his native Johnstown, in that crucial vote the white men at the polling locale refused to allow Williams to place his ballot in the box. Despite this very personal confrontation with legal barriers entrenching whiteness, Williams rather enjoyed the benefits his mission received in the form of throngs of curious visitors from being an exotic "white God-man." This title was a combination of the local terms for a Christian ("God man") and a settler in Liberia ("white"). Much like the missionary Williams, settler Diana James believed her whiteness proved a tool of "civilization." Writing to her former mistress in the States, James provided a "long catalogue about the Natives customs which I am in hopes that you have found very amusing." She concluded her letter with an account of a discussion she held with an unnamed native in which she inquired "how was it that the[y] could not read & write like white man (they call us all white man)." After receiving an unsatisfactory response, James told him that he could be the "same as white man" if he only applied himself to becoming civilized.[6]

Liberia's capacity for uplifting African Americans did not result from its lack of white privilege, as asserted by Frederickson, but rather by bestowing the privileges of whiteness upon African American settlers. Accounts of Liberia's warping effect on racial identities were scattered throughout colonizationist literature. In this manner, residents of the United States became intimately familiar with the African whiteness of Liberian settlers. Even as colonizationists nodded their heads in agreement with Mayes when he claimed that African Americans and Africans were of the same race, they were *simultaneously* aware that something had gone awry in the racial hierarchies of their colony. Not only were they aware, but many Euro-American colonizationist leaders embraced and celebrated these African definitions of whiteness. The tract *A Concise History of the Commencement, Progress and Present Condition of the American Colonies in Liberia*, written by a general agent of the ACS, described the Liberian settlers: "The Liberian is certainly a great man, and what is more, by the natives he is considered a white man, though many degrees from that stand—for to be thought acquainted with the white man's fashions, and to be treated as one, are considered as marks of great distinction among the Bassa and other nations." For other colonizationists, emigration to Liberia transformed the settler into a great man not only for Africans, but also for Americans. Andrew Hall, a settler in Africa's Maryland, wrote to an MSCS official in 1847, "I find it is true what you told me in your office that I would not be willing to come back to America to be called a negro." Although Hall did not suggest under what identities he would willingly return to the United States, the fact that Hall places the onus of the thought with the unnamed colonization official suggests the degrees of racial alchemy certain officials believed their colony wrought. Another Maryland colonizationist, Moses Sheppard, expressed great admiration for African taxonomy: "I am pleased with the meaning the native Africans give to the term 'white man' they make these words refer to intelligence rather than colour, the construction is a good one for knowledge is the same in all. minds [*sic*] as far as we know do not differ in complexion."[7]

Whiteness and blackness are not antipodes within this framework, but rather symbiotic partners in creating the elevated "civilization" of Liberia necessary to transform degraded American blackness into African greatness. These racial constructions were interrelated with the projections of space presented by both colonizationists in the United States and the Liberian settlers themselves. In essence, occupancy in the *space* of Liberia allowed settlers to claim to be both exotic "others" (a person of African descent who was also "white") and "civilized" because they had to defend that space, projected as a tiny United States regardless of the reality on the ground, against foreign barbarity.

While contemporaneous accounts of colonization have increasingly refocused the scholarly gaze upon the settlers and life within the colony itself, much work remains to reorient scholarship on colonization to include the active agency of both Africans and African Americans.[8] Colonizationists in the United States were not crafting their theories in a vacuum, but were actively engaging and being shaped by the letters, reports, and lectures of the Liberian settlers, many of whom either maintained contact with American correspondents or returned to the United States to travel.[9] Needless to say, the settlers' reports were filled with less-than-glowing opinions of the natives: "The people among whom we live are very ignorant and superstitious," "the natives about us are a lazy & idol people," "they are the most Savage, & blud thirsty people I ever saw." Even John Brown Russwurm, a towering figure in African American scholarship who one recent biographer has characterized as a "Pan-Africanist Pioneer," peppered his official reports with reminders to his employers that "we are in a land of savages."[10] When settler Samuel F. McGill returned to the United States and traveled through New England, he drew upon his experience in Africa when describing his nights without a bed as reducing himself "to sleep every night as a savage." Within this understanding of the colonizing mission, the continued use of "savage" makes sense, and it is important to remember that the colonizationist rhetoric was built upon a dialog between white colonizationists in the United States, white ACS officials in Africa, and African American settlers and officials in Africa.

The nearly ubiquitous use of the word "savage" or "barbarian" by settlers and American supporters of colonization alike underscores the complexity of this spatial logic. The expansion of Western power, combined with the growth of biological racism, led to an etymological evolution in the ways in which non-Western "others" transitioned from "savages" to "primitives." The transition is beguilingly significant. Savagery frames a horizontal relationship in which subjects are juxtaposed against an idealized vision of "civilization" and found wanting. Significantly, the concept lacks a temporal framework. Savages can become "civilized" by altering behavior and beliefs and adopting "civilized" modes of life. Conversely, primitivism replaces this framework by adding a temporal element. Within this model of thinking, Europeans (and Euro-Americans) have literally surpassed all others on the globe by attaining civilization more rapidly than others, which suggests something internally debased within the "primitive." To attain civilization, "primitives" cannot simply alter behavior as, being from a previous age, they lack the capacity to immediately adapt to the new ways but must progress through time to "catch up" to the more advanced civilization.[11]

Although Liberia was founded in this historical context, the term "primitive" is almost completely absent from colonizationist propaganda or settlers' reports. Instead, the preferred nomenclature was "savage." The colonizationists argued that the natives only "want but long and uninterrupted intercourse with enlightened nations, and the introduction of the Christian religion, to place them on a level with their more wealthy northern fellow-creatures."[12] Colonizationists held African society up to a Western prism and found it wanting, but assumed that their African American mediators provided the ideal go-betweens to coerce natives across the line of civilization. As such, their thinking reflected a spatial, horizontal interpretation of "civilization"; this was the civilizing mission of the colony and a foundational ideology of colonization thought: the mere fact of living within colonial Liberia in which settlers would control African savagery would simultaneously elevate settlers and natives. The only temporal element would be the time required to cohabit the same space so that natives could adopt settler culture. The problem lay in somehow incorporating the "savages" into this "civilized" American space without corrupting it, while also militarily defending against this ever-present African savagery. Separating and distinguishing between "civilization" and "savagery" was a spatial riddle that mapmakers attempted to solve. In their efforts to depict Liberia, the complexities and diversity of the colonial space presented them with great challenges.

While missionaries in Liberia were often attuned to the significant diversity surrounding them in order to propagate the Gospel in their converts' language, the words "savage" and "native" are used within the vast majority of settler correspondence papers over Liberia's diverse and evolving ethnoscape.[13] There were dozens of ethnic groups in the territory, speaking in languages from five different family groups. While some of the largest and most significant Liberian ethnic groups were identified by nineteenth-century observers, such as the Kpelle, Bassa, Kru, Grebo, Gola, Kissi, Dei, and Vai, these were, in turn, evolving identities profoundly shaped by the arrival of settlers from the Western Hemisphere.[14] Each possessing their own characteristics, cultures, languages, and motivations, these different groups at various times found the Americo-Liberians useful allies, bitter enemies, trading partners, helpful educators, annoying interlopers, and beneficial mediators in their conflicts with each other and with the settlers. Unfortunately, the settlers' dismissive and blanket descriptors often impede scholars who are left to use equally ill-defined terms—"African," "Native," and so forth—that likewise fail to denote the vast differences among these groups.

One exception is the independent colony of Maryland in Liberia, established by the MSCS in 1834. While the language of the settlers largely did not change, the creation of Liberia's Maryland did follow a different historical path than Monrovia. The MSCS had negotiated and purchased territory among several Grebo villages at Cape Palmas. Intriguingly, the Greboes were relative newcomers to Cape Palmas themselves. Grebo history recorded their origins in a handful of extended families forced from the African interior who arrived at the coast around the turn of the eighteenth century. Apparently due to overcrowding, the group separated to spread down the coast. The result was the formation of two rival factions—the Nyomowe and the Kudemowe—which were themselves divided into small autonomous towns; the ancestral alliances largely served the purpose of securing allies in times of war. Social rank in Grebo society was divided by age-based grades, and the two principal leaders of each village, the *bodio* and *wodoba*, were drawn from the town's population of men over the age of forty-five. While the *bodio* was the chief religious figure, the *wodoba* was usually the most influential man in the town (and often descended in some manner from the town's founder). While the *wodoba* held certain privileges and honors, he more readily functioned as the "first among equals" of the town's oldest men. Most American and European travelers to Cape Palmas, unfamiliar with the social make-up of Grebo society, often erroneously interpreted the *wodoba* as the town's king.[15]

The three village "kings" who signed the treaty that created Maryland in Liberia hoped to make their cape into a bustling entrepôt for American and European shipping and believed that an African American settlement would serve as the first step. As part of the treaty requirements, not only would none of the Grebo villages be removed from Cape Palmas, but the

Americans were also required to establish schools for each village. The Greboes hoped that access to a Western education and English-language skills would serve their children well as mercantile middlemen orchestrating the trade between the coast and West African interior. The Maryland settlement functioned quite differently from the visions colonizationists had for Monrovia. While the Greboes had desired the colony and sought to cooperate with its administrators to a certain degree, they also conceived themselves as economic rivals to the settlers; this caused immediate friction. Additionally, the Greboes were very much the American settlers' neighbors. Not only that, but Gbenelu, the largest Grebo village on the cape, actually lay right in the middle of the American settlement, much to the consternation of the settlers.

John Revey's two maps of Maryland in Liberia, drawn in 1838, are illustrative of the ways in which colonists conceived of the territory and the relationship between themselves and the natives. Revey was a member of the ACS's inaugural expedition aboard the *Elizabeth* in 1820, but by 1838 he was serving as colonial secretary to the MSCS's separate colony. Revey produced two maps. One provided a broad overview of the entire territory claimed by the Marylanders; the other focused on the colony's primary American settlement, Harper, and its agricultural satellite village of Latrobe. The entire mapmaking project was intimately connected to economic exploitation and exerting control. Governor John Brown Russwurm, coeditor of the first African American newspaper in the United States and the first person of African descent to be appointed governor of a Liberian colony, submitted Revey's maps to the MSCS Board of Managers to provide them with a visual understanding of their African claims. As the immediate impetus for commissioning the mapmaking project was the near loss of a European trading vessel off of Maryland's shore, Russwurm conceived of the project largely in economic terms. The recorded depths of the various points near Cape Palmas, along with dangerous submerged rocks, demonstrate the importance of shipping for both trade and the arrival of new settlers. A pair of anchors symbolically sketched northwest of the cape, where the bottom was reported "sandy," mark the prime anchorages for visiting ships and the most direct route to the settlement's wharf along the protected northern coast.[16]

Revey, however, conceived of his maps as portraying more than just nautical economic possibilities. In describing his cartographic intentions to the MSCS, Revey underscored that the map was designed to convey the most important elements of the colony. In addition to the economic potential of the colony—farms, inland waterways, and anchorages for ships—Revey also emphasized the spread of "civilization" in the form of Christianity, via missionary stations, and the orderly town, organized like any good American urban plan with scientific rigidity. Each section of Maryland Avenue, the primary thoroughfare of the American settlements, as it turns from its east-west axis to a precise northeast-southwest direction, is measured in rods. The bisecting roads, "Holmes Road," "Vermont Street," "Baltimore Street," belie the American origins of the colony. The farm lots of the settlers, nearly all displayed as perfectly rectangular, are numbered and labeled with both the plot's owner and the amount of acreage under cultivation. In combining two maps, one of the settlement and another of the entire territory claimed by Maryland in Liberia, Revey visually demarcated certain spaces as civilized Western-style private possessions while simultaneously claiming the land outside of the neat rectangles as potential areas for settler expansion. The only impediment to settler expansion, as projected by the map, is Mother Nature.[17]

The blank spaces of the Harper map surrounding the settler's rectangular plots are labeled with explanations for the end of development: "low land" and "sandy" terrain to the south of the farms nearer the ocean, "salt mangrove marshes" to the north and west along the Hoffman River, "swamps" near Mount Vaughn. Despite the environmental encroachments, Revey's rectangular plots march ever eastward, ending only with the page and the suggestion of unstoppable American agricultural expansion. Revey projected more than just American expansion, however, by conceding one corner of the Harper map to "Native Cassada fields," directly across the "Hoffman River" from Harper. In contrast to American expansionism, the four African settlements denoted within the confines of Harper are seemingly fed a by a single field planted with cassava, which Revey dismissed as a potential source of agricultural expansion due to sandy soil. Not only do the Africans farm this particular peninsula, but it is solely dedicated to a single crop and in poor soil to boot. There is no other notation of native spatial possessions aside from the navigational hazard of the "Devil Rocks or the Natives sacred rocks" and the "native cemetery" on tiny Auburn Island.[18]

Revey's concession that Maryland's African population laid claim to some territory was singular among maps of Liberia, which largely ignored African agricultural claims, but even this attempt to name the peninsula as a Grebo agricultural site concealed more than it revealed. Revey was correct in at least one regard: the soil on that peninsula probably was very sandy.

The poor soils of the Liberian coast forced its rice-dependent populations into an expansive system of crop rotation, meaning overgrown fields interpreted by American settlers as wasted territory were viewed by Greboes as active rice fields that were simply fallow.[19] Greboes at Cape Palmas grew more than cassava, and they certainly thought they possessed more arable land than Revey provided them on his map.

The most striking images, however, are the architectural drawings that symbolize the most significant Western-style buildings of the colonies: the agency structures, missionary stations, schools, and military fortifications. Presumably, Revey attempted to accurately depict the aesthetics of each structure within the confines of his artistic ability. The two-story agency house sits directly across from the squat, rectangular, single-story agency office. While many of the schools are depicted in a similar manner, the mission stations vary from the Presbyterian Fair Hope station, complete with triangular roof and what appears to be a porch, to the neighboring boxy two-story Methodist outpost named Mount Emory. The correlation between the "civilizing" mission of the Christian missionaries situated in the colony was underscored by the Protestant Episcopal schoolhouse oriented immediately outside the confines of "Joe Wah's towns." The various outbuildings of the easternmost colonial outpost, Mount Tubman, sitting dutifully on their hilltop, are encircled by a protective wooden palisade. Similarly, the town of Harper, situated on a peninsula, is protected from the neighboring African settlement with a small fortification and "Long Gun" protecting Maryland Avenue. The inclusion of this firepower projected the settler's power over their African neighbors, asserting dominance over savage African blackness and subsequently attaining an elevated status from Euro-Americans because of that dominance. This projection of violent power resonates with much of the correspondence emanating from the colony. Three years before Revey completed his map of Maryland in Liberia, the *Liberia Herald* responded to the massacre of a settlement organized by the Young Men's Colonization Society of Pennsylvania upon the pacifist principles of the organization's Quaker membership. The *Herald* echoed the claims of many settlers when it asserted the settlers' superior understanding of controlling African savagery over their patrons in the United States:

> What was the immediate cause of the attack we have not been able to learn, but we have no hesitancy in believing that the smallest show of military preparation would have prevented the attack. But the

principle on which the Colony was founded, is one, that forbids every thing like military preparation; consequently, they fell an easy prey to the villainous savages. With all deference, to the opinion of men, in almost every thing our superiors in wisdom, we beg leave, on this subject to differ, and we think our intercourse with the natives and consequent knowledge of their disposition, and habits, entitle us this privilege. We, as much as any one on earth, abhor, and deprecate the effusion of human blood; but we are conscious the way to prevent it, is not to be unprepared to resist the natives, but rather the most certain method to provoke it. Such is the dastardly, unprincipled disposition of these half cannibals, that nothing but a knowledge of superiority, in point of physical force, on the part of foreigners, will keep them to the terms of any compact made with them.[20]

Cartography provided a means of projecting that controlling and "civilizing" violence on Africans through depictions of how the colonial space was organized. There is order to Revey's cartographic world, "civilization" in the form of American architecture, and the necessary safeguards against encroaching savagery in the form of crude African structures. The principal design elements of Revey's maps are clear: American architecture, enlightened urban design founded on mathematical calculation, the "civilizing mission" of education and Christianity, and the necessary firepower and defensive structures to hold back African savagery that, even as it was drawn within the colonial sphere, was simultaneously projected beyond the pale of civilization.

In contrast to the careful street axes and farm lots of the American town, the four native settlements near Harper are written off as a jumbled and disorganized conglomeration of triangles. Although the shape vaguely echoes local domestic construction, round buildings with conical thatched roofs, there is little effort to reconstruct the same architectural flourishes depicted in the American frame buildings. A larger Grebo town simply has more triangles than a smaller one. These settlements either found themselves in the accompaniment of "civilizing" forces, like the Episcopal missionary station attached to "Joe Wah's towns," or as in the case of "King Freeman's Town," facing the barrel of a "Long Gun" which reminded all parties where the colonists believed their greatest external threat lay. Revey's solitary concession to their extensive road network was the "Native Road to Saurekah," a meandering line of dots originating from "Joe Wahs Town" north of Harper. In contrast, Maryland Avenue, denoted by two thick parallel lines representing a significant roadway, drives due east out of Harper, angles northeast with precision, and then cuts through the landscape to the prominent native town of Denah, situated on the Cavalla River. While Maryland Avenue was the main thoroughfare of Harper and Latrobe, most colonial accounts describe the eastern terminus of the avenue as the fortified outpost at Mount Tubman. There was a route to Denah from Harper, but it was a local path with none of the size or grandeur of Revey's boulevard. Governor Russwurm traveled the path in 1844 and 1845 to open communications between Harper and Denah and described the road as "a path worse than any I have ever seen, in fact, some parts were so bad as to have prevented a travel on horseback without danger."[21] Clearly, Russwurm was not impressed with the route he traversed six years after Revey portrayed a broad, straight thoroughfare.

In appropriating a native route as an extension of Liberian colonial authority, Revey reimagined the route as a flawless American road. Perhaps he was projecting an idealized future for Maryland Avenue constructed upon local foundations, but Revey understood the significance of projecting Liberian power into the interior. Denah was a strategically located town, and a "civilized" route there would expand Liberian power away from its coastal enclave and project it into the interior. The proper way to visually project that power onto the map was to reimagine an African road as a grand American boulevard. If the route was to be used by the settlers, it must be a "civilized" path.

The net effect of cartographic representations of colonial Liberia, of which Revey's maps are but a few indicative examples, was to constrain natives into isolated settlements residing within the territorial confines of the American colonies. They were under the civilizing control of the Americo-Liberian settlers but not really a part of the colonial hierarchy. They lacked agricultural exploits and habitation beyond their charted towns. They existed only within specific, chaotic settlements surrounded by the weapons of "civilization" in the form of missions, schools, and cannons and fortified hills. Of course, the effort to constrain chaotic Africanness to a few fixed points belied the reality of the colonial lived experience in which natives and settlers found themselves constantly in day-to-day interactions, something many settlers found a liability. Writing soon after arriving in the Maryland colony in July 1838, at the same historical moment that Revey was creating his map, settler Stephen Smith reported problems with the colony: "wee are al among the natives and thear is a nof [enough] of them heare to tend every foot of land that is heare and tha heave as much rite to the land as wee heave and as tha become inlightened theare woold require more room and wheare is it to come from." Sampson Caesar was also startled by the omnipresence of natives in Monrovia, although he found them a useful, though disconcerting, presence: "The natives are numerous in this place and they do the most of the work for the people in this place they will Steal every Chance." And Revey's own map of Maryland in Liberia inadvertently disputed the proposed separation between Africans and Americans. At the margins of the map, beyond the range of settler explorations, Revey still managed to include rough points of importance. Well to the north of the American settlements, "King Cavas Dominions" were reported to have populations between three and four thousand. Even more explicit, Revey was forced to estimate the course of the river near the seaside village called "Fishtown" by the Americans. He dutifully transcribed above the meandering stream "Course of the Fishtown River as described by the natives."[22]

The African assistance—presumably Grebo, but again the "natives" descriptor provides no guarantees—in creating this map raises the question of African responses to these settler efforts to depict simultaneous separation from and control over Africans. Given the remarkable diversity of African Liberians and the many different ways in which they engaged American settlers across space and time, it would be foolish to project the responses of the Cape Palmas Greboes onto the entirety of the Liberian coast. Yet, their actions in 1836, two years after the creation of the colony and during a period of strained settler-African relations, underscores both the complexity of life in Liberia and the sophistication of African responses.

As compared to the creation of Monrovia, which sparked an immediate and violent response from Africans, the early years of Maryland in Liberia were relatively peaceful. Yet, the neighboring Grebo villages and African American settlers found themselves in a constant struggle for power on the cape. Particularly galling to the settlers, often poor former slaves, were the repeated thefts of goods and supplies they attributed to the neighboring Greboes. By early 1836, the colony's governor sought an end to the growing crisis by declaring to the senior leaders of Gbenelu that settlers would henceforth indiscriminately confiscate any Grebo property of equal value to that of the claimed stolen goods.

The governor's plan was to force the African community to police its own or be subject to confiscation. The Grebo response took him by surprise. He reported back to his superiors in the United States: "But that what I had proposed was new to them, that they could not learn by their people who had visited the white mans country that any laws of that nature were ever made. That as we were one people & under one flag, I had no right to make one class more than another suffer for all the thefts." Noting the justice system established by the colonists, the Greboes demanded that a similar system be enacted for themselves. The Greboes considered Maryland in Liberia to be analogous to a "white man's country"—an argument that indicates the expansive travels of these seafarers—and that the laws in one must apply to the other. In lieu of an abusive system of justice, the Greboes conceded that they would police their own, but demanded a place within the colonial judiciary. Thus, the governor gave ground to African legal theory and found himself explaining to a board of governors in the United States why he had just appointed six Grebo constables and six Grebo justices of the peace.[23]

The Greboes not only conceived of themselves as within the colonial space, they also saw themselves as active partners within that space. This suggests that the Greboes certainly understood the legal implications of the deed signed by the *wodoba* of Gbenelu, Pah Nemah, more popularly known as "King Freeman" by the settlers.[24] While the Greboes had conceded to the MSCS the "power by its factor or agents to exercise all authority in the above named territory," the document also asserted that the Greboes "hereby acknowledge ourselves as members of the Colony of Maryland in Liberia, so far as to unite in common defence in case of War of foreign aggression."[25] Although their legal obligations were limited to military aid, the Greboes obviously perceived themselves as active members of the colony on equal footing with the settlers.

In fact, "King Freeman" hoped to circumvent the colonial administration entirely. Even before the colonial governor attempted to punish the Greboes for theft, "Freeman" had dispatched his translator and lieutenant, Simleh Ballah, on a mission to travel to Baltimore and speak directly to the board of managers of the Maryland colonization society. Ballah was instructed to verify the claims of the colonial governor and notify the board that "Freeman" appreciated the influx of trade goods into Cape Palmas. Ballah actually did address the board in June 1836 and personally received a set of laws they wished to be implemented in the colony. Unfortunately, it was the exact same law code they had already dispatched to their governor, and the diplomatic mission did not open future relations for the Greboes of Cape Palmas to directly negotiate with colonizationists in the United States.

Still, "Freeman" was reportedly pleased with the results of his own little exploratory expedition. Although he failed to establish himself on the same level as the settler governor in the eyes of colonizationists in the United

States, his representative had been received with remarkable decorum for an African traveling to a slave state on a diplomatic mission. Not only had Ballah resided with the colonization society's president during his American sojourn, but the colonizationists had likewise played (assuredly awkward) tour guides to Ballah, including a mandatory trip for tourists up the stairs of Baltimore's Washington Monument to view the harbor. Utilizing a white missionary as his "hand," "Freeman" dispatched a letter to the board upon Ballah's return, thanking them for their kind treatment of his "eyes" while in the United States. He claimed he was pleased with the MSCS's rules for governance and promised to implement them among his people. "Freeman" also reported that Ballah talked about the United States, and "Freeman" determined that it must be a "fine" country. What seemingly struck "Freeman" most forcibly was the economic power of the United States (probably reflecting a report of Ballah's panoramic view of Baltimore harbor). "Freeman" reported that "Soon Bello go for Merica first time long way bush & tell all man say he must make fine road & bring plenty trade for Cape Palmas." "Freeman" distorted the difference between the MSCS colony and the United States, as he was actually referring to a settler expedition that Ballah was escorting into the interior of Africa to secure trade routes. The missionary who transcribed the letter for "Freeman" explained to the board that the Greboes referred to the United States as "big Merica." The unspoken corollary to this formula would be that the colony clinging to the shores of Africa must be some sort of small America. Thus, "Bello go for Merica" meant that the Grebo diplomat would be working in the interests of both the colony and the United States, which were inseparable in the Grebo's eyes. For "Freeman," "Merica" was both in the Western Hemisphere and the tiny colonial outpost just beyond the pale of his village.[26]

What is remarkable about this Grebo construction of the colonial space is how similar it was to the hopes of the colonizationists and settlers. The Greboes conceived of the colony as another version of the United States, just as the colonizationists desired. Yet, while the settlers projected themselves as the unabashed masters of their little United States, a civilizing space in Africa projecting power over African barbarity, the Greboes sought to integrate themselves into this space as equal partners capable of negotiating directly with "big Merica." Of course, not all Africans shared the same relationship with the Liberian colonies as the Greboes, and even the Greboes changed their tactics and beliefs over time to address new crises; by the end of 1856 the Cape Palmas Greboes and Maryland in Liberia were at war. The sophistication of the Greboes' 1836 plans, however, underscores the important mission that map-making and arguments regarding space had for the settlers as well as just how much Revey's maps of Maryland in Liberia obscured as much as they revealed.

In separating natives from settlers and charting the "civilizing" influence of missionary stations and fictitious roads, Revey and his cartographer compatriots reinforced the imagery of the Liberian settler as a civilized "other" surrounded by chaotic savagery. In fact, the means by which the African Americans conceived of and organized their colony, a mathematical road grid connecting rectangular plots of land with Euro-American architectural features, contributed to their African neighbors' identification of the settlers as whites. This African whiteness, in turn, reinforced Euro-American perceptions of the colonial space as a portal by which American degradation could almost instantly become African civilization. Whiteness and blackness, civilization and savagery, walk hand-in-hand in this space as race is reimagined and projected, held to be something "here" and something very different "there" at the same time.

Aside from a solitary feature, the settlers never adopted Thornton's grandiose design for their settlement at Cape Mesurado. The one exception incorporated into Monrovia's city planning was a centrally placed defensive tower armed with cannons. With the assistance of the crew of the USS *Cyane,* construction on a Martello Tower began in 1823 immediately in the wake of a defeated pan-African assault on the infantile colony. The *Seventh Annual Report* of the ACS informed its membership, "This tower which is expected to bid defiance to barbarianism, has been called Stockton Castle. Africa will hereafter honour the men who are laboring for her deliverance."[27]

There is an unsettling assumption that only through violence and projecting power will the "barbarian" respect the efforts of the settlers "laboring for [Africa's] deliverance." Natives were within the colony's sphere of influence and also its greatest threat. The means to attaining "civilization" and greatness on the part of the settlers, those African whites, entailed physical control over savage blackness with its concomitant echoes of American slavery. Encoded alongside the straight-lines, American-style architecture, and fortifications was an embedded tension within the idealized landscape—that the liberty of one group necessitated the dominance of another. There is something suggestive and troubling in the perceived relationship between freedom and slavery when, even in unrealized dreams of the perfect society, Emancipation Street must terminate with a fortress.

Notes

1. *The First Annual Report of the American Society for Colonizing the Free People of Color of the United States: and the Proceedings of the Society at their Annual Meeting in the City of Washington, on the First Day of January, 1818* (Washington, D.C.: D. Rapine, 1818), 40; Marie Tyler-McGraw, *An African Republic: Black & White Virginians in the Making of Liberia* (Chapel Hill: University of North Carolina Press, 2007), 24; Claude A. Clegg III, *The Price of Liberty: African Americans and the Making of Liberia* (Chapel Hill: University of North Carolina Press, 2004), 30; George M. Frederickson, *The Black Image in the White Mind: The Debate on Afro-American Character and Destiny, 1817–1914* (New York: Harper & Row, 1971), 11–27.

2. Robert J. Breckinridge, *The Black Race: Some Reflections on Its Position and Destiny, as Connected with Our American Disposition. A Discourse Delivered Before the Kentucky Colonization Society, at Frankfort, on the 6th Day of February, 1851* (Frankfort, Ky.: A. G. Hodges, 1851), 17.

3. Henry Clay, *An Address, Delivered to the Colonization Society of Kentucky, at Frankfort, December 17, 1829* (Lexington, Ky.: Thomas Smith, 1829), 24; *First Annual Report of the American Society for Colonizing the Free People of Color of the United States*, 17; Daniel Mayes, "Address," in *The Proceedings of the Colonization Society of Kentucky with the Address of the Hon. Daniel Mayes, at the Annual Meeting, at Frankfort, December 1st, 1831* (Frankfort, Ky.: Commentator, n.d.), 23; Frederickson, *Black Image in the White Mind*, 110–17.

4. *The Sixth Annual Report of the American Society for Colonizing the Free People of Colour of the United States* (Washington, D.C.: Davis and Force, 1823), 13.

5. Hillary Teague, "Editorial," *Liberia Herald*, September 21, 1842; George R. McGill to John H. B. Latrobe, March 8, 1834, Records of the Maryland State Colonization Society, Maryland Historical Society, Baltimore (hereafter cited as MSCS).

6. Samuel Williams, *Four Years in Liberia: A Sketch of the Life of the Rev. Samuel Williams* (Philadelphia: King & Baird, 1857), 5–8, 35; Diana James to Sally Cocke, March 6, 1843, in Bell I. Wiley, ed., *Slaves No More: Letters from Liberia, 1833–1869* (Lexington: University Press of Kentucky, 1980), 57. These racial and religious terminologies were the sources of endless fascination for white American audiences and were often addressed at colonization meetings. For example, a public interview of Joseph Jones, a Liberian visiting the United States, occurred in Danville, Kentucky, on August 16, 1834. Jones was interviewed by supporters and opponents of colonization in a public forum. The record does not note whether a supporter or an opponent asked the twenty-second question: "Are colonists, as a body, called christians by the natives?" Jones responded, "They do not call them by this name, but call them all *white men.*—They use the expression a *God-man*, to mean what we do by a christian. They only call those they think to be good 'the God-men.' They make a difference as we do." See "The Colony at Liberia," *African Repository and Colonial Journal* 10, no. 10 (December 1834): 316.

7. Samuel Wikeson, *A Concise History of the Commencement, Progress and Present Condition of the American Colonies in Liberia* (Washington, D.C.: The Madisonian, 1839), 45; Andrew Hall to Maryland State Colonization Society, January 24, 1847, MSCS; Moses Sheppard to William Polk, May 15, 1838, MSCS.

8. The work of Tom W. Shick in the 1970s and 1980s was critical in turning this analytical focus onto the settlers and their lived experiences within Liberia. More recently, Marie Tyler-McGraw's aptly named *An African Republic: Black and White Virginians in the Making of Liberia* and James Sidbury's *Becoming African in America: Race and Nation in the Early Black Atlantic* have built upon this early foundation and integrated the experiences of African American settlers into their broader narratives. While there has been a shift to acknowledging the contributions of African Americans, the role Africans played in the colonization movement continues to be understudied. Claude A. Clegg's *The Price of Liberty: African Americans and the Making of Liberia* is the most successful monograph in incorporating African agency into the broader narrative of colonization.

9. "Report to the Pennsylvania Legislature," *African Repository and Colonial Journal* 16, no. 9 (May 1840): 137; "Colonization Society," *African Repository and Colonial Journal* 1, no. 10 (December 1825): 302.

10. Washington McDonogh to John McDonogh, December 28, 1845, in Wiley, ed., *Slaves No More*, 138; George R. McGill to Maryland State Colonization Society, July 12, 1832, MSCS; Matilda Lomax to Sally Cocke, July 4, 1848, in Wiley, ed., *Slaves No More*, 67; John B. Russwurm to John H. B. Latrobe, June 26, 1843, MSCS. Technically, Lomax's disparaging remarks were not directed towards the natives of Liberia, but rather a group of recently arrived "Congoes," or illegally enslaved Africans whose slave ship had been intercepted by a U.S. naval vessel. Whenever American ships liberated these slave voyages, the Africans were "returned" to Liberia regardless of their actual origins (which were very rarely near Liberia). The Americo-Liberians called these refugees "Congoes."

11. See, for example, Hayden White, "The Forms of Wildness: Archaeology of an Idea," in *Tropics of Discourse: Essays in Cultural Criticism* (Baltimore: Johns Hopkins University Press, 1978): 150–82; T. Carlos Jacques, "From Savages and Barbarians to Primitives: Africa, Social Typologies, and History in Eighteenth-Century French Philosophy," *History and Theory* 36, no. 2 (May 1997): 190–215. My thinking here is heavily indebted to Karen Piper, *Cartographic Fictions: Maps, Race, and Identity* (New Brunswick, N.J.: Rutgers University Press, 2002).

12. Samuel F. McGill to John H. B. Latrobe, August 11, 1837, MSCS; Samuel F. McGill to John H. B. Latrobe, April 28, 1838, MSCS.

13. J. Leighton Wilson, a Presbyterian missionary stationed among the Grebo of Harper, worked with the colony's African translator to learn the Grebo language in order to translate the Gospels and a hymnal. See Erskine Clarke, *By the Rivers of Water: A Nineteenth-Century Atlantic Odyssey* (New York: Basic Books, 2013), 101.

14. Contemporary Kru identity, for example, was initially a term utilized by external observers to describe a rather diverse population who adapted it to forge bonds between the urban connections of a Kru polity living in Monrovia and the rural Kru homelands along the southeastern coat of Liberia. See L. B. Breitborde, "City, Countryside, and Kru Ethnicity," *Africa* 61, no. 2 (1991): 186–201.

15. Richard L. Hall, *On Afric's Shore: A History of Maryland in Liberia, 1834–1857* (Baltimore: Maryland Historical Society, 2003), 54–55, 85–97.

16. After a brief period as an independent nation-state, Maryland in Liberia was annexed by the Republic of Liberia in 1857. Its territory now largely constitutes Liberia's

Maryland County. For a history of Maryland in Liberia, see Hall, *On Afric's Shore*; John B. Russwurm to John H. B. Latrobe, December 8, 1839, MSCS.

17. John Revey to John H. B. Latrobe, January 20, 1840, MSCS.

18. At some point after the installation of Russwurm as governor, the settlers renamed Auburn Island in honor of Russwurm. After war with the neighboring Africans in 1857 led to the annexation of the colony into the larger Republic of Liberia as Maryland County, the cessation of Grebo burials on Russwurm Island was the final constituent element of the peace treaty signed between the Greboes and Americo-Liberians. See "Treaty of Peace between the Government of Maryland in Liberia and the Grebo People," *Maryland Colonization Journal* 8, new ser., no. 24 (May 1857): 374–75.

19. Hall, *On Afric's Shore*, 82–84.

20. "Latest from Liberia," *African Repository and Colonial Journal* 11, no. 11 (November 1835): 338.

21. John Brown Russwurm, "Travel Journal to Denah on Cavally River," MSCS. Regarding the point at which Maryland Avenue ended, the MSCS Board of Managers reported in 1841 to the broader society the geographic features of the colony: "The principal town of the territory is on the promontory of Cape Palmas, and from this, the farms of the colonists extend for five miles into the interior, bordering upon roads graded and bridged for carriages. At the extremity of the Maryland Avenue, as it is called, is a small stockade [Mount Tubman], which forms at present the frontier post of the settlement." See "Communication from the Board of Managers of the Maryland State Colonization Society, To the President and Members of the Convention assembled in Baltimore on the 3d Day of June, 1841, in Reference to the Subject of Colonization," *Maryland Colonization Journal* 1, no. 1 (June 15, 1841): 3.

22. Stephen Smith to Zachariah Tippett, July 5, 1838, MSCS; Sampson Caesar to David Haselden, February 7, 1834, Liberian Letters: Samson Ceasar Letters, Electronic Text Center, University of Virginia Library, ead.lib.virginia.edu/vivaxtf/view?docId=uva-sc/viu02800.xml; Revey Map.

23. James Hall to John H. B. Latrobe, May 1, 1836, MSCS.

24. The American and Europeans traveling and settling in West Africa almost exclusively used sobriquets for Africans. Even when we have some indication of an African's actual name, such as in the case of Pah Nemah, it is usually filtered through an intermediary, a white missionary in his case. Depending upon the writer, these names could be spelled in many different fashions. The Deed for Cape Palmas, for example, named "Freeman" as "Parmah." Obviously, there is significant phonetic similarity between "Pah Nemah" and "Parmah." Unfortunately, subtle differences do exist. As such, I have elected to utilize the nickname "Freeman" in quotation marks here to maintain coherence in the narrative and cut down on confusion even as I emphasize the constructed nature of the name. Conversely, the name of "Freeman's" interpreter, Simleh Ballah, also called "Bill Williams" by the settlers, was uniformly spelled either "Ballah" or "Balla" by the settlers even as there was some discrepancy on the pronunciation of his first name. Given the near standardization of his last name, I have elected to retain "Ballah" in the text.

25. "Deed No. 1 From King Freeman and King Will, of Cape Palmas," MSCS.

26. "Selim Ballah," *African Repository and Colonial Journal* 13, no. 3 (March 1837): 101–3; Minutes of the Board of Managers of the MSCS, June 23 and July 8, 1836, MSCS;

J. Leighton Wilson and "King Freeman" [Pah Nemah] to the Board of Managers of the MSCS, September 5, 1836, MSCS.

27. "Extract of a Letter from Capt. R. T. Spence to J. Ashmun," *The Seventh Annual Report of the American Society for Colonizing the Free People of Colour of the United States* (Washington, D.C.: Davis & Force, 1824), 54–55.

14

Rewriting Their Own History; or, The Many Paul Cuffes

MATTHEW J. HETRICK

On January 2, 1811, Paul Cuffe set sail for Africa. He was traveling to the British colony of Sierra Leone to examine the prospects for African American emigration. Cuffe was the son of an African father and Wampanoag mother and had become wealthy through hard work in the shipping business. A devout Quaker, he sought to spread Christianity and civilization to Africa, all while making a profit. He found a hearty welcome at Sierra Leone and met with both the white governor and the local settlers. He visited the local tribes and then sailed for London to meet with the wealthy benefactors of the African Institution. Much encouraged by their support, and receiving positive coverage in the local newspapers, he sailed again for Sierra Leone with new trade goods. Staying there for two additional months, he even purchased a house.

By the time Cuffe returned to the United States in the spring of 1812, however, much had changed. The country was now at war with Great Britain, and the authorities impounded Cuffe's ship for trading with the enemy. In the end, this was the best thing that could have happened. Cuffe met privately with President James Madison as well as Secretary of State James Monroe. Both promised to secure his goods and support his plans for settlement in Sierra Leone.

As Cuffe traveled home from Washington he stopped in Baltimore, Philadelphia, and New York City to meet with local black leaders and encourage them to create "African Institutions." These were local organizations supported by African American leaders to promote emigration to Sierra Leone. He published a pamphlet explaining the prospects of the venture and corresponded with the new groups.

When Cuffe submitted a petition to go to Sierra Leone in 1814, it was debated on the floor of Congress but ultimately rejected due to the ongoing war. By 1815 he was both the wealthiest and the most famous black man in the country. Late that year, with the war now over, he set sail again for Sierra Leone. Nine families of thirty-eight people traveled with him. He stayed for two months to make sure they were properly settled, and then he returned to the United States. Although he lost money from the venture, his hopes had not dimmed.

Cuffe spent the rest of 1816 corresponding with his friends James Forten in Philadelphia and Peter Williams Jr. in New York, both the heads of their local African Institutions. Forten had read Cuffe's pamphlet on Sierra Leone to local gatherings, and Williams had spread information to combat rumors. Cuffe was planning to return to Sierra Leone, and he sought knowledgeable settlers to build a rice mill and open a school. Forten and Williams assured him that they had many more people interested in going to Africa. Given his fame and success, it is not surprising that two founders of the American Colonization Society wrote to Cuffe seeking his expertise and his blessing. Although he did not travel to the founding meeting that December, he did write to express his support.[1]

At one of the most frequently cited gatherings in the early republic, over three thousand African American men met in January of 1817 at Mother Bethel Church in Philadelphia. The local leaders of the African Institution had met beforehand to discuss the new ACS and the prospects of white support for their emigration plans. However, as Forten recounted to his friend Cuffe, the response of the local population was a tremendous "No." With James Forten as chair, the meeting adopted a series of resolutions: "Whereas our ancestors (not of choice) were the first successful cultivators" of America, we "feel ourselves entitled to participate in the blessings of her luxuriant soil, which their blood and sweat manured." They viewed "with deep abhorrence the unmerited stigma attempted to be cast upon the reputation of the free people of color" and vowed to "never separate ourselves voluntarily from the slave population of this country; they are our brethren by the ties of consanguinity, of suffering, and of wrong." These African Americans refused to be "cast into the savage wilds of Africa" with no training, science, or government, in something equivalent to a return to perpetual bondage. Forten told Cuffe that he still believed in emigration, but he bowed to the prevailing opinion. By that August, Forten was chairing another meeting of African Americans that attacked the ACS and loudly claimed their place in America. When Paul Cuffe died the following month, Peter Williams eulogized his friend to the local African Institution. Cuffe was a bastion of strength and achievement, and they must keep faith with his goal of settling in Africa.[2]

* * *

Recently many scholars have examined early African American interest in African colonization. Although the widespread rejection of the ACS from the 1820s onward is well known, there was diverse interest before then and even afterward; interest in leaving the country, often for the Caribbean or Canada, never really went away. While we now have a better understanding of the ebbs and flows of African American support for colonization, we still do not really understand how this earlier story was forgotten. It seems clear that important men from this period who lived into the 1830s, like Richard Allen and James Forten, willfully excised their interest in colonization from the public record.[3] But what about Paul Cuffe? How could African Americans write their own history as proud and successful citizens who belonged in America while accounting for someone who seemed so interested in leaving it?

The appropriation of Paul Cuffe began while he was still alive. Indeed, the last months of his life were taken up with not only the usual business matters and planning for a return to Sierra Leone, but in tracking down an impostor. The success and fame of Paul Cuffe made him a target for con artists, and word reached him that one was maligning his good name. This rogue had arrived in New Bedford, near Cuffe's home, claiming to be Richard Allen's son. He had even spoken from the pulpit. He then went to Boston, claiming to be Cuffe's brother-in-law, where he secured nine hundred dollars' worth of goods for New York City. Evading jail in Manhattan, he went to Albany, where he stole a set of clothes and a horse. Arriving in York, Pennsylvania, he claimed to be Paul Cuffe on his way to Congress with "plans for Civilizing Africa." This same story secured him a free hotel stay in Baltimore.

Cuffe protested that he would not mind so much the impugning of his good name, but his fame and support of African Americans made this "a national Concern. It is a Stain to the whole community of the African race."[4] This would not be the last time someone used the name of Paul Cuffe in matters of national concern for the whole race. Indeed, Cuffe would be held up repeatedly as a role model for Africans Americans.

A full decade after these events, on March 16, 1827, the first issue of *Freedom's Journal* appeared. Coedited by two black New Yorkers, Samuel

Cornish and John Russwurm, it established its purpose in the first article of the first issue. At a time "when so many schemes are in action concerning our people," it was more important than ever that African Americans "plead our own cause. Too long have others spoken for us." Following this not-so-oblique reference to the schemes of the ACS, they advised that this did not necessarily imply a rejection of Africa. "Useful knowledge of every kind, and every thing that relates to Africa, shall find a ready admission into our columns." As knowledge increased, this would prove "that the natives of it are neither so ignorant nor stupid as they have generally been supposed to be."[5]

Rejection of white-led schemes, like colonization, would find their place alongside the refutation of African inferiority. The very next article in that first issue would introduce the notion of black-led emigration (as opposed to the ACS's white-led colonization scheme) and prove what African Americans could achieve, both through the person of Paul Cuffe.

The "Memoirs of Capt. Paul Cuffe" appeared in the first five issues of the weekly paper, leading off every issue but the first one. Its pride of place cannot be accidental. Both the first installment and the last acknowledged that the material came from the *Liverpool Mercury*. That newspaper had published a lengthy biographical account of Cuffe when he arrived in England in the fall of 1811. The next year, the accounts were reprinted in a pamphlet. Since this memoir would form the basis of much of the future coverage of Cuffe, it makes sense to examine it more closely.[6]

The account, surely from Cuffe's own mouth, began with the story of his father, "a native of Africa." Through his intelligence and hard work, he purchased himself. After marrying a native woman, he purchased one hundred acres in Westport, Massachusetts. When Paul was only fourteen, his father died and "the care of supporting his mother and sisters devolved upon his brothers and himself." The American Revolution interrupted his career at sea, but it also afforded Cuffe his first opportunity to assert himself. Paul and his brother John refused to pay taxes to Massachusetts until they were afforded equal rights, including voting. Although they were ultimately forced to pay, their petition to the legislature was successful, "a day which ought to be gratefully remembered by every person of colour within the boundaries of Massachusetts, and the names of John and Paul Cuffe should always be united with its recollection." This anecdote and admonition ended the first installment of *Freedom's Journal*'s reprint and appeared verbatim many other times in future newspapers.

Subsequent reprints from the memoir recounted his trials and tribulations in the shipping business. Just as Cuffe became successful, he would lose it all to "the hazard of predatory warfare." Although he frequently returned to the family farm, he was never discouraged for long and, as soon as he had the funds, he returned to the sea to seek his fortune. Robbed again by pirates, he built another boat and continued to trade. Despite the misfortunes, "he possessed that inflexible spirit of perseverance and firmness of mind," and eventually his profits accrued. Although he received no formal education, at the time of his marriage he could read and write and "was so skilled in figures, that he was able to resolve all the common rules of arithmetical calculation," including navigation.

When Cuffe proposed opening a school for the local children, the "collision of opinion" stopped the measure. Instead, Cuffe paid for and built a schoolhouse on his own land for "all who pleased to send their children. How gratifying to humanity is this anecdote! And who, that justly appreciates human character, would not prefer Paul Cuffee, the offspring of an African Slave, to the proudest statesman that ever dealt out destruction amongst mankind?" This story and sentiment appeared word-for-word in the future published accounts of Paul Cuffe.

The concluding reprinted sections covered his whaling adventures and ongoing business success. By this point "Paul had turned his attention to the colony of Sierra Leone." He arrived in Liverpool in August of 1811 and was called to meet with "the Board of the African Institution, who were desirous of consulting with him as to the best means of carrying their benevolent views respecting Africa into effect." The account then ends with what can only be the Liverpudlian reporter's personal description of Cuffe's handsome appearance and Christian character.

The five installments in *Freedom's Journal* reprint the pamphlet almost verbatim. They paint a laudable portrait of overcoming obstacles toward financial success alongside strong support and sympathy for fellow members of the African race. However, the installments left out a very important part of the original document. The penultimate paragraph from the memoir, after the journeys to London and before the personal description, is missing from the reprinted material in *Freedom's Journal*. The original pamphlet notes: "He sailed from Liverpool on the 20th of September, to the honour of the British Government, with a license to prosecute his intended voyage to Sierra Leone. How animating a spectacle for the eye of humanity, to see a vessel trading to the port of Liverpool, commanded by a free and enlightened African; to behold him prosecuting another voyage to Africa, with a vessel not laden with instruments of cruelty and oppression, but manned with sable, yet free and respectable seamen, rescued from the galling chain of slavery, and employed in honourable commerce."[7] Perhaps the description of a return voyage to Africa simply ended up on the cutting-room floor of the New York offices but, seeing as how every other word made it in, this seems unlikely. Instead, the implication that Cuffe's interest continued past 1811—that the African sojourn was not a one-time venture—probably provoked uncomfortable questions in 1827, in the pages of a newspaper devoted to securing the place of African Americans in the United States, not in Africa. A major distinction between Cuffe's first voyage, included in the excerpt, and his later efforts, conveniently omitted by the editors, was that the first predated any national, white-led effort. It was clear of the taint of the American Colonization Society.

If the editors were hoping to minimize Cuffe's involvement with the ACS, it was convenient that the pamphlet ended in 1811, before Cuffe returned to Sierra Leone a third time in 1816 with actual settlers and before he corresponded with the founders of the ACS. In fact, Cornish and Russwurm had a source who could have filled in the missing later years of Cuffe's life, his close friend Peter Williams Jr.

Peter Williams Sr. was an enslaved man working for a tobacconist in New York City. His wife, a free emigrant from the West Indies, gave birth to their son, Peter Jr., in 1785, shortly after Peter Sr. purchased his own freedom. Peter Jr. was educated at the local African School and first came to public notice when, at the age of twenty-two, he gave a sermon on the abolition of the slave trade in 1808. That same year he helped organize the African Society for Mutual Relief, alongside Samuel Cornish. He also chaired the inaugural meeting of the African Dorcas Association, while John Russwurm served as secretary. Williams worked with both men to enroll children in the African School, where Paul Cuffe's sister was a teacher. Much like James Forten in Philadelphia, Williams helped to organize African Americans in defense of their city and their nation during the War of 1812. Williams became the first pastor at St. Philip's Episcopal Church when it opened in 1819; he continued there until his death in 1840.[8]

Williams was an active and frequent correspondent of Paul Cuffe. He saw that Cuffe's account of Sierra Leone was published in 1812, and he helped to spread the facts and counter misinformation about the venture. Perhaps his most notable connection came after Cuffe's death, when Williams eulogized his friend, a speech published the following year.[9] Williams connected the three nodes of Cuffe's life: "Europe and America mourn; and Africa, unhappy, bereaved Africa, pours a deluge of tears."

After recounting the anecdotes about the taxation petition and education, Williams spent much of the speech on the Sierra Leone adventure. Cuffe "recommended to the coloured people to form associations for the furtherance of the benevolent work in which he was engaged." Although the settlement of the thirty-eight passengers cost him between three and four thousand dollars, this was only "proof of the warmth of his benevolence, and of the purity and disinterestedness of his attachment to the African race." Even in his last days, "the subject of ameliorating the condition of his brethren, continued deeply impressed on his mind, and occupied his decaying powers in an extensive correspondence with friends." Cuffe "was gratified at finding his views adopted by a number of the most benevolent and influential men in the American Union," the founders of the ACS.

Leaving no doubt as to where Cuffe, and by extension Williams, stood, he ended the eulogy by reminding his audience that "Capt. C was an advocate of African colonization." Cuffe "wished to see that part of our nation," now "in a state of bondage and degradation in christian countries, returning to the land of their ancestors, carrying with them the light of science and religion, and diffusing it through those vast benighted regions." It was up to Williams and his audience to continue Cuffe's work, something the publication of this eulogy as a pamphlet was clearly meant to do.

If Williams was so close to Cuffe and so well-versed in his thoughts, why did he allow only a partial remembrance of the man to appear in the first issues of the first black newspaper? It was not that Williams was unfamiliar with the paper. He had served in many capacities with both Cornish and Russwurm and been present in Boston Crummell's house when the formation of the paper was first discussed. There were also copies of his 1818 pamphlet still circulating. Instead, it was the context that had changed. In the minds of Williams and other black abolitionists, now that the ACS was unmasked as a bastion of white racists and proslavery activists, any earlier support must be repudiated or ignored.

Yet, Williams's position was more nuanced than its public expression might suggest. After the deplorable Cincinnati race riot in 1829, Williams delivered a sermon advising that African Americans consider leaving the country. While the Declaration of Independence had secured freedom and happiness for millions, "the freedom which we have attained, is defective." For Williams, and for most African Americans—even those who supported resettlement—the ACS was a large part of the problem. Because of the society's rhetoric that African Americans suffered from a "degraded condition," whether they intended to or not, the ACS helped engender the "unreasonable, unrighteous, and cruel prejudice, which aims at nothing less than the forcing away of all the free coloured people of the United States to the distant shores of Africa." Williams did not necessarily reject Africa; instead, he suggested sending a few missionaries rather than wholesale colonization.

For the majority of the populace, however, he recommended Canada. Williams called on the broader community to raise funds and purchase lands for those driven out of Cincinnati: "Brethren, this scheme of colonization opens to us a brighter door of hope than has ever opened to us before, and has a peculiar charm upon our patronage, because it has originated among our own people. It is not of the devising of white men or foreigners, but of our own kindred and household."[10]

Even if he did not trust the ACS, Williams was tolerant of others who did. After publicly denouncing the ACS in *Freedom's Journal*, John Russwurm changed his mind two years later. Russwurm had come to believe that white prejudice was ineradicable and that the best hope for African Americans was Liberia. After his change of heart became public, detractors burned Russwurm in effigy as a traitor to the cause, but Peter Williams stood by him and supported his leaving.

Williams himself faced white violence in July of 1834 as a mob burned down his church and home. Adding grievous insult to injury, the local white bishop blamed Williams's activism for the attack. He ordered Williams to resign from the American Antislavery Society, a request to which Williams acquiesced.

The increasing white violence was a both a symbol and a cause of the growing passion over slavery and abolition. From widespread agreement that slavery was evil but would die a natural death, the country was increasingly divided over the issue. The rise of immediate abolition is traditionally dated to the publication of William Lloyd Garrison's *The Liberator* on January 1, 1831.

It is no coincidence that Garrison devoted many issues and a full-length book to attacking colonization and the ACS. Having been convinced of the evils of the ACS by black abolitionists like James Forten, Garrison's hatred was both genuine and tactical. Following in the tradition of black leaders, he used the racist language of the ACS to attack their motives and demonized gradualism to make immediate abolition seem a more realistic option. In a newspaper that railed against colonization and advocated immediate abolition alongside racial equality, Paul Cuffe would again make an appearance.

"Paul Cuffee" first appeared as a correspondent of *The Liberator* in the spring of 1831, even receiving a fan letter for his "noble sentiments." His first extended contribution, entitled "AVARICE," attacked greed in all its forms but especially that which "marred and desolated the peaceful habitations of ill-fated Africa." He even threatened holy retribution since "the Great Arbiter of nations has, in his infallible word, declared, that the wicked shall be punished, and that He will be the friend of the oppressed."[11] This "Paul Cuffee" was in fact Paul Cuffe Jr.

The son of the illustrious sea captain wrote again from Philadelphia the following January to attack colonization directly. Publisher Mathew Cary had issued a pamphlet on colonization that could not go unanswered, and who better than Paul Cuffe? Cary could not be "so woefully ignorant of the disposition of our people, in relation to the African colony: he must certainly have seen such resolutions as follow, coming from the people of color from every city and town north of the Potomac. 'We were born in this country, and this is our home—we will know no other.'" All attempts "to implant the desire of colonization in our hearts, will be forever futile." Of course, this ignored the actual history of Paul Cuffe Sr., something ardent colonizationists liked to point out. Even the pages of *The Liberator* mentioned this historical Paul Cuffe, though they never really addressed the seeming contradiction.[12]

In 1834, a notice from the Connecticut Colonization Society pointed out that the founders of the ACS visited with "Capt. Paul Cuffee" and in "consequence of these conferences, the American Colonization Society was formed." Unsurprisingly, Garrison took issue with this origin story. This "continued glorification" of the northern founders ignored the fact "that the Society originated in Virginia among the slaveholders. The *scheme* of Colonization is proved, beyond doubt, to have originated in the legislature of that State." Even while colonizationists continued to cite the name of Paul Cuffe, they "forgot to inform the audience that all these happy circumstances of kind treatment" predated "the Colonization Society, with all its corrupting and baleful influence upon prejudice."

Here Cuffe's support of the ACS is quickly explained as a product of an earlier time, thus leaving the tension between the father and the son unexamined and unresolved. Paul Cuffe was a true American success story and patriot and could therefore not be a proponent of African colonization. This friendly treatment toward the Cuffe name could be contrasted with the treatment of a more recent colonizationist: John Russwurm, who was attacked in print for being a dishonest bribe-taker.[13]

Throughout this period, as one Paul Cuffe sought to overwrite another, James Forten also reshaped the history of African American colonization. Forten, like Peter Williams Jr., was a friend and correspondent of the elder Paul Cuffe. He headed the Philadelphia African Institution, just as Williams headed the New York one, and he expressed his interest in the ACS during its early days, just not publicly. By the 1830s those days were a distant memory. In 1835 a newspaper editor contacted James Forten when a colonizationist claimed he had never heard of the Philadelphia meeting opposing colonization. Forten set him straight: "It was the largest meeting of colored persons ever convened in Philadelphia, I will say 3000, though I might safely add 500 more." When asked if they were interested in African colonization, the response was "one *long, loud,* ay, TREMENDOUS NO, for, this vast audience seemed as if it would bring down the walls of the building. Never did there appear a more unanimous opinion. Every heart seemed to feel that it was a *life and death question.*" From the very beginning, "when the monster came in a guise to deceive some of our firmest friends, who hailed it as the dawning of a brighter day for our oppressed race," and by this Forten could only mean Paul Cuffe, "even then, we penetrated through its thickly-laid covering, and beheld it prospectively as the scourge which in after years was to grind us to the earth, and by a series of unrelenting persecution, force us into involuntary exile."[14]

Forten had been sharing this version for years. It appeared in Garrison's *Thoughts on African Colonization,* and he had personally shared it with white colonizationists in his home, but it differed in important ways from what he wrote immediately after the meeting. In a private letter to Paul Cuffe in January of 1817, Forten shared that there were actually three meetings. The Philadelphia African Institution met to consider the newly formed ACS at Richard Allen's house. They then met with Robert Finley, correspondent of Cuffe and a prime motivator behind the ACS, at the home of another local minister, Absalom Jones. Only then did they attend "a large meeting of males at the Rev. Allen's Church."

Forten confirmed that "Three thousand at least attended, and there was not one sole that was in favor of going to Africa," but the story seems more complicated than his later accounts suggest. The leaders of the African Institution, Cuffe's allies and fellow emigration enthusiasts, "have agreed to remain silent, as the people here both White and Coloured are decided against the measure." While Forten believed "that they will never become a people until they come out from amongst the white people," he was "determined to remain silent, except as to my opinion which I freely give when asked."[15] This contemporary, private account hints at some of the complexity and ambiguity that African Americans had since removed.

By the 1850s the place of African Americans in the United States seemed ever more tenuous, and the ACS was resurgent. William Cooper Nell was an African American historian who worked with both Garrison and Frederick Douglass. His book *The Colored Patriots of the American Revolution* was both a synthesis of many disparate accounts and pamphlets but also a demand for black equality. By documenting the historical presence and patriotism of African Americans, Nell could refute ever-present arguments about black inferiority and challenge colonizationists demanding their removal.

Nell included a detailed biographical sketch of Paul Cuffe, drawn from the familiar 1812 memoir but also using the 1818 address of Peter Williams. Unlike *Freedom's Journal,* Nell edited and rewrote some of the passages, but many of the same anecdotes about the petition, schoolhouse, and perseverance reappeared. In the final paragraph, Nell admitted that Cuffe "turned his attention to the British settlement at Sierra Leone, being induced to believe, from various communications he had received from Europe and other sources, that his endeavors to contribute to its welfare, and to that of his fellow-men, might not be ineffectual." This passage was drawn verbatim from the memoir, but Nell then added events that could only come from the address of Peter Williams. Upon Cuffe's return to Sierra Leone, he suggested improvements and helped create a Friendly Society "composed principally of respectable men of color." Nell ended with: "Paul Cuffe terminated his labors and his life, which he departed in peace, the 7th of the 9th mo., 1817, being then in the fifty-ninth year of his age." There was no mention of a return voyage with thirty-eight colonists in 1816, no discussion of the African Institutions, indeed no mention of colonization at all, any of which could easily be found in Nell's sources.[16]

The previous year, Frederick Douglass published an account that could certainly have used Nell's more accurate description. On the last page of the newspaper, under the heading "Miscellaneous," he published a brief sketch of "Paul Cuffee." Douglass misconstrued some facts, writing that Paul Cuffe was a slave in Boston who purchased both his freedom and one hundred acres, things that were true of Paul Cuffe's father. He then gained firmer footing by discussing his sailing ventures and petition to the state legislature, which "procured for the free negroes of that State all the privileges of white citizens; and not of this alone, for others soon followed the example of Massachusetts; and thus Paul Cuffee became a benefactor to the whole colored population of North America."

Douglass seemed to frame Cuffe's life as both a morality tale and an adventure story. He stressed the successes and failures of Cuffe's early efforts and, especially, his trouble with pirates. Douglass included the anecdote about building a schoolhouse and even quoted from the *Mercury* account. However, Cuffe's interest in Sierra Leone was only "proof of the disposition for practical good," and received very little mention, certainly much less than appeared in the source from which he quoted. Douglass concluded that after Cuffe "imparted valuable information and advice" to the London African Institute "he returned to America, to spend the remainder of his days in the enjoyment of that competency which he had so well earned, and which enabled him to obey the promptings of his warm and generous heart." There were, per usual, no mentions of any later adventure. Douglass did not even know when Cuffe had died, though he did declare him "God's Image in Ebony."[17]

By this point Paul Cuffe's life was just a source for anecdotes and stories. Following the Dred Scott ruling in 1857, Garrison reprinted one anecdote from the *New Bedford Standard* to complain about Chief Justice Roger Taney's decision. In a piece entitled "Paul Cufe and President Madison," Cuffe's all-black crew was shamefully abused and detained by a government inspector in Norfolk. He then met with President Madison and, using the informal address of a Quaker, said, "James, I have been put to much trouble, and have been abused." The president promptly ordered the release of Cuffe's ship, "and although the collector believed black men had no rights that white men were bound to respect, yet he was bound, in this instance, to respect the rights of Capt. Cuffe." Even Madison "regarded Capt. Cuffe as a citizen of the United States, and considered that he had rights which the President of the United States was bound to respect."

This story actually conflates two events. Cuffe had been detained early in his career when entering Virginia, but he had the proper papers and it was resolved. It was only later, after trading with Sierra Leone, that Cuffe met with President Madison to secure the release of his ship and the government's support for colonization. Of course, accuracy and complexity were beside the point. Instead, here was a historical example of a U.S. president recognizing the very rights that the Dred Scott decision repudiated. The fact that both Madison and Cuffe supported African colonization seemed merely incidental.[18]

After the reprinted section, Garrison added the usual description of Cuffe's appearance and character. He then recounted the story of Cuffe "securing the elective franchise to the colored citizens of Massachusetts." To his credit, Garrison directed his readers to Nell's book, from which he had surely drawn his more accurate information. Of course Garrison had another source of information on Paul Cuffe—himself. He had heard ACS officials citing Paul Cuffe for years and had challenged them on the facts. He had corresponded with Paul Cuffe's son and James Forten. He surely knew some of the complex truth about Cuffe's early interest in colonization, even if he believed that Cuffe would have changed his mind, as Forten had, if only he had lived longer. But maybe that story was too confusing and too complex to tell.

Paul Cuffe was a successful, ambitious, complicated man. He fought for African American equality while seeking a better home in Africa. He believed in black leadership while corresponding with white colonizationists. Cuffe owned two homes, one in Massachusetts and one in Sierra Leone. These facts were widely known and much discussed during and immediately after his life, but within a decade any hint of this complexity was gone. It was not simply forgotten; it was rewritten. Men who knew the real Paul Cuffe elided the last years of his life and his interest in colonization. Instead, they emphasized the uncontroversial portions about equality and uplift, voting and education. Paul Cuffe became a Horatio Alger story of success through hard work and perseverance while his interest in African colonization was ignored. In the 1830s any black support for the ACS was vilified as wrong-headed and traitorous; witness the treatment of John Russwurm. Times may have changed, and both the aged James Forten and Paul Cuffe Jr. may have been correct in their assumptions that Paul Cuffe would not have supported what the ACS had become, but they never addressed the issue.

By the 1850s the life of Paul Cuffe was a comforting source of anecdotes and examples of black success to combat white prejudice. Anyone who knew the truth about Cuffe's complex life and his interest in African colonization was either dead or not talking. This rewriting of history was so convincing and so powerful that the actual history of African American interest in colonization would take many years to be uncovered.

Notes

1. The best single volume on Cuffe remains Lamont D. Thomas, *Rise to Be a People: A Biography of Paul Cuffe* (Urbana: University of Illinois Press, 1986). There is also good biographical information in *Captain Paul Cuffe's Logs and Letters, 1808–1817: A Black Quaker's "Voice from Within the Veil,"* ed. Rosalind Cobb Wiggins (Washington, D.C.: Howard University Press, 1996), and James Sidbury, *Becoming African in America: Race and Nation in the Early Black Atlantic* (New York: Oxford University Press, 2007), 145–79. There has been some inconsistency on the spelling of his last name, but I will use the more common "Cuffe," except when quoting.

2. The fullest primary account of the January meeting is James Forten to Paul Cuffe, January 25, 1817, in *Cuffe's Logs and Letters,* 501–3. The best secondary account is Gary Nash, *Forging Freedom: The Formation of Philadelphia's Free Black Community, 1720–1840* (Cambridge, Mass.: Harvard University Press, 2003), beginning on page 238. The quotation from the January meeting is from *A Documentary History of the Negro People in the United States,* ed. Herbert Aptheker (New York: Citadel Press, 1969), 71. The meeting that August is recounted in *Early Negro Writing, 1760–1837,* ed. Dorothy Porter (Boston: Beacon Press, 1971), 265.

3. Richard S. Newman, *Freedom's Prophet: Bishop Richard Allen, the AME Church, and the Black Founding Fathers* (New York: New York University Press, 2008); Julie Winch, *A Gentleman of Color: The Life of James Forten* (Oxford, U.K.: Oxford University Press, 2002).

4. Paul Cuffe to James Forten, January 23, 1817, and Paul Cuffe to Joseph Jessop, January 26, 1817, *Cuffe's Logs and Letters,* 499–501.

5. "To Our Patrons," *Freedom's Journal,* March 16, 1827.

6. "Memoirs of Paul Cuffee," *Liverpool Mercury,* October 4 and 11, 1811, and *Memoir of Paul Cuffee, A Man of Colour: to which is subjoined The Epistle of the Society of Sierra Leone in Africa* (York, U.K.: C. Peacock, 1812).

7. *Memoir of Paul Cuffee,* 22–3; "Memoirs of Capt. Paul Cuffee (Concluded)," *Freedom's Journal,* April 13, 1827.

8. Accounts of Peter Williams Jr. can be found in Leslie M. Harris, *In the Shadow of Slavery: African Americans in New York City, 1626–1863* (Chicago: University of Chicago Press, 2003), and Leslie M. Alexander, *African or American? Black Identity and Political Activism in New York City, 1784–1861* (Urbana: University of Illinois Press, 2008), among other places.

9. Peter Williams, *A Discourse Delivered on the Death of Capt. Paul Cuffe, before the New-York African Institution, in the African Methodist Episcopal Church, October 21, 1817* (New York; rpt., York, U.K.: Hargrove, Gawthorp, and Cobb, 1818).

10. Peter Williams, *A Discourse Delivered in St. Philip's Church for the Benefit of the Coloured Community of Wilberforce, in Upper Canada, on the Fourth of July, 1830* (New York: G. F. Bunce, 1830); rpt. in *Early Negro Writing,* 294–302.

11. The first mention is from March 12, and the column appears on April 9, with the fan letter on April 23.

12. "Letter to Editor about Mathew Cary's Pamphlet on colonization," *The Liberator,* January 28, 1832. Although it is possible that "Paul Cuffee" was a pseudonym, it seems very

unlikely. Other authors hid their identity by using a single initial, "R," or a clear obfuscation, "Man of Colour" (usually James Forten). All full names seem to be genuine, and *The Liberator* was familiar with the family; they announced the death of Paul Cuffe's widow on August 31, 1855. It also seems unlikely that the family would have allowed the appropriation of his name, given the history, without protest.

13. For historical Paul Cuffe, see *The Liberator,* March 2, 1833, and June 21, 1834. For the example of Russwurm, see April 9 and 16, 1831, among many others.

14. Rpt. from *New-England Spectator* in *The Liberator,* August 1, 1835.

15. James Forten to Paul Cuffe, January 25, 1817, *Cuffe's Logs and Letters,* 501–3.

16. William Cooper Nell, *The Colored Patriots of the American Revolution, With Sketches of Several Distinguished Colored Persons: To Which is Added a Brief Survey of the Condition and Prospects of Colored Americans* (Boston: Robert F. Wallcut, 1855; electronic edition, 1999), 73–86. (The electronic work is the property of the University of North Carolina at Chapel Hill. It may be used freely by individuals for research, teaching, and personal use as long as this statement of availability is included in the text.) Nell's citation is to "Address of Peter Williams, delivered in 1812, published in Liverpool Mercury," but this can only be a conflation of the two sources. He includes information not in the original *Mercury* publication, but found in Williams's address, and Peter Williams's name appears nowhere in the *Mercury*. For more on Nell's work and life, see: Stephen G. Hall, *A Faithful Account of the Race: African American Historical Writing in Nineteenth Century America* (Chapel Hill: University of North Carolina Press, 2009), esp. 94–104; John Ernest, *Liberation Historiography: African American Writers and the Challenge of History, 1794–1861* (Chapel Hill: University of North Carolina Press, 2004), esp. 132–53.

17. "Paul Cuffee," *Frederick Douglass' Paper,* September 29, 1854. The last appellation is suggestive, though not conclusive, that Douglass knew something of Cuffe's true history and interest in colonization. Douglass used the same description for his erstwhile ally Martin Delany, who was also interested in African colonization at this time.

18. *The Liberator,* September 18, 1857.

15

The Changing Legacy of Civil War Colonization

PHILLIP W. MAGNESS

On January 2, 1863, a strongly worded yet anonymous editorial appeared in the Washington *Daily Morning Chronicle.* Its purpose was to fortify the Emancipation Proclamation of the previous day, and in so doing leave no uncertainty as to the moral significance of this action. The editorialist delineated what he perceived to be three specific justifications for the president's decision. The first two foreshadowed the proclamation's subsequent reputation, emphasizing its effect upon the army—now openly permitted to entice and employ freed African Americans in its ranks—and upon the nation—by initiating the end of slavery. The third justification enlisted the proclamation's supposed effect "upon mankind," though it struck a chord very different from what a modern reader might expect. The writer informed his audience that "this day is also the initial point of separation of the black from the white race."

The author's purpose was to tout the policy of colonizing African Americans, with their consent, in the tropical regions of the Caribbean, South America, and Africa, a central theme of Lincoln's own annual message to Congress just one month before. The proclamation would signal the beginning of "an eventual exodus from the United States." It would bring about "a successful and prosperous colonization within the tropics of this continent of the black nation today liberated by the President's wise and just decree."[1]

Any discussion of Civil War–era colonization is inextricably linked to its public espousal by Lincoln and a number of failed "experiments" undertaken by his administration. Readers of the anonymous essay knew well the president's affinity for the policy. Curiously enough, the January 2 editorial may be the closest thing to a formal explication of Lincoln's most famous act to emerge concurrently from the White House, and thus a direct insight into his own understanding of its intent, as the hidden author was in all likelihood John G. Nicolay, the president's personal secretary.[2]

A stark contrast may be seen between this editorial and customary interpretations of the Emancipation Proclamation on January 1, 1863, as a departure point in Lincoln's attachment to voluntary black resettlement. Indeed it is almost a cliché for historians to observe—and extract interpretive meaning from—two textual distinctions between the final proclamation and its precursor of September 22, 1862. The later document added the enlistment of black soldiers while saying nothing of the "preliminary" measure's promise of colonization, along with compensation for slave-owners, leading numerous scholars to read a presidential departure from these policies into the textual omissions of January 1, 1863.[3]

This self-reinforcing scholarly obsession with a rejection of colonization creates a number of problems from an evidentiary front. Lincoln plainly did not cede his longstanding interest in compensated emancipation after January 1, 1863, seeking instead to attach it to the contemporaneous creation of West Virginia as well as an emancipation bill for Missouri later that spring. He even held out the offer of payment for the South's slaves as late as the Hampton Roads Conference of February 1865.[4] Colonization too carried a post-emancipation design even in its public articulations, Lincoln having pressed it upon the black community to address a time "even when you cease to be slaves."[5] Thus Nicolay's editorial appears as a consistent articulation of the same, its explicit colonization appeal raising an uncomfortable oversight in the common historiography of a closely studied event.

Yet Nicolay is not alone in presenting this complication. A comparable observation might be made of a second anonymous dispatch to the *New York Examiner* a few days prior in which William O. Stoddard, another member of Lincoln's secretarial pool, predicted the revival of the president's "Emigration Scheme" after it was temporarily sidetracked by the December 1862 cabinet crisis. In addition, any conscious exclusion of colonization from the final Emancipation Proclamation would have surely provoked the ire of Postmaster General Montgomery Blair, its chief promoter in the cabinet. Yet Blair offered not a word of protest over the allegedly abandoned policy when he submitted his suggested edits to the proclamation a day prior, and furthermore continued to publicly identify it as the administration's policy thereafter. In each case, these witnesses possessed a firsthand awareness that has nearly disappeared in modern assessments. Black colonization was still very much alive in January 1863, and was in fact being carried out by Lincoln in direct conjunction with emancipation.[6]

Anonymity aside, it is unlikely that an observer in early 1863 would have found colonization out of character for the Lincoln White House. A month prior the president had informed Congress, "I can not make it better known than it already is that I strongly favor colonization" while outlining a detailed program of gradual, compensated emancipation and voluntary resettlement of the freed slaves abroad.[7] He offered this commitment under the authority of two congressional appropriations during the previous year. When measured by $600,000 in appropriated funds and the establishment of an Emigration Office to administer them, the Civil War years may well constitute the high-water mark of federal interest in the entire colonization enterprise.

Lincoln's Second Annual Message, in December 1862, linked these policies to the forthcoming Emancipation Proclamation, announcing, "Nor will the war nor proceedings under the proclamation of September 22, 1862, be stayed because of the recommendation of this plan."[8] Lincoln similarly connected both policies with the District of Columbia Emancipation Act of April 16, 1862, and, less known but equally significant, urged these features upon two black emigrationists the following day.[9]

In keeping with this pattern, the events directly surrounding the signing of the Emancipation Proclamation lend credence to the expectations set forth in Nicolay's editorial. Lincoln spent the better part of the evening of December 31 engaged in discussion over a colonization project for the Île à Vache, an island off the coast of Haiti, to be launched concurrently with the more famous proclamation of the following day. Final negotiations commenced at the White House at around 9 p.m. with the president joined by Sen. James R. Doolittle of Wisconsin, Francis P. Blair Sr.—the family's famous powerbroker patriarch—and Bernard Kock, the lessee of the island. Blair's daughter Elizabeth referenced the event as a contract for "Des Vache or some such name," noting her father and "Mr. Doolittle think it the beginning of the 2nd great Exodus." Perhaps aware of growing opposition in his own party, Lincoln also reportedly instructed Kock that "under no consideration was he to impart to any members of the Cabinet except Mr. Seward and Judge Blair the existence of his contract." Lincoln actually gave his approval the following morning as Kock and Doolittle returned with the finished contract for a signature, only hours before the Emancipation Proclamation was issued.[10]

If anything, Lincoln's actions after January 1, 1863, show a sustained if little-noticed pattern of personal involvement in colonization, a policy he reportedly referred to as his "hobby." Lincoln broached the subject in at least eight documented meetings with prospective colonization partners at the White House between January and November 1863, to say nothing of accompanying conversations with cabinet officials and subordinates that they surely provoked.[11] Nor were these simple courtesies to friends or fleeting encounters with visitors. Lincoln launched a "second wave" of colonization projects in 1863, and more than once rescued them from growing opposition in his own cabinet—opposition from an insubordinate Edwin M. Stanton, who moved to block emigration agents from competing with black troop recruitment; from a corrupt John P. Usher, who had personal interests in a competing colonization scheme that fell out of presidential favor; and from a philosophically opposed William H. Seward, who became habitually lackadaisical when implementing presidential directives involving colonization.[12]

One needn't rehash the entire history of Civil War colonization to know that it faltered. Blair's "exodus" was not to be, nor was the Emancipation Proclamation the "point of separation" anticipated in Nicolay's editorial. Aside from a small handful of wartime emigrants who traveled to Liberia with government funding, Lincoln's policies yielded no permanent resettlements abroad. Of the wartime ventures, the Haitian project—which ended in disaster in March 1864—and another aborted effort in the Chiriqui region of modern-day Panama from the fall of 1862 are the most familiar.[13] Less known are the 1863 ventures. While awaiting the resolution of the Île à Vache contract and still engaging the American Colonization Society over a small number of individual emigrants to Liberia, Lincoln turned to the European powers in early 1863 and spent the better part of a year pressing for colonization via diplomatic channels. This yielded a "second wave" of colonization attempts, the most developed one in British Honduras by way of a June 1863 agreement with two land agents under the supervision of the British Colonial Office. He also sought a similar arrangement with Dutch Suriname, prepared in a signed treaty with the Netherlands in late 1863 but never submitted for ratification.[14] These projects all stalled by early 1864, an indeterminate hold placed upon them as the raging Civil War assumed priority and politics on both sides of the Atlantic intervened.

Many modern explanations for colonization's demise revolve around "the question of exactly when—or even if—[Lincoln] relinquished his idea of settling black people outside the country," to quote Michael Vorenberg.[15] John Hay seemingly supplied this answer on July 1, 1864, writing in a diary entry—often assumed to be the final word on the matter—that the president had "sloughed off" colonization shortly after Congress rescinded its funding in an amendment to a massive budget bill. This curiously worded entry, falling far short of the conclusiveness some attach to it, conceals a story that has less to do with Lincoln than with those around him. Wartime colonization succumbed to a mixture of political maneuvering in Congress, administrative infighting among those charged with its execution, and the idea's failure to gain traction within the black community, as well as common instances of corruption, incompetence, and insubordination that plagued its execution *despite* Lincoln's articulated "honest desire" to see it carried through.[16]

Nor did Lincoln's own interests wane as quickly as Hay's diary suggests. According to James Mitchell, the president's colonization commissioner, Lincoln deemed the repeal of colonization an "unfriendly" amendment to a needed budget bill. Shortly thereafter Lincoln assisted Mitchell with filing a legal brief to have his suspended salary restored in the wake of Congress's action, though in late 1864 he reportedly asked Mitchell to hold off on further colonization work "for the time being" on account of a then-pending "attempt of the men of Richmond to arm and emancipate their negroes" lest it divert manpower from the army and inadvertently prolong the war. Once signs of an approaching Union victory became a reality, Mitchell resumed preparations for what might be the only direct glimpse of the administration's second-term colonization policy from a wartime source. On January 31, 1865—the day the House passed the Thirteenth Amendment—he met with Rep. Thaddeus Stevens to discuss a plan for the partial restoration of the colonization office budget. Stevens cosigned a memorandum to the president indicating his willingness to advance the measure, his endorsement noting "I cheerfully recommend the above named settlement." No action came from the effort in the wake of Lincoln's assassination, though Mitchell always maintained that the president intended to house a colonization function in the newly formed Freedmen's Bureau.[17]

Without wading into the speculative territory of what, if anything, might have become of this or any other remnant of the wartime colonization policy had Lincoln lived to complete his second term, it is sufficient to note that the corpus of colonization source material generated between the Emancipation Proclamation and the Civil War's conclusion diverges in significant ways from its assumed abandonment on January 1, 1863, or even with the later ambiguously phrased diary entry of Hay. Accepting that it is nearly impossible to dissociate wartime colonization from the chief executive who oversaw it—policies do not simply will themselves into existence and persist in adverse political conditions without a person to drive them—a question may nonetheless be raised as to how the course of historical inquiry into this subject moved so far astray from the analytical discovery and contextual interpretation of its progression to such a narrow and singular question of timing in the person of Abraham Lincoln.

Civil War Colonization Recollected

In 1866 the painter Francis Bicknell Carpenter recounted an anecdote from James C. Derby concerning a conversation with William H. Seward. A New York acquaintance of the Seward family, Derby had been a visitor to the secretary's room during the long recovery from the coordinated attempt on his life on the night of Lincoln's death. Seward offered his guest a comment about the late president: "No knife was ever sharp enough to divide us upon any question of public policy, though we frequently came to the same conclusion through different processes of thought." Seward could only recall one disagreement: "His 'colonization' scheme . . . which I opposed on the self-evident principle that all natives of a country have an equal right to its soil."[18] That the bedridden secretary of state pointed to colonization as his sole substantive point of divergence from Lincoln must surely reveal his assessment of the conviction with which the latter adhered to the idea.

Seward's remarks also share a common forthrightness in conceding Lincoln's affection for voluntary black resettlement. The first "historians" of colonization were the numerous contemporaries who left behind reminiscences of their own part in the wartime experiments. The history of colonization was already being written in some quarters before Lee even laid down his sword at Appomattox. Like Seward's story to Derby, these accounts almost uniformly present colonization as a true reflection of Lincoln's beliefs and seldom hint that he ever departed from them, except by occasional supposition about his public silence emanating from those who were not at the heart of the administration.[19]

Colonization received one of its first specific "historical" elaborations in the 1864 campaign biography of Lincoln by *New York Times* editor Henry J. Raymond. The pertinent chapter provided summary details of Chiriqui and Île à Vache, the latter somewhat tersely worded owing to Raymond's own financial involvement in a still-boiling controversy about the failed scheme's unpaid contracts. Kock also weighed in with a little-noticed defense of his role in Île à Vache published in 1864, as did two investors in the scheme. One of these men, Charles K. Tuckerman, later reprised his account in an article for the *Magazine of American History*.[20]

The British projects of the "second wave" received their first public airing in an obscure 1864 pamphlet by Charles Babcock, a free African American who accompanied an investigative mission to the site. James Mitchell published a fuller account of the British projects in late 1865 to somewhat wider notice, hoping to prod Congress into resuming colonization in fulfillment of the "settled policy" of the martyred president. Mitchell would also share details of this venture later in life, apparently with the confidence of many high-ranking contemporaries.[21] When President Ulysses S. Grant attempted to annex the Dominican Republic in 1872, spurred in part by a desire to give African Americans an option of escaping racial oppression in the South, Lincoln's memory was quickly attached to the cause. Though their views on colonization diverged, Mitchell maintained a postwar acquaintance with Sen. Charles Sumner of Massachusetts, the main annexation critic. At Sumner's request, Mitchell wrote down his recollections of Lincoln's colonization views to illustrate their dissimilarity from the treaty—the memo being published in summary form many years later. Mitchell's recollections also received a public forum in an 1894 interview with the *St. Louis Globe-Democrat*—part of an effort by the paper's editor, Walter B. Stevens, to compile anecdotes of Lincoln from the dwindling number of the living who knew him.[22]

Beginning in the early 1870s another Lincoln cabinet official, Gideon Welles, offered his own accounts of wartime colonization as part of a series of articles for the *Galaxy* magazine, written to dispel other writers who credited Seward with wartime leadership at Lincoln's expense. Welles's account is in accord with the Nicolay editorial and other events of January 1863. Emancipation and colonization, he notes, "were in [Lincoln's] mind indispensably and indissolubly connected." In a shot at both Seward and the radicals, he chided those who wrapped themselves in the Emancipation Proclamation but "omit to mention that colonization" was an intended part of this policy. Welles, whose revelations about colonization actually chafe with his tendency to portray Lincoln as eminently pragmatic, used the example to illustrate the uncertainties of a post-slavery United States while cautioning against the tendency to evaluate emancipation with the benefit of hindsight. For his own part, Welles doubted whether Lincoln "would not have hesitated longer in issuing the decree of emancipation had he been aware that colonization would not be accepted as an accompaniment." Such sentiments were fairly common among those wartime figures who reflected upon colonization, with George Julian and Carl Schurz wondering essentially the same thing.[23]

Reminiscence-era colonization accounts also came from the diplomats Elisha O. Crosby, who recounted a colonization overture to Guatemala in his memoirs, and Charles A. Leas, the source of a posthumously published anecdote about Lincoln's colonization interests in Latin America. The 1907 memoirs of Army Chaplain John Eaton contain a brief conversation with Lincoln about the disease-plagued Île à Vache project in the summer of 1863. D. C. Donnohue, the government agent who oversaw the Île à Vache rescue mission, recounted how Lincoln, still described as "a firm believer in colonization" who was "instrumental" in supporting the Haitian venture, tapped him as an antislavery moderate over Charles Sumner's agitation for a more radical candidate. Treasury official Lucius Chittenden similarly related his role in arranging a meeting between the president and the promoter of a domestic colonization scheme, as did a diary entry of Treasury clerk Donald MacLeod in reference to Liberia. An elderly Samuel Pomeroy also granted an interview to the *Baltimore Sun* in 1890 to recount his role in the Chiriqui venture, albeit expectedly without reference to the allegations of personal graft on the colonization account that plagued him for some years after.[24]

Though divergent in their politics and, in some cases, character, each of these witnesses treated colonization as a perfectly genuine and intended—albeit failed—program of the president. Of equal note, many of these sources are all but unknown in the modern literature with even well-regarded figures such as Welles receiving only passing attention where colonization is concerned.[25]

One contrasting exception that still retains modern appeal is the monumental ten-volume biography of Lincoln by his secretaries Nicolay and Hay, serialized beginning in 1886. In many respects Nicolay and Hay produced the first attempt at a formal retrospective history of wartime colonization, as opposed to simply reminiscing upon its particular facets or—like Raymond—providing a less-than-impartial commentary on events that were still in play. Mirroring other first-generation writers, they offered a candid but respectful assessment of Lincoln's interest in the policy. "Lincoln was a firm believer in colonization," though he also "did not shut his eyes to its difficulties." Nicolay and Hay offered their own synopses of the Chiriqui and Île à Vache projects by drawing upon personal familiarity and access to Lincoln's papers. In describing them as the "only two [that] commended themselves to the special attention of the President," they had the unfortunate if unintended effect of obscuring subsequent scholarship and directing its attention entirely to these two projects.[26] Nicolay and Hay can hardly be faulted here—there is no indication that either secretary took part in Lincoln's direct negotiations with the British authorities in 1863, and they were probably unaware of the unratified Dutch treaty's existence. Such was the effect of the close guard Lincoln kept around the policy that no single member of his administration knew the full extent of his colonization program, though several witnessed its many components.

Despite their oversights, Nicolay and Hay formalized wartime colonization as a subject of historical inquiry and did so at a point of transition in its study.[27] The ensuing years would see both the introduction of a more formal secondary literature on the subject and the growing politicization of Lincoln's connection to it, still almost universally acknowledged, but with increasingly complex interpretations and claimants.

Between History, Politics, and Contested Memory

It can be stated with absolute certainty that Union Gen. Benjamin F. Butler arrived at the White House on the morning of April 11, 1865, for a private meeting with Abraham Lincoln. Among the more colorful characters to emerge from the war, Butler was an archetypal political general—a popular if incessant self-promoter who compensated for his dubious military skill with a strong legal mind and the ability to rouse up a crowd. Despite later contrary and somewhat caricatured assessments, he was actually "a kind of favorite with the President," to quote Stoddard. Or in Butler's admittedly opportune self-assessment, "Mr. Lincoln's relations with myself were perfectly kindly from the day I first saw him, in April 1861, to the day of his death."[28]

What happened next is arguably the most heavily contested detail of the wartime colonization program. As Butler reported some two decades later, Lincoln approached him about resuming colonization. Fearing that the former slaves would be "but little better off with their masters than they were before," the president solicited a proposal from Butler to transport up to 150,000 African Americans to Panama, where they would be employed in the construction of a canal. Once established, they would "form a colony there which will protect the canal and the interest of the United States" while also providing grounds to petition Congress for additional funding for the transport of their families and future emigrants. "There is meat in that, General Butler," the president responded, directing him to investigate the subject and report on its practicality. Butler never had the chance, with Booth's bullet claiming Lincoln's life three days later.[29]

Interest in Butler's story derives largely from its implications to the timing question. If ignored or rejected, it permits room for an evolutionary narrative on Lincoln and colonization; if accepted, it carries the implication that "Lincoln continued to his dying day to deny the possibility of racial harmony" in the United States, to quote George Fredrickson.[30] It might also be noted that, if accurate, Butler's story offers the final glimpse of a postwar path-not-taken, itself signifying a turning point in the larger history of the colonization movement. Butler's story gained its widest audience from its final telling in the general's 1892 autobiography. Its presentation there shows clear signs of distance from the event as well as Butler's own enrichments, and whereas a number of recent historians have seized upon these issues to question the authenticity of the entire episode, it should also be noted that the anecdote appeared in at least two earlier and less problematic iterations and garnered widespread acceptance in an age when many Lincoln contemporaries were still alive to contest any perceived libels upon his memory.[31]

The earliest and most succinct version originated from the pen of another in an August 1884 *New York Times* article. The account is brief, specific, and fits the known timeline of Butler's documented meeting on April 11. Butler's political notoriety was near its peak at the time. He had just completed a tumultuous term as governor of Massachusetts, and offered his name to the Greenback Party as a spoiler candidate in the approaching presidential election. Yet the article had little to do with either. It was actually posted some two weeks prior by an unnamed European correspondent for the *Times* and bore little direct relevance to the general's politicking beyond a biographical backstory.[32]

Whatever its origin, the story did not begin to gain traction for another two years when Butler, by then largely retired from electoral politics, authored the first of his own accounts. He provided this longer version in response to a solicitation from Allen Thorndike Rice, editor of the *North American Review,* for a forthcoming book of Lincoln reminiscences. Owing to failing eyesight in his old age, Butler composed the piece by way of dictation to a stenographer. He submitted the contribution as a loose collection of anecdotes "which I have been withholding from the public" in anticipation of a memoir, and with instructions for Rice to arrange and edit them as he saw fit. Like the *Times* account, the Rice version's timeline is consistent with the April 11 encounter. It also adds details that may strengthen Butler's claim, including familiarity with an earlier colonization "provision at Demerara"—a possible reference to the British Guyana scheme of 1863, which was not public knowledge at the time—and awareness of Lincoln and Seward's longstanding interest in an isthmian canal.[33]

Again writing by dictation, Butler committed the third and best-known version of the story to print in his 1892 autobiography. Unsurprisingly for a document written over twenty-five years after the event, it suffers from an imprecision that obscures the date of the interview and tends to further inflate the dialogue of the two prior versions. Yet it also entered the anecdote into the mainline of Lincoln's biography, at least for some decades following its publication. Butler's near-legendary habits of self-promotion actually worked to the advantage of the story's dissemination. Prepublication promotional materials for the book touted a chapter that would reveal the general's interest in the Panama Canal "before DeLesseps ever dreamed" of such a project. Notably, the publicity campaign showed far more interest in attaching Butler's name to this engineering feat than highlighting a colonizationist motive that 1890s readers would have found in full keeping with what they already knew of the late president. Even Butler's own political career included numerous dalliances with Liberian colonization and Grant's Dominican annexation scheme in the 1870s, suggesting an air of presentism among those skeptics who interpret the story as an attempt to posthumously impugn a "less enlightened" Lincoln.[34]

Characteristically, Butler also saw to it that his opus received wide distribution. He purchased what may well be over a thousand complimentary copies and mailed them "to every state governor in the Union; the United States Senators; to the members of the cabinet; to the ex-Presidents; the ex-Vice Presidents, and ex-members of the Cabinets; the leading clergymen . . . college professors . . . financiers . . . railroad men, and manufacturers." Recipients who returned notes of praise for the work included Benjamin Harrison, Oliver O. Howard, Julia Dent Grant, Oliver Wendell Holmes, Thomas Brackett Reed, Andrew Carnegie, and Frederick Douglass.[35] While it is difficult to say if any readers subjected the colonization story to scrutiny, its publication does not appear to have elicited any objection from still-living witnesses to Lincoln's presidency even as other aspects of Butler's book—particularly his portrayal of a long-festering rift with the late Admiral David Dixon Porter and some uncomplimentary language about John Hay—certainly did.

Starting in the 1880s, the precedent of the wartime colonization movement and Lincoln's name in particular lent credence to another political appropriation of a more sinister character in the rise of the Jim Crow South. An 1890 bill promoted by segregationist senators John Tyler Morgan of

Alabama and Matthew C. Butler of South Carolina sought five million dollars in federal expenditures to affect the relocation of African Americans abroad, sparking an extended debate that frequently appealed to the wartime precedent. Lincoln's name was similarly appropriated by William Patrick Calhoun, a grand-nephew of the famous South Carolina senator, who promoted a viciously racist and forced deportationist variant of the scheme on the pretext that the "Negro Question . . . has two ways of being settled—colonization or extermination."[36]

At a time of growing historical vilification of the Reconstruction-era Radical Republicans, colonization ironically helped to rehabilitate Lincoln's appeal to white supremacists. After Mitchell's death in 1903 a reporter who viewed his now-lost files from the wartime Emigration Office noted they contained "ample proof" that Lincoln intended the separation of the races—something he readily connected to segregation.[37] A more famous and notorious exhibition of these sentiments came from the pen of Thomas Dixon, who portrayed the late president favorably in his *Clansman* trilogy—a venomous homage to the Ku Klux Klan that is best known from its film adaptation, *The Birth of a Nation*.

To Dixon, Lincoln's attachment to colonization was his most admirable characteristic—proof that "he never believed it possible to assimilate the Negro into our national life." The resulting fictionalized Lincoln turns history on its head and acquires Dixon's own distinctive brand of overt separatism couched in racial evolutionary differences whereas the actual Lincoln, even though misguided in his design, turned to colonization only as a means of affecting peace by offering blacks an exit from the very same breed of Klan-like violence so brazenly glorified in Dixon's works. Yet this portrayal also serves as a reminder of the slippery pathway from wartime colonization to white-supremacist thought. The fictional Lincoln outlines his colonization plan as a conscious part of Dixon's depiction of the Emancipation Proclamation—a chilling juxtaposition in light of the Nicolay editorial and Île à Vache negotiations of its actual circumstance. Dixon also dealt with the Butler story, by then well engrained into Lincoln's biography, with an oddly similar swapping of motives. Whereas Butler almost certainly played up his own credit for the canal-building proposal, Dixon saw in him only a radical naysayer offering a "famous, false and facetious report" to dissuade Lincoln from the idea of separating the races by questioning its feasibility.[38]

Dixon is symptomatic of the poisoning effects of white supremacist thought upon the early twentieth-century political climate. Numerous

African Americans nonetheless answered him, and did so by forcefully asserting their own agency in a historical discussion that generally neglected it. Booker T. Washington regarded the entire colonization enterprise as a path not taken and therefore no longer subject to renewal. "Here we are and to stay," declared a similar editorial in an African American paper, citing open knowledge of Lincoln's commitment to voluntary resettlement. "Ten million people are on the ground, and the quicker white people recognize the fact that they cannot ignore us the better it will be for all concerned."[39] Others still saw some hope in seeking a more welcoming home abroad but, echoing wartime black emigrationists like Henry Highland Garnet, Martin Delany, and John Willis Menard, insisted any nascent "Back to Africa" enterprise be undertaken on their own terms and at their own direction.

A somewhat more benign claimant to colonization "history" also emerged in 1906 in the character of J. B. Merwin, a Union Army chaplain turned temperance preacher who transformed a single wartime encounter with Lincoln into a lecture-circuit career. Further illustrating the dissemination of the Butler story, Merwin actually wrote himself into it as a messenger tasked with delivering a memorandum about the proposed canal. This invention in turn permitted him to claim an audience with Lincoln on the eve of his assassination, wherein the president allegedly offered his support for the cause of alcohol prohibition.[40]

Insofar as the politicization of wartime colonization history in the early twentieth century ranged from the trifling to the maliciously racist, it represented a shift away from the revelatory character of the earlier reminiscence phase. The emerging historical profession offered something of a corrective to this course that continued until the mid-twentieth century, simultaneously bringing a detailed narrative of the wartime colonization experience to light and offering a depoliticized interpretation. Walter L. Fleming published the first attempt at an academic history of colonization in 1914. The contextual history he offered was in many ways a product of its time and of the Dunning School disposition. For instance, there is little room for black agency in Fleming's account save the portrayal of a largely ignorant and helpless people being defrauded by colonization swindlers, though he also pressed the distinction between colonization history and its more recent white-supremacist incarnations by timing the last serious projects to the close of the war.[41]

In 1919 Charles H. Wesley, the pioneering African American historian, published the first detailed examination of Lincoln's own stake in colonization since Nicolay and Hay, notably pressing its heretofore neglected tension with his legacy as the "Great Emancipator." The article presaged much of the modern debate, or at least its implications if one is to seriously consider the evidence of Lincoln's attachment to the scheme. Wesley challenged an emergent portrayal of Lincoln in popular memory, if not necessarily professional history, "as the champion of the race's equality," though he did so through a measured analysis of the available evidence.[42]

With popular Lincoln biography mired in a hagiographic phase, colonization disappeared from serious political discussion by the 1930s save for occasional fringe manifestation in such figures as segregationist Sen. Theodore Bilbo of Mississippi.[43] After Fleming and Wesley, most early scholarly examinations of the policy came from African American historians who directly pressed its racial implications. Carter G. Woodson bluntly described Lincoln as a colonizationist who doubted "that the two races could dwell together in peace" and wished to resettle African Americans in "some neglected part of the earth." W. E. B. DuBois dealt frankly with its meaning to Lincoln in his groundbreaking 1935 book *Black Reconstruction*, acknowledging that the sixteenth president "simply could not envisage free Negroes in the United States." This was not gratuitous disparagement but fealty to truth, for DuBois's Lincoln "was a man—a big, inconsistent, brave man" and indeed "big enough to be inconsistent" per a famous earlier assessment.[44]

By mid-century a new generation of scholars began to grapple with further challenges posed by colonization. Thus, Richard Hofstadter enlisted it as part of the Whig antislavery formula to frame his iconoclastic reexamination of Lincoln's antislavery reputation, and David Herbert Donald cited it to illustrate a pragmatic moderation in Lincoln's politics. A specialized colonization literature also emerged at mid-century, aided by both new manuscript accessions and a growing interest in African American history.[45] Freed from an earlier and uglier era of separatist politics, colonization now forced historians to account for the realities of uncomfortable, though not unfamiliar, racial aspects of the war. Yet colonization studies also came of age amidst the ongoing challenges of the civil rights era, and with them an ongoing reassessment of Lincoln's own racial legacy.

Discovery, Denial, and Renewal

In 1950 Warren A. Beck submitted a historical survey of the Chiriqui scheme and other isthmian colonization ventures to the *Abraham Lincoln Quarterly*. The manuscript originally enlisted Butler's reminiscence as evidence that Lincoln explored the resumption of Central American colonization on the eve of his death, and perhaps never abandoned the policy. As Beck revealed the following year in a letter to Paul J. Scheips, Lincoln scholar Roy P. Basler, the journal's editor, "persuaded him prior to the publication of his article to reconsider his manuscript conclusion that Lincoln never really gave up the idea of colonization." As Basler indicated, the story "ran counter to the established scholarly opinion on the subject." Beck accordingly dropped the matter and adopted Hay's report that Lincoln "sloughed off" the policy as its final word.[46]

Where this opinion had been "established" Basler did not note. In fact his assessment actually runs contrary to the thrust of the colonization literature available at this point, although it was perhaps truer to a Lost Cause strain of biography that gratuitously disparaged the "Beast" Butler. Basler may have been calling upon his own familiarity as editor of Lincoln's *Collected Works*, in which case it warrants mention that multiple colonization-specific Lincoln documents were unknown to him and have since come to light.[47] Fleming, Wesley, and DuBois offered no indication that Lincoln ever shed the policy and viewed the particulars of Butler's story as broadly consistent with this reading. The same year Scheips diverged from Basler, concluding Butler was "at least worth noting" on account of the evidence of Lincoln's abandoning the scheme being far from conclusive.[48] Yet the direction of subsequent scholarship has tended toward Basler's view, and indeed pushed it well beyond.

Since the onset of the civil rights era, the questions of Lincoln's beliefs on slavery and, more broadly, his conceptualization of race have attained renewed significance.[49] The challenges posed by colonization in each instance have fed the search for what essentially amounts to an exculpatory narrative around Lincoln—one that reconciles the evidence of wartime colonization with the ethical distaste it brings to modern readers, while allowing Lincoln to either correct for this "mistake" later in his presidency or escape its acknowledged errors completely.

To this end, the dominant historiographical trends of the past half-century have sought to either demonstrate Lincoln's intellectual evolution beyond colonization—essentially a change of heart from a view it is still conceded he once held—or to recast the entire policy as a conscious but benevolent political deception, never intended for any real purpose but to ease the process of emancipation before a largely bigoted and anti-black northern public. The latter view in particular has gained widespread adherence owing to its exonerative appeal. Donald Fehrenbacher thus describes colonization as a "psychological safety valve," and James McPherson calls it a "sugar coat" to the "strong pill" of emancipation—a palliative approach to the disease of slavery. Gabor Boritt similarly deems it a "lullaby" that "served its purpose" in facilitating emancipation, though "never a great cause" to which the president had any deep personal commitment.[50] Yet as Lincoln never actually articulated this "lullaby" or "palliative" strategy, it necessarily rests upon an esoteric extraction of unspoken intentions from his words, even drawing its language from an unrelated descriptor Lincoln applied to shaky arguments for the Kansas-Nebraska Act—"a palliation—a lullaby"—in 1854.

Both the evolutionary and lullaby explanations easily, if erroneously, attach to the Emancipation Proclamation, which either serves as a possible departure point for Lincoln's evolution, or a *fait accompli* in that the palliative ruse had run its course. Such may be the unavoidable risk of interpreting historical events through the lens of a single mover, and particularly a celebrated one. More curious though is the vigor in which the modern exculpatory narrative has been asserted around colonization, and the number of instances where a thinly attested diminution of the policy from Lincoln's actions and thoughts has degraded into outright incredulity at any suggestion otherwise. For many years it was commonplace—and may yet still be—to completely discount the Butler anecdote on the basis of Mark Neely's insightful but ultimately flawed deconstruction of the details of timing in the 1892 autobiography.[51] More alarming is the vigor with which Butler is dismissed.

To this end, a highly public spat over colonization evidence between the novelist Gore Vidal and historian Richard Nelson Current in 1988 resulted in the latter making charges of willful misrepresentation and declaring "the question of Butler's veracity has long since ceased to be one that scholarly historians or biographers dispute."[52] Michael Lind drew similar rebuke in 2005 for both portraying Lincoln as a genuine colonizationist and attempting to rehabilitate Butler's account. Allen C. Guelzo slammed him for repeating a demonstrated "fabrication" in Butler. James M. McPherson went further, charging Lind with taking "Lincoln quotations out of context and then supply[ing] an artificial context to sustain his thesis." McPherson then vigorously pressed a lullaby explanation for the entire colonization venture on account of an asserted but factually contradicted silence by Lincoln after January 1, 1863.[53]

Attesting to their long historical interconnectedness, denunciations of this type also migrate somewhat fluidly between the particulars of Butler's anecdote and general associations of Lincoln with colonization, even when both subjects are taken up cautiously and in cognizance of the controversies involved. In 2009 Sean Wilentz savaged an intentionally delicate attempt by Henry Louis Gates Jr. to update the colonization evidence through its neglected post-emancipation phase—"a wild goose chase" evincing "credulity about historical sources" as Wilentz put it. Certain that Lincoln dropped the entire colonization enterprise after 1863 and dismissive of the very idea of reinvestigating the "flawed" Butler anecdote, he chides somewhat patronizingly that "almost any scholar in the field could have told Gates" of these alleged faults and saved him the trouble.[54]

In a more recent exchange with the author of this chapter, Guelzo pushes even further. The result reveals the extreme aversion in some quarters to even countenancing the possibility of a Lincoln who was also a genuine colonizationist. After misreading Lincoln's endorsement on a widely attested post–emancipation colonization agreement with Great Britain, Guelzo's only recourse is to deny the authenticity of records with clear historical provenance. In the bizarre resulting impasse, even primary sources are set aside to service a faulty historiographical convention that predates their rediscovery.[55]

Though these responses by no means encompass the whole of the discipline, they do suggest an ongoing struggle to take colonization seriously wherever Lincoln is involved. Much of the controversy reflects a simple resistance to incorporating numerous primary colonization sources that were unknown when many modern beliefs about Lincoln's racial views took hold. In addition to the documents that were missed in Basler's accounting of Lincoln's papers, these include hundreds of pages of recently rediscovered diplomatic records in the archival holdings of the United Kingdom, Belize, Jamaica, the Netherlands, and Denmark.[56]

It would exceed the scope of the present inquiry to debate the gravity of the wartime colonization, further rehash the particulars of the Butler evidence, identify the contestants for the moment at which Lincoln reputedly evolved beyond colonization, if ever, or review how one might extract a hidden pattern of palliatives and lullabies from Lincoln's known and overtly colonizationist pronouncements. It is however entirely fair and appropriate to note that the relatively recent attachment of a sense of finality to the study of colonization, along with repetitive deference to the authority of a secondary literature when evaluating primary sources overlooked in the very same body of scholarship, yields a highly problematic "consensus."

Lullabies and evolutions alike have trouble accounting for evidence that

Lincoln pressed forward on colonization after the Emancipation Proclamation or that Nicolay's editorial promised as much. Lincoln pursued additional schemes in the West Indies through the end of 1863 and clearly had more to say on the matter in 1864 than a single ambiguous entry in John Hay's diary reveals. Discussions of salvaging the Emigration Office and reviving some iteration of the colonization venture after the war entered serious political consideration in early 1865. A Lincoln without a serious stake in colonization is also in conflict with the Lincoln portrayed by virtually all who were involved in the wartime colonization enterprise and took it to represent the president's true and honest beliefs. To the contrary, the history of colonization's political course actually defies all the purported benefits of a palliation for emancipation. Even where Lincoln evolved toward a cautious support for black voting rights at the end of his life, it conflates loose synonymy with parity to suggest that Lincoln found this 1865 development any more "inconsistent" with colonization than the written opinion by Attorney General Edward Bates affirming free black citizenship in November 1862.[57]

Rather, most arguments in this vein involve some degree of looking backward to absolve the past of its recognized faults. Indeed it might be said that the relatively recent push to get Lincoln "off the hook" for colonization has led us down a path of unattested supposition of motive and flawed conclusions from only partially engaged evidence, all wrapped in a normative framework with a suspiciously strong resemblance to a late twentieth-century understanding of racial politics at the expense of its nineteenth-century context.

While finding the lullaby thesis contradicted on an evidentiary front and the evolutionary change of heart in want of demonstration beyond a level of conjecture extracted from gaps in activity and perceived presidential silence, the present discussion does not purport to offer an alternative thesis so much as a call for the resumption of a prior line of empirically grounded inquiry. Civil War–era colonization needs a thorough reexamination to account for what we have learned in the past half-century or more, and one that may require resetting the board to shed the burdens of "consensus" in instances where the secondary literature has gone astray.

Moving forward, some further interpretive considerations should also be taken into account. Specifically, historians would do well to discard the implicit Manichean characteristics of colonization where Lincoln is concerned. Both experiential hindsight and ethical evaluation have correctly deemed the colonization enterprise racist, retrograde, and generally neglectful of its intended participants. To project these demons backward onto Lincoln, or conversely absolve him of their stain through rhetorical sleights of hand, accomplishes little more than bludgeoning the past for what it was or was not. In moving beyond this habit, even while his critics persist, we will find in Lincoln a measured, flawed, and entirely human colonizationist, perhaps guilty of racial paternalism toward African Americans, though hardly a malevolent actor or forerunner to the turn-of-the-century segregationists who later claimed him in a direct inversion of his actual motive and always-voluntary position. Recovery of this nuanced approach is a necessary and overdue maturation for Lincoln studies, though also tellingly one that would do much to revive the older line of inquiry typified by Wesley and DuBois, analytical and open in its criticism though also respectful of its subject and valuing evidence over polemic.[58]

Perhaps the contentiousness of colonization is a reflection of its own past, replete with political uses and abuses that persist today in a different form. In Lincoln's case, colonization strikes a nerve precisely because it is disconcerting as both an attempted policy and a path not taken. Yet rather than objecting to the existence of something distasteful, historians should be seeking to understand it, knowing full well that open scholarly inquiry must permit the possibility of unaccounted evidence and, on a subject replete with information gaps and ambiguous source materials, the liberty of diverse interpretation.

Notes

1. "The Proclamation," *Washington Daily Morning Chronicle*, January 2, 1863, in Michael Burlingame, ed., *With Lincoln in the White House: Letters, Memoranda, and Other Writings of John G. Nicolay, 1860–1865* (Carbondale: Southern Illinois University Press, 2000), 99–102.

2. Nicolay's personal scrapbook of his own writings at the Library of Congress contains a copy of this editorial. While its colonizationist message has somewhat surprisingly escaped significant attention, the editorial's association with Nicolay is widely established. See Burlingame, ed., *With Lincoln*, 225; Allen C. Guelzo, *Lincoln's Emancipation Proclamation* (New York: Simon & Schuster, 2006), 186; James Oakes, *Freedom National: The Destruction of Slavery in the United States*, (New York: W. W. Norton, 2012), 370.

3. See discussion in Phillip S. Paludan, "Lincoln and Colonization: Policy or Propaganda?" *Journal of the Abraham Lincoln Association* 25 (2004): 23–37. Examples include Gabor Boritt, *The Lincoln Enigma: The Changing Faces of an American Icon* (Oxford, U.K.: Oxford University Press, 2001), 14; Douglas R. Egerton, "A Measure Alike Military and Philanthropic: Historians and the Emancipation Proclamation," *Pennsylvania Magazine of History and Biography* 137 (January 2013): 111; Louis P. Masur, *Lincoln's Hundred Days:*

The Emancipation Proclamation and the War for the Union (Cambridge, Mass.: Harvard University Press, 2012), 197; Eric Foner, *The Fiery Trial: Abraham Lincoln and American Slavery* (New York: W. W. Norton, 2011), 258; Louis Gerteis, "Slaves, Servants, and Soldiers," in William A. Blair and Karen Fisher Young, eds., *Lincoln's Proclamation: Emancipation Reconsidered* (Chapel Hill: University of North Carolina Press, 2009), 176; Stephen B. Oates, *Abraham Lincoln: The Man Behind the Myths* (New York: HarperCollins, 2009), 113; Chandra Manning, *What This Cruel War Was Over* (New York: Vintage, 2007) 86; Oakes, *Freedom National*, 282.

4. Lincoln to the Senate and House of Representatives [February 5, 1865], in Roy P. Basler et al., eds., *Collected Works of Abraham Lincoln* (New Brunswick, N.J.: Rutgers University Press, 1953–1955), vol. 8: 260–61 (hereafter *CW*). Alexander Stephens, Robert M. T. Hunter, and John A. Campbell all similarly recalled Lincoln's offer. "The Terms Offered the South at the Fortress Monroe Conference," *Augusta Chronicle*, June 7, 1865; "The South: Talk with an Ex–United States Justice, John A. Campbell," *New York Herald*, December 9, 1872; "Mr. R. M. T. Hunter's Address," *Alexandria Gazette*, October 14, 1873.

5. "Address on Colonization," August 14, 1862, *CW* 5: 372.

6. Michael Burlingame, ed., *Dispatches from Lincoln's White House: The Anonymous Civil War Journalism of Presidential Secretary William O. Stoddard* (Lincoln: University of Nebraska Press, 2002), 128; Montgomery Blair, "Notes on the Emancipation Proclamation," December 31, 1862, Abraham Lincoln Papers, Library of Congress (hereafter cited as AL-LOC); Montgomery Blair, *Comments on the Policy Inaugurated by the President, in a Letter and Two Speeches* (New York: Hall, Clayton, and Medole Printers, 1863).

7. "Annual Message to Congress," December 1, 1862, *CW* 5: 520.

8. Ibid.

9. "Eulogy on Henry Clay," *CW* 2: 121–32. The little-known meeting on Liberian colonization took place between Lincoln, Alexander Crummell, and J. D. Johnson on April 17, 1862. See Johnson to Lincoln, March 3, 1863, Miscellaneous Letters, reel 8, Slave Trade and Negro Colonization Records; Lincoln to Crummell and Johnson, May 5, and Crummell and Johnson to the editor, May 10, 1862; *Boston Herald*, May 15, 1862.

10. Elizabeth Blair Lee to Samuel Phillips Lee, December 31, 1862, in Virginia Jeans Laas, ed., *Wartime Washington: The Civil War Letters of Elizabeth Blair Lee* (Urbana: University of Illinois Press, 1991), 223; John T. Doyle, "An Episode of the Civil War," *Overland Monthly*, May 1887, 541; Bernard Kock, *Statement of Facts in Relation to the Settlement on the Island of A'Vache, near Hayti, W.I., of a Colony under Bernard Kock, with Documentary Evidence and Affidavits* (New York: William C. Bryant, 1864), 4–5.

11. Lyons, Dispatch No. 69, January 23, 1863, and No. 78, January 27, 1863, in James J. Barnes and Patience M. Barnes, *The American Civil War through British Eyes* (Kent, Ohio: Kent State University Press, 2005), vol. 2: 305, 306–8; Lincoln to John P. Usher, January 30, 1863, in U.S. Department of the Interior, Slave Trade and Negro Colonization Records, RG 48, M160, National Archives and Records Administration, College Park, Maryland (hereafter STNCR); Charles K. Tuckerman, "President Lincoln and Colonization," *Magazine of American History* 16 (October 1886); Revised Contract with Paul M. Forbes and Charles K. Tuckerman, April 6, 1863, and Lincoln to Usher, April 13, 1863, STNCR; John Hodge to Lyons, June 13, 1863, as enclosed in Russell to Lyons, No. 567, June 19, 1863, FO 5/934, National Archives of the United Kingdom, Kew; Abraham Lincoln, pass for Hodge and S.

R. Dickson, June 13, 1863, STNCR; James Mitchell (interview), "Lincoln and the Negro," *St. Louis Daily Globe-Democrat,* August 26, 1894; LeVere et al. "Address to the President of the United States," November 5, 1863, AL-LOC; McLain to Hall, November 7, 1863, American Colonization Society Papers, Library of Congress. The above-noted instances notwithstanding, Douglas R. Egerton has recently maintained that "scholars have yet to identify any reliable presidential endorsements of colonization after the final Proclamation" ("A Measure Alike Military and Philanthropic," 111).

12. Phillip W. Magness and Sebastian N. Page, *Colonization after Emancipation: Lincoln and the Movement for Black Resettlement* (Columbia: University of Missouri Press, 2011), 34–37, 41.

13. Warren A. Beck, "Lincoln and Negro Colonization in Central America," *Abraham Lincoln Quarterly* 6, no. 3 (1950): 162–83; Paul J. Scheips, "Lincoln and the Chiriqui Colonization Project," *Journal of Negro History* 37 (1952): 418–53; Sebastian N. Page, "Lincoln and Chiriqui Colonization Revisited," *American Nineteenth Century History* 12 (2011), 289–325; Willis D. Boyd, "The Île à Vache Colonization Venture," *Americas* 16, no. 1 (July 1959): 45–62; James D. Lockett, "Abraham Lincoln and Colonization: An Episode That Ends in Tragedy at L'Île à Vache, Haiti, 1863–1864," *Journal of Black Studies* 21 (1991): 428–44.

14. Magness and Page, *Colonization after Emancipation*; Phillip W. Magness, "The British Honduras Colony: Black Emigrationist Support for Colonization in the Lincoln Presidency," *Slavery & Abolition* 34, no. 1 (2013) 39–60; Robert F. Durden, *James Shepherd Pike: Republicanism and the American Negro, 1850–1882* (Durham, N.C.: Duke University Press, 1957), 86–93; Michael J. Douma, "Hoe verder zonder slaven? Het kolonisatie project van Amerikaanse vrijgelaten slaven op de Surinaame plantages, 1862–1866," *Geschiedenis Magazine* 4 (2013): 14–19.

15. Michael Vorenberg, "Slavery Reparations in Theory and Practice," in Brian R. Dirck, ed., *Lincoln Emancipated: The President and the Politics of Race,* (DeKalb: Northern Illinois University Press, 2007), 119.

16. John Hay, *Inside Lincoln's White House: The Complete Civil War Diary of John Hay,* ed. Michael Burlingame and John R. T. Ettlinger (Carbondale: Southern Illinois University Press, 1997), 217; Hodge to Lyons, July 9, 1863, National Archives of the United Kingdom, Kew, CO 318/239. For further detail of the causes of colonization's failure see Magness and Page, *Colonization after Emancipation,* chap. 8.

17. Enclosure of James Mitchell in James Hughes and J. W. Denver to Andrew Johnson, June 16, 1865, Miscellaneous Letters of the Department of State, RG 59, National Archives and Records Administration; Mitchell and Thaddeus Stevens (endorsement), Memorandum to Abraham Lincoln, February 1, 1865, enclosed in Mitchell to Hugh McCulloch, August 1865, Miscellaneous Letters of the Department of the Treasury. Stevens's sometimes-assumed hostility to colonization has also been overstated. Though he voiced displeasure with the president's Chiriqui project, he was actually the author of the original colonization appropriation in July 1862 and inserted it into the bill at Lincoln's request. See Mitchell to Lincoln, July 3, 1863, AL-LOC; Smith to Stevens, July 3, 1863, Papers of Caleb Blood Smith, Huntington Library; and Stevens to Salmon P. Chase, August 25, 1862, in Beverly W. Palmer and Holly B. Ochoa, eds., *The Selected Papers of Thaddeus Stevens* (Pittsburg: University of Pittsburgh Press, 1997), vol. 1: 319–20. Former congressman Lemuel D. Evans published a corroborating account of a February 1865 conversation with Stevens in 1869,

indicating the latter's consideration of resuming colonization at the time (Evans, *Speech of Hon. L. D. Evans: On the Condition of Texas, and the Formation of New States* [n.p., 1869], 4). Several letters suggest that Mitchell was being considered for a role with the newly created Freedmen's Bureau at the time of Lincoln's assassination. See Richard Yates to Lincoln, March 6, 1865, and James Speed, Joseph A. Wright et al. to Lincoln, undated [1865], Register of Letters Received, Bureau of Refugees, Freedmen, and Abandoned Lands, National Archives and Records Administration (NARA) Record Group (RG) 105, M752.

18. Francis B. Carpenter, *Six Months at the White House with Abraham Lincoln* (1866; rpt., Lincoln: University of Nebraska Press, 1995), 291.

19. A number of recent works have given undue emphasis in this regard to British commentators Frederick Milnes Edge and Harriet Martineau, both of whom deprecated the sincerity of Lincoln's colonization policy from afar, despite having no direct knowledge of its formation.

20. Henry J. Raymond, *The History and Administration of President Lincoln* (New York: J. C. Derby & N. C. Miller, 1864), 469–73. See also "Candor," "Letters to the Editor," *New York Times*, May 27, 1864; Kock, *Statement of Facts*; Charles K. Tuckerman and Paul M. Forbes, "Papers relating to the colonization experiment at A'Vache, Hayti, W.I." (ca. 1864); Tuckerman, "President Lincoln and Colonization."

21. Charles Babcock, *British Honduras, Central America: A Plain Statement to the Colored People of the U.S. who Contemplate Emigration* (Salem, Mass.: C. Babcock, 1863); James Mitchell, *Brief on Emigration and Colonization* (Washington, D.C.: M. Polkinhorn & Son, 1865).

22. "The Real Object of Dominican Annexation," *Richmond Whig*, March 14, 1871; Sumner to Mitchell, July 5, 1871, rpt. in "The Western Question," *Atlanta Constitution*, March 25, 1894; Mitchell, "Lincoln and the Negro," *St. Louis Daily Globe-Democrat*, August 26, 1894.

23. Gideon Welles, "Administration of Abraham Lincoln," *Galaxy* 24, no. 4 (1877): 439–40, 444; George Julian in Allen Thorndike Rice, ed., *Reminiscences of Abraham Lincoln by Distinguished Men of His Time* (New York: North American Publishing, 1886), 61–62; Carl Schurz, "Abraham Lincoln," *Atlantic Monthly* 67, no. 404 (1891): 733–34.

24. Elisha O. Crosby and Charles A. Barker, *Memoirs of Elisha O. Crosby* (San Marino, Calif.: Huntington Library, 1945), 87; "Reminiscence of Lincoln," *Daily Inter-Ocean*, February 12, 1896; John Eaton, *Grant, Lincoln and the Freedmen: Reminiscences of the Civil War* (New York: Longmans & Green, 1907), 91–92; "A Pioneer in Politics," *Indianapolis News*, November 8, 1895; Lucius E. Chittenden, *Recollections of President Lincoln and His Administration* (New York: Harper & Brothers, 1891), 336–40; Entry of October 23, 1862, Donald MacLeod Diary, MacLeod Family Papers, Virginia Historical Society, Richmond; "Negro Emigration: An Experiment by the Government During the War," *Baltimore Sun*, February 26, 1890.

25. Welles's articles were widely acclaimed at the time of their publication, including an endorsement by the late president's son. See Robert Todd Lincoln to William Burnside, June 19, 1883, in Robert Todd Lincoln Papers, vol. 9, Abraham Lincoln Presidential Library, Springfield, Illinois. By comparison, Welles's *Galaxy* articles are omitted entirely from James M. McPherson's single-volume standard, *Battle Cry of Freedom* (Oxford, U.K.: Oxford University Press, 1988). Guelzo's reminiscence-heavy history *Lincoln's*

Emancipation Proclamation evinces awareness of the articles, but makes no use of Welles's extended commentary upon the role of colonization in the Emancipation Proclamation.

26. John Nicolay and John Hay, *Abraham Lincoln: A History* (New York: Century Co., 1890), 355, 357.

27. The principal surviving participants in wartime colonization died within a few years of Nicolay (d. 1901) and Hay's (d. 1905) writing, including Usher (d. 1889), Pomeroy (d. 1891), and Mitchell (d. 1903).

28. John Hay to Benjamin F. Butler, April 10, 1865, Butler Papers, Library of Congress (hereafter BFB-LOC); William O. Stoddard, *Inside the White House in War Times: Memoirs and Reports of Lincoln's Secretary*, ed. Michael Burlingame (Lincoln: University of Nebraska Press, 2000), 83. Butler to Seward Baker, June 12, 1884, BFB-LOC.

29. Benjamin F. Butler, *Autobiography and Personal Reminiscences of Major-General Benjamin F. Butler* (Boston: A. M. Thayer, 1892), 903–8.

30. George Fredrickson, "A Man but Not a Brother: Abraham Lincoln and Racial Equality," *Journal of Southern History* 41 (1975): 56–57.

31. Phillip W. Magness, "Benjamin Butler's Colonization Testimony Reevaluated," *Journal of the Abraham Lincoln Association* 29 (2008): 1–28.

32. "Spain to Abandon Cuba," *New York Times*, August 20, 1884. One possible candidate for its source is the article's main subject, Sidney Webster, a close friend and legal associate of Butler.

33. Butler to Rice, June 25, 1885; August 12, 1885, in BFB-LOC. Rice, ed., *Reminiscences of Abraham Lincoln*, 150.

34. For a textual comparison of the three accounts, see Magness and Page, *Colonization after Emancipation*, 112–13. See also "Ben Butler's Big Book: Quite a Remarkable Volume," *Chicago Herald*, March 8, 1891; Jaros to Butler, March 2, 1891 (misfiled in March 1892), BFB-LOC.

35. Jaros to Butler, January 29, 1892, BFB-LOC. O. O. Howard to Butler, February 11, 1892; Oliver Wendell Holmes to Butler, February 19, 1892; Julia Dent Grant to Butler, March 24, 1892, BFB-LOC. Endorsements of Harrison, Douglass, Carnegie, and Reed, among others, in A. M. Thayer & Co. promotional leaflet (ca. 1892); Jaros to Butler, March 17, 1892, BFB-LOC.

36. "Negro Emigration: Interesting Debate in the Senate over Mr. Butler's Proposition," *New York Herald*, January 17, 1890; "The Negro Question: Latest Comments On The Subject By Mr. Calhoun," *Augusta Chronicle*, June 2, 1889; William P. Calhoun, *The Caucasian and the Negro in the United States: They Must Separate. If Not, then Extermination. A Proposed Solution: Colonization* (Columbia, S.C.: R. L. Bryan Co., 1902), 134. A similar argument appears in William Passmore Pickett, *The Negro Problem: Abraham Lincoln's Solution* (New York: G. P. Putnam's Sons, 1909).

37. "Lincoln and Segregation," *Macon Telegraph*, September 13, 1904; Phillip W. Magness, "Mitchell and the Mystery of the U.S. Emigration Office Papers," *Journal of the Abraham Lincoln Association* 32 (2011): 50–62.

38. Thomas Dixon, "Booker T. Washington and the Negro," *Indianapolis Freeman*, September 9. 1905; "Thomas Dixon—Intimate Study of a Picturesque Personality," *Cleveland Plain-Dealer*, January 29, 1905; Dixon, *A Man of the People: A Drama of Abraham Lincoln* (New York: D. Appleton & Co, 1920), 47.

39. "Lincoln and the Panama Canal," *Chicago Defender,* April 12, 1913.

40. "Lincoln Fellowship," *New York Tribune,* June 28, 1907; Richard F. Hamm, "The Prohibitionists' Lincoln," *Illinois Historical Journal,* 86, Summer 1993, 104.

41. Fleming was a primary figure of the Dunning School, a group of early twentieth-century historians who approached the Civil War era with an emphasis upon the position of southern whites and an accompanying deep racial conservatism. Thomas L. Fleming, "Deportation and Colonization: An Attempted Solution to the Race Problem," in William A. Dunning, ed., *Studies in Southern History and Politics* (New York: Columbia University Press, 1914), 3–30.

42. Charles A. Wesley, "Lincoln's Plan for Colonizing Emancipated Negroes," *Journal of Negro History* 6 (1919): 8, 21. See also Andrew N. Cleven, "Some Plans for Colonizing Liberated Negro Slaves in Hispanic America," *Journal of Negro History* 11 (January 1926): 35–49.

43. This culminated in a viciously racist and utterly bizarre episode when Bilbo and his frequent collaborator Ernest Sevier Cox invoked Lincoln's colonization program to urge African Americans to repatriate themselves. See Theodore G. Bilbo, *Take Your Choice: Separation or Mongrelization* (Poplarville, Miss.: Dream House, 1947).

44. Carter G. Woodson, "Negro History Week," *New York Amsterdam News,* February 8, 1936; W. E. B. DuBois, *Black Reconstruction in America* (New York: Harcourt Brace, 1935) 82; W. E. B. DuBois, "Abraham Lincoln," *The Crisis* 24, no. 3 (July 1922).

45. Richard Hofstadter, *The American Political Tradition and the Men Who Made It* (New York: A. A. Knopf, 1948), 167; David H. Donald, *Lincoln Reconsidered: Essays on the Civil War Era* (New York: A. A. Knopf, 1956), 126–27; Luveta Gresham, "Colonization Proposals for Free Negroes and Contrabands During the Civil War," *Journal of Negro Education* 16 (1947): 28–33; Benjamin Quarles, *The Negro in the Civil War* (Boston: Little, Brown, 1953); Marvin R. Cain, "Lincoln's Views on Slavery and the Negro: A Suggestion," *Historian* 26 (August 1964): 502–20; James M. McPherson, "Abolitionist and Negro Opposition to Colonization During the Civil War," *Phylon* 26, no. 4 (1965): 391–99; Harold S. Smith, "Negro Colonization during the Civil War," master's thesis, University of Wisconsin–Madison, 1941; Robert Benson Leard, "Civil War Attempts at Negro Colonization," master's thesis, University of California, 1948; Willis D. Boyd, "Negro Colonization in the National Crisis, 1860–1870," PhD diss., University of California–Los Angeles, 1953; Tinsley L. Spraggins, "Economic Aspects of Negro Colonization During the Civil War," PhD diss., American University, 1957.

46. Beck, "Lincoln and Negro Colonization in Central America"; David Brion Davis, "Reconsidering the Colonization Movement: Leonard Bacon and the Problem of Evil," *Intellectual History Newsletter* 14 (1992); Scheips, "Lincoln and the Chiriqui Colonization Project," 449 n57.

47. See Lincoln to Crummell and Johnson, May 5, 1862 (rpt. in *Boston Herald,* May 15, 1862); Lincoln, appointment of James Mitchell, August 4, 1862, STNCR; Lincoln, Amended Chiriqui Article, September 15, 1862, STNCR; Lincoln to Usher regarding Chauncey Leonard, January 30, 1863, STNCR; Lincoln to Usher extending the Île-à-Vache contract, April 13, 1863, STNCR; Pass for Hodge and Dickson, June 13, 1863 (copies in National Archives of the United Kingdom, Kew; National Archives of Jamaica, Spanish Town; and Belize

Archives and Records Service, Belmopan); and Lincoln to Bates, September 9, 1864 (original lost, logged in NARA, RG 60, Entry 7).

48. Several early historians accepted Butler's account. See William Eleroy Curtis, *Abraham Lincoln* (Philadelphia: J. P. Lippincott, 1902), 334; Edward McMahon, "Lincoln the Emancipator," *Pacific Historical Review* 5, no. 1 (1936): 24; Hans Trefousse, *Ben Butler: The South Called Him Beast!* (New York: Twayne Publishers, 1957), 179. Carl Sandburg notably does not wade into the colonization matter despite referencing the episode as an illustration of Butler's tendencies of language (Sandburg, *Abraham Lincoln: The War Years* [New York: Harcourt, Brace, 1939], vol. 4: 26). Scheips, "Lincoln and the Chiriqui Colonization Project," 449.

49. For an illustrative example, also invoking colonization, see Ludwell H. Johnson, "Lincoln and Equal Rights: The Authenticity of the Wadsworth Letter," *Journal of Southern History* 32 (1966): 83–87; Harold M. Hyman, "Lincoln and Equal Rights for Negroes: The Irrelevancy of the 'Wadsworth Letter,'" *Civil War History* 12, no. 3 (1966): 258–66; Ludwell H Johnson, "Lincoln and Equal Rights: A Reply," *Civil War History* 13, no. 1 (1967): 66–73.

50. Donald E. Fehrenbacher, *Lincoln in Text and Context* (Stanford, Calif.: Stanford University Press, 1989), 111; James M. McPherson, *Ordeal by Fire: The Civil War and Reconstruction* (New York: A. A. Knopf, 1982), 277; James M. McPherson, *Tried by War: Lincoln as Commander in Chief* (New York: Penguin, 2009), 128. Boritt, *Lincoln Enigma*, 13–14. For a full discussion of the evolutionary "change of heart" argument and "lullaby" thesis of colonization, see Magness and Page, *Colonization After Emancipation*, 8–9, and George M. Fredrickson, *Big Enough to Be Inconsistent: Abraham Lincoln Confronts Slavery and Race* (Cambridge, Mass.: Harvard University Press, 2008), 110–11. A nuanced example of the evolutionary narrative may also be found in Eric Foner, "Lincoln on Colonization," in Foner, ed., *Our Lincoln: New Perspectives on Lincoln and His World* (New York: W. W. Norton, 2008), 135–66.

51. For early doubters of Butler, see Donald E. Fehrenbacher, "Only His Stepchildren: Lincoln and the Negro," *Civil War History* 20 (December 1974): 308; Gabor S. Boritt, "The Voyage to the Colony of Lincolnia," *Historian* 37, no. 4 (August 1975): 619–32. Johnson ("Lincoln and Equal Rights") and Fredrickson ("A Man but Not a Brother") attempted to revive the story. See also Neely, "Abraham Lincoln and Black Colonization: Benjamin Butler's Spurious Testimony," *Civil War History* 25 (1979): 77–83; Magness, "Butler's Colonization Testimony."

52. Gore Vidal and Richard N. Current, "Vidal's Lincoln: An Exchange," *New York Review of Books*, April 28, 1988. See also Frank J. Williams, "Gore Vidal on Lincoln," *Los Angeles Times*, April 24, 1988.

53. Ironically, Guelzo cites the Wadsworth Letter, a posthumous Lincoln forgery from September 1865, as further evidence to dismiss colonization and Butler's story. Allen C. Guelzo, "Two Cheers for Lincoln," *Books and Culture: A Christian Review*, January–February 2006; James M. McPherson, "Twist and Shout," *The Nation*, June 13, 2005; Michael Lind, "Lincoln & Race," and James M. McPherson, "A reply to Michael Lind," *New York Review of Books*, March 29, 2007.

54. Henry Louis Gates Jr. and Donald Yacovone, *Lincoln on Race and Slavery* (Princeton, N.J.: Princeton University Press, 2009); Sean Wilentz, "Who Lincoln Was," *New Republic*, July 15, 2009, 40.

55. Allen C. Guelzo, "Review: Colonization after Emancipation," *Journal of the Abraham Lincoln Association* 34 (2013): 83, 85–86, 87; Phillip W. Magness and Sebastian N. Page, "Lincoln, Colonization, and Evidentiary Standards: A Response to Allen C. Guelzo," May 1, 2013, SSRN: ssrn.com/abstract=2267625.

56. Michael J. Douma and Anders Bo Rasmussen, "The Danish St Croix Project: Revisiting the Lincoln Colonization Program with Foreign-language Sources." *American Nineteenth Century History* 15, no. 3 (2014): 311–42.

57. Mark E. Neely, "Colonization and the Myth that Lincoln Prepared the People for Emancipation," in Blair and Young, eds., *Lincoln's Proclamation*, 45–74. Bates's opinion, affirming in a particular instance that the "free man of color . . . if born in the United States, is a citizen of the United States," was issued on November 29, 1862, just two days before Lincoln's strong endorsement of colonization in his Second Annual Message. See Edward Bates, *Opinion of Attorney General Bates on Citizenship* (Washington, D.C.: Government Printing Office, 1862).

58. Many recent attempts to link colonization to Lincoln's legacy have come from a segment of the literature that John M. Barr dubs the "anti-Lincoln tradition." See Barr, "The Anti-Lincoln Tradition in American Life," PhD diss., University of Houston, 2010. The primary examples in this genre are Lerone Bennett Jr., *Forced Into Glory: Abraham Lincoln's White Dream* (Chicago: Johnson Publishing Co., 1999), and Thomas DiLorenzo, *The Real Lincoln* (New York: Forum/Random House, 2002). Colonization has also seen a recent and more nuanced critical assessment among a growing minority of Civil War specialists, including Richard J. Blackett, "Lincoln and Colonization," *OAH Magazine of History*, October 2007; Paul D. Escott, *What Shall We Do with the Negro? Lincoln, White Racism, and Civil War America* (Charlottesville: University of Virginia Press, 2009); Gates and Yacovone, *Lincoln on Race and Slavery*; Nicholas Guyatt, "A Topic Best Avoided," *London Review of Books*, December 1, 2011, 27–31; Brian R. Dirck, *Lincoln and White America* (Lawrence: University Press of Kansas, 2012); as well as the author of this chapter.

16

Rethinking Colonization in the Early United States

NICHOLAS GUYATT

Between the American Revolution and the Confederate surrender at Appomattox, the black population in the United States increased by more than 3.5 million. Across the same period, the total number of African Americans who left the United States under the aegis of colonization was around 20,000. By 1865, colonization had removed around one-half of one-hundredth of 1 percent of the black population increase since 1776, and had been denounced as "an impossible idea" (Thaddeus Stevens), "absurd" (Charles Sumner), and "a hideous and barbarous humbug" (John Hay, channeling Abraham Lincoln). Given these meager results, and the ultimate triumph of emancipation without black removal, did colonization really have much impact? How would we measure its significance, beyond noting that the stated aim of colonizationists was spectacularly unsuccessful? This essay addresses these questions by reframing the colonization movement's origins and assumptions. By restoring colonization to its proper contexts, we can appreciate the full extent of its legacy.[1]

One of the earliest attempts to explain the meaning of colonization remains among the most influential. In the late 1820s and early 1830s, a series of black and white abolitionists led by David Walker and William Lloyd Garrison insisted that the American Colonization Society (ACS) was a proslavery conspiracy. While members of the colonization society styled themselves as liberal thinkers—enlightened, benevolent, disdainful of prejudices—and couched their proposals in the language of philanthropy, abolitionists judged them to be gullible at best, depraved at worst. The ACS, according to Walker's 1829 *Appeal to the Colored Citizens of the World*, was "got up by a gang of slave-holders to select the free people of color from among the slaves, that our more miserable brethren may be the better secured in ignorance and wretchedness, to work their farms and dig their mines." This view created enormous controversy in the 1830s, but was widely accepted by historians of colonization in the twentieth century. Even contemporary scholars who acknowledge the antislavery leanings of many ACS supporters draw attention to the society's slaveholding members, sketching a complex coalition between unwitting antislavery "moderates" and conniving proslavery diehards. The principal insight of Garrison and Walker—that the ACS could not be considered a genuinely antislavery organization—continues to inform our understanding of the entire colonization movement.[2]

Similarly, since the publication of Winthrop Jordan's pioneering study *White over Black* in 1968, historians have tended to see colonization as part of America's journey "toward a white man's country." While some scholars have acknowledged the curiously double-edged nature of colonization rhetoric, and the insistence of many colonization proponents on black ability and the unity of the human species, the temptation to conflate colonization with white supremacy has been considerable. These familiar approaches to black removal—which code colonization as racist in its intentions and proslavery in its effects—have prevented us from confronting an awkward truth. Many colonization supporters considered themselves to be passionately opposed to both slavery and prejudice, and yet they placed their faith in the proposition that justice and equality could be secured through a physical separation of the races. To understand the unsettling logic of this proposition, we need to examine the motives and tactics of the ACS more closely, and to look beyond the society towards the full range of colonization thinking in the early United States.[3]

* * *

From the 1770s onward, black and white reformers discussed colonization in an unambiguously antislavery register. These conversations were international, uniting philanthropists in London with free black pioneers in Sierra Leone and "enlightened" planters in the Caribbean. Among the most influential figures in this early debate was William Thornton, whose career captures the cosmopolitan milieu of colonization's formative years.

Thornton was born in 1759 into a family of Quaker slaveholders on the Caribbean island of Tortola. During his long schooling in Europe, while Thornton paid his bills with income drawn from his family's plantation, he became immersed in the rising antislavery sentiment of London and Paris. Having decided to resolve the contradiction between his means and his ideals, he returned to Tortola in 1786 to persuade his mother and stepfather to free the family's slaves. When they dismissed his request, Thornton quit the Caribbean for Philadelphia, where he joined the Pennsylvania Abolition Society. Thornton's family had rejected his suggestion that black people could live freely alongside their former masters. Acknowledging "the prejudices of my parents" as "shackles to the mind," Thornton sought an emancipation plan that would accommodate their misgivings.[4]

The idea of colonization had come to Thornton through his sojourn in Europe. In Paris, he had befriended the entomologist Henry Smeathman, and was fascinated by his proposal for a West African outpost settled by free blacks. In 1786 and 1787, as Thornton visited free black churches and meeting halls along the Eastern Seaboard of the United States, he presented his own plan for a settlement "on the Tooth or Ivory Coast of Africa" in which blacks "who are now free in America and Europe" would be joined by freed slaves from the Caribbean and the United States. Thornton was received politely by white and black audiences, and took encouragement from the news that Smeathman's West Africa plan had been implemented by a group of British reformers led by Granville Sharp.

Unfortunately, this first experiment in antislavery colonization went disastrously awry. The settlement of Sierra Leone, hamstrung by poor planning and ravaged by bad weather, collapsed within a matter of months. Thornton was undeterred. He sent Sharp his condolences but insisted that a new wave of settlers could learn from the experiment's failure.[5]

In spite of his British influences, Thornton had no patience with the emerging symbiosis of antislavery and imperialism. Black emigrants should prosper in Africa as "an independent people," he insisted, without obligations to an imperial sponsor. ("I hate the word *colony*," he told an English correspondent.) In October 1789, Thornton shared his ideas with a new friend he had made at his lodging house in Philadelphia: James Madison, the most influential member of the new House of Representatives. The Virginian was so taken with Thornton's scheme that he wrote his own endorsement of colonization, which Thornton sent to his friends at the Société des Amis des Noirs in Paris. While Thornton's courting of French abolitionists offers another indication of colonization's currency within the international antislavery movement, Madison was focused on American realities. The "benevolent experiment" of an African colony "might prove a great encouragement to manumission in the Southern parts of the U.S. and even afford the best hope yet presented of putting an end to the slavery in which not less than 600,000 unhappy negroes are now involved." Madison—future president of both the United States and the American Colonization Society—insisted that a black settlement in Africa would "induce the humanity of Masters, and by degrees both the humanity and policy of the Governments, to forward the abolition of slavery in America."[6]

The humanity of masters was hard to discern in the House of Representatives, at least among the members from the Lower South, when an abolitionist petition signed by Benjamin Franklin was presented to Congress in February of the following year. "The Gentlemen from S. Carolina & Georgia are intemperate beyond all example and even all decorum," Madison wrote a friend. While he hoped that their "virulent" views would backfire, providing "the patrons of Humanity & Freedom" with an opening in the fight against slavery, his conservative instincts easily checked his antislavery sentiment. Under pressure from the Lower South, but at the direction of Madison, Congress in 1790 confirmed its abdication from the slavery debate for a generation. A disappointed William Thornton chose to make a renewed assault on the planters of Tortola, insisting that slavery violated the foundational principle "that every man is equally entitled to the protection of life, liberty and property." But his focus on "the rights of man" failed to sway the slaveholders in the island's assembly, and Thornton returned to the United States to pursue new enthusiasms.[7]

Over the next three decades, Thornton became a prominent public figure. He won a competition to design the Capitol building in the new federal city of Washington; he directed the U.S. Patent Office for nearly three decades; and he vigorously promoted the revolutions in Latin America. But Thornton never abandoned his view that colonization was the key to emancipation. In 1802, he urged Thomas Jefferson to buy Puerto Rico as a refuge for free blacks. Two years later, he proposed a black colony in the American West, reasoning that Native Americans might benefit from the proximity of an industrious and civilized black population. In a letter to Henry Clay in 1816, Thornton gave his blessing to the new American Colonization Society, aligning his life's efforts with the promise of the ACS. The "liberal policy" adopted by the earliest proponents of colonization might now be revived in the work of the society, or so Thornton hoped. In the process, slavery—the "darkest stain" on America's career—would "be finally rendered subservient to the work of heaven."[8]

Thornton's plans were typical of the early wave of colonization enthusiasm in the United States, which was marked by a churning sense of slavery's injustice. Colonization proponents were keenly aware of the British experiment in Sierra Leone, both as an inspiration and as a source of embarrassment as that settlement struggled for stability. There was a lively debate on the best location for a colony, with proponents variously looking to the American West, the Caribbean, and Africa. Colonization supporters were awkwardly cognizant that a key rationale for removing blacks after emancipation was the impermeability of white prejudice. It would be an exaggeration to argue that the prejudice of others was the only reason advanced for black removal. William Thornton, like Thomas Jefferson in the *Notes on the State of Virginia,* warned that former slaves might seek revenge against their masters for the evils of slavery. Jefferson even flirted with the argument that blacks were permanently inferior to whites, though in this he was an outlier. The vast majority of antislavery theorists viewed the challenges of emancipation in environmental terms. Slavery had denied African Americans an education, and had offered perverse incentives to embrace bad habits. Government and philanthropic societies might reverse the effects of slavery after emancipation, but antislavery writers promoted colonization as a shortcut: a colony would externalize the process of recovering blacks from their "degradation" and, in theory, speed the prospects of abolition.[9]

During the early years of colonization enthusiasm, free blacks themselves devised numerous plans for settlement outside the United States. In 1773, four Massachusetts slaves asked the colonial assembly to help them "transport ourselves to some part of the coast of *Africa.*" In 1787, a group in Boston petitioned the General Court for assistance in "return[ing] to Africa, our native country." In 1795, James McKenzie, the secretary of the African Society in Providence, traveled to Sierra Leone to assess the progress of the colonists. Most notably, in 1811 the Massachusetts sea captain Paul Cuffe made his first trip to Sierra Leone, and thereafter promoted emigration from the United States to West Africa. Here, too, the international dimension of early colonization initiatives was decisive. Cuffe, who may have attended Thornton's colonization talks in the 1780s, was asked to visit Sierra Leone by James Pemberton, the president of the Pennsylvania Abolition Society, who, in turn, had helped to animate William Thornton's initial interest in the subject. Pemberton had been directed toward Sierra Leone by the African Institution, the London-based benevolent society established by the alumni of the British campaign against the slave trade. The institution's leading light, Thomas Clarkson, endorsed various colonization schemes from the American interior to Haiti to West Africa, and relayed suggestions to his American correspondents.[10]

Free blacks embraced colonization primarily as a response to northern white prejudice, but the prospect of self-improvement in a new environment had a broader appeal: a thriving and self-governing settlement outside the United States would vindicate black ability against the calumnies of slaveholders and the prejudices of white New Englanders. In this respect, both black and white promoters of emigration were inspired by an antislavery colonization movement that was transnational in its character and which spanned the Atlantic world.

* * *

The idea that colonization and antislavery were incompatible was forged in 1817, as the new American Colonization Society burst into life. Robert Finley, the New Jersey clergyman who helped found the society, asked Paul Cuffe in 1816 to endorse the ACS at its inaugural meeting in December. While Cuffe's reply came too late, and the dignitaries who assembled in Washington to christen the ACS were conspicuously white, Cuffe congratulated Finley in January 1817 on the "great and laborious task you are engaged in," even offering suggestions for where a new colony might be located. When Finley approached the leaders of Philadelphia's free black community that same month, he met with a similarly warm response. James Forten, who had been following Cuffe's African initiatives for many years, was particularly receptive. But when the ACS plans were conveyed to a mass meeting of three thousand free blacks, Forten received a setback. "There was not one soul that was in favor of going to Africa," he wrote Cuffe. Free blacks "will never become a people until they come out from amongst the white people," he concluded. "But as the majority is decidedly against me, I am determined to remain silent."[11]

Forten crisply summarized the case against the ACS: free blacks believed that "the slave holders want to get rid of them so as to make their property more secure." Given the high visibility of slaveholders like Henry Clay and Robert Goodloe Harper in the ACS leadership, black skeptics wanted more from the ACS than the reassurance that colonization would be voluntary. But the society's managers feared that an overtly antislavery message would complicate their courting of federal officials and alienate ambivalent slaveholders in the South. (Ironically, it was Harper who provided the most full-throated endorsement of the ACS's antislavery intentions.) During the newspaper wars that raged in Philadelphia in 1817, defenders of the ACS lamented the failure of its white and black critics to acknowledge that colonization and abolition were inextricably linked; that "the axe is to be laid to the root of SLAVERY" by colonization, and that a colony would provide refuge both to free blacks and to "those that may hereafter be emancipated." But the finessing of this question in the society's official pronouncements deepened the reluctance of free blacks to accept its overtures. By the end of 1817, James Forten had joined the majority in opposition to the ACS.[12]

Those who doubted the viability of the ACS's plans or the purity of its intentions did not necessarily reject the principle of colonization. Paul Cuffe thought that an ACS colony bordering Sierra Leone should be supplemented by another on the outskirts of the United States, offsetting the logistical challenges of an African exodus. In January 1817, free blacks in Washington declared "our dislike to colonize in Africa" but proposed "the colonizing of the free people of color on the waters of the Missouri river, under the government of the United States." James Forten, who in 1819 confirmed his opposition to "any plan of colonization without the American continent or islands," became closely involved in plans for black emigration to Haiti. Despite the consistent opposition of free blacks to the new ACS colony of Liberia, thousands left for the Caribbean during the 1820s.[13]

The tendency of historians to assume a divergence between antislavery sentiment and colonization enthusiasm has made it harder for us to understand (or even acknowledge) the proliferation of emigration schemes beyond Liberia. This supposed divergence has also led us to expect a conversion narrative in which antislavery radicals are first duped by colonization principles before triumphantly renouncing them. James Forten was initially enthusiastic toward the ACS, but changed his mind within a matter of months. William Lloyd Garrison lectured at a fundraising event for the ACS before becoming its most obstreperous critic. James Birney, the Kentucky reformer, worked as an ACS agent in the South before his dramatic conversion to abolitionism. Ranked against these figures, and their hard-won embrace of a "genuine" antislavery, we have Gary Nash's disappointed assessment of those reformers who embraced the ACS in the face of free black opposition: "Support for colonization became the safety valve of those suffering a failure of nerve in the antislavery cause." The assumption that a true commitment to antislavery relied on an anti-colonization epiphany overlooks the fact that most ACS supporters believed slavery was an evil. Even critics of the ACS explored emigrationist alternatives to Liberia, and the notion that slavery could be undermined by a program of racial separation attained considerable momentum within and beyond the ACS's support base.[14]

During the late 1810s, when state abolition societies assembled for their national convention, the intentions and prospects of the ACS were keenly debated. The 1818 convention lamented that colonization would "eternize the bondage of those of the African race." The following year, having received a pro-colonization message from Thomas Clarkson, the convention rejected the ACS while urging "a removal into the interior of our own country." A western refuge for free blacks could earn territorial status from the federal government, soften the hostilities of the western Indians towards the United States, and offer "the incentive to individual emancipation" to southern slaveholders. The convention's meetings throughout the 1820s balanced skepticism towards the ACS with enthusiasm for other colonization schemes until, at the 1829 meeting, even Liberia received a cautious welcome from the delegates. "Your committee do not look to the transportation of the whole coloured population from this country, at any period," declared Thomas Earle of the Pennsylvania Abolition Society, but "partial emigration may greatly aid the cause" of emancipation.[15]

Other opponents of slavery experienced a similar thawing towards colonization. The ACS won support after 1817 from William Short, who had previously recommended intermarriage between the races to his mentor Thomas Jefferson, and from Edward Coles, the protégé of James Madison who, as governor of Illinois, led the fight against the introduction of slavery to the state in 1824. Short and Coles supported the ACS for the rest of their lives, and made generous bequests to the society. Benjamin Lundy, the pioneering antislavery editor, printed essays in support of Liberian and Haitian emigration before pursuing colonization schemes in Canada and Texas. When William Lloyd Garrison finally persuaded William Wilberforce to reject Liberia, Wilberforce endorsed a black colony in the American West with settlers "represented on the floor of Congress." Even James Birney, the most celebrated convert from colonizationism to abolitionism in the 1830s, urged African Americans two decades later to consider emigration to Liberia. During the colonization society's two public crises of legitimacy—under attack from free blacks in 1817, and from abolitionists in the early 1830s—it retained considerable appeal among antislavery "moderates" who rejected the charge that colonization was a front for slavery.[16]

* * *

To many historians, the efforts to remove America's black population confirmed a transition from environmental understandings of human difference to indelible hierarchies of race. In Winthrop Jordan's celebrated account of the origins of racism in North America, white proponents of black emigration initially identified the prejudices of less enlightened whites as the rationale for black removal, but eventually embraced those prejudices as "objective assessments of the realities of Negro inferiority." (Jordan dated this shift to the second decade of the nineteenth century.) Other scholars have blurred the distinction between environmental arguments and "hard" racism in the promotion of black emigration. John Wood Sweet notes that, in the 1820s, the ACS "attracted widespread support for its assertion that American prejudice—or black inferiority, it didn't make any practical difference—was too ingrained to be overcome." In reference to the Whig Party's embrace of colonization in the 1830s, James Brewer Stewart observes that, "in the end, Democrats' blunt racism and Whiggery's more genteel appeals to colonization amounted to the same thing. African Americans must be branded by pigmentation alone as members of a perpetually inferior race." In these accounts, colonization seems to have slipped entirely from the liberal moorings evident in William Thornton's long advocacy of black removal.[17]

But to conflate colonization with the triumph of "hard" racism is to miss its central appeal to white reformers: it allowed them to reconcile "all men are created equal" with the permanent exile of people of color. George Fredrickson's startling observation that one can read the vast promotional literature of the ACS in the 1820s "without finding a single clear and unambiguous assertion of the Negro's inherent and unalterable inferiority to whites" is worth recalling here. Before 1830, science and religion offered little succor to the view that blacks were permanently inferior to whites, but a recognition of racial universalism suggested two things: that slavery should be abolished without delay, and that blacks should receive the same rights and privileges as whites. Since the 1780s, environmental theorists had argued against immediate abolition by invoking the damage done to black people by slavery: "degradation" was a social rather than a biological phenomenon, but freed blacks would need education and support to sustain equal citizenship and overturn white prejudice. Colonization offered a way to outsource this difficult work and avert the prospect of a multiracial citizenry. In this sense, David Walker was right to identify a "colonizing trick" in the early United States, but wrong to locate its origins in proslavery. The real achievement of colonization was to allow liberal whites to indulge antislavery sentiments without a commitment to integration.[18]

Since the 1790s, antislavery thinkers had fretted that emancipation would lead to racial amalgamation. David Rice, the Methodist preacher who led the fight against slavery in the Kentucky constitutional convention in 1792, confessed that amalgamation would ensue despite the "prejudices of education" among white people. In 1798, the Virginian diplomat and businessman William Short reassured Thomas Jefferson that racial mixing would not endanger the republic. (Jefferson carefully avoided replying to Short's letter, which he received shortly after Sally Hemings gave birth to his son, Beverley.) In the early 1800s the Princeton University president, Samuel Stanhope Smith, offered his students a hybrid plan in which colonization prepared the way for amalgamation: blacks would be removed to the American West, whites would be paid to marry them in the new settlement, and the success of this mixed-race laboratory would erode the prejudices of the East.

In the main, however, white reformers gratefully identified colonization as an alternative to amalgamation. David Rice had conquered his aversion to racial mixing: "My own pride remonstrates against it," he admitted, "but it does not influence my judgement, nor affect my conscience." William Thornton, who was generally scrupulous in his defense of black ability, was less successful: "If the taste of a white man should be so depraved as to prefer a black to a white, they ought to be joined, for it would be injustice to permit such depravity to contaminate a white woman." The question would not arise, though, because Thornton "did not mean to leave the blacks subjected to remain, when emancipated, in the bosom of that country where they had been slaves."[19]

Environmental arguments for black emigration undoubtedly reinforced and amplified stereotypes. As Joanne Pope Melish has argued, colonization proponents caricatured African American communities of diverse achievements and means as uniformly "degraded." But the universalist underpinnings of colonization rhetoric—the sense that blacks could prove their equality with whites, if placed in propitious surroundings—reconciled white liberals to removal plans that might otherwise seem distressingly illiberal. This "enlightened" sensibility, informed by natural-rights thinking and the promises of the Declaration of Independence, resonated beyond the northern states.

Many slaveholders in the Upper South saw an obvious contradiction between slavery and "all men are created equal." As Lacy Ford has argued, the "discourses of colonization" that flowed through the South had a dominant polarity: colonization held an antislavery charge. This produced considerable enthusiasm for the ACS in the Upper South, where the white public could imagine a gradual end to slavery, and considerable opposition in the lower South, where hostility towards gradualism and federally sponsored emancipation was widespread. While abolitionists later accused the ACS of playing both ends against the middle, colonization debates in the South actually sharpened the lines between antislavery and proslavery sentiment.[20]

Consider, for example, the 1826 controversy between Virginia slaveholders John White Nash and William Fitzhugh in the pages of the *Richmond Enquirer*. Nash, a member of the state assembly, complained that, despite its public advocacy of free black removal, the colonization society secretly desired general emancipation. To Nash's surprise, Fitzhugh—an ACS vice-president—confessed that this had been the plan all along. ACS supporters refused to accept slavery as "an evil entailed upon us forever," Fitzhugh boasted, before supplying an alarmingly specific estimate of how the "ulterior object" of the society could be achieved: the removal of every black person from the United States, free and enslaved, would cost around fifty million dollars, and might be accomplished within "twenty or thirty years."[21]

Similar arguments punctuated the debates in the Virginia Assembly in the aftermath of Nat Turner's 1831 uprising. Of the forty or so members who addressed the topics of emancipation and colonization in January 1832, nearly half invoked natural-rights arguments against the maintenance of slavery. Many pointed to a contradiction between slavery and the political creed of the United States, and the majority stated openly that slavery was an evil. A handful ventured the claim that blacks were permanently inferior to whites, and only one argued that free blacks should be removed from Virginia to bolster slavery.[22]

William H. Roane of Hanover County was one of the few speakers to challenge the relevance of the Declaration of Independence to the debate. Admitting that his views might "shock the tender nerves," he denied "that all men are by nature equal," or that "the flat-nosed, woolly-headed black native" was "equal to the straight haired white man of Europe." More typical was the insistence of James McDowell that even "the most decided enemies of abolition" acknowledged the evils of slavery; the slave was "soiled in his character and degraded in his fortunes," but "still a member of a common race and still entitled, as such, to our sympathy and kindness." McDowell was from the Upcountry region, where fewer than 25 percent of the population was black.

Philip Bolling, on the other hand, represented Buckingham County, where blacks easily outnumbered whites. For Bolling, the proslavery minority in the assembly reflected "the power of deep-rooted prejudice over the mind of man." Deep down, everyone knew that slavery was wrong: "There is a still small voice which speaks to the heart of man in a tone too clear and distinct to be disregarded. It tells him that every system of slavery is based upon injustice and oppression." Bolling's solution was a program of gradual emancipation and colonization in Liberia, and he was confident that the "rapid progress of liberal feelings" would speed his ideas to fruition.[23]

* * *

Henry Clay had been president of the American Colonization Society for almost fifteen years when he addressed its annual meeting in Washington in January 1851. Presenting himself as the "sole survivor" of the ACS's founding generation, he announced the society's best year in terms of fundraising and the recruitment of colonists. Northern abolitionists—"or at least all the moderate and rational portion of them"—were finally choosing colonization over immediatism. It would take a century or more to effect the removal of black people from America, Clay suggested, but in the meantime delegates should treat blacks with kindness and empathy: "It is not their fault, that they are a debased and degraded set." Clay invoked misfortune rather than biology to explain black deviance: "The whites themselves, if placed in the condition of the free people of color in the United States, would like them be addicted to vice, and would be exposed to the perpetration of crime in the same way that they are." Colonization offered a new beginning for black people and a chance to emulate the storied settlement of North America. Having compared Liberia to Jamestown and Plymouth Rock, Clay took his seat "amidst great applause."[24]

While the rhetoric of the ACS remained remarkably consistent across four decades, by 1850 the antislavery rationale for colonization faced mounting demographic and political challenges. Fewer than ten thousand blacks had emigrated to Liberia. The ACS retained support in the Upper South, but the explosive growth of the internal slave trade—which transferred slaves to the Cotton Belt rather than Liberia—illustrated the limits of the society's reach.

As Henry Clay and his colleagues fixed colonization's antislavery effects on improbably distant horizons, they invited criticism even from their friends. Thomas Clarkson, who had kept faith with the colonization society throughout the 1830s despite considerable pressure from abolitionists, eventually conceded that the designs of the ACS were "entirely impracticable." The trickle of Liberian emigrants and the unchecked expansion of southern slavery had led Clarkson to examine the ACS "with new eyes." After years of steadfast support, Clarkson now beheld a "diabolical scheme."[25]

But while the ACS struggled to sell its vision of national unity amidst a deepening sectionalism, the underlying idea of black removal proved durable and elastic. After 1848, planters in the Deep South watched with alarm as Upper South assemblies expanded manumission and emigration initiatives. In the North, meanwhile, radical abolitionists could never quite purge their ranks of backsliders. James Birney's beleaguered endorsement of African emigration in 1852 was trumpeted by the ACS. Still more embarrassingly, in the conclusion of *Uncle Tom's Cabin*, Harriet Beecher Stowe sent her hero, George Harris, to Liberia.

That a fiercely antislavery novel should stage its happy ending in Africa struck some readers as incongruous. Stowe, wounded by the complaints of abolitionists, reassured the 1853 meeting of the American and Foreign Antislavery Society that she did not support "coercive" emigration. Instead, she sympathized with "the whole colored race, whether in Canada, the West Indies, or in Liberia," and she viewed the West African colony as "one of the means of elevating them." The abolitionist delegates were inclined to accept Stowe's explanation. In a telling admission of the state of race relations in the North, one of them admitted that "it was a very natural resource for the novelist, in looking out for a place of rest and safety, to set the black man down in Africa."[26]

While the ACS continued to court antislavery moderates in the North in the 1850s, free blacks and radical whites promoted Haiti, Central and South America, or the western frontier as alternatives to Africa. These were responses to northern prejudice rather than schemes for southern emancipation. The Fugitive Slave Act had nationalized the hold of tyranny, according to the black emigrationist Martin Delany, leaving African Americans even in the northern states as "slaves in the midst of freedom."

In the sphere of national politics, the resurgence of colonization in the 1850s had a more obvious antislavery cast. While the Whigs clung to black colonization in the 1830s and 1840s against the quickening eddies of sectionalism, the new Republican Party vowed to freeze the growth of slavery in the western territories. This brought into question Republicans' long-term intentions towards the institution. Colonization allowed Republican orators to galvanize their hostility toward slavery with a commitment to racial separation. In his celebrated speech at Peoria in 1854, Abraham Lincoln admitted the lure of immediate abolition and colonization; but the practical obstacles to settling so many people at once in Africa were so daunting that "systems of gradual emancipation" would be more effective. In the speeches of Lincoln and his Republican colleagues, antislavery, colonization, and gradualism became mutually reinforcing.[27]

As the prospect of a confrontation between the Republican Party and the South seemed ever more likely during the 1850s, party members saw the American Colonization Society as inadequate to the task ahead. Liberia was too far from the United States; its capacity to absorb huge numbers of migrants was open to question; the task of managing colonization seemed better suited to the government than to a private concern like the ACS. James Doolittle of Wisconsin, addressing the U.S. Senate in 1859, suggested a creative reworking of the Republican homesteading policy as an alternative to Liberian emigration. While the West would provide land for white settlers, the "luxuriant tropical regions of America" might supply "homesteads for our free colored men." Francis and Montgomery Blair, the influential Missouri politicians, envisaged a black exodus to Central America that would transform the region into "our India" (albeit "under happier auspices"). And, after Lincoln's inauguration in 1861, his administration sought colonization agreements with Mexico, Haiti, Honduras, Guatemala, Costa Rica, Nicaragua, and Brazil. Officials of the ACS were torn between dismissing these alternatives as visionary and lobbying Lincoln to direct his enthusiasm towards Africa.[28]

The federal government proved no better than the ACS at promoting black colonization. Beyond a disastrous attempt to resettle hundreds of freed people off the coast of Haiti in 1863, the Lincoln administration made no progress toward its stated goal of a permanent separation of the races. Some historians have concluded from this that the Republican colonization program was a clever ruse to lull a reluctant public into accepting emancipation. Others have suggested that Lincoln and his colleagues "outgrew" their early interest in racial separation. The most compelling explanation for colonization's failure in the 1860s is the same one that accounts for its limited progress since 1817: the vast majority of free blacks refused to consent to their expatriation, especially under circumstances in which they had strong reasons to doubt that a new home would bring self-determination and prosperity. As long as colonization remained voluntary, the prospect of a sweeping relocation of African Americans remained vanishingly small.[29]

A more complicated question is why colonization survived for as long as it did, given its painfully slow progress and the extent of free black skepticism towards Liberia. We usually answer this by insisting that the ACS was all things to all of its supporters, who clung to its ambiguities amidst a stiffening sectionalism.

While this may account for the Whig embrace of the 1830s and 1840s, it does not explain the broader appeal of colonization in the early republic. Even if we focus narrowly on the ACS, it is time to discard the idea that its membership was divided neatly between proslavery and antislavery elements. The vast majority of ACS followers believed that slavery was an evil, and that colonization would satisfy the dictates of conscience without requiring immediate emancipation or racial integration. While its radical critics denounced the ACS as a tool of the slave power, the society continued to draw support from northerners who saw no practical alternative to gradualism and emigration. When these antislavery "moderates" found a new political home in the Republican Party, they developed colonization proposals which were unencumbered by the baggage of the ACS, and which could be embraced by the federal government rather than private philanthropy.

If colonization had been a proslavery conspiracy, as David Walker and William Lloyd Garrison famously claimed, we would expect its influence to end abruptly with the Emancipation Proclamation. Even if we conceive of colonization in antislavery terms, we might expect its swift demise in 1863: Lincoln's proclamation vindicated the immediatists' call for a sudden overthrow of the slave system without the crutch of black resettlement. But the idea of separating the races continued to circulate after emancipation, for the same reason colonization rose to prominence in the early republic: it underpinned a widespread aversion among white people to integration. "All men are created equal" was tremendously useful to the antislavery cause, but it allowed defenders of the slave system to insist that emancipation would lead to civil, political, and social equality between the races. During his debates with Abraham Lincoln in the summer of 1858, Stephen Douglas tirelessly repeated the line that abolition and intermarriage were synonymous. Colonization supplied an obvious and welcome riposte: equality could be secured through separation.

Colonization allowed antislavery moderates to acknowledge popular prejudices against racial mixing, and to avoid commitments to equal citizenship after emancipation. From this vantage point, much of the opprobrium leveled at colonization by abolitionists (and historians) seems misplaced. What should trouble us is not the supposed racism of colonization's many proponents, but their enduring confidence that they could promote grand schemes of segregation while insisting that they weren't racists.[30]

Historian Gabor Boritt has argued that Lincoln's embrace of colonization had a "mostly beneficial" effect during the Civil War, allowing white Americans to imagine the end of slavery despite their ingrained prejudices against integration. But Boritt concedes that this mental maneuver made it harder for whites "to confront realistically the problem of the black man in America" after emancipation. We can only speculate on the damage done to the prospects of integration by the long hold of separatist thinking on the imagination of antislavery "moderates."

The task of Reconstruction was undoubtedly complicated by the lack of any widespread commitment to a society in which equality could be realized without physical separation. Colonization's grounding in a liberal understanding of human universalism—or even an expansive reading of the Declaration of Independence—made this separatist logic both insidious and tenacious. It is not surprising, therefore, that colonization schemes captured the attention of Lincoln, Andrew Johnson, and Ulysses S. Grant in the years after 1863. The embedded logic of separate-but-equal may also explain why so many northerners who cheered the downfall of slavery could reconcile themselves to the redemption of the South in 1877.[31]

Frederick Douglass understood the threat posed by colonization to the idea of a race-blind republic. In 1852, he hoped that the movement for black removal would be eclipsed by a growing public enlightenment on questions of race. "The Jim Crow pew" and the "Jim Crow car" were, he insisted, "becoming relics of American barbarism." His optimism was misplaced, as he himself soon admitted. The "barbarism" of racial separation survived the Civil War and helped to structure American life for another century because many of its proponents saw it as unimpeachably liberal. The reassurance provided by colonization on this question was its most important legacy.[32]

Notes

1. Thaddeus Stevens to John Hutchins, August 27, 1865, in Beverly Wilson Palmer and Holly Byers Ochoa, eds., *The Selected Papers of Thaddeus Stevens* (Pittsburgh: University of Pittsburgh Press, 1997–98), vol. 2: 11. Charles Sumner to Carl Schurz, August 28, 1865, in Beverly Wilson Palmer, ed., *The Selected Letters of Charles Sumner* (Boston: Northeastern University Press, 1990), vol. 2: 330. John Hay, entry for July 1, 1864, in Michael Burlingame, ed., *Inside Lincoln's White House: The Complete Civil War Diary of John Hay* (Carbondale: Southern Illinois University Press, 1997), 217.

2. David Walker, *Walker's Appeal, in Four Articles, Together with a Preamble to the Colored Citizens of the World* (Boston: Printed for the Author, 1829), 55. See also William Lloyd Garrison, *Thoughts on African Colonization: or an Impartial Exhibition of the Doctrines, Principles and Purpose of the American Colonization Society, together with the Resolutions, Addresses and Remonstrances of the Free People of Color* (Boston: Garrison and Knapp, 1832). For interpretations that link colonization and proslavery, see Paul Goodman, *Of One Blood: Abolitionism and the Origins of Racial Equality* (Berkeley: University of California Press, 1998), 14, 16, 130; C. Peter Ripley, ed., *The Black Abolitionist Papers* (Chapel Hill: University of North Carolina Press, 1991), vol. 3: 7; James Sidbury, *Becoming African in America: Race and Nation in the Early Black Atlantic* (New York: Oxford University Press, 2007), 168; and Charles F. Irons, *The Origins of Proslavery Christianity: White and Black Evangelicals in Colonial and Antebellum Virginia* (Chapel Hill: University of North Carolina Press, 2008), 102. For the idea of the ACS as delicately balanced between proslavery and antislavery wings, see Douglas Egerton, "'Its Origin Is Not a Little Curious': A New Look at the American Colonization Society," *Journal of the Early Republic* 5 (1985): 463–80; and Eva Shepard Wolf, *Race and Liberty in the New Nation: Emancipation in Virginia from the Revolution to Nat Turner's Rebellion* (Baton Rouge: Louisiana State University Press, 2009), 167–70. Manisha Sinha shuttles between these two interpretations, but consistently denies that colonization can be considered a part of the "antislavery movement" in antebellum America (*The Slave's Cause: A History of Abolition* [New Haven, Conn.: Yale University Press, 2016]).

3. Winthrop D. Jordan, *White over Black: American Attitudes toward the Negro, 1550–1812* (Chapel Hill: University of North Carolina Press, 1968), 566.

4. William Thornton to John Coakley Lettsom, November 18, 1786, in C. M Harris, ed., *Papers of William Thornton*, vol. 1: *1781–1802* (Charlottesville: University Press of Virginia, 1995), 31, 113–15. See also Gordon S. Brown, *Incidental Architect: William Thornton and the Cultural Life of Early Washington, D.C., 1794–1828* (Athens: Ohio University Press, 2009); P. J. Staudenraus, *The African Colonization Movement, 1816–1865* (New York: Columbia University Press, 1961), 5–8; and Christopher Leslie Brown, *Moral Capital: Foundations of British Abolitionism* (Chapel Hill: University of North Carolina Press, 2006), 317–18, 438–39.

5. "General Outlines of a Settlement on the Tooth or Ivory Coast of Africa," *Papers of William Thornton* 1: 38–41; Thornton to Lettsom, November 15, 1788, *Papers of William Thornton* 1: 77–79; Lettsom to Thornton, January 29, 1789, *Papers of William Thornton* 1: 86–96; Thornton to Sharp, November 13, 1789, *Papers of William Thornton* 1: 113–15. Harris, "Introduction," *Papers of William Thornton*, xl–xliv.

6. Thornton to Lettsom, July 26, 1788, *Papers of William Thornton* 1: 70–75. James Madison, "Memorandum on an African Colony for Freed Slaves," in Charles F. Hobson and Robert A. Rutland, eds., *The Papers of James Madison* (Charlottesville: University Press of Virginia, 1979), vol. 12: 437–38. See also Marie-Jeanne Rossignol, "Jacques-Pierre Brissot and the Fate of Atlantic Antislavery during the Age of Revolutionary Wars," in Richard Bessel et al., eds., *War, Empire and Slavery, 1770–1830* (Houndmills, U.K.: Palgrave Macmillan, 2010), 139–56.

7. James Madison to Benjamin Rush, March 20, 1790, in Hobson and Rutland, eds., *Papers of James Madison* 13: 109. "To the President and Members of the Council of the

Virgin Islands," February 22, 1791, in *Papers of William Thornton* 1: 129-30. Jabez Doty to Thornton, February 25, 1791, in *Papers of William Thornton* 1: 130-32. William Thornton, *Political Economy: Founded in Justice and Humanity, in a Letter to a Friend* (Washington, D.C.: Samuel Harrison Smith, 1804), 3, 6. On the House debate on abolition, see George William Van Cleve, *A Slaveholders' Union: Slavery, Politics, and the Constitution in the Early American Republic* (Chicago: University of Chicago Press, 2010), 187-203.

8. "Suggestion to Buy Porto Rico for Free Negroes," in Gaillard Hunt, *William Thornton and Negro Colonization* (Worcester, Mass.: American Antiquarian Society, 1921), 24-26. Thornton, *Political Economy*, 23. "To the Honorable Henry Clay," in Hunt, *William Thornton*, 28-32.

9. Thomas Jefferson, *Notes on the State of Virginia* (Paris: n.p., 1785), 252, 263-65. Thornton, *Political Economy*, 21. For early colonization proposals and endorsements, see Ferdinando Fairfax, "Plan for Liberating the Negroes within the United States," *American Museum* 8 (1790): 285-87; [Moses Fisk], *Tyrannical Libertymen: A Discourse upon Negro-Slavery in the United States* (Hanover, N.H.: The Eagle Office, 1795); St. George Tucker, *A Dissertation on Slavery* (Philadelphia: Mathew Cary, 1796); and John Parrish, *Remarks on the Slavery of the Black People* (Philadelphia: Kimber, Conrad & Co., 1806). See also Beverly C. Tomek, *Colonization and Its Discontents: Emancipation, Emigration, and Antislavery in Antebellum Pennsylvania* (New York: New York University Press, 2011), 18-37; and Wolf, *Race and Liberty*, 101-9.

10. Guyatt, *Bind Us Apart: How Enlightened Americans Invented Racial Segregation* (New York: Basic Books, 2016), 210-11, 259-62. Floyd J. Miller, *The Search for a Black Nationality: Black Emigration and Colonization, 1787-1863* (Urbana: University of Illinois Press, 1975), 9-53. James Pemberton to Paul Cuffe, June 8 and September 27, 1808, in Rosalind Cobb Wiggins, ed., *Captain Paul Cuffe's Logs and Letters, 1808-1817* (Washington, D.C.: Howard University Press, 1996), 77-80, 56. Thomas Clarkson to Henri Christophe, February 20, 1819, in Earl Leslie Griggs and Clifford H. Prator, eds., *Henry Christophe and Thomas Clarkson: A Correspondence* (Berkeley: University of California Press, 1952), 124-25. See also James T. Campbell, *Middle Passages: African American Journeys to Africa, 1787-2005* (New York: Penguin, 2006), 16-39; Jeffrey A. Fortin, "Cuffe's Black Atlantic World, 1808-1817," *Atlantic Studies* 4 (2007): 245-66; Wayne Ackerson, *The African Institution (1807-1827) and the Antislavery Movement in Great Britain* (Lampeter, Wales: Edwin Mellen Press, 2005), 72-76; and Lamont D. Thomas, *Rise to Be a People: A Biography of Paul Cuffe* (Urbana: University of Illinois Press, 1986). On the conviction of free black emigration supporters that colonization would hasten American abolition, see Miller, *Search for a Black Nationality*, 4, 13, 22, 44-45, 87, 93, 128. This view was fiercely contested by other free blacks; see John Russwurm's editorial in *Freedom's Journal*, January 25, 1828, 175; and Joanne Pope Melish, *Disowning Slavery: Gradual Emancipation and "Race" in New England, 1780-1860* (Ithaca, N.Y.: Cornell University Press, 1998), 267.

11. Cuffe to Robert Finley, January 8, 1817, in Wiggins, ed., *Cuffe's Logs and Letters*, 492-93. James Forten to Cuffe, January 25, 1817, in Wiggins, ed., *Cuffe's Logs and Letters*, 501-3. See also Julie Winch, *A Gentleman of Color: The Life of James Forten* (New York: Oxford University Press, 2002), 181-95; Gary B. Nash, *Forging Freedom: The Formation of Philadelphia's Black Community, 1720-1840* (Cambridge, Mass.: Harvard University Press, 1988), 235-42; and Richard S. Newman, *Freedom's Prophet: Bishop Richard Allen, the AME*

Church, and the Black Founding Fathers (New York: New York University Press, 2008), 183–209.

12. Forten to Cuffe, January 25, 1817, in Wiggins, ed., *Cuffe's Logs and Letters*, 502. "Colonization," *Poulson's Daily Advertiser*, August 12, 1817, 3. "Colonization of Africa," *Poulson's Daily Advertiser*, July 10, 1817, 3. "Colonization of the Free People of Colour," *Poulson's Daily Advertiser*, August 11, 1817, 2. On Robert Goodloe Harper, see Eric Robert Papenfuse, *The Evils of Necessity: Robert Goodloe Harper and the Moral Dilemma of Slavery* (Philadelphia: American Philosophical Society, 1997). On the development of free black opposition to the ACS, see Tomek, *Colonization and Its Discontents*, 132–50.

13. Cuffe to James Brian, January 16, 1817, in Wiggins, ed., *Cuffe's Logs and Letters*, 498. "At a Meeting of Free People of Colour," *Poulson's Daily Advertiser*, January 10, 1817, 3. "The Colonization Scheme," *Niles' Weekly Register*, November 27, 1819, 201. On Haitian emigration schemes, see Chris Dixon, *African America and Haiti: Emigration and Black Nationalism in the Nineteenth Century* (Westport, Conn.: Greenwood Press, 2000), 24–52; Newman, *Freedom's Prophet*, 238–63; Winch, *Gentleman of Color*, 209–20; and Bruce Dain, *A Hideous Monster of the Mind: American Race Theory in the Early Republic* (Cambridge, Mass.: Harvard University Press, 2003), 93–104.

14. Winch, *Gentleman of Color*, 197–206. Eric Burin, *Slavery and the Peculiar Solution: A History of the American Colonization Society* (Gainesville: University Press of Florida, 2005), 21–22. Betty Fladeland, *James Gillespie Birney: Slaveholder to Abolitionist* (Ithaca, N.Y.: Cornell University Press, 1955), 75–89. Gary B. Nash, *First City: Philadelphia and the Forging of Historical Memory* (Philadelphia: University of Pennsylvania Press, 2002), 187. Manisha Sinha makes a problematic distinction between "emigration," which she uses to describe black-authored schemes for racial separation, and "colonization," which she sees as synonymous with the activities of the American Colonization Society. (Her index entry for colonization directs readers to the entry for the ACS.) This overlooks the ubiquity and complexity of colonization proposals before the founding of the ACS in 1816, and the continuing popularity of schemes that combined antislavery and black resettlement through the rise of the Republican Party (*Slave's Cause*, 161–91, 743).

15. *Minutes of the Proceedings of a Special Meeting of the Fifteenth Convention for Promoting the Abolition of Slavery* (Philadelphia: Hall & Atkinson, 1818), 38, 47–54, 67–68. *Minutes of the Sixteenth American Convention, for Promoting the Abolition of Slavery* (Philadelphia: William Fry, 1819), 28–30, 38, 50–56. *Minutes of the Twenty-First Biennial American Convention for Promoting the Abolition of Slavery* (Philadelphia: Thomas B. Town, 1829), 28–35. The appendix to the 1829 minutes reprinted a letter from the New York Manumission Society proposing that, if black people were to be colonized anywhere, "there is no place so eligibly situated for this purpose as Texas" (51).

16. Edward Coles to Roberts Vaux, February 8, 1826, box 2, folder 20, Roberts Vaux Papers, Historical Society of Pennsylvania; and William Short to Vaux, December 13, 1830, box 3, folder 12, Roberts Vaux Papers. Kurt E. Leichtle and Bruce G. Carveth, *Crusade Against Slavery: Edward Coles, Pioneer of Freedom* (Carbondale: Southern Illinois University Press, 2011); and George Green Shackelford, *Jefferson's Adoptive Son: The Life of William Short, 1759–1848* (Lexington: University Press of Kentucky, 1993), 165–66, 175–77. On Lundy, see Merton L. Dillon, *Benjamin Lundy and the Struggle for Negro Freedom* (Champaign: University of Illinois Press, 1966), 87–103, 165–205; and Dain, *Hideous Monster*

of Mind, 102-3. James G. Birney, *Examination of the Supreme Court of the United States* (Cincinnati: Truman & Spofford, 1852), 43-46. For Wilberforce's plan, see G. B. Stebbins, *Facts and Opinions, Touching the Real Origin, Character, and Influence of the American Colonization Society* (Boston: John P. Jewett and Co., 1853), 215-24.

17. Jordan, *White over Black*, 569. John Wood Sweet, *Bodies Politic: Negotiating Race in the American North, 1730-1830* (Baltimore: Johns Hopkins University Press, 2003), 405. James Brewer Stewart, "The Emergence of Racial Modernity and the Rise of the White North, 1790-1840," *Journal of the Early Republic* 18 (1998): 181-217, 208. See also Lacy K. Ford, *Deliver Us from Evil: The Slavery Question in the Old South* (New York: Oxford University Press, 2009), 302; Melish, *Disowning Slavery*, 198; Goodman, *Of One Blood*, 19-21; Claude A. Clegg III, *The Price of Liberty: African Americans and the Making of Liberia* (Chapel Hill: University of North Carolina Press, 2004), 33; and Bruce Laurie, *Beyond Garrison: Antislavery and Social Reform* (Cambridge, U.K.: Cambridge University Press, 2004), 87. Douglas Egerton rejects the historiographical presumption that the ACS was proslavery, but condemns the colonization society's "institutionalized racism." See Egerton, "Averting a Crisis: The Proslavery Critique of the American Colonization Society," *Civil War History* 43 (1997): 142-56.

18. George M. Fredrickson, *The Black Image in the White Mind: The Debate on Afro-American Character and Destiny, 1817-1914* (New York: Harper & Row, 1971), 12.

19. David Rice, *Slavery Inconsistent with Justice and Good Policy, Proved by a Speech Delivered in the Convention, Held at Danville, Kentucky* (Philadelphia: Parry Hall, 1792), 26. William Short to Thomas Jefferson, February 27, 1798, in Barbara B. Oberg, ed., *The Papers of Thomas Jefferson* (Princeton, N.J.: Princeton University Press, 2003), vol. 30: 146-154. Samuel Stanhope Smith, *The Lectures, Corrected and Improved, Which Have Been Delivered For a Series of Years, in the College of New Jersey* (Trenton: Daniel Fenton, 1812), vol. 2: 176-77. Thornton, *Political Economy*, 21.

20. Melish, *Disowning Slavery*, 198.

21. On the persistence of antislavery sentiment and ACS support in the Upper South, see Ford, *Deliver Us from Evil*, 299-328.

22. Erik S. Root, ed., *Sons of the Fathers: The Virginia Slavery Debates of 1831-32* (Lanham, Md.: Lexington Books, 2010). See also Ford, *Deliver Us from Evil*, 361-89; and Alison Goodyear Freehling, *Drift Toward Dissolution: The Virginia Anti-Slavery Debates of 1831-1832* (Baton Rouge: Louisiana State University Press, 1982), esp. 170-95.

23. Root, *Sons of the Fathers*, 125, 239, 244, 292, 297, 298.

24. "Speech of the Hon. H. Clay," *African Repository* 26 (1851): 105-14.

25. Stebbins, *Facts and Opinions*, 215-24. "Governor Hunt on Colonization," *African Repository* 28 (1852): 33-37. On the ACS's failure to make inroads in the Lower South, see Ford, *Deliver Us from Evil*, 388-89.

26. "James G. Birney on Colonization," *African Repository* 28 (1852): 144-46. *Thirteenth Annual Report of the American and Foreign Anti-Slavery Society* (New York: Published for the Society, 1853), 192-93. George Fredrickson located *Uncle Tom's Cabin* within a resurgence of "antislavery colonizationist thinking" in the early 1850s, noting that Stowe's brother, Henry Ward Beecher, "made exactly the same kind of endorsement of colonization" (*Black Image in the White Mind*, 115-17). See also Elizabeth Ammons, "Freeing the Slaves and Banishing the Blacks: Racism, Empire, and Africa in *Uncle Tom's Cabin*," in

Ammons, ed., *Harriet Beecher Stowe's Uncle Tom's Cabin: A Casebook* (New York: Oxford University Press, 2007), 227–46.

27. Martin Robison Delany, *The Condition, Emigration, and Destiny of the Colored People of the United States, Politically Considered* (Philadelphia: Martin Delany, 1852), 155, 27, 159–208. Abraham Lincoln, "Speech at Peoria, Illinois," in Roy P. Basler, ed., *The Collected Works of Abraham Lincoln* (New Brunswick, N.J.: Rutgers University Press, 1953–55), vol. 2: 255–56. On Delany and the resurgence of black interest in colonization after 1850, see Burin, *Slavery and the Peculiar Solution*, 27–33; Dixon, *African America and Haiti*, 66–127; Campbell, *Middle Passages*, 54–90; Miller, *Search for a Black Nationality*, 115–69; and Tomek, *Colonization and Its Discontents*, 187–218.

28. *Congressional Globe*, 35th Cong., 2nd Sess., February 9, 1859, 907; February 16, 1859, 1056. Frank P. Blair Jr., *The Destiny of the Races of this Continent* (Washington, D.C.: Buell & Blanchard, 1859), 23–24. *Papers Relating to Foreign Affairs* (Washington, D.C.: Government Printing Office, 1862), vol. 1: 703, 881–910. On the Republican embrace of colonization, see Eric Foner, *The Fiery Trial: Abraham Lincoln and American Slavery* (New York: Norton, 2010), 123–31; James D. Bilotta, *Race and the Rise of the Republican Party* (New York: P. Lang, 1992), 262–76; and Sharon Hartman Storm, "Labor, Race and Colonization: Imagining a Post-Slavery World in the Americas," in Steven Mintz and John Stauffer, eds., *The Problem of Evil: Slavery, Freedom, and the Ambiguities of American Reform* (Amherst: University of Massachusetts Press, 2007), 260–75. On the progress of colonization planning during the Lincoln administration, see Foner, *Fiery Trial*, 221–27; Thomas Schoonover, "Misconstrued Mission: Expansionism and Black Colonization in Mexico and Central America during the Civil War," *Pacific Historical Review* 49 (1980): 607–20; Phillip W. Magness and Sebastian N. Page, *Colonization After Emancipation: Lincoln and the Movement for Black Resettlement* (Columbia: University of Missouri Press, 2011); and Sebastian N. Page, "Lincoln and Chiriquí Colonization Revisited," *American Nineteenth Century History* 12 (2011): 289–325. For an ACS critique of federal colonization proposals, see "Annual Meeting of the American Colonization Society," *African Repository* 38 (1862): 47–48.

29. Advocates of the "lullaby thesis" claim that Lincoln endorsed black resettlement tactically, promoting emancipation to a public that was not yet ready for black citizenship. See, for instance, James M. McPherson, *Battle-Cry of Freedom* (New York: Oxford University Press, 1988), 508. Advocates of the "growth thesis" view Lincoln as sincere in his endorsement of colonization but increasingly open to enlightened and inclusive understandings of black ability. See, for instance, Foner, *Fiery Trial*, 244, 288–89. The fullest account of this debate is in Sebastian N. Page, "The American Civil War and Black Colonization," DPhil thesis, University of Oxford, 2012, 16–80.

30. My argument here builds on William Freehling's insistence that we look beyond the impracticability of colonization in assessing its influence and legacy: "'Absurd' Issues and the Causes of the Civil War: Colonization as a Test Case," in Freehling, *The Reintegration of American History: Slavery and the Civil War* (New York: Oxford University Press, 1994), 138–57.

31. G. S. Boritt, "The Voyage to the Colony of Lincolnia: The Sixteenth President, Black Colonization, and the Defense Mechanism of Avoidance," *Historian* 37 (1975): 619–32, 631. On removal schemes after 1863, see Magness and Page, *Colonization after Emancipation*;

Nicholas Guyatt, "America's Conservatory: Race, Reconstruction and the Santo Domingo Controversy," *Journal of American History* 97 (2011): 974–1000; Guyatt, "'An Impossible Idea?' The Curious Career of Internal Colonization," *Journal of the Civil War Era* 4 (2014): 234–63; and Guyatt, "'The Future Empire of the Freedmen': Republican Colonization Schemes in Texas and Mexico, 1861–1865," in Adam I. Arenson and Andrew R. Graybill, eds., *Civil War Wests: Testing the Limits of the United States* (Berkeley: University of California Press, 2015), 95–117.

32. "Mr. Birney on Colonization," *Frederick Douglass' Paper,* February 12, 1852.

Contributors

Eric Burin is professor of history at the University of North Dakota.

Andrew Diemer is associate professor of history at Towson University. He is author of *The Politics of Black Citizenship: Free African Americans in the Mid-Atlantic Borderland, 1817–1863*, and *Vigilance: The Life of William Still, Father of the Underground Railroad*.

David F. Ericson is an instructor in political science at Cleveland State University.

Bronwen Everill is a fellow and lecturer in history at Gonville & Caius College, University of Cambridge.

Nicholas Guyatt is university lecturer in American history and fellow of Trinity Hall, University of Cambridge.

Debra Newman Ham is retired professor of history at Morgan State University.

Matthew J. Hetrick is a teacher at the Bryn Mawr School in Baltimore.

Gale L. Kenny is assistant professor of religious studies at Barnard College, Columbia University.

Phillip W. Magness is academic program director at the Institute for Humane Studies at George Mason University, where he also teaches in the School of Policy, Government, and International Affairs.

Brandon Mills is associate professor of history at the University of Colorado–Denver.

Robert Murray is assistant professor of history at Mercy College in Dobbs Ferry, New York.

Sebastian N. Page is a researcher at Hertford College, University of Oxford.

Daniel Preston is editor of the Papers of James Monroe at the University of Mary Washington in Fredericksburg, Virginia.

Beverly C. Tomek is associate provost for curriculum and student achievement and associate professor of history at the University of Houston–Victoria.

Andrew N. Wegmann is assistant professor of history at Delta State University.

Nicholas P. Wood is assistant professor at Spring Hill College, where he teaches early American history.

Ben Wright is assistant professor of history at the University of Texas at Dallas.

Index

Abolition: gradual, 4, 13, 112, 142–43, 152, 254–56; immediate, 9, 34, 43; motivation for, 3–4
Adams, John Quincy, 115, 137–38, 153, 172–73, 237
African Civilization Society, 218
African Education Society, 41, 43
African Institution, 288–90, 292, 297, 298, 333
African Squadron, 112, 113, 117–18, 122, 175
Allen, Richard, 61, 62, 290
Alligator, 114, 236, 238, 239, 246
amalgamation, 4, 5, 42, 44, 141, 337, 338
American Bible Society, 13
American Board of Commissioners for Foreign Missions, 13, 33, 35–36, 42, 44
American Colonization Society (ACS): and antislavery, 112, 115, 117, 147, 155–56, 162, 209, 211, 332, 340–41; and black resistance, 8, 63, 159, 211, 289, 336; and black support, 6–8, 12, 21, 71, 214; and conversion in Africa, 35; and forced removal, 8–9, 174, 210–11, 314, 334, 341; founding of, 135, 229–30, 250; and manumission, 249, 256; as moderate antislavery alternative, 336; as proslavery, 249–50, 329, 336; and recaptured Africans, 112–15, 146, 154, 207–8; and Republican Party, 207–8; and slaveholders, 6, 8, 13, 112, 134–36, 155, 161, 207; and slave trade, 19, 22, 59, 111–23, 136–37, 146, 148–50, 175, 176; and state funding, 119; and westward expansion, 167–71; and women settlers, 90
American Missionary Association, 45
Andover Theological Seminary, 35–37, 45
Andrus, Joseph, 234, 236, 239
Ashmun, Jehudi, 24, 73–74, 114–15, 194

Augusta, 231, 234, 238
Ayres, Eli, 114, 237, 238–45

Bacon, Ephraim, 63, 234–36, 239
Bacon, Leonard, 13, 15, 33, 36, 45; on Charles Caldwell's work, 37; on immediate abolition, 43–44; *A Plea for Africa*, 38, 40
Bacon, Samuel, 50, 65, 239
Bassa, 94, 95, 102, 103, 105, 175, 271, 274
Benezet, Anthony, 54, 57–58
Birney, James G., 335, 336, 341
Blair, Francis P., Sr., 305, 342
Blair, Montgomery, 209, 216, 304, 342
Blyden, Edward W., 76, 82–83
Boso, Sao, 238, 244
Boudinot, Elias, 42
Boyer, Jean Pierre, 53
Branagan, Thomas, 168
Buchanan, James, 112, 121, 207–8
Buchanan, Thomas, 80, 117, 197
Butler, Benjamin F., 311–12, 315, 316, 318–19
Buxton, Thomas Fowell, 11

Caldwell, Elias B., 37, 58–59, 149
Carey, Mathew, 15, 23, 296
Cary (Carey), Lott, 18, 41, 63, 70; as leader in Liberia, 72–73, 78, 80, 90; and opposition to ACS, 71; and Providence Baptist Church, 70
Chiriqui Resettlement, 209–15, 216, 306, 308, 310, 316
Clarkson, Thomas, 333, 336, 340–41
Clay, Henry, 14, 58, 112, 159, 332, 334; and corrupt bargain, 115; and slave trade suppression, 123; and state funding for colonization, 116, 150, 151, 174

Coates, Benjamin, 15
Coker, Daniel, 50, 63, 65, 90, 233–35
Colonization: and Africans, 272; and antislavery, 115, 117, 147, 155–56, 162, 209, 211, 249–50, 254, 259, 261, 334; and black resistance, 8, 63, 159, 211, 252–53, 307, 342; and black support, 6–8, 12, 21, 71, 214; diplomatic value of, 118, 121; during the Civil War, 206–20; and emancipation, 304; and free blacks, 251–52, 255–56, 333–34; and gradual emancipation, 249–50, 251, 254–61, 262; and immigration into US, 250–64; and imperialism, 166–79, 184–85, 193–200, 331; importance of federal support, 111–23, 142, 146, 149–51, 156, 172–73, 207–8, 343; and Indian removal, 251–52; legacy of, 2, 13–14, 17, 21, 178–79, 329, 344; as middle ground in slavery debates, 143, 162, 207, 250, 256, 316, 332, 343–44; motives of supporters, 1–2, 6, 8, 10, 12–17, 50, 140, 146, 150, 155–60, 249–50, 259, 329–44; practicality of, 250–51; and race, 267–83, 294, 330, 336–37; and Republican Party, 207, 209, 258, 262, 263, 341, 342, 343; and slavery, 254; and Whig Party, 256, 316, 337, 343
Committee on Commerce, U.S. House of Representatives, 175–76
Cornish, Samuel, 290–91, 293
Crandall, Prudence, 35, 44–45
Crawford, William H., 138, 153–54
Cresson, Elliott, 15
Crittenden, John, 119
Crowther, Samuel, 79
Crummell, Alexander, 9, 15, 80–82, 90, 210
Cuffe, Paul, 7, 11, 12, 21, 41, 62, 168, 171, 230, 288, 333–35
Cugoano, Ottobah, 6
Cyane, 231–32, 283

Dei, 196, 197, 200, 229, 238, 242–46, 274
Delany, Martin R., 9, 10, 15, 22, 315, 341
Dominican annexation, 313
Doolittle, James R., 209, 305, 342
Douglas, Stephen A., 119, 343
Douglass, Frederick, 298–99, 313, 344

Elizabeth, 50, 114, 231, 236, 238, 275
Emancipation Proclamation, 211, 213–15, 220, 303–4, 309, 314, 318, 320, 343
emigration, 9, 15, 220; as means of black independence, 9; as opposed to colonization, 12, 71, 293; in response to Fugitive Slave Law of 1850, 119
Emigration Office, 305, 314, 320
Equiano, Olaudah, 7, 9
Everett, Edward, 119, 176

Fillmore, Millard, 119, 207
Finley, Robert, 18, 56, 58; as American Colonization Society (ACS) founder, 13, 170, 334; on the slave trade, 59; *Thoughts on the Colonization of Free Blacks*, 52
Forten, James, 7, 12, 15, 61–62, 289–93, 297, 300, 334–35
free labor ideology, 258
free produce, 9
Frelinghuysen, Theodore, 53, 116
Fugitive Slave Act: of 1793, 9; of 1850, 9, 119, 341

Gabriel's Rebellion, 130–33, 168
Garnet, Henry Highland, 9, 95, 218, 315
Garrison, William Lloyd, 1–2, 8–13, 39, 65, 249, 295–300, 329, 335, 343
Gola, 76, 105, 196, 197, 200, 238, 245, 274
Grand Bassa, 233, 234–37, 239, 241, 243, 245
Grant, Ulysses S., 309, 344
Great Commission, 91, 104
Grebo, 99, 105, 175, 270, 274–77, 280–83, 285, 286
Gurley, Ralph R., 23, 36, 42, 211, 215, 216; and Africa, 56; and black missionaries, 64

Haitian emigration, 52–53, 62, 206–13, 305, 310, 333, 335, 342. *See also* Île à Vache
Harper, Robert Goodloe, 123, 139, 334
Hay, John, 306–7, 310–11, 313, 315, 320, 329

Indian Removal, 8, 140–41, 169–70, 174
Ingersoll, Joseph, 253
Île à Vache, 215, 217, 218, 305, 306, 308, 310, 314

Jackson, Andrew, 8, 112–13, 115–17, 174
Jefferson, Thomas, 4, 6, 8, 130–32, 263, 332, 333, 336; and Native Americans, 8, 140–41; and race, 333, 338
Jones, Absalom, 60, 61–62

Kansas-Nebraska Act, 121, 213
King Freeman. *See* Nemah, Pah

King Jack Ben, 235, 241
King Naimbanna, 57; and son John, 57
King Peter, 229, 238, 239–44
King, Rufus, 132, 161
King Sherbro, 232
Kissi, 105, 274
Kizell, John, 230–31, 235
Kock, Bernard, 215, 216, 305, 308
Kpelle, 81, 105, 197, 274
Kru, 101–3, 105, 175, 197, 274, 285, 286

Liberia, 5, 8, 11, 15, 19, 34, 184, 268, 310; and diplomatic recognition, 10, 111, 206–9; governing structure, 197–99; and imperialism, 16–17, 18, 19–20, 22, 185–86, 200–201; independence, 80, 119, 177–78, 198, 201, 216; and missionaries, 43; and racial ideology, 187, 199, 201; and schools, 41; as U.S. first overseas colony, 123, 178–79, 184–85, 193–200; and women, 90–91
Lincoln, Abraham, 15, 21, 143, 263, 343, 344; and abolition, 342; as colonizationist, 208–10, 214, 218–19, 303–21, 342; and race, 321; and recognition of Liberian independence, 119, 209

Madison, James, 288, 299, 331–32, 336
Mandingo, 76, 105
Mary Caroline Stevens, 208
Maryland Colonization Society, 195–96, 217, 252, 270, 271, 274–83
Massachusetts Colonization Society, 208
McLain, William, 209, 211, 212, 215, 216
Menard, John W., 214, 216–17, 315
Mercer, Charles Fenton, 112, 115–16, 120, 133, 157, 158, 230–31, 267; and federal funding for American Colonization Society (ACS), 150, 160; as founder of ACS, 13, 15, 135–37, 148; and free black removal, 140, 148, 252; and slave trade, 136, 150–53, 162
Mill, John S., 239, 243
Mills, Samuel J., 13, 36, 170, 230
Missouri Compromise, 19, 146, 157, 158
Missouri Crisis, 36, 138–39, 142, 146, 152–62, 260
Mitchell, James, 212, 214, 215, 216–17, 218, 307, 309, 314
Monroe, James, 19, 111, 115–16, 129–43, 153, 172, 231, 237, 288; and Gabriel's Conspiracy, 130, 133; and Monrovia, 139; and Sierra Leone, 149; and slave trade, 134, 139, 154; antislavery views, 129–30; as slave owner, 131–33
Mother Bethel African Methodist Episcopal Church, 61–62, 289

Nautilus, 63, 70, 114, 234
Nell, William Cooper, 298, 300
Nemah, Pah, 281
New Jersey Colonization Society, 53
New York State Colonization Society, 195, 208
Nicolay, John G., 304–6, 310–11, 314, 315, 320

Panama Canal, 311, 313
Parrott, Russell, 61–62
Pennsylvania Abolition Society (PAS), 5, 331, 333, 336
Pennsylvania Colonization Society, 162, 195, 215, 208
Philadelphia Colonization Society, 162
Pinney, John B., 78, 208, 210, 211, 215–17

Quakers. *See* Society of Friends

Randolph, John, 112, 147–49, 157, 159, 161
Redpath, James, 208, 211, 212
Roberts, Joseph J., 79–80, 102, 117, 120, 199, 212
Russwurm, John Brown, 15, 41, 195, 272, 275, 279, 290–91, 293

Second Confiscation Act, 211, 213
Second Great Awakening, 36, 75, 79
Senate Committee on Foreign Relations, 174
Seward, William H., 212, 213, 215, 216–17, 305–6, 308, 309
Seys, John, 78–80, 83, 212
Shark, 114
Sharp, Granville, 6, 10, 54, 184, 188–89, 196, 331
Sierra Leone, 5–7, 10, 11, 15, 19, 132, 148, 168, 229–33, 331; as destination for American blacks, 149–50, 171; and imperialism, 184–85, 187–93; and missionaries, 57, 63–64; as inspiration for American Colonization Society (ACS), 172, 332; and suppression of slave trade, 152
Sierra Leone Company, 55, 57, 189
Sierra Leone Council, 192
Sigourney, Lydia, 15, 23, 33, 39
Slave Trade Act of 1819, 146, 150–51, 153, 154, 157, 160, 162, 172, 208, 230–31

Slave Trade Committee, 149, 151, 153
Slave Trade Law of 1807, 151
Smith, Gerrit, 37–38
Society of Friends, 3, 149, 277, 288, 299, 330
Stanton, Edwin M., 217, 306
Stevens, 214, 216, 218
Stevens, Thaddeus, 24, 307, 329
Stiles, Ezra, 53, 55
Stockton, Robert, 114, 229–30, 236–46
Sumner, Charles, 209, 262, 309, 310, 328

Tazewell, Littleton Waller, 115, 119, 174
Teague, Collin, 63
Teague, Hilary, 70
Thompson, Elizabeth Mars, 91, 94, 103–4
Thompson, Smith, 114, 136, 238, 245
Thornton, William, 268, 330–33, 338
Turner, Nat, 43, 255, 339

Vai, 76, 81, 101, 102, 105, 197, 245, 274
Vaux, Roberts, 159, 162
Vermont Colonization Society, 40
Virginia Colonization Society, 118, 141, 161–62, 195

Walker, David, 8, 40, 65, 329, 337, 343
Washington, Bushrod, 112, 157
Washington, George, 8, 194
Webster-Ashburton Treaty, 118, 175
Webster, Daniel, 112, 116, 118, 176, 238
Welles, Gideon, 309, 310
Wheatley, Phillis, 55–56, 63
Women's Baptist Missionary Society, 95
Women's Home Missionary Society, 100

Young Men's Colonization Society of Pennsylvania, 277

SOUTHERN DISSENT

Edited by Stanley Harrold and Randall M. Miller

The Other South: Southern Dissenters in the Nineteenth Century, by Carl N. Degler, with a new preface (2000)
Crowds and Soldiers in Revolutionary North Carolina: The Culture of Violence in Riot and War, by Wayne E. Lee (2001)
"Lord, We're Just Trying to Save Your Water": Environmental Activism and Dissent in the Appalachian South, by Suzanne Marshall (2002)
The Changing South of Gene Patterson: Journalism and Civil Rights, 1960–1968, edited by Roy Peter Clark and Raymond Arsenault (2002; first paperback edition, 2020)
Gendered Freedoms: Race, Rights, and the Politics of Household in the Delta, 1861–1875, by Nancy D. Bercaw (2003)
Civil War on Race Street: The Civil Rights Movement in Cambridge, Maryland, by Peter B. Levy (2003)
South of the South: Jewish Activists and the Civil Rights Movement in Miami, 1945–1960, by Raymond A. Mohl, with contributions by Matilda "Bobbi" Graff and Shirley M. Zoloth (2004)
Throwing Off the Cloak of Privilege: White Southern Women Activists in the Civil Rights Era, edited by Gail S. Murray (2004)
The Atlanta Riot: Race, Class, and Violence in a New South City, by Gregory Mixon (2004)
Slavery and the Peculiar Solution: A History of the American Colonization Society, by Eric Burin (2005; first paperback edition, 2008)
"I Tremble for My Country": Thomas Jefferson and the Virginia Gentry, by Ronald L. Hatzenbuehler (2006; first paperback edition, 2009)
From Saint-Domingue to New Orleans: Migration and Influences, by Nathalie Dessens (2007)
Higher Education and the Civil Rights Movement: White Supremacy, Black Southerners, and College Campuses, edited by Peter Wallenstein (2008)
Burning Faith: Church Arson in the American South, by Christopher B. Strain (2008; first paperback edition, 2020)
Black Power in Dixie: A Political History of African Americans in Atlanta, by Alton Hornsby Jr. (2009; first paperback edition, 2016)
Looking South: Race, Gender, and the Transformation of Labor from Reconstruction to Globalization, by Mary E. Frederickson (2011; first paperback edition, 2012)
Southern Character: Essays in Honor of Bertram Wyatt-Brown, edited by Lisa Tendrich Frank and Daniel Kilbride (2011)
The Challenge of Blackness: The Institute of the Black World and Political Activism in the 1970s, by Derrick E. White (2011; first paperback edition, 2012)
Quakers Living in the Lion's Mouth: The Society of Friends in Northern Virginia, 1730–1865, by A. Glenn Crothers (2012; first paperback edition, 2013)

Unequal Freedoms: Ethnicity, Race, and White Supremacy in Civil War–Era Charleston, by Jeff Strickland (2015)

Show Thyself a Man: Georgia State Troops, Colored, 1865–1905, by Gregory Mixon (2016)

The Denmark Vesey Affair: A Documentary History, edited by Douglas R. Egerton and Robert L. Paquette (2017; first paperback edition, 2022)

New Directions in the Study of African American Recolonization, edited by Beverly C. Tomek and Matthew J. Hetrick (2017; paperback edition, 2022)

Everybody's Problem: The War on Poverty in Eastern North Carolina, by Karen M. Hawkins (2017)

The Seedtime, the Work, and the Harvest: New Perspectives on the Black Freedom Struggle in America, edited by Jeffrey L. Littlejohn, Reginald K. Ellis, and Peter B. Levy (2018; first paperback edition, 2019)

Fugitive Slaves and Spaces of Freedom in North America, edited by Damian Alan Pargas (2018; first paperback edition, 2020)

Latino Orlando: Suburban Transformation and Racial Conflict, by Simone Delerme (2020)

Slavery and Freedom in the Shenandoah Valley during the Civil War Era, by Jonathan A. Noyalas (2021; paperback edition, 2022)

The Citizenship Education Program and Black Women's Political Culture, by Deanna M. Gillespie (2021)

www.ingramcontent.com/pod-product-compliance
Lightning Source LLC
Chambersburg PA
CBHW030235240426

43663CB00037B/515